BELIEVE

LIVING THE STORY OF THE BIBLE
TO BECOME LIKE JESUS

SELECTIONS FROM THE KING JAMES VERSION

BELIEVE

LIVING THE STORY OF THE BIBLE
TO BECOME LIKE JESUS

GENERAL EDITOR
RANDY FRAZEE

ZONDERVAN®

ZONDERVAN
Believe, KJV
Copyright © 2015 by Zondervan

Requests for information should be addressed to:
Zondervan, 3900 Sparks Drive SE, Grand Rapids, Michigan, 49546

Assistant Editor: Randy Larson

All Scripture quotations are taken from The Holy Bible, King James Version.

Any Internet addresses (websites, blogs, etc.) and telephone numbers in this book are offered as a resource. They are not intended in any way to be or imply an endorsement by Zondervan, nor does Zondervan vouch for the content of these sites and numbers for the life of this book.

Cover design: Extra Credit Projects

Printed in the United States of America

15 16 17 18 19 20 21 22 23 24 25 /DCI/ 15 14 13 12 11 10 9 8 7 6 5 4 3 2 1

Table of Contents

BE

Who Am I Becoming?

Preface

A distinguished sociologist embarked on a quest to answer this question, "How did the marginal Jesus movement become the dominant religious force in the Western world within just a few centuries?" By his estimates the number of Christians grew to 33,882,008 believers by AD 350.[1] A movement that started with Jesus and a handful of his followers grew at an amazing rate! This professor was not a personal follower of Jesus but was mesmerized by the influence of Jesus' life on the entire world.

What he discovered in his adventures through history was a group of very common, ordinary folks who ended up doing uncommon, extraordinary things. These people valued others who were looked down upon. When two devastating epidemics of measles and smallpox wiped out one-fourth to one-third of the population of the Roman Empire, these Christ-followers not only nursed their own but also took in those whose families cast them out into the streets to die. People flocked to this new community — a community founded on a rare expression of love. Anyone who said "yes" to Jesus' invitation to life was welcomed.

At the end of the unbelieving social scientist's extensive search, he wrote these words: "Therefore, as I conclude this study, I find it necessary to confront what appears to me to be *the ultimate factor* in the rise of Christianity ... I believe that it was the religion's particular doctrines that permitted Christianity to be among the most sweeping and successful revitalization movements in history. And it was the way these doctrines took on actual flesh, the way they directed organizational actions and individual behavior that led to the rise of Christianity."[2]

In a nutshell, the early Christians BELIEVED. They simply, by faith, believed with their whole hearts the powerful truths taught in the Scriptures. It changed them from the inside out. Their loving and courageous actions toward their family, neighbors and

---

1. Rodney Stark, *The Rise of Christianity: A Sociologist Reconsiders History* (New Jersey: Princeton University Press, 1996), 10.
2. Ibid., 211.

even strangers were merely outpourings of the love that was flowing from inside them. What are the core truths these followers believed that so radically changed their lives for the good? These truths make up the content of the book you now hold in your hands — *Believe*.

As you read the first core belief about God, remember *Believe* is an action word. God is personally watching over you as you embark on this journey. He doesn't want you to just believe in your head these truths; he wants you to believe with your whole heart his Word as the operating system for your life. He wants to transform your life and family for good and forever. He wants you to join the movement. He wants to put the "extra" in your "ordinary" so you can live an "extraordinary" life in Christ. What he did so radically in the beginning, he is doing again today, if you will only BELIEVE.

Here is my prayer for you:

"Father, you fully know the reader who holds this book in their hands. You know them by name. You love them deeply — always have, always will. As they embark on this amazing journey, give them the faith to believe your truths with their whole heart. Work within them. Let that good work push out to their mouth, ears, hands and feet to positively affect the people you have placed around them. As they finish reading the last page, may they whisper to you and then shout to the world — I BELIEVE!"

— Randy Frazee
General Editor

Introduction

All scripture is *given by inspiration of God, and* is *profitable for doctrine, for reproof, for correction, for instruction in righteousness.*
                                                                    2 Timothy 3:16

Book Sections

As you journey through *Believe*, you will read three ten-chapter sections:

THINK. The first ten chapters of *Believe* detail the core BELIEFS of the Christian life. Together they answer the question, "What do I believe?"

ACT. The second ten chapters discuss the core PRACTICES of the Christian life. Together they answer the question, "What should I do?"

BE. The final ten chapters contain the core VIRTUES of the Christian life. Together they answer the question, "Who am I becoming?"

Scripture

Believe includes the actual, God-breathed words of the Bible. This is not one person's or one church's words on these important, life-altering topics. The Bible text alone is our source of teaching on each of these truths. *Believe* contains portions of Scripture that were thoughtfully and carefully excerpted from the Bible because they speak directly to the core belief, practice or virtue. You will read an Old Testament story, a New Testament story and several supporting texts from throughout the Bible. The Scripture text used in *Believe* is taken from the King James Version (KJV).

Chapter Structure

Each chapter contains several elements to guide you through your *Believe* journey.

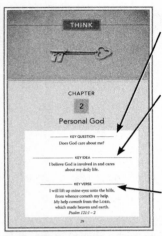

The Keys

Key Question

The key question poses the problem or issue the chapter will grapple with.

Key Idea

The key idea gives you words to use to express your beliefs. Try memorizing the key ideas so you "know that you know" what you believe.

Key Verse

The key verse for each belief is the most important Scripture about that subject. The 30 key verses are also important to commit to memory, so you have the power of God's Word at the ready when you need it.

Our Map

The Our Map section orients you to the belief, practice or virtue you are about to explore. You will get the big picture of what the chapter is about and see a preview of the topics that will be covered.

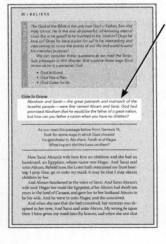

Transitions

The transition paragraphs between the Scripture text appear *in italic*. They were written to guide you through the chapter and connect the dots between each story. The transitions have been carefully crafted to avoid telling you what to believe; it is important that the Scripture itself be the driver of what you decide to believe. These segments aid you in digging into the meaning and significance of the Scripture.

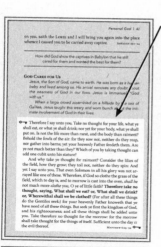

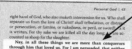

Key Stories

Look for Key Story symbols at the beginning and end of one Old Testament and one New Testament story in each chapter. The Bible characters in these stories best exemplify that belief, practice or virtue.

Core Truths

As you read the Scripture text, you will see core truths or main ideas bolded. The core truth is the essence of the message of that Scripture and helps you understand why that particular passage was selected to convey that truth.

Reflection Questions

There are five reflection questions embedded in each chapter. These questions and suggestions are there to help you get the most out of your reading. When you come to a question, pause and reflect. You will grow to understand the Bible better if you take the time to explore the issues raised by these questions. You can record your answers and observations in a journal, the companion study guide or right in your book. Then talk about your discoveries with someone. Sharing your thoughts with others is a great way to dig deeper into what you've learned.

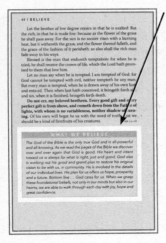

What We Believe

At the conclusion of each chapter, the What We Believe section wraps it all up. The big ideas of the belief, practice or virtue are recapped in a helpful summary so you can recall everything you learned in the chapter and put it all together in a cohesive way.

Back of the Book

At the back of the book, the epilogue gives you an idea of the global impact this story has had on the world. You'll also find the Chart of References, which lists every Scripture reference in the book.

Take It to the Next Level

Believe is a full Bible-engagement campaign with resources for an entire church, school or small group to experience together. If you have experienced *The Story* and are wondering what's next and how to go deeper, then *Believe* is the next step for you. If you haven't experienced *The Story* and are looking for a tool to help you and your church, organization or small group understand the Bible as one overarching narrative, then *The Story* will also be a useful resource for you to explore your faith. For more on *Believe* and *The Story*, check out www.thestory.com and www.believethestory.com.

What Do I Believe?

A good man out of the good treasure
of his heart bringeth forth that which is good;
and an evil man out of the evil treasure
of his heart bringeth forth that which is evil:
for of the abundance of the heart his mouth speaketh.
Luke 6:45

What we believe in our hearts will define who we become. God wants you to become like Jesus. This is who God created you to be. It is the most truthful and powerful way to live. The journey to *becoming* like Jesus begins by *thinking* like Jesus.

The following ten chapters will introduce and expose you to the key beliefs of the Christian life. These beliefs were not only taught by Jesus but also modeled by Jesus when he walked this earth. Because we live from the heart, embracing these core truths in both our minds and our hearts is the first step to truly becoming like Jesus.

Each of the following chapters contains Scripture passages from Genesis to Revelation focused on a particular belief. You are about to discover what God wants you to know and believe about these important topics. Embark on each page with a passion to learn and understand. Then prayerfully ask, "What do *I* believe?"

Fully adopting these fantastic truths in your heart may not come at the end of reading the chapter. If you are honest, it may take a while, and that is okay. The Christian life is a journey. There are no shortcuts. As each of the key concepts takes up residence in your heart it, with the amazing help of God's presence in your life, will change your life for the good.

When you start *thinking* like Jesus, you are well on your way to *becoming* like Jesus.

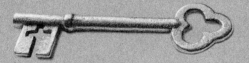

CHAPTER

1

God

———— KEY QUESTION ————

Who is God?

———— KEY IDEA ————

I believe the God of the Bible is the only true God —
Father, Son and Holy Ghost.

———— KEY VERSE ————

The grace of the Lord Jesus Christ,
and the love of God, and the communion
of the Holy Ghost, *be* with you all. Amen.
2 Corinthians 13:14

OUR MAP

Belief in God is the very foundation of the Christian faith. Christianity is the only spiritual belief system that emanates from a Creator-God who had no beginning, who interacts with his creation as a plural entity and who exhibits preeminence over all other gods and beings.

We will be reading Scripture passages in this chapter that describe how we know about God, all aspects of his essence and what they mean to us:

- God Reveals Himself
- The One True God
- God in Three Persons: Father, Son and Holy Ghost
- The Trinity in Our Lives

GOD REVEALS HIMSELF

Everything begins with God. The Bible never seeks to defend the existence of God. It is assumed. God has revealed himself so powerfully through his creation—both at the macro and micro level—that at the end of the day, no one will have an excuse for not putting their trust in him.

In the beginning God created the heaven and the earth.

GENESIS 1:1

The heavens declare the glory of God;
    and the firmament sheweth his handywork.
Day unto day uttereth speech,
    and night unto night sheweth knowledge.
There is no speech nor language,
    where their voice is not heard.
Their line is gone out through all the earth,
    and their words to the end of the world.
In them hath he set a tabernacle for the sun.   PSALM 19:1–4

For the invisible things of him from the creation of the world are clearly seen, being understood by the things that are made, *even* his eternal power and Godhead; so that they are without excuse.   ROMANS 1:20

In what ways do you see the invisible qualities
of God revealed in nature?

THE ONE TRUE GOD

*From beginning to end, the Bible reveals that there is only one
true God. But who is he? The book of Deuteronomy looks back
at how Moses had led the Israelites out of slavery in Egypt. During that time God, through the ten plagues, had revealed himself as the one true, all-powerful God over Pharaoh. Now a new
generation had grown up in the wilderness and was poised to
inherit the land God had promised Abraham. Moses offered the
second generation a series of farewell speeches to remind them
to choose, worship and follow the one true God—the God of
Abraham, Isaac and Jacob. If they did, all would go well for
them.*

Now these are the commandments, the statutes, and the judgments, which the LORD your God commanded to teach you, that
ye might do *them* in the land whither ye go to possess it: that thou
mightest fear the LORD thy God, to keep all his statutes and his
commandments, which I command thee, thou, and thy son, and
thy son's son, all the days of thy life; and that thy days may be prolonged. Hear therefore, O Israel, and observe to do *it*; that it may
be well with thee, and that ye may increase mightily, as the LORD
God of thy fathers hath promised thee, in the land that floweth
with milk and honey.

Hear, O Israel: The LORD our God *is* one LORD. And thou
shalt love the LORD thy God with all thine heart, and with all thy
soul, and with all thy might. And these words, which I command
thee this day, shall be in thine heart. And thou shalt teach them
diligently unto thy children, and shalt talk of them when thou sittest in thine house, and when thou walkest by the way, and when
thou liest down, and when thou risest up. And thou shalt bind
them for a sign upon thine hand, and they shall be as frontlets between thine eyes. And thou shalt write them upon the posts of thy
house, and on thy gates. DEUTERONOMY 6:1–9

What are some of the main points
of God's requirements for his people? Why do
you think he emphasized these things?

After Moses died, Joshua became the next great leader of the Israelites. He was charged with leading the people into the promised land. God was with them and fought for them as they began conquering the land. Under Joshua's leadership the Israelites remained steady in their devotion to God. Before Joshua died, he gathered the people together and issued them a stiff challenge to choose to serve the Lord, the one true God.

And Joshua gathered all the tribes of Israel to Shechem, and called for the elders of Israel, and for their heads, and for their judges, and for their officers; and they presented themselves before God.

And Joshua said unto all the people, Thus saith the LORD God of Israel, Your fathers dwelt on the other side of the flood in old time, *even* Terah, the father of Abraham, and the father of Nachor: and they served other gods. And I took your father Abraham from the other side of the flood, and led him throughout all the land of Canaan, and multiplied his seed, and gave him Isaac. And I gave unto Isaac Jacob and Esau: and I gave unto Esau mount Seir, to possess it; but Jacob and his children went down into Egypt.

I sent Moses also and Aaron, and I plagued Egypt, according to that which I did among them: and afterward I brought you out. And I brought your fathers out of Egypt: and ye came unto the sea; and the Egyptians pursued after your fathers with chariots and horsemen unto the Red sea. And when they cried unto the LORD, he put darkness between you and the Egyptians, and brought the sea upon them, and covered them; and your eyes have seen what I have done in Egypt: and ye dwelt in the wilderness a long season.

And I brought you into the land of the Amorites, which dwelt on the other side Jordan; and they fought with you: and I gave them into your hand, that ye might possess their land; and I destroyed them from before you. Then Balak the son of Zippor, king of Moab, arose and warred against Israel, and sent and called Balaam the son of Beor to curse you: But I would not hearken unto Balaam; therefore he blessed you still: so I delivered you out of his hand.

And ye went over Jordan, and came unto Jericho: and the men of Jericho fought against you, the Amorites, and the Perizzites, and the Canaanites, and the Hittites, and the Girgashites, the Hivites, and the Jebusites; and I delivered them into your hand. And I sent the hornet before you, which drave them out from before you, *even* the two kings of the Amorites; *but* not with thy sword, nor with thy bow. And I have given you a land for which ye did not labour, and cities which ye built not, and ye dwell in them; of the vineyards and oliveyards which ye planted not do ye eat.

Now therefore fear the LORD, and serve him in sincerity and in truth: and put away the gods which your fathers served on the other side of the flood, and in Egypt; and serve ye the LORD. And if it seem evil unto you to serve the LORD, choose you this day whom ye will serve; whether the gods which your fathers served that were on the other side of the flood, or the gods of the Amorites, in whose land ye dwell: but as for me and my house, we will serve the LORD.

And the people answered and said, God forbid that we should forsake the LORD, to serve other gods; for the LORD our God, he *it is* that brought us up and our fathers out of the land of Egypt, from the house of bondage, and which did those great signs in our sight, and preserved us in all the way wherein we went, and among all the people through whom we passed: And the LORD drave out from before us all the people, even the Amorites which dwelt in the land: *therefore* will we also serve the LORD; for he *is* our God.

And Joshua said unto the people, Ye cannot serve the LORD: for he *is* an holy God; he *is* a jealous God; he will not forgive your transgressions nor your sins. If ye forsake the LORD, and serve strange gods, then he will turn and do you hurt, and consume you, after that he hath done you good.

And the people said unto Joshua, Nay; but we will serve the LORD.

And Joshua said unto the people, Ye *are* witnesses against yourselves that ye have chosen you the LORD, to serve him.

And they said, *We are* witnesses.

Now therefore put away, *said he*, the strange gods which *are* among you, and incline your heart unto the LORD God of Israel.

And the people said unto Joshua, The LORD our God will we serve, and his voice will we obey.

So Joshua made a covenant with the people that day, and set them a statute and an ordinance in Shechem. And Joshua wrote these words in the book of the law of God, and took a great stone, and set it up there under an oak, that *was* by the sanctuary of the LORD.

And Joshua said unto all the people, Behold, this stone shall be a witness unto us; for it hath heard all the words of the LORD which he spake unto us: it shall be therefore a witness unto you, lest ye deny your God.

So Joshua let the people depart, every man unto his inheritance.

And it came to pass after these things, that Joshua the son of Nun, the servant of the LORD, died, *being* an hundred and ten years old. And they buried him in the border of his inheritance in Timnath-serah, which *is* in mount Ephraim, on the north side of the hill of Gaash.

And Israel served the LORD all the days of Joshua, and all the days of the elders that overlived Joshua, and which had known all the works of the LORD, that he had done for Israel.   JOSHUA 24:1–31

Unfortunately the Israelites failed to keep their promise to follow only God. Through the people's repeated disobedience, God weakened Israel's influence—445 years after Joshua died— by dividing them into two kingdoms: the northern kingdom of Israel and the southern kingdom of Judah. Israel did not have one good king during its more than 200 years of existence. King Ahab was particularly wicked, as he introduced the worship of the pagan god Baal to Israel. But God demonstrated through the prophet Elijah that he, the Lord, not Baal or any other "god," is the one true God.

Ahab went to meet Elijah. And it came to pass, when Ahab saw Elijah, that Ahab said unto him, *Art* thou he that troubleth Israel?

And he answered, I have not troubled Israel; but thou, and thy father's house, in that ye have forsaken the commandments of the

LORD, and thou hast followed Baalim. Now therefore send, *and* gather to me all Israel unto mount Carmel, and the prophets of Baal four hundred and fifty, and the prophets of the groves four hundred, which eat at Jezebel's table.

So Ahab sent unto all the children of Israel, and gathered the prophets together unto mount Carmel. **And Elijah came unto all the people, and said, How long halt ye between two opinions? if the LORD *be* God, follow him: but if Baal, *then* follow him.**

And the people answered him not a word.

Then said Elijah unto the people, I, *even* I only, remain a prophet of the LORD; but Baal's prophets *are* four hundred and fifty men. Let them therefore give us two bullocks; and let them choose one bullock for themselves, and cut it in pieces, and lay *it* on wood, and put no fire *under*: and I will dress the other bullock, and lay *it* on wood, and put no fire *under*: And call ye on the name of your gods, and I will call on the name of the LORD: and the God that answereth by fire, let him be God.

And all the people answered and said, It is well spoken.

And Elijah said unto the prophets of Baal, Choose you one bullock for yourselves, and dress *it* first; for ye *are* many; and call on the name of your gods, but put no fire *under*.

And they took the bullock which was given them, and they dressed *it*, and called on the name of Baal from morning even until noon, saying, O Baal, hear us. But *there was* no voice, nor any that answered. And they leaped upon the altar which was made.

And it came to pass at noon, that Elijah mocked them, and said, Cry aloud: for he *is* a god; either he is talking, or he is pursuing, or he is in a journey, *or* peradventure he sleepeth, and must be awaked. And they cried aloud, and cut themselves after their manner with knives and lancets, till the blood gushed out upon them. And it came to pass, when midday was past, and they prophesied until the *time* of the offering of the *evening* sacrifice, that *there was* neither voice, nor any to answer, nor any that regarded.

And Elijah said unto all the people, Come near unto me. And all the people came near unto him. And he repaired the altar of the LORD *that was* broken down. And Elijah took twelve stones, according to the number of the tribes of the sons of Jacob, unto whom the word of the LORD came, saying, Israel shall be thy name.

And with the stones he built an altar in the name of the LORD: and he made a trench about the altar, as great as would contain two measures of seed. And he put the wood in order, and cut the bullock in pieces, and laid *him* on the wood, and said, Fill four barrels with water, and pour *it* on the burnt sacrifice, and on the wood.

And he said, Do *it* the second time. And they did *it* the second time.

And he said, Do *it* the third time. And they did *it* the third time. And the water ran round about the altar; and he filled the trench also with water.

And it came to pass at *the time of* the offering of the *evening* sacrifice, that Elijah the prophet came near, and said, LORD God of Abraham, Isaac, and of Israel, let it be known this day that thou *art* God in Israel, and *that* I *am* thy servant, and *that* I have done all these things at thy word. Hear me, O LORD, hear me, that this people may know that thou *art* the LORD God, and *that* thou hast turned their heart back again.

Then the fire of the LORD fell, and consumed the burnt sacrifice, and the wood, and the stones, and the dust, and licked up the water that *was* in the trench.

And when all the people saw *it*, they fell on their faces: and they said, The LORD, he *is* the God; the LORD, he *is* the God.

And Elijah said unto them, Take the prophets of Baal; let not one of them escape. And they took them: and Elijah brought them down to the brook Kishon, and slew them there.   1 KINGS 18:16–40

Why did God have to prove over and
over that he is the one true God?

GOD IN THREE PERSONS: FATHER, SON AND HOLY GHOST

Throughout the Old Testament, people were invited to worship the one true God, but what do we know about this God of miracles and creative wonder? Christians believe God is actually three persons, a "Trinity." Though the word "Trinity" isn't found in the Bible, in the very beginning of God's story, the creation story, we see hints that God is plural. Genesis 1:26 says, "And God said, Let *us make man in **our** image, after **our** likeness." God is himself a mini-community.*

The creation story tells us we were created in God's image. When he made the first human (Adam), God wanted him to experience the community and relationship that has eternally existed within the Trinity. That's why he made Eve. Notice that Adam and Eve were not two separate beings. Eve came out of Adam, and they became two distinct persons who shared one being, like God. God is three distinct persons who share a single being.

These *are* the generations of the heavens and of the earth when they were created, in the day that the LORD God made the earth and the heavens,

And every plant of the field before it was in the earth, and every herb of the field before it grew: for the LORD God had not caused it to rain upon the earth, and *there was* not a man to till the ground. But there went up a mist from the earth, and watered the whole face of the ground. **And the LORD God formed man** *of* **the dust of the ground, and breathed into his nostrils the breath of life; and man became a living soul.**

And the LORD God planted a garden eastward in Eden; and there he put the man whom he had formed. And out of the ground made the LORD God to grow every tree that is pleasant to the sight, and good for food; the tree of life also in the midst of the garden, and the tree of knowledge of good and evil.   GENESIS 2:4–9

And the LORD God took the man, and put him into the garden of Eden to dress it and to keep it. And the LORD God commanded the man, saying, Of every tree of the garden thou mayest freely eat. But of the tree of the knowledge of good and evil, thou shalt not eat of it: for in the day that thou eatest thereof thou shalt surely die.

And the LORD God said, *It is* **not good that the man should be alone; I will make him an help meet for him.**

And out of the ground the LORD God formed every beast of the field, and every fowl of the air; and brought *them* unto Adam to see what he would call them: and whatsoever Adam called every living creature, that *was* the name thereof.

And Adam gave names to all cattle, and to the fowl of the air, and to every beast of the field; but for Adam there was not found an help meet for him. And the LORD God caused a deep sleep to fall upon Adam, and he slept: and he took one of his ribs, and closed up the flesh instead thereof; **And the rib, which the LORD God had taken from man, made he a woman, and brought her unto the man.**

And Adam said, This *is* now bone of my bones, and flesh of my flesh: she shall be called Woman, because she was taken out of Man. **Therefore shall a man leave his father and his mother, and shall cleave unto his wife: and they shall be one flesh.**

GENESIS 2:15–24

Recalling Genesis 1:26, "And God said, Let us make man in our image, after our likeness." God as a plural being is clearly evident from the very beginning of the Bible. But what are the identities of the individual persons of God, and how are they just one being? How do they interact? The opening words of John's Gospel makes the answer more clear.

In the beginning was the Word, and the Word was with God, and the Word was God. The same was in the beginning with God. All things were made by him; and without him was not any thing made that was made. In him was life; and the life was the light of men. And the light shineth in darkness; and the darkness comprehended it not.

JOHN 1:1–5

The "Word" here refers to Jesus. John refers to him as "God," as divine. John also says Jesus was there in the beginning. Jesus, the divine Word, partnered with God to create all that we see and all that we have yet to see.

So who were the other members of the Trinity? The second sentence of the Bible tells us that the Holy Ghost, also known as the Spirit of God, was also present at creation: "And the earth was without form, and void; and darkness was upon the face of the deep. And the Spirit of God moved upon the face of the waters" (Genesis 1:2). Jesus and the Spirit were at the creation of the world; these two persons are God. Is that it? Who else makes up the person of God? Fast-forward to the baptism of Jesus at the age of 30 to discover the answer. As you read this account, look for the appearance of all three persons of the Trinity.

Now in the fifteenth year of the reign of Tiberius Caesar, Pontius Pilate being governor of Judaea, and Herod being tetrarch of Galilee, and his brother Philip tetrarch of Ituraea and of the region of Trachonitis, and Lysanias the tetrarch of Abilene, Annas and Caiaphas being the high priests, the word of God came unto John the son of Zacharias in the wilderness. And he came into all the country about Jordan, preaching the baptism of repentance for the remission of sins; As it is written in the book of the words of Esaias the prophet, saying,

The voice of one crying in the wilderness, Prepare ye the way of the Lord, make his paths straight. Every valley shall be filled, and every mountain and hill shall be brought low; and the crooked shall be made straight, and the rough ways *shall be* made smooth; And all flesh shall see the salvation of God.   LUKE 3:1–6

And as the people were in expectation, and all men mused in their hearts of John, whether he were the Christ, or not; John answered, saying unto *them* all, I indeed baptize you with water; but one mightier than I cometh, the latchet of whose shoes I am not worthy to unloose: he shall baptize you with the Holy Ghost and with fire: Whose fan *is* in his hand, and he will throughly purge his floor, and will gather the wheat into his garner; but the chaff he will burn with fire unquenchable. And many other things in his exhortation preached he unto the people.   LUKE 3:15–18

Now when all the people were baptized, it came to pass, that Jesus also being baptized, and praying, the heaven was opened, And the Holy Ghost descended in a bodily shape like a dove upon him, and a voice came from heaven, which said, Thou art my beloved Son; in thee I am well pleased.

And Jesus himself began to be about thirty years of age, being (as was supposed) the son of Joseph, which was *the son* of Heli.

                    LUKE 3:21–23

Three distinct persons are fully revealed in Scripture to make up the identity of the one true God: the Father, the Son Jesus and the Holy Ghost. And all three were involved at the baptism of Jesus—the Father spoke, the Son was baptized and the Holy Ghost descended on the Son. Throughout the centuries, followers of Jesus have come to call the one true God the Trinity, three persons who share one being. As difficult as this concept is to understand, it is important to our lives.

In what ways have you experienced God as Father?
As Jesus the Son? As the Holy Ghost?

THE TRINITY IN OUR LIVES

In the spirit of Joshua of the Old Testament, in the early church Paul called people to declare the identity of the one true God. During his travels Paul went to the great Areopagus in Athens, Greece. The intellectual people who lived there created an altar to many gods. Notice how they even created an altar dedicated "to the unknown God" in case they missed one and therefore offended them. Paul declares the identity of this God as the one who created everything in the beginning (see Genesis 1–2) and is now revealed in the second person of the Trinity, Jesus Christ. His words to the people of Athens are applicable to all those who believe—God is everywhere and there is nothing in this world that his hand has not touched. The Trinity is woven into every aspect of our lives.

Now while Paul waited for them at Athens, his spirit was stirred in him, when he saw the city wholly given to idolatry. Therefore disputed he in the synagogue with the Jews, and with the devout persons, and in the market daily with them that met with him. Then certain philosophers of the Epicureans, and of the Stoicks, encountered him. And some said, What will this babbler say? other some, He seemeth to be a setter forth of strange gods: because he preached unto them Jesus, and the resurrection. And they took him, and brought him unto Areopagus, saying, May we know what this new doctrine, whereof thou speakest, *is*? For thou bringest certain strange things to our ears: we would know therefore what these things mean. (For all the Athenians and strangers which were there spent their time in nothing else, but either to tell, or to hear some new thing.)

Then Paul stood in the midst of Mars' hill, and said, *Ye* men of Athens, I perceive that in all things ye are too superstitious. For as I passed by, and beheld your devotions, I found an altar with this inscription, TO THE UNKNOWN GOD. Whom therefore ye ignorantly worship, him declare I unto you.

God that made the world and all things therein, seeing that he is Lord of heaven and earth, dwelleth not in temples made with hands; Neither is worshipped with men's hands, as though he needed any thing, seeing he giveth to all life, and breath, and all things; And hath made of one blood all nations of men for to dwell on all the face of the earth, and hath determined the times before appointed, and the bounds of their habitation; That they should seek the Lord, if haply they might feel after him, and find him, though he be not far from every one of us: For in him we live, and move, and have our being; as certain also of your own poets have said, For we are also his offspring.

Forasmuch then as we are the offspring of God, we ought not to think that the Godhead is like unto gold, or silver, or stone, graven by art and man's device. And the times of this ignorance God winked at; but now commandeth all men every where to repent: Because he hath appointed a day, in the which he will judge the world in righteousness by *that* man whom he hath ordained; *whereof* he hath given assurance unto all *men*, in that he hath raised him from the dead.

And when they heard of the resurrection of the dead, some mocked: and others said, We will hear thee again of this *matter*. So Paul departed from among them. Howbeit certain men clave unto him, and believed: among the which *was* Dionysius the Areopagite, and a woman named Damaris, and others with them.

ACTS 17:16–34

What is meant by the phrase Paul quoted: "For in him
we live, and move, and have our being?" Why do you think
this needed to be said to this group of Athenians?

The power and identity of the one true God are highlighted throughout Paul's writing, including the last words of 2 Corinthians, which he penned with the benediction below.

The grace of the Lord Jesus Christ, and the love of God, and the communion of the Holy Ghost, *be* with you all. Amen.

2 CORINTHIANS 13:14

Notice how all three members of the Trinity are involved in our lives. God, the Father, loves us and sought a way for us to come back into a relationship with him. Jesus, the second person of the Trinity, provided the way back to God by offering himself as a sacrifice in our place. Now that we believe, the Holy Ghost, the third person of the Trinity, fellowships with us as we journey through life, guiding and comforting us every step of the way.

WHAT WE BELIEVE

The Bible never tries to prove the existence of God—his existence is simply an assumed fact. God has clearly revealed himself through creation, in events such as Jesus' baptism and in our own consciences, leaving everyone without excuse in the end. The key question we asked at the beginning of this chapter comes down to the declaration of who the one true God is. The God who protected Israel and demonstrated power over false gods declares, "I AM!"

The journey of faith begins with our belief in God. Like the Israelites of the Old Testament and the early Christians of the New Testament, we too are called to make a personal declaration. Do we believe in the one true God? Do we accept the Bible's revelation that God exists in three persons?

CHAPTER

2

Personal God

―――――― KEY QUESTION ――――――

Does God care about me?

――――――― KEY IDEA ―――――――

I believe God is involved in and cares
about my daily life.

――――――― KEY VERSE ―――――――

I will lift up mine eyes unto the hills,
from whence cometh my help.
My help *cometh* from the LORD,
which made heaven and earth.
Psalm 121:1 – 2

29

The God of the Bible is the only true God—Father, Son and Holy Ghost. He is the one all-powerful, all-knowing eternal God. But is he good? Is he involved in his creation? Does he love us? Does he have a plan for us? Is he interceding and intervening to move the events of our life and world toward his intended purpose?

We can consider these questions as we read the Scripture passages in this chapter that explore three ways God shows us he is a personal God:

- God Is Good
- God Has a Plan
- God Cares for Us

GOD IS GOOD

Abraham and Sarah—the great patriarch and matriarch of the Israelite people—were first named Abram and Sarai. God had promised Abraham that he would be the father of a great nation, but how can you father a nation when you have no children?

As you read the passage below from Genesis 16,
look for some ways in which God showed
his goodness to Abraham, Sarah and Hagar.
What impact did this have on them?

Now Sarai Abram's wife bare him no children: and she had an handmaid, an Egyptian, whose name *was* Hagar. And Sarai said unto Abram, Behold now, the LORD hath restrained me from bearing: I pray thee, go in unto my maid; it may be that I may obtain children by her.

And Abram hearkened to the voice of Sarai. And Sarai Abram's wife took Hagar her maid the Egyptian, after Abram had dwelt ten years in the land of Canaan, and gave her to her husband Abram to be his wife. And he went in unto Hagar, and she conceived.

And when she saw that she had conceived, her mistress was despised in her eyes. And Sarai said unto Abram, My wrong *be* upon thee: I have given my maid into thy bosom; and when she saw that she had conceived, I was despised in her eyes: the LORD judge between me and thee.

But Abram said unto Sarai, Behold, thy maid *is* in thy hand; do to her as it pleaseth thee. And when Sarai dealt hardly with her, she fled from her face.

And the angel of the LORD found her by a fountain of water in the wilderness, by the fountain in the way to Shur. And he said, Hagar, Sarai's maid, whence camest thou? and whither wilt thou go?

And she said, I flee from the face of my mistress Sarai.

And the angel of the LORD said unto her, Return to thy mistress, and submit thyself under her hands. And the angel of the LORD said unto her, I will multiply thy seed exceedingly, that it shall not be numbered for multitude.

And the angel of the LORD said unto her, Behold, thou *art* with child, and shalt bear a son, and shalt call his name Ishmael; because the LORD hath heard thy affliction. And he will be a wild man; his hand *will be* against every man, and every man's hand against him; and he shall dwell in the presence of all his brethren.

And she called the name of the LORD that spake unto her, Thou God seest me: for she said, Have I also here looked after him that seeth me? Wherefore the well was called Beer-lahai-roi; behold, *it is* between Kadesh and Bered.

And Hagar bare Abram a son: and Abram called his son's name, which Hagar bare, Ishmael. And Abram *was* fourscore and six years old, when Hagar bare Ishmael to Abram.   GENESIS 16:1–16

Abraham and Sarah tried to "help God out" by having Abraham father a child with Hagar. What resulted was a debacle for everyone involved. But in this story, we see the beginning of a pattern—God takes our messes and turns them into something good. Hagar involuntarily became party to Abraham's and Sarah's lack of faith. Yet God heard her cries and helped her. The story continues . . .

And the LORD visited Sarah as he had said, and the LORD did unto Sarah as he had spoken. For Sarah conceived, and bare Abraham a son in his old age, at the set time of which God

had spoken to him. And Abraham called the name of his son that was born unto him, whom Sarah bare to him, Isaac. And Abraham circumcised his son Isaac being eight days old, as God had commanded him. And Abraham was an hundred years old, when his son Isaac was born unto him.

And Sarah said, God hath made me to laugh, *so that* **all that hear will laugh with me.** And she said, Who would have said unto Abraham, that Sarah should have given children suck? for I have born *him* a son in his old age.

And the child grew, and was weaned: and Abraham made a great feast the *same* day that Isaac was weaned. And Sarah saw the son of Hagar the Egyptian, which she had born unto Abraham, mocking. Wherefore she said unto Abraham, Cast out this bondwoman and her son: for the son of this bondwoman shall not be heir with my son, *even* with Isaac.

And the thing was very grievous in Abraham's sight because of his son. And God said unto Abraham, Let it not be grievous in thy sight because of the lad, and because of thy bondwoman; in all that Sarah hath said unto thee, hearken unto her voice; for in Isaac shall thy seed be called. And also of the son of the bondwoman will I make a nation, because he *is* thy seed.

And Abraham rose up early in the morning, and took bread, and a bottle of water, and gave *it* unto Hagar, putting *it* on her shoulder, and the child, and sent her away: and she departed, and wandered in the wilderness of Beer-sheba.

And the water was spent in the bottle, and she cast the child under one of the shrubs. And she went, and sat her down over against *him* a good way off, as it were a bow shot: for she said, Let me not see the death of the child. And she sat over against *him*, and lift up her voice, and wept.

And God heard the voice of the lad; and the angel of God called to Hagar out of heaven, and said unto her, What aileth thee, Hagar? fear not; for God hath heard the voice of the lad where he *is***. Arise, lift up the lad, and hold him in thine hand; for I will make him a great nation.**

And God opened her eyes, and she saw a well of water; and she went, and filled the bottle with water, and gave the lad drink.

And God was with the lad; and he grew, and dwelt in the wilderness, and became an archer. And he dwelt in the wilderness of Paran: and his mother took him a wife out of the land of Egypt.

GENESIS 21:1–21

Even though Hagar and Ishmael weren't main characters in the Biblical story line, God still provided for them and promised to bless their descendants. He did this because he is a compassionate and personal God.

Another Biblical character in whose life we see how much God is involved and cares about his people is David, the poet, singer, shepherd, warrior and king, who wrote and sang from a deep well of faith as he journeyed through life and encountered the one true God. David composed many of the psalms found in our Bible: he wrote as a shepherd boy while gazing at the billions of stars God created; he wrote while being chased down by King Saul; he wrote while he was king of Israel; and he wrote as he was coming to the end of his life on earth. The songs that David and the other psalmists wrote express their personal and intimate relationship with God.

O LORD, our Lord,
   how excellent *is* thy name in all the earth!
Who hast set thy glory
   above the heavens.
Out of the mouth of babes and sucklings
   hast thou ordained strength because of thine enemies,
   that thou mightest still the enemy and the avenger.
When I consider thy heavens,
   the work of thy fingers,
the moon and the stars,
   which thou hast ordained;
What is man, that thou art mindful of him?
   and the son of man, that thou visitest him?

For thou hast made him a little lower than the angels,
   and hast crowned him with glory and honour.
Thou madest him to have dominion over the works
      of thy hands;
   thou hast put all *things* under his feet:

All sheep and oxen, yea,
    and the beasts of the field;
The fowl of the air,
    and the fish of the sea,
    and whatsoever passeth through the paths of the seas.

O LORD, our Lord,
    how excellent *is* thy name in all the earth!   PSALM 8:1–9

The LORD *is* my shepherd; I shall not want.
    He maketh me to lie down in green pastures:
he leadeth me beside the still waters.
    He restoreth my soul.
He leadeth me in the paths of righteousness
    for his name's sake.
Yea, though I walk
    through the valley of the shadow of death,
I will fear no evil:
    for thou *art* with me;
thy rod and thy staff they comfort me.

Thou preparest a table before me
    in the presence of mine enemies:
thou anointest my head with oil;
    my cup runneth over.
Surely goodness and mercy shall follow me
    all the days of my life:
and I will dwell in the house of the LORD for ever.
                                        PSALM 23:1–6

O LORD, thou hast searched me,
    and known *me*.
Thou knowest my downsitting and mine uprising,
    thou understandest my thought afar off.
Thou compassest my path and my lying down,
    and art acquainted *with* all my ways.
For *there is* not a word in my tongue,
    but, lo, O LORD, thou knowest it altogether.
Thou hast beset me behind and before,
    and laid thine hand upon me.

Such knowledge *is* too wonderful for me;
    it is high, I cannot *attain* unto it.

Whither shall I go from thy spirit?
    or whither shall I flee from thy presence?
If I ascend up into heaven, thou *art* there:
    if I make my bed in hell, behold, thou *art there.*
If I take the wings of the morning,
    and dwell in the uttermost parts of the sea;
Even there shall thy hand lead me,
    and thy right hand shall hold me.
If I say, Surely the darkness shall cover me;
    even the night shall be light about me.
Yea, the darkness hideth not from thee;
    but the night shineth as the day:
    the darkness and the light *are* both alike *to thee.*

For thou hast possessed my reins:
    thou hast covered me in my mother's womb.
I will praise thee; for I am fearfully *and* wonderfully made:
    marvellous *are* thy works;
    and *that* my soul knoweth right well.
My substance was not hid from thee,
    when I was made in secret,
    and curiously wrought in the lowest parts of the earth.
Thine eyes did see my substance, yet being unperfect;
    and in thy book all *my members* were written,
    which in continuance were fashioned, when *as yet there*
        was none of them.
How precious also are thy thoughts unto me, O God!
    how great is the sum of them!
If I should count them,
    they are more in number than the sand:
    when I awake, I am still with thee.   PSALM 139:1–18

How have you experienced God's personal knowledge
of you? When have you known he was
searching your heart? What was the result?

I will extol thee, my God, O king;
 and I will bless thy name for ever and ever.
Every day will I bless thee;
 and I will praise thy name for ever and ever.

Great *is* the LORD, and greatly to be praised;
 and his greatness *is* unsearchable.
One generation shall praise thy works to another,
 and shall declare thy mighty acts.
I will speak of the glorious honour of thy majesty,
 and of thy wondrous works.
And *men* shall speak of the might of thy terrible acts:
 and I will declare thy greatness.
They shall abundantly utter the memory of thy great
  goodness,
 and shall sing of thy righteousness.

The LORD *is* gracious, and full of compassion;
 slow to anger, and of great mercy.

The LORD *is* good to all:
 and his tender mercies *are* over all his works.
All thy works shall praise thee, O LORD;
 and thy saints shall bless thee.
They shall speak of the glory of thy kingdom,
 and talk of thy power;
To make known to the sons of men his mighty acts,
 and the glorious majesty of his kingdom.
Thy kingdom *is* an everlasting kingdom,
 and thy dominion *endureth* throughout all generations.

The LORD upholdeth all that fall,
 and raiseth up all *those that be* bowed down.
The eyes of all wait upon thee;
 and thou givest them their meat in due season.
Thou openest thine hand,
 and satisfiest the desire of every living thing.

The LORD *is* righteous in all his ways,
 and holy in all his works.

The Lord *is* nigh unto all them that call upon him,
 to all that call upon him in truth.
He will fulfil the desire of them that fear him:
 he also will hear their cry, and will save them.
The Lord preserveth all them that love him:
 but all the wicked will he destroy.

My mouth shall speak the praise of the Lord:
 and let all flesh bless his holy name
 for ever and ever.

Psalm 145:1–21

God Has a Plan

Forty years after David's death, the nation of Israel was torn apart, and what resulted were two nations: the northern kingdom of Israel and the southern kingdom of Judah. All the kings of Israel did evil in the eyes of the Lord. In Judah, only a handful of kings were good. One of them was Hezekiah. He courageously served the Lord in perilous times.

Then when he was about thirty-eight years old, Hezekiah became ill and was about to die. He was devastated and pleaded with the Lord for mercy. In response, the Lord sent him a shocking message and a tender change of plan. We know from the Bible that God has a plan for our individual lives and has our days numbered. This story shows how God will hear our prayers and see our tears. He may not answer us in the way we desire, but he will sometimes alter the plan he has for us at our request.

In those days was Hezekiah sick unto death. And the prophet Isaiah the son of Amoz came to him, and said unto him, Thus saith the Lord, Set thine house in order; for thou shalt die, and not live.

Then he turned his face to the wall, and prayed unto the Lord, saying, I beseech thee, O Lord, remember now how I have walked before thee in truth and with a perfect heart, and have done *that which is* good in thy sight. And Hezekiah wept sore.

And it came to pass, afore Isaiah was gone out into the middle court, that the word of the Lord came to him, saying, **Turn again, and tell Hezekiah the captain of my people, Thus saith the Lord, the God of David thy father, I have heard thy prayer,**

**I have seen thy tears: behold, I will heal thee: on the third day
thou shalt go up unto the house of the LORD. And I will add
unto thy days fifteen years;** and I will deliver thee and this city
out of the hand of the king of Assyria; and I will defend this city for
mine own sake, and for my servant David's sake.

And Isaiah said, Take a lump of figs. And they took and laid *it*
on the boil, and he recovered.   2 KINGS 20:1–7

> *While Hezekiah's story focuses on the length of his life, Jeremi-
> ah's story goes all the way back before he was born. Jeremiah
> was a prophet who lived in the time of the divided kingdom. He
> lived in the southern kingdom of Judah and prophesied to the
> people there of their coming conquest and exile by the Babylo-
> nians. In the lives of both Hezekiah and Jeremiah, God was not
> distant or ambivalent, but near and loving. Notice how specific
> and detailed God's warnings were, and yet how he assured Jer-
> emiah of his intervention and protection.*

The words of Jeremiah the son of Hilkiah, of the priests that
were in Anathoth in the land of Benjamin: To whom the word of
the LORD came in the days of Josiah the son of Amon king of Judah, in the thirteenth year of his reign. It came also in the days
of Jehoiakim the son of Josiah king of Judah, unto the end of the
eleventh year of Zedekiah the son of Josiah king of Judah, unto the
carrying away of Jerusalem captive in the fifth month.

Then the word of the LORD came unto me, saying, **Before I
formed thee in the belly I knew thee; and before thou camest
forth out of the womb I sanctified thee,** *and* **I ordained thee a
prophet unto the nations.**

Then said I, Ah, Lord GOD! behold, I cannot speak: for I *am* a
child.

But the LORD said unto me, Say not, I *am* a child: for thou shalt
go to all that I shall send thee, and whatsoever I command thee
thou shalt speak. Be not afraid of their faces: for I *am* with thee to
deliver thee, saith the LORD.

Then the LORD put forth his hand, and touched my mouth.
And the LORD said unto me, Behold, I have put my words in thy
mouth. See, I have this day set thee over the nations and over the

kingdoms, to root out, and to pull down, and to destroy, and to throw down, to build, and to plant.

Moreover the word of the LORD came unto me, saying, Jeremiah, what seest thou?

And I said, I see a rod of an almond tree.

Then said the LORD unto me, Thou hast well seen: for I will hasten my word to perform it.

And the word of the LORD came unto me the second time, saying, What seest thou?

And I said, I see a seething pot; and the face thereof *is* toward the north.

Then the LORD said unto me, Out of the north an evil shall break forth upon all the inhabitants of the land. For, lo, I will call all the families of the kingdoms of the north, saith the LORD. And they shall come, and they shall set every one his throne at the entering of the gates of Jerusalem, and against all the walls thereof round about, and against all the cities of Judah. And I will utter my judgments against them touching all their wickedness, who have forsaken me, and have burned incense unto other gods, and worshipped the works of their own hands.

Thou therefore gird up thy loins, and arise, and speak unto them all that I command thee: be not dismayed at their faces, lest I confound thee before them. For, behold, I have made thee this day a defenced city, and an iron pillar, and brasen walls against the whole land, against the kings of Judah, against the princes thereof, against the priests thereof, and against the people of the land. And they shall fight against thee; but they shall not prevail against thee; for I *am* with thee, saith the LORD, to deliver thee.   JEREMIAH 1:1–19

Jeremiah's role was to reveal the overall plan God was unfolding through Israel. He warned the southern kingdom of Judah about their unfaithfulness and God's pending discipline. He knew up front that they would not listen, but his task was simply to be faithful and courageous and to deliver the message from God. Three times the dreaded Babylonians attacked Jerusalem and carried away some of the people to Babylon. In 597 BC, after the second deportation, God gave Jeremiah the assignment of writing a letter to those exiles to remind them that, as Jeremiah had experienced personally, God had a grand and good plan for their lives.

Now these *are* the words of the letter that Jeremiah the prophet sent from Jerusalem unto the residue of the elders which were carried away captives, and to the priests, and to the prophets, and to all the people whom Nebuchadnezzar had carried away captive from Jerusalem to Babylon; (After that Jeconiah the king, and the queen, and the eunuchs, the princes of Judah and Jerusalem, and the carpenters, and the smiths, were departed from Jerusalem;) By the hand of Elasah the son of Shaphan, and Gemariah the son of Hilkiah, (whom Zedekiah king of Judah sent unto Babylon to Nebuchadnezzar king of Babylon) saying,

Thus saith the LORD of hosts, the God of Israel, unto all that are carried away captives, whom I have caused to be carried away from Jerusalem unto Babylon; Build ye houses, and dwell *in them*; and plant gardens, and eat the fruit of them; Take ye wives, and beget sons and daughters; and take wives for your sons, and give your daughters to husbands, that they may bear sons and daughters; that ye may be increased there, and not diminished. And seek the peace of the city whither I have caused you to be carried away captives, and pray unto the LORD for it: for in the peace thereof shall ye have peace. For thus saith the LORD of hosts, the God of Israel; Let not your prophets and your diviners, that *be* in the midst of you, deceive you, neither hearken to your dreams which ye cause to be dreamed. For they prophesy falsely unto you in my name: I have not sent them, saith the LORD.

For thus saith the LORD, That after seventy years be accomplished at Babylon I will visit you, and perform my good word toward you, in causing you to return to this place. **For I know the thoughts that I think toward you, saith the LORD, thoughts of peace, and not of evil, to give you an expected end.** Then shall ye call upon me, and ye shall go and pray unto me, and I will hearken unto you. And ye shall seek me, and find *me*, when ye shall search for me with all your heart. And I will be found of you, saith the LORD: and I will turn away your captivity, and I will gather you from all the nations, and from all the places whither I have driven you, saith the LORD; and I will bring you again into the place whence I caused you to be carried away captive. JEREMIAH 29:1–14

How did God show the captives in Babylon that he still cared for them and wanted the best for them?

GOD CARES FOR US

Jesus, the Son of God, came to earth. He was born as a human baby and lived among us. His arrival removes any doubt about the nearness of God in our lives. Jesus is Immanuel, "God with us."

When a large crowd assembled on a hillside by the sea of Galilee, Jesus taught this weary and worn bunch about the intimate involvement of God in their lives.

Therefore I say unto you, Take no thought for your life, what ye shall eat, or what ye shall drink; nor yet for your body, what ye shall put on. Is not the life more than meat, and the body than raiment? Behold the fowls of the air: for they sow not, neither do they reap, nor gather into barns; yet your heavenly Father feedeth them. Are ye not much better than they? Which of you by taking thought can add one cubit unto his stature?

And why take ye thought for raiment? Consider the lilies of the field, how they grow; they toil not, neither do they spin: And yet I say unto you, That even Solomon in all his glory was not arrayed like one of these. Wherefore, if God so clothe the grass of the field, which to day is, and to morrow is cast into the oven, *shall he* not much more *clothe* you, O ye of little faith? **Therefore take no thought, saying, What shall we eat? or, What shall we drink? or, Wherewithal shall we be clothed?** (For after all these things do the Gentiles seek:) for your heavenly Father knoweth that ye have need of all these things. But seek ye first the kingdom of God, and his righteousness; and all these things shall be added unto you. Take therefore no thought for the morrow: for the morrow shall take thought for the things of itself. Sufficient unto the day *is* the evil thereof. MATTHEW 6:25–34

Why does Jesus want us to refrain from worry?
How does freedom from worry demonstrate confidence
in God's provision and care?

After Jesus' death on the cross, he ascended back to the Father in heaven. Then God the Holy Ghost descended on all who believed in Jesus. The dwelling place for God was no longer in temples built by human hands but in the spirits of his people. From the inside out the Holy Ghost speaks to us, ministers to us, affirms us, directs us, challenges us and empowers us. With pen in hand, the apostle Paul instructed the church that gathered in Rome of this great truth.

Therefore, brethren, we are debtors, not to the flesh, to live after the flesh. For if ye live after the flesh, ye shall die: but if ye through the Spirit do mortify the deeds of the body, ye shall live.

ROMANS 8:12–13

Likewise the Spirit also helpeth our infirmities: for we know not what we should pray for as we ought: but the Spirit itself maketh intercession for us with groanings which cannot be uttered. And he that searcheth the hearts knoweth what *is* the mind of the Spirit, because he maketh intercession for the saints according to *the will of* God.

And we know that all things work together for good to them that love God, to them who are the called according to *his* purpose. For whom he did foreknow, he also did predestinate *to be* conformed to the image of his Son, that he might be the firstborn among many brethren. Moreover whom he did predestinate, them he also called: and whom he called, them he also justified: and whom he justified, them he also glorified.

What shall we then say to these things? **If God *be* for us, who *can be* against us? He that spared not his own Son, but delivered him up for us all, how shall he not with him also freely give us all things?** Who shall lay any thing to the charge of God's elect? *It is* God that justifieth. Who *is* he that condemneth? *It is* Christ that died, yea rather, that is risen again, who is even at the right hand of God, who also maketh intercession for us. Who shall separate us from the love of Christ? *shall* tribulation, or distress, or persecution, or famine, or nakedness, or peril, or sword? As it is written, For thy sake we are killed all the day long; we are accounted as sheep for the slaughter.

Nay, in all these things we are more than conquerors through him that loved us. For I am persuaded, that neither death, nor life, nor angels, nor principalities, nor powers, nor things present, nor things to come, nor height, nor depth, nor any other creature, shall be able to separate us from the love of God, which is in Christ Jesus our Lord. Romans 8:26–39

What amazing love God has for his people! In the spirit of this love, James, the half brother of Jesus, wrote a practical letter to Jesus' early disciples. He reminded them that God is involved in and cares about their daily lives—although they too had a role to play. As believers, we can acknowledge God's involvement in our lives, even during seasons of trial. We can seek God and ask him for wisdom. We must also be careful not to blame God for our trials and temptations and realize that every good gift comes from his hands.

As you read the passage below from James 1, ask yourself:
How does God show his care and concern
for us when we go through difficult seasons in life?

James, a servant of God and of the Lord Jesus Christ, to the twelve tribes which are scattered abroad, greeting.

My brethren, count it all joy when ye fall into divers temptations; Knowing *this*, that the trying of your faith worketh patience. But let patience have *her* perfect work, that ye may be perfect and entire, wanting nothing. If any of you lack wisdom, let him ask of God, that giveth to all *men* liberally, and upbraideth not; and it shall be given him. But let him ask in faith, nothing wavering. For he that wavereth is like a wave of the sea driven with the wind and tossed. For let not that man think that he shall receive any thing of the Lord. A double minded man *is* unstable in all his ways.

Let the brother of low degree rejoice in that he is exalted: But the rich, in that he is made low: because as the flower of the grass he shall pass away. For the sun is no sooner risen with a burning heat, but it withereth the grass, and the flower thereof falleth, and the grace of the fashion of it perisheth: so also shall the rich man fade away in his ways.

Blessed *is* the man that endureth temptation: for when he is tried, he shall receive the crown of life, which the Lord hath promised to them that love him.

Let no man say when he is tempted, I am tempted of God: for God cannot be tempted with evil, neither tempteth he any man: But every man is tempted, when he is drawn away of his own lust, and enticed. Then when lust hath conceived, it bringeth forth sin: and sin, when it is finished, bringeth forth death.

Do not err, my beloved brethren. Every good gift and every perfect gift is from above, and cometh down from the Father of lights, with whom is no variableness, neither shadow of turning. Of his own will begat he us with the word of truth, that we should be a kind of firstfruits of his creatures. JAMES 1:1–18

WHAT WE BELIEVE

The God of the Bible is the only true God and is all-powerful and all-knowing. As we read the pages of the Bible we discover over and over again that God is good. His heart and intent toward us is always for what is right, just and good. God also is working out his good and grand plan to restore his original vision to be with us, in community. He is involved in the details of our individual lives. His plan for us offers us hope, prosperity and a future. Bottom line ... God cares for us. When we grasp these foundational beliefs, not only in our minds but also in our hearts, we are able to walk through each day with joy, hope and great confidence.

CHAPTER

3

Salvation

---------- KEY QUESTION ----------

How do I have a relationship with God?

---------- KEY IDEA ----------

I believe a person comes into a right relationship
with God by God's grace through faith in Jesus Christ.

---------- KEY VERSE ----------

For by grace are ye saved through faith;
and that not of yourselves: *it is* the gift of God:
Not of works, lest any man should boast.
Ephesians 2:8 – 9

OUR MAP

We have discovered so far that the God of the Bible is the one true God—Father, Son and Holy Ghost. We have also discovered he is not a distant deity, uninterested in our world and our lives; he is personal and near. He is utterly good. He has a plan and purpose for our lives. He cares deeply for us. Now we turn to what may be the most important question of all, "How do I come into a relationship with God?"

In this chapter we will be reading a collection of Scripture passages about salvation that has all the makings of the greatest love story ever told:

- The Problem: We Are Not Born Into a Relationship With God
- The Solution: There Is Only One Solution and Our Good God Provided It
- The Outcome: A Lasting Relationship With Our Loving God

THE PROBLEM: WE ARE NOT BORN INTO A RELATIONSHIP WITH GOD

Satan, the great deceiver, clothed himself as a serpent, one of God's good creatures, and set out to trick Adam and Eve into disobeying their gracious God. After creating Adam and Eve, God told them not to eat of the fruit of a certain tree in the garden of Eden. But Satan suggested that God wasn't being honest when he warned of the results of eating the forbidden fruit. The great deceiver's ploy succeeded, and Adam and Eve willfully rejected God and his promise of life together with them in the garden.

The consequences of Adam and Eve's rebellion were passed on to their offspring and then again and again to every generation since. Every human born receives this "virus" at conception and then acts out of this nature throughout their life. The Bible calls it sin. It causes death—both the physical death of our bodies and the spiritual death of separation from God.

And the LORD God planted a garden eastward in Eden; and there he put the man whom he had formed. And out of the ground made the LORD God to grow every tree that is pleasant to the sight, and good for food; the tree of life also in the midst of the garden, and the tree of knowledge of good and evil. GENESIS 2:8–9

And the LORD God took the man, and put him into the garden of Eden to dress it and to keep it. And the LORD God commanded the man, saying, Of every tree of the garden thou mayest freely eat: But of the tree of the knowledge of good and evil, thou shalt not eat of it: for in the day that thou eatest thereof thou shalt surely die. GENESIS 2:15–17

Now the serpent was more subtil than any beast of the field which the LORD God had made. And he said unto the woman, Yea, hath God said, Ye shall not eat of every tree of the garden?

And the woman said unto the serpent, We may eat of the fruit of the trees of the garden: But of the fruit of the tree which *is* in the midst of the garden, God hath said, Ye shall not eat of it, neither shall ye touch it, lest ye die.

And the serpent said unto the woman, Ye shall not surely die: For God doth know that in the day ye eat thereof, then your eyes shall be opened, and ye shall be as gods, knowing good and evil.

And when the woman saw that the tree *was* good for food, and that it *was* pleasant to the eyes, and a tree to be desired to make *one* wise, she took of the fruit thereof, and did eat, and gave also unto her husband with her; and he did eat. And the eyes of them both were opened, and they knew that they *were* naked; and they sewed fig leaves together, and made themselves aprons.

And they heard the voice of the LORD God walking in the garden in the cool of the day: and Adam and his wife hid themselves from the presence of the LORD God amongst the trees of the garden. And the LORD God called unto Adam, and said unto him, Where *art* thou?

And he said, I heard thy voice in the garden, and I was afraid, because I *was* naked; and I hid myself.

And he said, Who told thee that thou *wast* naked? Hast thou eaten of the tree, whereof I commanded thee that thou shouldest not eat?

And the man said, The woman whom thou gavest *to be* with me, she gave me of the tree, and I did eat.

And the LORD God said unto the woman, What *is* this *that* thou hast done?

And the woman said, The serpent beguiled me, and I did eat.

And the LORD God said unto the serpent, Because thou hast done this, thou *art* cursed above all cattle, and above every beast of the field; upon thy belly shalt thou go, and dust shalt thou eat all the days of thy life: And I will put enmity between thee and the woman, and between thy seed and her seed; it shall bruise thy head, and thou shalt bruise his heel.

Unto the woman he said, I will greatly multiply thy sorrow and thy conception; in sorrow thou shalt bring forth children; and thy desire *shall be* to thy husband, and he shall rule over thee.

And unto Adam he said, Because thou hast hearkened unto the voice of thy wife, and hast eaten of the tree, of which I commanded thee, saying, Thou shalt not eat of it: Cursed *is* the ground for thy sake; in sorrow shalt thou eat *of* it all the days of thy life; Thorns also and thistles shall it bring forth to thee; and thou shalt eat the herb of the field; In the sweat of thy face shalt thou eat bread, till thou return unto the ground; for out of it wast thou taken: for dust thou *art*, and unto dust shalt thou return.

And Adam called his wife's name Eve; because she was the mother of all living.

Unto Adam also and to his wife did the LORD God make coats of skins, and clothed them. And the LORD God said, Behold, the man is become as one of us, to know good and evil: and now, lest he put forth his hand, and take also of the tree of life, and eat, and live for ever. **Therefore the LORD God sent him forth from the garden of Eden, to till the ground from whence he was taken. So he drove out the man; and he placed at the east of the garden of Eden Cherubims, and a flaming sword which turned every way, to keep the way of the tree of life.** GENESIS 3:1–24

How would you describe Adam and Eve's life
in the garden with God before they disobeyed him?
What was life with God like for them afterward?

The Solution: There Is Only One Solution and Our Good God Provided It

When Adam and Eve sinned, God set into motion his plan to get people back into a relationship with him. When he replaced their clothes of fig leaves with the skins of animals, he signaled something important — it would take the blood of another to cover the sins of humankind. God began by the founding of a brand-new nation through which he would reveal himself and his plan to restore humankind. For more than 1,600 years, every Biblical story of the chosen people of Israel would point to the coming of the solution.

One of the earliest examples of this "blood covering" took place as God was preparing to deliver Israel from 400 years of captivity in Egypt. God chose Moses as his messenger to Pharaoh to demand that he release God's people from slavery and let them take possession of the promised land. But Pharaoh was hardhearted and would not let the people leave. To make Pharaoh understand and believe in God's power, God issued ten brutal plagues on Egypt and its people. The tenth and final plague foreshadows the ultimate solution of deliverance from humankind's slavery to sin.

And the LORD said unto Moses, Yet will I bring one plague *more* upon Pharaoh, and upon Egypt; afterwards he will let you go hence: when he shall let *you* go, he shall surely thrust you out hence altogether. Speak now in the ears of the people, and let every man borrow of his neighbour, and every woman of her neighbour, jewels of silver, and jewels of gold. And the LORD gave the people favour in the sight of the Egyptians. Moreover the man Moses *was* very great in the land of Egypt, in the sight of Pharaoh's servants, and in the sight of the people.

And Moses said, Thus saith the LORD, About midnight will I go out into the midst of Egypt: And all the firstborn in the land of Egypt shall die, from the firstborn of Pharaoh that sitteth upon his throne, even unto the firstborn of the maidservant that *is* behind the mill; and all the firstborn of beasts. And there shall be a great cry throughout all the land of Egypt, such as there was none like it, nor shall be like it any more. But against any of the children of Israel shall not a dog move his tongue, against man or beast: that ye may know how that the LORD doth put a difference between the Egyptians and Israel. And all these thy servants shall come down unto me, and bow down themselves unto me, saying, Get thee out, and all the people that follow thee: and after that I will go out. And he went out from Pharaoh in a great anger.

And the LORD said unto Moses, Pharaoh shall not hearken unto you; that my wonders may be multiplied in the land of Egypt. And Moses and Aaron did all these wonders before Pharaoh: and the LORD hardened Pharaoh's heart, so that he would not let the children of Israel go out of his land.

And the LORD spake unto Moses and Aaron in the land of Egypt, saying, This month *shall be* unto you the beginning of months: it *shall be* the first month of the year to you. Speak ye unto all the congregation of Israel, saying, In the tenth *day* of this month they shall take to them every man a lamb, according to the house of *their* fathers, a lamb for an house: And if the household be too little for the lamb, let him and his neighbour next unto his house take *it* according to the number of the souls; every man according to his eating shall make your count for the lamb. Your lamb shall be without blemish, a male of the first year: ye shall take *it* out from the sheep, or from the goats: And ye shall keep it up until the fourteenth day of the same month: and the whole assembly of the congregation of Israel shall kill it in the evening. And they shall take of the blood, and strike *it* on the two side posts and on the upper door post of the houses, wherein they shall eat it. And they shall eat the flesh in that night, roast with fire, and unleavened bread; *and* with bitter *herbs* they shall eat it. Eat not of it raw, nor sodden at all with water, but roast *with* fire; his head with his legs, and with the purtenance thereof. And ye shall let nothing of it remain until the morning; and that which remaineth of it until the morning ye shall burn with fire. And thus shall ye eat it; *with* your loins girded, your shoes on your feet, and your staff in your hand; and ye shall eat it in haste: it *is* the LORD's passover.

For I will pass through the land of Egypt this night, and will smite all the firstborn in the land of Egypt, both man and beast; and against all the gods of Egypt I will execute judgment: I *am* the LORD. And the blood shall be to you for a token upon the houses

where ye *are*: and when I see the blood, I will pass over you, and
the plague shall not be upon you to destroy *you*, when I smite the
land of Egypt.

EXODUS 11:1—12:13

What are the similarities between the sacrificed lamb
and the sacrifice of Jesus? What type of "Passover" has
been caused by Jesus' blood applied to our lives?

**Then Moses called for all the elders of Israel, and said
unto them, Draw out and take you a lamb according to your
families, and kill the passover. And ye shall take a bunch of
hyssop, and dip *it* in the blood that *is* in the bason, and strike
the lintel and the two side posts with the blood that *is* in the
bason; and none of you shall go out at the door of his house
until the morning. For the LORD will pass through to smite
the Egyptians; and when he seeth the blood upon the lintel,
and on the two side posts, the LORD will pass over the door,
and will not suffer the destroyer to come in unto your houses
to smite *you*.**

And ye shall observe this thing for an ordinance to thee and
to thy sons for ever. And it shall come to pass, when ye be come
to the land which the LORD will give you, according as he hath
promised, that ye shall keep this service. And it shall come to
pass, when your children shall say unto you, What mean ye by
this service? That ye shall say, It *is* the sacrifice of the LORD's passover, who passed over the houses of the children of Israel in Egypt,
when he smote the Egyptians, and delivered our houses. And the
people bowed the head and worshipped. And the children of Israel went away, and did as the LORD had commanded Moses and
Aaron, so did they.

And it came to pass, that at midnight the LORD smote all the
firstborn in the land of Egypt, from the firstborn of Pharaoh that
sat on his throne unto the firstborn of the captive that *was* in the
dungeon; and all the firstborn of cattle. And Pharaoh rose up in
the night, he, and all his servants, and all the Egyptians; and there
was a great cry in Egypt; for *there was* not a house where *there was*
not one dead.

And he called for Moses and Aaron by night, and said, Rise up, *and* get you forth from among my people, both ye and the children of Israel; and go, serve the LORD, as ye have said.   EXODUS 12:21–31

About 700 years after the exodus and 700 years before the birth of Jesus, God inspired the prophet Isaiah to speak on his behalf. The following prophecy about the Lord's "suffering servant" takes the concept of blood sacrifice and the Passover lamb to a new level. This Scripture, which is quoted more often in the New Testament than any other Old Testament passage, also foretells the mission of the One who will provide the way for our sins to be forgiven.

Recalling the details of Jesus' time on earth,
look for similarities between Jesus' life and Isaiah's
prophecy of the "suffering servant."

Behold, my servant shall deal prudently, he shall be exalted and extolled, and be very high. As many were astonied at thee; his visage was so marred more than any man, and his form more than the sons of men: So shall he sprinkle many nations; the kings shall shut their mouths at him: for *that* which had not been told them shall they see; and *that* which they had not heard shall they consider.

Who hath believed our report? and to whom is the arm of the LORD revealed? For he shall grow up before him as a tender plant, and as a root out of a dry ground: he hath no form nor comeliness; and when we shall see him, *there is* no beauty that we should desire him. He is despised and rejected of men; a man of sorrows, and acquainted with grief: and we hid as it were *our* faces from him; he was despised, and we esteemed him not.

Surely he hath borne our griefs, and carried our sorrows: yet we did esteem him stricken, smitten of God, and afflicted. **But he *was* wounded for our transgressions, *he was* bruised for our iniquities: the chastisement of our peace *was* upon him; and with his stripes we are healed.** All we like sheep have gone astray; we have turned every one to his own way; and the LORD hath laid on him the iniquity of us all.

He was oppressed, and he was afflicted, yet he opened not his mouth: he is brought as a lamb to the slaughter, and as a sheep before her shearers is dumb, so he openeth not his mouth. He was taken from prison and from judgment: and who shall declare his generation? for he was cut off out of the land of the living: for the transgression of my people was he stricken. And he made his grave with the wicked, and with the rich in his death; because he had done no violence, neither *was any* deceit in his mouth.

Yet it pleased the LORD to bruise him; he hath put *him* to grief: when thou shalt make his soul an offering for sin, he shall see *his* seed, he shall prolong *his* days, and the pleasure of the LORD shall prosper in his hand. He shall see of the travail of his soul, *and* shall be satisfied: by his knowledge shall my righteous servant justify many; for he shall bear their iniquities. Therefore will I divide him *a portion* with the great, and he shall divide the spoil with the strong; because he hath poured out his soul unto death: and he was numbered with the transgressors; and he bare the sin of many, and made intercession for the transgressors.   ISAIAH 52:13—53:12

God's ultimate solution to our problem of separation from him was poignantly demonstrated and graphically foretold over hundreds of years of Jewish history. When God spared the Israelites through the sacrifice of their Passover lambs, his point was inescapable. When Isaiah foresaw one who would be "wounded for our transgressions" and "bruised for our iniquities," the identity of the suffering servant was undeniable. The ritual and the prophecy were fulfilled when the Messiah Jesus was crucified on a cross for the sins of humankind. God's plan, set into motion in the garden of Eden, was at long last finished.

[Jesus] said unto his disciples, Ye know that after two days is *the feast of* the passover, and the Son of man is betrayed to be crucified.

Then assembled together the chief priests, and the scribes, and the elders of the people, unto the palace of the high priest, who was called Caiaphas, and consulted that they might take Jesus by subtilty, and kill *him*.   MATTHEW 26:1–4

Then the soldiers of the governor took Jesus into the common hall, and gathered unto him the whole band *of soldiers*. And they stripped him, and put on him a scarlet robe. And when they had platted a crown of thorns, they put *it* upon his head, and a reed in his right hand: and they bowed the knee before him, and mocked him, saying, Hail, King of the Jews! And they spit upon him, and took the reed, and smote him on the head. And after that they had mocked him, they took the robe off from him, and put his own raiment on him, and led him away to crucify *him*.

And as they came out, they found a man of Cyrene, Simon by name: him they compelled to bear his cross. And when they were come unto a place called Golgotha, that is to say, a place of a skull, They gave him vinegar to drink mingled with gall: and when he had tasted *thereof*, he would not drink. And they crucified him, and parted his garments, casting lots: that it might be fulfilled which was spoken by the prophet, They parted my garments among them, and upon my vesture did they cast lots. And sitting down they watched him there; And set up over his head his accusation written, THIS IS JESUS THE KING OF THE JEWS.

Then were there two thieves crucified with him, one on the right hand, and another on the left. And they that passed by reviled him, wagging their heads, And saying, Thou that destroyest the temple, and buildest *it* in three days, save thyself. If thou be the Son of God, come down from the cross. Likewise also the chief priests mocking *him*, with the scribes and elders, said, He saved others; himself he cannot save. If he be the King of Israel, let him now come down from the cross, and we will believe him. He trusted in God; let him deliver him now, if he will have him: for he said, I am the Son of God. The thieves also, which were crucified with him, cast the same in his teeth.

Now from the sixth hour there was darkness over all the land unto the ninth hour. And about the ninth hour Jesus cried with a loud voice, saying, Eli, Eli, lama sabachthani? that is to say, My God, my God, why hast thou forsaken me?

Some of them that stood there, when they heard *that*, said, This *man* calleth for Elias.

And straightway one of them ran, and took a spunge, and filled *it* with vinegar, and put *it* on a reed, and gave him to drink. The rest said, Let be, let us see whether Elias will come to save him.

Jesus, when he had cried again with a loud voice, yielded up the ghost.

And, behold, the veil of the temple was rent in twain from the top to the bottom; and the earth did quake, and the rocks rent; And the graves were opened; and many bodies of the saints which slept arose, and came out of the graves after his resurrection, and went into the holy city, and appeared unto many.

Now when the centurion, and they that were with him, watching Jesus, saw the earthquake, and those things that were done, they feared greatly, saying, Truly this was the Son of God.

And many women were there beholding afar off, which followed Jesus from Galilee, ministering unto him: Among which was Mary Magdalene, and Mary the mother of James and Joseph, and the mother of Zebedee's children.

When the even was come, there came a rich man of Arimathaea, named Joseph, who also himself was Jesus' disciple. He went to Pilate, and begged the body of Jesus. Then Pilate commanded the body to be delivered. And when Joseph had taken the body, he wrapped it in a clean linen cloth, And laid it in his own new tomb, which he had hewn out in the rock: and he rolled a great stone to the door of the sepulchre, and departed. And there was Mary Magdalene, and the other Mary, sitting over against the sepulchre.

Now the next day, that followed the day of the preparation, the chief priests and Pharisees came together unto Pilate, saying, Sir, we remember that that deceiver said, while he was yet alive, After three days I will rise again. Command therefore that the sepulchre be made sure until the third day, lest his disciples come by night, and steal him away, and say unto the people, He is risen from the dead: so the last error shall be worse than the first.

Pilate said unto them, Ye have a watch: go your way, make *it* as sure as ye can. So they went, and made the sepulchre sure, sealing the stone, and setting a watch.

In the end of the sabbath, as it began to dawn toward the first *day* of the week, came Mary Magdalene and the other Mary to see the sepulchre.

And, behold, there was a great earthquake: for the angel of the Lord descended from heaven, and came and rolled back the stone from the door, and sat upon it. His countenance was like lightning, and his raiment white as snow: And for fear of him the keepers did shake, and became as dead *men*.

And the angel answered and said unto the women, Fear not ye: for I know that ye seek Jesus, which was crucified. He is not here: for he is risen, as he said. Come, see the place where the Lord lay. And go quickly, and tell his disciples that he is risen from the dead; and, behold, he goeth before you into Galilee; there shall ye see him: lo, I have told you.

And they departed quickly from the sepulchre with fear and great joy; and did run to bring his disciples word. And as they went to tell his disciples, behold, Jesus met them, saying, All hail. And they came and held him by the feet, and worshipped him. Then said Jesus unto them, Be not afraid: go tell my brethren that they go into Galilee, and there shall they see me.   MATTHEW 27:27—28:10

THE OUTCOME: A LASTING RELATIONSHIP
WITH OUR LOVING GOD

Even with all the incredible stories connecting the dots from the promised Messiah to the person Jesus, most members of the nation of Israel didn't recognize or accept Jesus as the Savior of the world. They didn't recognize the One who would provide the way for our sin to be forgiven so we could enter into a personal relationship with God, overcome death and have eternal life. John tells the story of one Jewish religious leader who approached Jesus at night to probe his true identity and mission.

There was a man of the Pharisees, named Nicodemus, a ruler of the Jews: The same came to Jesus by night, and said unto him, Rabbi, we know that thou art a teacher come from God: for no man can do these miracles that thou doest, except God be with him.

Jesus answered and said unto him, Verily, verily, I say unto thee, Except a man be born again, he cannot see the kingdom of God.

Nicodemus saith unto him, How can a man be born when he is old? can he enter the second time into his mother's womb, and be born?

Jesus answered, Verily, verily, I say unto thee, Except a man be born of water and *of* the Spirit, he cannot enter into the kingdom of God. That which is born of the flesh is flesh; and that which is born of the Spirit is spirit. Marvel not that I said unto thee, Ye must be born again. The wind bloweth where it listeth, and thou hearest the sound thereof, but canst not tell whence it cometh, and whither it goeth: so is every one that is born of the Spirit.

Nicodemus answered and said unto him, How can these things be?

Jesus answered and said unto him, Art thou a master of Israel, and knowest not these things? Verily, verily, I say unto thee, We speak that we do know, and testify that we have seen; and ye receive not our witness. If I have told you earthly things, and ye believe not, how shall ye believe, if I tell you *of* heavenly things? And no man hath ascended up to heaven, but he that came down from heaven, *even* the Son of man which is in heaven. And as Moses lifted up the serpent in the wilderness, even so must the Son of man be lifted up: That whosoever believeth in him should not perish, but have eternal life.

For God so loved the world, that he gave his only begotten Son, that whosoever believeth in him should not perish, but have everlasting life. For God sent not his Son into the world to condemn the world; but that the world through him might be saved. He that believeth on him is not condemned: but he that believeth not is condemned already, because he hath not believed in the name of the only begotten Son of God. And this is the condemnation, that light is come into the world, and men loved darkness rather than light, because their deeds were evil. For every one that doeth evil hateth the light, neither cometh to the light, lest his deeds should be reproved. But he that doeth truth cometh to the light, that his deeds may be made manifest, that they are wrought in God.   JOHN 3:1–21

Nicodemus was not the only person who heard and believed Christ's good news. After Jesus ascended back to the Father following his resurrection, the Holy Ghost came down on the disciples as Jesus had promised, and the church was born. Peter exited the upper room and gave a powerful sermon to the thousands of people who gathered in Jerusalem for the Pentecost celebration. Read carefully his final challenge and celebrate the outcome.

Therefore let all the house of Israel know assuredly, that God hath made that same Jesus, whom ye have crucified, both Lord and Christ.

Now when they heard *this*, they were pricked in their heart, and said unto Peter and to the rest of the apostles, Men *and* brethren, what shall we do?

Then Peter said unto them, Repent, and be baptized every one of you in the name of Jesus Christ for the remission of sins, and ye shall receive the gift of the Holy Ghost. For the promise is unto you, and to your children, and to all that are afar off, *even* as many as the Lord our God shall call.

And with many other words did he testify and exhort, saying, Save yourselves from this untoward generation. Then they that gladly received his word were baptized: and the same day there were added *unto them* about three thousand souls.   ACTS 2:36–41

In his letter to the church at Rome, the apostle Paul—who was called by God to tell this good news to the rest of the world—further reinforces what we must do to receive this gift of grace.

Wherefore, as by one man sin entered into the world, and death by sin; and so death passed upon all men, for that all have sinned:

(For until the law sin was in the world: but sin is not imputed when there is no law. Nevertheless death reigned from Adam to Moses, even over them that had not sinned after the similitude of Adam's transgression, who is the figure of him that was to come.

But not as the offence, so also *is* the free gift. For if through the offence of one many be dead, much more the grace of God, and the gift by grace, *which is* by one man, Jesus Christ, hath abounded unto many. And not as *it was* by one that sinned, *so is* the gift: for the judgment *was* by one to condemnation, but the free gift *is* of many offences unto justification. **For if by one man's offence death reigned by one; much more they which receive abundance of grace and of the gift of righteousness shall reign in life by one, Jesus Christ.)**

Therefore as by the offence of one *judgment came* upon all men to condemnation; even so by the righteousness of one *the free gift came* upon all men unto justification of life. For as by one man's disobedience many were made sinners, so by the obedience of one shall many be made righteous.

Moreover the law entered, that the offence might abound. But where sin abounded, grace did much more abound: That as sin hath reigned unto death, even so might grace reign through righteousness unto eternal life by Jesus Christ our Lord. Romans 5:12–21

Brethren, my heart's desire and prayer to God for Israel is, that they might be saved. For I bear them record that they have a zeal of God, but not according to knowledge. For they being ignorant of God's righteousness, and going about to establish their own righteousness, have not submitted themselves unto the righteousness of God. For Christ *is* the end of the law for righteousness to every one that believeth.

For Moses describeth the righteousness which is of the law, That the man which doeth those things shall live by them. But the righteousness which is of faith speaketh on this wise, Say not in thine heart, Who shall ascend into heaven? (that is, to bring Christ down *from above:*) Or, Who shall descend into the deep? (that is, to bring up Christ again from the dead.) But what saith it? The word is nigh thee, *even* in thy mouth, and in thy heart: that is, the word of faith, which we preach; **That if thou shalt confess with thy mouth the Lord Jesus, and shalt believe in thine heart that God hath raised him from the dead, thou shalt be saved. For with the heart man believeth unto righteousness; and with the mouth confession is made unto salvation.** For the scripture saith, Whosoever believeth on him shall not be ashamed. For there is no difference between the Jew and the Greek: for the same Lord over all is rich unto all that call upon him. For whosoever shall call upon the name of the Lord shall be saved. Romans 10:1–13

Why is it important to both believe in our hearts and profess with our mouths that Jesus is Lord?

The apostle Paul opens his letter to the church at Ephesus with the declaration that God had accomplished his intended outcome of providing to humanity the way of salvation. As you read these beautiful words, celebrate in your heart that the one true personal God of the universe wants to be in a relationship with you.

Blessed *be* the God and Father of our Lord Jesus Christ, who hath blessed us with all spiritual blessings in heavenly *places* in Christ: According as he hath chosen us in him before the foundation of the world, that we should be holy and without blame before him in love: Having predestinated us unto the adoption of children by Jesus Christ to himself, according to the good pleasure of his will, To the praise of the glory of his grace, wherein he hath made us accepted in the beloved. **In whom we have redemption through his blood, the forgiveness of sins, according to the riches of his grace; Wherein he hath abounded toward us in all wisdom and prudence;** Having made known unto us the mystery of his will, according to his good pleasure which he hath purposed in himself: That in the dispensation of the fulness of times he might gather together in one all things in Christ, both which are in heaven, and which are on earth; *even* in him:

In whom also we have obtained an inheritance, being predestinated according to the purpose of him who worketh all things after the counsel of his own will: That we should be to the praise of his glory, who first trusted in Christ. In whom ye also *trusted*, after that ye heard the word of truth, the gospel of your salvation: in whom also after that ye believed, ye were sealed with that holy Spirit of promise, Which is the earnest of our inheritance until the redemption of the purchased possession, unto the praise of his glory. Ephesians 1:3–14

Can you pinpoint a moment or chart a sequence
of moments in time when you realized that Christ died for you?
How would you describe that process?

WHAT WE BELIEVE

Before the creation of the world, God had a Plan B in place for humanity to be in relationship with him. Sure enough, Plan B became necessary when Adam and Eve ate the forbidden fruit, ushering in sin and death to all. But thanks to the sacrifice of the second person of the Trinity—the Son—the way was provided to come back to God through faith in Jesus Christ. If we believe this truth, not only in our heads but also in our hearts, and publicly confess it for the world to hear, we will be saved.

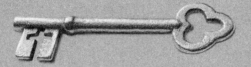

CHAPTER

4

The Bible

─────── KEY QUESTION ───────

How do I know God and his will for my life?

─────── KEY IDEA ───────

I believe the Bible is the inspired Word of God
that guides my beliefs and actions.

─────── KEY VERSE ───────

All scripture *is* given by inspiration of God, and *is* profitable
for doctrine, for reproof, for correction, for instruction
in righteousness: That the man of God may be perfect,
throughly furnished unto all good works.

2 Timothy 3:16 – 17

OUR MAP

How do we know God? How do we understand and see the world we live in? How do we grasp where we came from and why we are here? How do we know where this story is ultimately heading? The answer is profound—God reveals himself and his grand plan to us. Our role is to listen and believe.

By simply looking at nature and the world around us we can conclude there is a God. But how do we learn about this God? How do we come into a full relationship with God? What are his plans and purposes for us? What are the principles he wants us to live by to guide us into his truth? The answer to all of these questions is found in God's revelation to us—the Bible.

In this chapter we will read some of God's messages in Scripture that clearly convey his will and discover why the Bible holds such power for the Christian:

- *God Speaks*
- *The Authority of Scripture*
- *The Purpose of Scripture*

GOD SPEAKS

The Bible repeatedly records that God communicated to his people at specific times with specific messages. In some cases, such as with Moses at the burning bush, God spoke audibly. In other instances he spoke through dreams, visions or less direct impressions. But the words of the Lord were always given to his people to reveal his plan for them and then recorded in the Scriptures for the benefit of all humanity. God spelled out his story in the Bible because he loves us.

Now Moses kept the flock of Jethro his father in law, the priest of Midian: and he led the flock to the backside of the desert, and came to the mountain of God, *even* to Horeb. And the angel of the LORD appeared unto him in a flame of fire out of the midst of a bush: and he looked, and, behold, the bush burned with fire, and the bush *was* not consumed. And Moses said, I will now turn aside, and see this great sight, why the bush is not burnt.

And when the LORD saw that he turned aside to see, God called unto him out of the midst of the bush, and said, Moses, Moses.

And he said, Here *am* I.

And he said, Draw not nigh hither: put off thy shoes from off thy feet, for the place whereon thou standest *is* holy ground. Moreover he said, I *am* the God of thy father, the God of Abraham, the God of Isaac, and the God of Jacob. And Moses hid his face; for he was afraid to look upon God.

And the LORD said, I have surely seen the affliction of my people which *are* in Egypt, and have heard their cry by reason of their taskmasters; for I know their sorrows; And I am come down to deliver them out of the hand of the Egyptians, and to bring them up out of that land unto a good land and a large, unto a land flowing with milk and honey; unto the place of the Canaanites, and the Hittites, and the Amorites, and the Perizzites, and the Hivites, and the Jebusites. Now therefore, behold, the cry of the children of Israel is come unto me: and I have also seen the oppression wherewith the Egyptians oppress them. Come now therefore, and I will send thee unto Pharaoh, that thou mayest bring forth my people the children of Israel out of Egypt.

And Moses said unto God, Who *am* I, that I should go unto Pharaoh, and that I should bring forth the children of Israel out of Egypt?

And he said, Certainly I will be with thee; and this *shall be* a token unto thee, that I have sent thee: When thou hast brought forth the people out of Egypt, ye shall serve God upon this mountain.

And Moses said unto God, Behold, *when* I come unto the children of Israel, and shall say unto them, The God of your fathers hath sent me unto you; and they shall say to me, What *is* his name? what shall I say unto them?

And God said unto Moses, I AM THAT I AM: and he said, Thus shalt thou say unto the children of Israel, I AM hath sent me unto you.

And God said moreover unto Moses, Thus shalt thou say unto the children of Israel, The LORD God of your fathers, the God of Abraham, the God of Isaac, and the God of Jacob, hath sent me unto you: This *is* my name for ever, and this *is* my memorial unto all generations.

Go, and gather the elders of Israel together, and say unto them, The Lord God of your fathers, the God of Abraham, of Isaac, and of Jacob, appeared unto me, saying, I have surely visited you, and *seen* that which is done to you in Egypt: And I have said, I will bring you up out of the affliction of Egypt unto the land of the Canaanites, and the Hittites, and the Amorites, and the Perizzites, and the Hivites, and the Jebusites, unto a land flowing with milk and honey.

And they shall hearken to thy voice: and thou shalt come, thou and the elders of Israel, unto the king of Egypt, and ye shall say unto him, The Lord God of the Hebrews hath met with us: and now let us go, we beseech thee, three days' journey into the wilderness, that we may sacrifice to the Lord our God. And I am sure that the king of Egypt will not let you go, no, not by a mighty hand. And I will stretch out my hand, and smite Egypt with all my wonders which I will do in the midst thereof: and after that he will let you go.

And I will give this people favour in the sight of the Egyptians: and it shall come to pass, that, when ye go, ye shall not go empty: But every woman shall borrow of her neighbour, and of her that sojourneth in her house, jewels of silver, and jewels of gold, and raiment: and ye shall put *them* upon your sons, and upon your daughters; and ye shall spoil the Egyptians.

And Moses answered and said, But, behold, they will not believe me, nor hearken unto my voice: for they will say, The Lord hath not appeared unto thee.

And the Lord said unto him, What *is* that in thine hand?

And he said, A rod.

And he said, Cast it on the ground.

And he cast it on the ground, and it became a serpent; and Moses fled from before it. And the Lord said unto Moses, Put forth thine hand, and take it by the tail. And he put forth his hand, and caught it, and it became a rod in his hand: That they may believe that the Lord God of their fathers, the God of Abraham, the God of Isaac, and the God of Jacob, hath appeared unto thee.

And the Lord said furthermore unto him, Put now thine hand into thy bosom. And he put his hand into his bosom: and when he took it out, behold, his hand *was* leprous as snow.

And he said, Put thine hand into thy bosom again. And he put his hand into his bosom again; and plucked it out of his bosom, and, behold, it was turned again as his *other* flesh.

And it shall come to pass, if they will not believe thee, neither hearken to the voice of the first sign, that they will believe the voice of the latter sign. And it shall come to pass, if they will not believe also these two signs, neither hearken unto thy voice, that thou shalt take of the water of the river, and pour *it* upon the dry *land*: and the water which thou takest out of the river shall become blood upon the dry *land*.

And Moses said unto the LORD, O my Lord, I *am* not eloquent, neither heretofore, nor since thou hast spoken unto thy servant: but I *am* slow of speech, and of a slow tongue.

And the LORD said unto him, Who hath made man's mouth? or who maketh the dumb, or deaf, or the seeing, or the blind? have not I the LORD? Now therefore go, and I will be with thy mouth, and teach thee what thou shalt say.

And he said, O my Lord, send, I pray thee, by the hand *of him whom* thou wilt send.

And the anger of the LORD was kindled against Moses, and he said, *Is* not Aaron the Levite thy brother? I know that he can speak well. And also, behold, he cometh forth to meet thee: and when he seeth thee, he will be glad in his heart. And thou shalt speak unto him, and put words in his mouth: and I will be with thy mouth, and with his mouth, and will teach you what ye shall do. And he shall be thy spokesman unto the people: and he shall be, *even* he shall be to thee instead of a mouth, and thou shalt be to him instead of God. And thou shalt take this rod in thine hand, wherewith thou shalt do signs.   EXODUS 3:1—4:17

What can we learn about God's character
from the story of Moses and the burning bush? How did
Moses react to this direct communication from God?
How would you respond in a similar situation?

---

*The Lord spoke mostly through prophets in the Old Testament
and through Jesus and the apostles in the New Testament. After*

Jesus' death on the cross and miraculous resurrection, two of his followers were walking on the road from Jerusalem to Emmaus. Jesus came up and started walking with them and talking about his identity, though they were kept from recognizing him at first. Soon after, Jesus appeared to them again once they rejoined the disciples. It is significant that to prove to them he was the Messiah, he drew from the Old Testament. Jesus obviously understood these writings to be inspired by God.

And beginning at Moses and all the prophets, [Jesus] expounded unto them in all the scriptures the things concerning himself.

And they drew nigh unto the village, whither they went: and he made as though he would have gone further. But they constrained him, saying, Abide with us: for it is toward evening, and the day is far spent. And he went in to tarry with them.

And it came to pass, as he sat at meat with them, he took bread, and blessed *it*, and brake, and gave to them. And their eyes were opened, and they knew him; and he vanished out of their sight. **And they said one to another, Did not our heart burn within us, while he talked with us by the way, and while he opened to us the scriptures?**

And they rose up the same hour, and returned to Jerusalem, and found the eleven gathered together, and them that were with them, Saying, The Lord is risen indeed, and hath appeared to Simon. And they told what things *were done* in the way, and how he was known of them in breaking of bread.

And as they thus spake, Jesus himself stood in the midst of them, and saith unto them, Peace *be* unto you.

But they were terrified and affrighted, and supposed that they had seen a spirit. And he said unto them, Why are ye troubled? and why do thoughts arise in your hearts? Behold my hands and my feet, that it is I myself: handle me, and see; for a spirit hath not flesh and bones, as ye see me have.

And when he had thus spoken, he shewed them *his* hands and *his* feet. And while they yet believed not for joy, and wondered, he said unto them, Have ye here any meat? And they gave him a piece of a broiled fish, and of an honeycomb. And he took *it*, and did eat before them.

And he said unto them, These *are* the words which I spake unto you, while I was yet with you, that all things must be fulfilled, which were written in the law of Moses, and *in* the prophets, and *in* the psalms, concerning me.

Then opened he their understanding, that they might understand the scriptures, And said unto them, Thus it is written, and thus it behoved Christ to suffer, and to rise from the dead the third day: And that repentance and remission of sins should be preached in his name among all nations, beginning at Jerusalem. And ye are witnesses of these things. And, behold, I send the promise of my Father upon you: but tarry ye in the city of Jerusalem, until ye be endued with power from on high.   LUKE 24:27–49

How did Jesus help his disciples
understand who he was and why he came?

Before appearing to the Eleven in Jerusalem, Jesus appeared to Peter, also known as Simon, who, after denying Jesus, went on to become a faithful follower of Christ and a key leader in the early church.

Like other leaders of the church, Peter sent letters to those early believers; those letters are preserved in the Bible in the New Testament. He wrote this letter to one of the churches because false teaching was infiltrating the church and causing followers to stray from God's Word. Peter wrote to them to shepherd them back toward the truth. In the process, he provided insight into the origin of Scripture and how followers can use it to guide their lives.

As you read the passage below from 2 Peter 1,
think about how God, through Scripture, built a case
for the identity and purpose of Jesus.

Simon Peter, a servant and an apostle of Jesus Christ, to them that have obtained like precious faith with us through the righteousness of God and our Saviour Jesus Christ:

Grace and peace be multiplied unto you through the knowledge of God, and of Jesus our Lord.

According as his divine power hath given unto us all things that *pertain* unto life and godliness, through the knowledge of him that hath called us to glory and virtue: Whereby are given unto us exceeding great and precious promises: that by these ye might be partakers of the divine nature, having escaped the corruption that is in the world through lust.

And beside this, giving all diligence, add to your faith virtue; and to virtue knowledge; And to knowledge temperance; and to temperance patience; and to patience godliness; And to godliness brotherly kindness; and to brotherly kindness charity. For if these things be in you, and abound, they make *you that ye shall* neither *be* barren nor unfruitful in the knowledge of our Lord Jesus Christ. But he that lacketh these things is blind, and cannot see afar off, and hath forgotten that he was purged from his old sins.

Wherefore the rather, brethren, give diligence to make your calling and election sure: for if ye do these things, ye shall never fall: For so an entrance shall be ministered unto you abundantly into the everlasting kingdom of our Lord and Saviour Jesus Christ.

Wherefore I will not be negligent to put you always in remembrance of these things, though ye know *them*, and be established in the present truth. Yea, I think it meet, as long as I am in this tabernacle, to stir you up by putting *you* in remembrance; Knowing that shortly I must put off *this* my tabernacle, even as our Lord Jesus Christ hath shewed me. Moreover I will endeavour that ye may be able after my decease to have these things always in remembrance.

For we have not followed cunningly devised fables, when we made known unto you the power and coming of our Lord Jesus Christ, but were eyewitnesses of his majesty. For he received from God the Father honour and glory, when there came such a voice to him from the excellent glory, This is my beloved Son, in whom I am well pleased. And this voice which came from heaven we heard, when we were with him in the holy mount.

We have also a more sure word of prophecy; whereunto ye do well that ye take heed, as unto a light that shineth in a dark place, until the day dawn, and the day star arise in your hearts: **Knowing**

this first, that no prophecy of the scripture is of any private interpretation. For the prophecy came not in old time by the will of man: but holy men of God spake *as they were* moved by the Holy Ghost.   2 PETER 1:1–21

THE AUTHORITY OF SCRIPTURE

To understand the power of the authority of Scripture, we must go back to the early days of Israel. With a mighty hand God led the Israelites out of slavery in Egypt. While they were in the wilderness, God made preparations for them to enter into the land of Canaan that he had promised to Abraham 600 years earlier. Soon God descended from the heavens to Mount Sinai to meet with his servant Moses and the people and proclaim to them the Ten Commandments. These laws, spoken directly by God to Moses, guided the values and behavior of the Israelites.

In the third month, when the children of Israel were gone forth out of the land of Egypt, the same day came they *into* the wilderness of Sinai. For they were departed from Rephidim, and were come *to* the desert of Sinai, and had pitched in the wilderness; and there Israel camped before the mount.

And Moses went up unto God, and the LORD called unto him out of the mountain, saying, Thus shalt thou say to the house of Jacob, and tell the children of Israel; Ye have seen what I did unto the Egyptians, and *how* I bare you on eagles' wings, and brought you unto myself. Now therefore, if ye will obey my voice indeed, and keep my covenant, then ye shall be a peculiar treasure unto me above all people: for all the earth *is* mine: And ye shall be unto me a kingdom of priests, and an holy nation. These *are* the words which thou shalt speak unto the children of Israel.

And Moses came and called for the elders of the people, and laid before their faces all these words which the LORD commanded him. And all the people answered together, and said, All that the LORD hath spoken we will do. And Moses returned the words of the people unto the LORD.

And the LORD said unto Moses, Lo, I come unto thee in a thick cloud, that the people may hear when I speak with thee, and believe thee for ever. And Moses told the words of the people unto the LORD.   EXODUS 19:1–9

And it came to pass on the third day in the morning, that there were thunders and lightnings, and a thick cloud upon the mount, and the voice of the trumpet exceeding loud; so that all the people that *was* in the camp trembled. And Moses brought forth the people out of the camp to meet with God; and they stood at the nether part of the mount. **And mount Sinai was altogether on a smoke, because the Lord descended upon it in fire: and the smoke thereof ascended as the smoke of a furnace, and the whole mount quaked greatly. And when the voice of the trumpet sounded long, and waxed louder and louder, Moses spake, and God answered him by a voice.** Exodus 19:16–19

⚷ And God spake all these words, saying, I *am* the Lord thy God, which have brought thee out of the land of Egypt, out of the house of bondage.

Thou shalt have no other gods before me.

Thou shalt not make unto thee any graven image, or any likeness *of any thing* that *is* in heaven above, or that *is* in the earth beneath, or that *is* in the water under the earth: Thou shalt not bow down thyself to them, nor serve them: for I the Lord thy God *am* a jealous God, visiting the iniquity of the fathers upon the children unto the third and fourth *generation* of them that hate me; And shewing mercy unto thousands of them that love me, and keep my commandments.

Thou shalt not take the name of the Lord thy God in vain; for the Lord will not hold him guiltless that taketh his name in vain.

Remember the sabbath day, to keep it holy. Six days shalt thou labour, and do all thy work: But the seventh day *is* the sabbath of the Lord thy God: *in it* thou shalt not do any work, thou, nor thy son, nor thy daughter, thy manservant, nor thy maidservant, nor thy cattle, nor thy stranger that *is* within thy gates: For *in* six days the Lord made heaven and earth, the sea, and all that in them *is*, and rested the seventh day: wherefore the Lord blessed the sabbath day, and hallowed it.

Honour thy father and thy mother: that thy days may be long upon the land which the Lord thy God giveth thee.

Thou shalt not kill.

Thou shalt not commit adultery.

Thou shalt not steal.

Thou shalt not bear false witness against thy neighbour.

Thou shalt not covet thy neighbour's house, thou shalt not covet thy neighbour's wife, nor his manservant, nor his maidservant, nor his ox, nor his ass, nor any thing that *is* thy neighbour's.

And all the people saw the thunderings, and the lightnings, and the noise of the trumpet, and the mountain smoking: and when the people saw *it*, they removed, and stood afar off. And they said unto Moses, Speak thou with us, and we will hear: but let not God speak with us, lest we die.

And Moses said unto the people, Fear not: for God is come to prove you, and that his fear may be before your faces, that ye sin not.

And the people stood afar off, and Moses drew near unto the thick darkness where God *was*.   EXODUS 20:1–21 ⚷

Are the Ten Commandments as relevant today
as they were when Moses delivered
them to the Israelites? How?

God's words carry the authority of the One who speaks them. Examples of the authority of Scripture are found throughout the Bible — in both the Old and New Testaments. For instance, immediately after John baptized Jesus, the Spirit led Jesus into the wilderness where Satan sought to take advantage of Jesus' isolation, hunger and physical exhaustion. But God's power was revealed in Jesus' interactions with Satan; Jesus quoted Scripture three times — twice from Deuteronomy and once from Psalms — as his authority to overcome each temptation. Despite facing genuine temptations at a time when he was vulnerable, Jesus remained rooted in the principles recorded in God's Word.

⚷ Then was Jesus led up of the Spirit into the wilderness to be tempted of the devil. And when he had fasted forty days and forty nights, he was afterward an hungred. And when the tempter came to him, he said, If thou be the Son of God, command that these stones be made bread.

But he answered and said, It is written, Man shall not live

by bread alone, but by every word that proceedeth out of the mouth of God.

Then the devil taketh him up into the holy city, and setteth him on a pinnacle of the temple, And saith unto him, If thou be the Son of God, cast thyself down: for it is written, He shall give his angels charge concerning thee: and in *their* hands they shall bear thee up, lest at any time thou dash thy foot against a stone.

Jesus said unto him, It is written again, Thou shalt not tempt the Lord thy God.

Again, the devil taketh him up into an exceeding high mountain, and sheweth him all the kingdoms of the world, and the glory of them; And saith unto him, All these things will I give thee, if thou wilt fall down and worship me.

Then saith Jesus unto him, Get thee hence, Satan: for it is written, Thou shalt worship the Lord thy God, and him only shalt thou serve.

Then the devil leaveth him, and, behold, angels came and ministered unto him. MATTHEW 4:1–11

Jesus himself relied on Scripture, and he passed on his reverence for the authority of God's Word to his followers. One faithful follower, the apostle Paul, was languishing near death in a dungeon in Rome. Despite his suffering, one of his main priorities was passing the mantle of leadership to young pastors like Timothy. In his final charge to Timothy, Paul encouraged him to continue to follow Scripture, God's Word.

But thou hast fully known my doctrine, manner of life, purpose, faith, longsuffering, charity, patience, Persecutions, afflictions, which came unto me at Antioch, at Iconium, at Lystra; what persecutions I endured: but out of *them* all the Lord delivered me. Yea, and all that will live godly in Christ Jesus shall suffer persecution. But evil men and seducers shall wax worse and worse, deceiving, and being deceived. But continue thou in the things which thou hast learned and hast been assured of, knowing of whom thou hast learned *them*; And that from a child thou hast known the holy scriptures, which are able to make thee wise unto salvation through faith which is in Christ Jesus. **All scripture *is***

given by inspiration of God, and is profitable for doctrine, for reproof, for correction, for instruction in righteousness: That the man of God may be perfect, throughly furnished unto all good works. 2 TIMOTHY 3:10–17

THE PURPOSE OF SCRIPTURE

Because the collection of sacred writings, or Scriptures, came from God, it is referred to as the Word of God. In the Old Testament, Isaiah spoke for the Lord during a difficult season in Israel's history. Because the people of the northern kingdom of Israel had perpetually disregarded God and his Word, the nation was destroyed by the Assyrians. The Lord revealed to Isaiah that his own nation, the southern kingdom of Judah, would likewise be conquered—by the Babylonians. But God's prophet, under the inspiration of the Holy Ghost, also looked many years ahead and foretold Judah's restoration following the Babylonian exile. He reminded the Israelites that God's Word is eternal, and that God always accomplishes his purposes.

The voice said, Cry. And he said, What shall I cry?

All flesh *is* grass, and all the goodliness thereof *is* as the flower of the field: The grass withereth, the flower fadeth: because the spirit of the LORD bloweth upon it: surely the people *is* grass. **The grass withereth, the flower fadeth: but the word of our God shall stand for ever.** ISAIAH 40:6–8

Seek ye the LORD while he may be found, call ye upon him while he is near: Let the wicked forsake his way, and the unrighteous man his thoughts: and let him return unto the LORD, and he will have mercy upon him; and to our God, for he will abundantly pardon.

For my thoughts *are* not your thoughts, neither *are* your ways my ways, saith the LORD. For *as* the heavens are higher than the earth, so are my ways higher than your ways, and my thoughts than your thoughts. **For as the rain cometh down, and the snow from heaven, and returneth not thither, but watereth the earth, and maketh it bring forth and bud, that it may give seed to the sower, and bread to the eater: So shall my word be that goeth**

forth out of my mouth: it shall not return unto me void, but it shall accomplish that which I please, and it shall prosper *in the thing* whereto I sent it. For ye shall go out with joy, and be led forth with peace: the mountains and the hills shall break forth before you into singing, and all the trees of the field shall clap *their* hands. Instead of the thorn shall come up the fir tree, and instead of the brier shall come up the myrtle tree: and it shall be to the Lord for a name, for an everlasting sign *that* shall not be cut off.

ISAIAH 55:6–13

The writer of the book of Hebrews builds on the idea that God breathed life into things—including the words of the Bible. Scripture is dynamic and alive and has a way of "getting under our skin."

For the word of God *is* quick, and powerful, and sharper than any twoedged sword, piercing even to the dividing asunder of soul and spirit, and of the joints and marrow, and *is* a discerner of the thoughts and intents of the heart. Neither is there any creature that is not manifest in his sight: but all things *are* naked and opened unto the eyes of him with whom we have to do.

HEBREWS 4:12–13

In what ways have you experienced the Word of God as "quick and powerful" in your own spiritual life?

Throughout the Bible the writers warned readers that they should not add or take away from God's Word. God has given and preserved his Word for us so we can rely on it to guide our lives into all truth and according to God's good plan. Therefore, Christians revere the Bible and affirm its right to command our beliefs and actions.

Moses writes,

Now therefore hearken, O Israel, unto the statutes and unto the judgments, which I teach you, for to do *them*, that ye may live, and go in and possess the land which the Lord God of your fathers giveth you. Ye shall not add unto the word which I command you, neither shall ye diminish *ought* from it, that ye may keep the commandments of the LORD your God which I command you.

DEUTERONOMY 4:1–2

In the book of Proverbs, Agur declares,

> Every word of God *is* pure:
>> he *is* a shield unto them that put their trust in him.
> Add thou not unto his words,
>> lest he reprove thee, and thou be found a liar.

PROVERBS 30:5–6

John, the author of Revelation, writes,

For I testify unto every man that heareth the words of the prophecy of this book, If any man shall add unto these things, God shall add unto him the plagues that are written in this book: And if any man shall take away from the words of the book of this prophecy, God shall take away his part out of the book of life, and out of the holy city, and *from* the things which are written in this book.

REVELATION 22:18–19

WHAT WE BELIEVE

How do we know God and his will for our lives? The loving, personal, one true God speaks to us. Throughout history God has spoken through dreams, visions and even burning bushes. The primary way God reveals himself and his truth to us today is through the Bible. Because these words are from God, we can give it the rightful authority to guide our lives. Whatever God promises in his Word will come to pass and accomplish his purposes. Do you believe the Bible is the Word of God and has the right to command your beliefs and actions?

CHAPTER

5

Identity in Christ

--- KEY IDEA ---

Who am I?

--- KEY IDEA ---

I believe I am significant because of
my position as a child of God.

--- KEY VERSE ---

But as many as received him, to them
gave he power to become the sons of God,
even to them that believe on his name.
John 1:12

OUR MAP

When we open the pages of the Bible, God's trusted revelation to us, we discover that the one true God—Father, Son and Holy Ghost—is involved in and cares about our daily lives. We also learn that he has provided the way for us to come into a personal relationship with him through faith in Jesus Christ. When we believe and receive this gift of grace, we become a new person with a new identity and a new outlook on life. Our worth is no longer defined by what we do, but by who we know. We are significant because we are children of God.

Who am I? In the following pages, soak in God's truth about:

- Our New Name
- A New Covenant
- Our Adoption
- Being an Heir of God

OUR NEW NAME

During Bible times, a person's name was more than simply a reference to one's family or a way to uniquely identify someone; typically it characterized something about them. There are several instances recorded in the Bible of God giving a person a new name. When God renamed a person, he was establishing for them a new identity and marking that he was changing their mission or place in life. This was the case with Abram (meaning "exalted father"), whose name God changed to Abraham (meaning "father of many"). The meaning of the name "Abraham" represented God's plan to make Abraham's offspring into the great nation of Israel—and eventually into the body of Christ through Abraham's spiritual descendants.

And when Abram was ninety years old and nine, the LORD appeared to Abram, and said unto him, I *am* the Almighty God; walk before me, and be thou perfect. And I will make my covenant between me and thee, and will multiply thee exceedingly.

And Abram fell on his face: and God talked with him, saying,

As for me, behold, my covenant *is* with thee, and thou shalt be a father of many nations. Neither shall thy name any more be called Abram, but thy name shall be Abraham; for a father of many nations have I made thee. And I will make thee exceeding fruitful, and I will make nations of thee, and kings shall come out of thee. And I will establish my covenant between me and thee and thy seed after thee in their generations for an everlasting covenant, to be a God unto thee, and to thy seed after thee. GENESIS 17:1–7

God's promise to make Abraham a great nation seemed laughable, given the ages of Abraham and Sarah. But God followed through on his promise and gave them a son when Abraham was one hundred years old and Sarah was ninety. God gave him the name Isaac, which means "he laughs."

Then Abraham fell upon his face, and laughed, and said in his heart, Shall *a child* be born unto him that is an hundred years old? and shall Sarah, that is ninety years old, bear? GENESIS 17:17

And God said, Sarah thy wife shall bear thee a son indeed; and thou shalt call his name Isaac: and I will establish my covenant with him for an everlasting covenant, *and* with his seed after him. GENESIS 17:19

And the LORD visited Sarah as he had said, and the LORD did unto Sarah as he had spoken. For Sarah conceived, and bare Abraham a son in his old age, at the set time of which God had spoken to him. And Abraham called the name of his son that was born unto him, whom Sarah bare to him, Isaac. And Abraham circumcised his son Isaac being eight days old, as God had commanded him. And Abraham was an hundred years old, when his son Isaac was born unto him.

And Sarah said, God hath made me to laugh, *so that* all that hear will laugh with me. And she said, Who would have said unto Abraham, that Sarah should have given children suck? for I have born *him* a son in his old age. GENESIS 21:1–7

God gave Abraham and Sarah new names to
represent their new identities and their covenant with God.
Looking back on the time since you first
encountered God, what would your new name
be if you could pick one? Why?

A New Covenant

In Old Testament times, God provided his people with a prom-
ise termed the old covenant, which included his directions to his
people under Moses' leadership. A covenant is a binding agree-
ment between two parties, in this case God and Israel, that lays
out what each side promises to do. The prophet Jeremiah, how-
ever, foretold of a new covenant—a new deal God had in the
works—that would redefine the identity of God's people. This
time it involved more than just a name change. The old covenant
changed God's people from the outside in; the new covenant
changes us from the inside out.

**Behold, the days come, saith the Lord, that I will make a
new covenant with the house of Israel, and with the house of
Judah:** Not according to the covenant that I made with their fathers in the day *that* I took them by the hand to bring them out of
the land of Egypt; which my covenant they brake, although I was
an husband unto them, saith the Lord:

But this *shall be* the covenant that I will make with the house of
Israel; After those days, saith the Lord, I will put my law in their
inward parts, and write it in their hearts; and will be their God,
and they shall be my people. And they shall teach no more every
man his neighbour, and every man his brother, saying, Know the
Lord: for they shall all know me, from the least of them unto the
greatest of them, saith the Lord: **for I will forgive their iniquity,
and I will remember their sin no more.**   Jeremiah 31:31–34

What are the main points of God's new covenant? What effect
does the new covenant have on our identity?

Jesus Christ fulfilled the requirements of the old covenant God made with Moses and ushered in a new season of amazing grace. Those who embrace this new covenant and turn from their sins will have their sins wiped away and will receive a new identity.

That was the true Light, which lighteth every man that cometh into the world. He was in the world, and the world was made by him, and the world knew him not. He came unto his own, and his own received him not. But as many as received him, to them gave he power to become the sons of God, *even* to them that believe on his name: Which were born, not of blood, nor of the will of the flesh, nor of the will of man, but of God.   JOHN 1:9–13

As you read the passage below from Hebrews 10, compare and contrast the sacrifices made to fulfill the requirements of the old covenant with the sacrifice of Jesus that sealed the new covenant.

For the law having a shadow of good things to come, *and* not the very image of the things, can never with those sacrifices which they offered year by year continually make the comers thereunto perfect. For then would they not have ceased to be offered? because that the worshippers once purged should have had no more conscience of sins. But in those *sacrifices there is* a remembrance again *made* of sins every year. For *it is* not possible that the blood of bulls and of goats should take away sins.

Wherefore when he cometh into the world, he saith, Sacrifice and offering thou wouldest not, but a body hast thou prepared me: In burnt offerings and *sacrifices* for sin thou hast had no pleasure. Then said I, Lo, I come (in the volume of the book it is written of me,) to do thy will, O God. Above when he said, Sacrifice and offering and burnt offerings and *offering* for sin thou wouldest not, neither hadst pleasure *therein*; which are offered by the law; Then said he, Lo, I come to do thy will, O God. He taketh away the first, that he may establish the second. By the which will we are sanctified through the offering of the body of Jesus Christ once *for all.*

And every priest standeth daily ministering and offering

oftentimes the same sacrifices, which can never take away sins: But this man, after he had offered one sacrifice for sins for ever, sat down on the right hand of God; From henceforth expecting till his enemies be made his footstool. For by one offering he hath perfected for ever them that are sanctified.

Whereof the Holy Ghost also is a witness to us: for after that he had said before, This *is* the covenant that I will make with them after those days, saith the Lord, I will put my laws into their hearts, and in their minds will I write them; And their sins and iniquities will I remember no more.

Now where remission of these *is, there is* no more offering for sin.   Hebrews 10:1–18

Our Adoption

The beautiful thing about God's kingdom is that all those who welcome Jesus as their Lord are given the opportunity to accept a new identity through him. This is illustrated poignantly through the story of a crooked tax collector named Zacchaeus. Tax collectors were among the most despised people in Israel because they chose to work for Rome and were making themselves rich by gouging their fellow Jews. But the story of Zacchaeus shows that even the outcast can be adopted by God and made new.

And *Jesus* entered and passed through Jericho. And, behold, *there was* a man named Zacchaeus, which was the chief among the publicans, and he was rich. And he sought to see Jesus who he was; and could not for the press, because he was little of stature. And he ran before, and climbed up into a sycomore tree to see him: for he was to pass that *way*.

And when Jesus came to the place, he looked up, and saw him, and said unto him, Zacchaeus, make haste, and come down; for to day I must abide at thy house. And he made haste, and came down, and received him joyfully.

And when they saw *it*, they all murmured, saying, That he was gone to be guest with a man that is a sinner.

And Zacchaeus stood, and said unto the Lord; Behold, Lord, the half of my goods I give to the poor; and if I have taken any thing from any man by false accusation, I restore *him* fourfold.

And Jesus said unto him, This day is salvation come to this house, forsomuch as he also is a son of Abraham.   LUKE 19:1–9 🗝

The people in the early church were living examples of the changes that resulted from following Jesus. The letter to the Romans was written by the apostle Paul to present the full picture of the new covenant—its cost, the payment exacted for it and the promise it holds for those who agree to it. Follow along as Paul starts with our position in sin and the payment required to release us from its power, and he finishes with a glorious description of how our adoption into God's family gives us a new identity.

As it is written, There is none righteous, no, not one: There is none that understandeth, there is none that seeketh after God. They are all gone out of the way, they are together become unprofitable; there is none that doeth good, no, not one. Their throat *is* an open sepulchre; with their tongues they have used deceit; the poison of asps *is* under their lips: Whose mouth *is* full of cursing and bitterness: Their feet *are* swift to shed blood: Destruction and misery *are* in their ways: And the way of peace have they not known: There is no fear of God before their eyes.

Now we know that what things soever the law saith, it saith to them who are under the law: that every mouth may be stopped, and all the world may become guilty before God. Therefore by the deeds of the law there shall no flesh be justified in his sight: for by the law *is* the knowledge of sin.

But now the righteousness of God without the law is manifested, being witnessed by the law and the prophets; Even the righteousness of God *which is* by faith of Jesus Christ unto all and upon all them that believe: for there is no difference: For all have sinned, and come short of the glory of God; Being justified freely by his grace through the redemption that is in Christ Jesus: Whom God hath set forth *to be* a propitiation through faith in his blood, to declare his righteousness for the remission of sins that are past, through the forbearance of God; To declare, *I say*, at this time his righteousness: that he might be just, and the justifier of him which believeth in Jesus.   ROMANS 3:10–26

Therefore being justified by faith, we have peace with God through our Lord Jesus Christ: By whom also we have access by faith into this grace wherein we stand, and rejoice in hope of the glory of God.   ROMANS 5:1–2

For when we were yet without strength, in due time Christ died for the ungodly. For scarcely for a righteous man will one die: yet peradventure for a good man some would even dare to die. But God commendeth his love toward us, in that, while we were yet sinners, Christ died for us.

Much more then, being now justified by his blood, we shall be saved from wrath through him. For if, when we were enemies, we were reconciled to God by the death of his Son, much more, being reconciled, we shall be saved by his life. And not only *so*, but we also joy in God through our Lord Jesus Christ, by whom we have now received the atonement.   ROMANS 5:6–11

What shall we say then? Shall we continue in sin, that grace may abound? God forbid. How shall we, that are dead to sin, live any longer therein? Know ye not, that so many of us as were baptized into Jesus Christ were baptized into his death? Therefore we are buried with him by baptism into death: that like as Christ was raised up from the dead by the glory of the Father, even so we also should walk in newness of life.

For if we have been planted together in the likeness of his death, we shall be also *in the likeness* of *his* resurrection: **Knowing this, that our old man is crucified with *him*, that the body of sin might be destroyed, that henceforth we should not serve sin. For he that is dead is freed from sin.**   ROMANS 6:1–7

As you read Romans 8:1 – 25 below, look for what God gives
to those who find their identity in Jesus Christ.

There is therefore now no condemnation to them which are in Christ Jesus, who walk not after the flesh, but after the Spirit. For the law of the Spirit of life in Christ Jesus hath made me free from the law of sin and death. For what the law could not do, in that it was weak through the flesh, God sending his own Son in the likeness of sinful flesh, and for sin, condemned sin in the flesh: That the righteousness of the law might be fulfilled in us, who walk not after the flesh, but after the Spirit.

For they that are after the flesh do mind the things of the flesh; but they that are after the Spirit the things of the Spirit. For to be carnally minded *is* death; but to be spiritually minded *is* life and peace. Because the carnal mind *is* enmity against God: for it is not subject to the law of God, neither indeed can be. So then they that are in the flesh cannot please God.

But ye are not in the flesh, but in the Spirit, if so be that the Spirit of God dwell in you. Now if any man have not the Spirit of Christ, he is none of his. And if Christ *be* in you, the body *is* dead because of sin; but the Spirit *is* life because of righteousness. But if the Spirit of him that raised up Jesus from the dead dwell in you, he that raised up Christ from the dead shall also quicken your mortal bodies by his Spirit that dwelleth in you.

Therefore, brethren, we are debtors, not to the flesh, to live after the flesh. For if ye live after the flesh, ye shall die: but if ye through the Spirit do mortify the deeds of the body, ye shall live.

For as many as are led by the Spirit of God, they are the sons of God. **For ye have not received the spirit of bondage again to fear; but ye have received the Spirit of adoption, whereby we cry, Abba, Father. The Spirit itself beareth witness with our spirit, that we are the children of God: And if children, then heirs; heirs of God, and joint-heirs with Christ; if so be that we suffer with *him*, that we may be also glorified together.**

For I reckon that the sufferings of this present time *are* not worthy *to be compared* with the glory which shall be revealed in us. For the earnest expectation of the creature waiteth for the manifestation of the sons of God. For the creature was made subject to vanity, not willingly, but by reason of him who hath subjected *the same* in hope, Because the creature itself also shall be delivered from the bondage of corruption into the glorious liberty of the children of God.

For we know that the whole creation groaneth and travaileth in pain together until now. And not only *they*, but ourselves also, which have the firstfruits of the Spirit, even we ourselves

groan within ourselves, waiting for the adoption, *to wit,* **the re-demption of our body.** For we are saved by hope: but hope that is seen is not hope: for what a man seeth, why doth he yet hope for? But if we hope for that we see not, *then* do we with patience wait for *it.*   ROMANS 8:1–25

BEING AN HEIR OF GOD

One of Paul's favorite themes throughout his writings is our iden-tity in Christ. He writes in Romans 8:1–25 about how we need to live by the Spirit in order to fully experience our new identity. When he wrote to the believers in Ephesus, he eloquently laid out the incredible reality of our magnificent heritage, made pos-sible by God's great love.

And you *hath he quickened,* who were dead in trespasses and sins; Wherein in time past ye walked according to the course of this world, according to the prince of the power of the air, the spir-it that now worketh in the children of disobedience: Among whom also we all had our conversation in times past in the lusts of our flesh, fulfilling the desires of the flesh and of the mind; and were by nature the children of wrath, even as others. But God, who is rich in mercy, for his great love wherewith he loved us, Even when we were dead in sins, hath quickened us together with Christ, (by grace ye are saved;) And hath raised *us* up together, and made *us* sit together in heavenly *places* in Christ Jesus: That in the ages to come he might shew the exceeding riches of his grace in *his* kindness toward us through Christ Jesus. For by grace are ye saved through faith; and that not of yourselves: *it is* the gift of God: Not of works, lest any man should boast. For we are his workmanship, created in Christ Jesus unto good works, which God hath before ordained that we should walk in them.

Wherefore remember, that ye *being* in time past Gentiles in the flesh, who are called Uncircumcision by that which is called the Circumcision in the flesh made by hands; That at that time ye were without Christ, being aliens from the commonwealth of Is-rael, and strangers from the covenants of promise, having no hope, and without God in the world: But now in Christ Jesus ye who sometimes were far off are made nigh by the blood of Christ.

For he is our peace, who hath made both one, and hath broken down the middle wall of partition *between us*; Having abolished in his flesh the enmity, *even* the law of commandments *contained* in ordinances; for to make in himself of twain one new man, *so* making peace; And that he might reconcile both unto God in one body by the cross, having slain the enmity thereby: And came and preached peace to you which were afar off, and to them that were nigh. For through him we both have access by one Spirit unto the Father.

Now therefore ye are no more strangers and foreigners, but fellowcitizens with the saints, and of the household of God; And are built upon the foundation of the apostles and prophets, Jesus Christ himself being the chief corner *stone*; In whom all the building fitly framed together groweth unto an holy temple in the Lord: In whom ye also are builded together for an habitation of God through the Spirit.

For this cause I Paul, the prisoner of Jesus Christ for you Gentiles, If ye have heard of the dispensation of the grace of God which is given me to you-ward: How that by revelation he made known unto me the mystery; (as I wrote afore in few words, Whereby, when ye read, ye may understand my knowledge in the mystery of Christ) Which in other ages was not made known unto the sons of men, as it is now revealed unto his holy apostles and prophets by the Spirit; That the Gentiles should be fellowheirs, and of the same body, and partakers of his promise in Christ by the gospel:

Whereof I was made a minister, according to the gift of the grace of God given unto me by the effectual working of his power. Unto me, who am less than the least of all saints, is this grace given, that I should preach among the Gentiles the unsearchable riches of Christ; And to make all *men* see what *is* the fellowship of the mystery, which from the beginning of the world hath been hid in God, who created all things by Jesus Christ: To the intent that now unto the principalities and powers in heavenly *places* might be known by the church the manifold wisdom of God, According to the eternal purpose which he purposed in Christ Jesus our Lord: In whom we have boldness and access with confidence by the faith of him. Wherefore I desire that ye faint not at my tribulations for you, which is your glory.

For this cause I bow my knees unto the Father of our Lord Jesus Christ, Of whom the whole family in heaven and earth is named, That he would grant you, according to the riches of his glory, to be strengthened with might by his Spirit in the inner man; That Christ may dwell in your hearts by faith; that ye, being rooted and grounded in love, May be able to comprehend with all saints what *is* the breadth, and length, and depth, and height; And to know the love of Christ, which passeth knowledge, that ye might be filled with all the fulness of God.

Now unto him that is able to do exceeding abundantly above all that we ask or think, according to the power that worketh in us, Unto him *be* glory in the church by Christ Jesus throughout all ages, world without end. Amen.　　　　EPHESIANS 2:1—3:21

The church at Corinth in Greece was blessed with spiritual gifts but struggled to grasp the full meaning and freedom of being heirs with Christ. Paul wrote passionately to help them understand their new identity and to call them to live up to it in their daily lives. And as he did in his letter to the Ephesians, he also exalted the reality and importance of their life together as the body of Christ.

Know ye not that ye are the temple of God, and *that* the Spirit of God dwelleth in you? If any man defile the temple of God, him shall God destroy; for the temple of God is holy, which *temple* ye are.　　　　1 CORINTHIANS 3:16—17

What? know ye not that your body is the temple of the Holy Ghost *which is* in you, which ye have of God, and ye are not your own?　　　　1 CORINTHIANS 6:19

For as the body is one, and hath many members, and all the members of that one body, being many, are one body: so also *is* Christ. For by one Spirit are we all baptized into one body, whether *we be* Jews or Gentiles, whether *we be* bond or free; and have been all made to drink into one Spirit. For the body is not one member, but many.　　　　1 CORINTHIANS 12:12—14

The apostle Peter felt as deeply about these new realities as the apostle Paul. He wrote to believers scattered throughout Asia Minor (in modern-day Turkey), reinforcing the new identity they had in Christ. Though his readers consisted of both Jewish and Gentile Christians, Peter used lofty words like "chosen" and "holy" that previously had been reserved for the people of Israel.

Peter, an apostle of Jesus Christ, to the strangers scattered throughout Pontus, Galatia, Cappadocia, Asia, and Bithynia,

Elect according to the foreknowledge of God the Father, through sanctification of the Spirit, unto obedience and sprinkling of the blood of Jesus Christ: Grace unto you, and peace, be multiplied.

Blessed *be* the God and Father of our Lord Jesus Christ, which according to his abundant mercy hath begotten us again unto a lively hope by the resurrection of Jesus Christ from the dead, To an inheritance incorruptible, and undefiled, and that fadeth not away, reserved in heaven for you, Who are kept by the power of God through faith unto salvation ready to be revealed in the last time.

1 Peter 1:1–5

Seeing ye have purified your souls in obeying the truth through the Spirit unto unfeigned love of the brethren, *see that ye* love one another with a pure heart fervently: Being born again, not of corruptible seed, but of incorruptible, by the word of God, which liveth and abideth for ever. 1 Peter 1:22–23

To whom coming, *as unto* a living stone, disallowed indeed of men, but chosen of God, *and* precious, Ye also, as lively stones, are built up a spiritual house, an holy priesthood, to offer up spiritual sacrifices, acceptable to God by Jesus Christ. Wherefore also it is contained in the scripture, Behold, I lay in Sion a chief corner stone, elect, precious: and he that believeth on him shall not be confounded. Unto you therefore which believe *he is* precious: but unto them which be disobedient, the stone which the builders disallowed, the same is made the head of the corner, And a stone of stumbling, and a rock of offence, *even to them* which stumble at the word, being disobedient: whereunto also they were appointed.

But ye *are* a chosen generation, a royal priesthood, an holy nation, a peculiar people; that ye should shew forth the praises of him who hath called you out of darkness into his marvellous light: Which in time past *were* not a people, but *are* now the people of God: which had not obtained mercy, but now have obtained mercy.

1 PETER 2:4–10

Highlight or underline all the phrases that speak
to our new identity in Christ.

WHAT WE BELIEVE

Who am I? As the key verse declares in John 1:12, when we believe and receive Jesus Christ as our Savior, we are given a new name, a new unconditional covenant. We are adopted. We become heirs of all that belongs to God—and so much more. As we face each day, our worth is not up for grabs. Our identity is rooted firmly and permanently in our honored position as children of God. We do not live our lives to prove who we are but to express who we are in Christ.

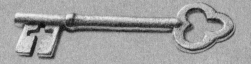

CHAPTER

6

Church

──────── KEY QUESTION ────────

How will God accomplish his plan?

──────────── KEY IDEA ────────────

I believe the church is God's primary way
to accomplish his purposes on earth.

──────────── KEY VERSE ────────────

But speaking the truth in love, [we]
may grow up into him in all things,
which is the head, *even* Christ.
Ephesians 4:15

OUR MAP

The first five key beliefs we have read so far are mostly vertical in nature—they deal with our relationships with God. The God of the Bible is the one true God who is involved in and cares about our daily lives. This God has provided the way for us to come into a relationship with him through faith in Jesus Christ. God revealed this to us along with a road map (the Bible) for our lives. This special book is from God and therefore has the right to command our beliefs and actions. We who embrace these beliefs and receive Jesus as our Savior from sin are given a new identity. From that moment on we can find our significance not in our performance but in our position as children of God.

The final set of five beliefs is more horizontal in nature—they deal with our relationship with others. Out of our relationship with God we engage our world in a purposeful and fruitful way. How will God accomplish the plan for humanity he has laid out in the Bible? God has chosen to use two communities he created—the ancient nation of Israel and the church—to accomplish his purposes on earth. If you are a Christian, you are a part of this community.

In this chapter we will explore the following regarding the church:

- *Founding*
- *Expansion*
- *Plan and Purpose*

FOUNDING

From the very beginning God had a vision to be with his people in perfect community. When the first two humans—Adam and Eve—rejected this vision and were escorted from the garden of Eden, God began to unveil a plan to provide the way back to him.

God's plan consisted of making Abraham's offspring into a great nation. From this single nation would come the solution for all people of all nations to come back into a relationship with the one true God. Thus the story of Israel pointed people of all nations to Abraham's descendant Jesus and was part of God's plan to restore a relationship with his people.

Again we return to the story of Abraham (Abram) where we can see the beginnings of God's covenant with a people who came to be known as Israel. It starts with God's call to Abram and Abram's amazing response of complete faith and trust.

Now the Lord had said unto Abram, Get thee out of thy country, and from thy kindred, and from thy father's house, unto a land that I will shew thee: And I will make of thee a great nation, and I will bless thee, and make thy name great; and thou shalt be a blessing: And I will bless them that bless thee, and curse him that curseth thee: and in thee shall all families of the earth be blessed.

So Abram departed, as the Lord had spoken unto him; and Lot went with him: and Abram *was* seventy and five years old when he departed out of Haran. And Abram took Sarai his wife, and Lot his brother's son, and all their substance that they had gathered, and the souls that they had gotten in Haran; and they went forth to go into the land of Canaan; and into the land of Canaan they came.

And Abram passed through the land unto the place of Sichem, unto the plain of Moreh. And the Canaanite *was* then in the land. And the Lord appeared unto Abram, and said, Unto thy seed will I give this land: and there builded he an altar unto the Lord, who appeared unto him.

And he removed from thence unto a mountain on the east of Beth-el, and pitched his tent, *having* Beth-el on the west, and Hai on the east: and there he builded an altar unto the Lord, and called upon the name of the Lord.

And Abram journeyed, going on still toward the south.

Genesis 12:1–9

After these things the word of the Lord came unto Abram in a vision, saying, Fear not, Abram: I *am* thy shield, *and* thy exceeding great reward.

And Abram said, Lord God, what wilt thou give me, seeing I go childless, and the steward of my house *is* this Eliezer of Damascus? And Abram said, Behold, to me thou hast given no seed: and, lo, one born in my house is mine heir.

And, behold, the word of the Lord *came* unto him, saying, This shall not be thine heir; but he that shall come forth out of thine own bowels shall be thine heir. And he brought him forth abroad, and said, Look now toward heaven, and tell the stars, if thou be able to number them: and he said unto him, So shall thy seed be.

And he believed in the LORD; and he counted it to him for righteousness.   GENESIS 15:1–6

> At this time and place in history, a covenant was a type of promise. The covenant described in the following verses is a covenant that would have been made between a king and a subject. The narrative describes the establishment of a covenant between God and Abram, initiated by God himself. God was making an unconditional promise (not dependent on Israel's obedience). By God's mighty hand the descendants of Abram survived and God accomplished his plan through them.

And [the LORD] said unto him, I *am* the LORD that brought thee out of Ur of the Chaldees, to give thee this land to inherit it.

And he said, Lord GOD, whereby shall I know that I shall inherit it?

And he said unto him, Take me an heifer of three years old, and a she goat of three years old, and a ram of three years old, and a turtledove, and a young pigeon.

And he took unto him all these, and divided them in the midst, and laid each piece one against another: but the birds divided he not. And when the fowls came down upon the carcases, Abram drove them away.

And when the sun was going down, a deep sleep fell upon Abram; and, lo, an horror of great darkness fell upon him. And he said unto Abram, Know of a surety that thy seed shall be a stranger in a land *that is* not theirs, and shall serve them; and they shall afflict them four hundred years; And also that nation, whom they shall serve, will I judge: and afterward shall they come out with great substance. And thou shalt go to thy fathers in peace; thou shalt be buried in a good old age. But in the fourth generation they shall come hither again: for the iniquity of the Amorites *is* not yet full.

And it came to pass, that, when the sun went down, and it was dark, behold a smoking furnace, and a burning lamp that passed between those pieces. In the same day the LORD made a covenant with Abram, saying, Unto thy seed have I given this land, from the river of Egypt unto the great river, the river Euphrates: The Kenites, and the Kenizzites, and the Kadmonites, and the Hittites, and the Perizzites, and the Rephaims, and the Amorites, and the Canaanites, and the Girgashites, and the Jebusites.

GENESIS 15:7–21

The covenant with Abram was the beginning of God's long and complicated relationship with the nation of Israel. The Old Testament of the Bible contains the details of this relationship, but as we have read in previous chapters, a new covenant was instituted. In the end, God's plan was accomplished through Israel and the new covenant was ushered in when the Messiah was born.

As Jesus was nearing his crucifixion, he told the disciples what was ahead and explained their role in accomplishing God's ultimate vision for the coming kingdom. This exchange highlights that God's plan for believers is still in force; the vision is for believers to come together in a new community that continues to this day. And here Jesus speaks of the founding of that community—the church.

When Jesus came into the coasts of Caesarea Philippi, he asked his disciples, saying, Whom do men say that I the Son of man am?

And they said, Some *say that thou art* John the Baptist: some, Elias; and others, Jeremias, or one of the prophets.

He saith unto them, But whom say ye that I am?

And Simon Peter answered and said, Thou art the Christ, the Son of the living God.

And Jesus answered and said unto him, Blessed art thou, Simon Bar-jona: for flesh and blood hath not revealed *it* unto thee, but my Father which is in heaven. And I say also unto thee, That thou art Peter, and upon this rock I will build my church; and the gates of hell shall not prevail against it. And I will give unto thee the keys of the kingdom of heaven: and whatsoever thou shalt bind on earth shall be bound in heaven: and whatsoever thou shalt loose on earth shall be loosed in heaven.

MATTHEW 16:13–19

Look back over the last two stories of Abraham (see
Genesis 12:1–9; 15:1–6,7–21) and Peter (see Matthew 16:13–19).
What was Abraham's response that was "counted ... to him
for righteousness"? How did Peter respond when Jesus asked,
"Whom say ye that I am?" How are these responses related?

---

*After the resurrection and ascension of Jesus, God formed this
community, called the church, led by his disciples. The story of
the church points people of all nations to the second coming of
Christ when he will fully restore God's original vision.*

*Forty days after Jesus' resurrection and just before his ascension
back to the Father, Jesus visited with his disciples and gave
them his final instructions. Luke, who also wrote the Gospel bearing
his name, recorded the incident in the book of Acts. The
result? The church was born!*

The former treatise have I made, O Theophilus, of all that Jesus
began both to do and teach, Until the day in which he was taken
up, after that he through the Holy Ghost had given commandments
unto the apostles whom he had chosen: To whom also he
shewed himself alive after his passion by many infallible proofs,
being seen of them forty days, and speaking of the things pertaining
to the kingdom of God: And, being assembled together with
them, commanded them that they should not depart from Jerusalem,
but wait for the promise of the Father, which, *saith he*, ye have
heard of me. For John truly baptized with water; but ye shall be
baptized with the Holy Ghost not many days hence.

When they therefore were come together, they asked of him,
saying, Lord, wilt thou at this time restore again the kingdom to
Israel?

**And he said unto them, It is not for you to know the times
or the seasons, which the Father hath put in his own power.
But ye shall receive power, after that the Holy Ghost is come
upon you: and ye shall be witnesses unto me both in Jerusalem,
and in all Judaea, and in Samaria, and unto the uttermost part
of the earth.**

And when he had spoken these things, while they beheld, he was taken up; and a cloud received him out of their sight.

And while they looked stedfastly toward heaven as he went up, behold, two men stood by them in white apparel; Which also said, Ye men of Galilee, why stand ye gazing up into heaven? this same Jesus, which is taken up from you into heaven, shall so come in like manner as ye have seen him go into heaven. ACTS 1:1–11

How did God equip the people of the early church
to carry out their mission to spread the gospel of Jesus Christ?

For the next ten days, Jesus' followers—about 120 men and women—met together. They joined together continually in prayer in anticipation of what was about to happen. After they became filled with the Holy Spirit, Peter used the "keys of the kingdom" that Jesus had mentioned earlier. Peter announced that the door of the kingdom had been unlocked.

And when the day of Pentecost was fully come, they were all with one accord in one place. And suddenly there came a sound from heaven as of a rushing mighty wind, and it filled all the house where they were sitting. And there appeared unto them cloven tongues like as of fire, and it sat upon each of them. And they were all filled with the Holy Ghost, and began to speak with other tongues, as the Spirit gave them utterance.

And there were dwelling at Jerusalem Jews, devout men, out of every nation under heaven. Now when this was noised abroad, the multitude came together, and were confounded, because that every man heard them speak in his own language. And they were all amazed and marvelled, saying one to another, Behold, are not all these which speak Galilaeans? And how hear we every man in our own tongue, wherein we were born? Parthians, and Medes, and Elamites, and the dwellers in Mesopotamia, and in Judaea, and Cappadocia, in Pontus, and Asia, Phrygia, and Pamphylia, in Egypt, and in the parts of Libya about Cyrene, and strangers of Rome, Jews and proselytes, Cretes and Arabians, we do hear them speak in our tongues the wonderful works of God. And they were all amazed, and were in doubt, saying one to another, What meaneth this?

Others mocking said, These men are full of new wine.

But Peter, standing up with the eleven, lifted up his voice, and said unto them, Ye men of Judaea, and all *ye* that dwell at Jerusalem, be this known unto you, and hearken to my words: For these are not drunken, as ye suppose, seeing it is *but* the third hour of the day. But this is that which was spoken by the prophet Joel; And it shall come to pass in the last days, saith God, I will pour out of my Spirit upon all flesh: and your sons and your daughters shall prophesy, and your young men shall see visions, and your old men shall dream dreams: And on my servants and on my handmaidens I will pour out in those days of my Spirit; and they shall prophesy: And I will shew wonders in heaven above, and signs in the earth beneath; blood, and fire, and vapour of smoke: The sun shall be turned into darkness, and the moon into blood, before that great and notable day of the Lord come: And it shall come to pass, *that* whosoever shall call on the name of the Lord shall be saved.

Ye men of Israel, hear these words; Jesus of Nazareth, a man approved of God among you by miracles and wonders and signs, which God did by him in the midst of you, as ye yourselves also know: Him, being delivered by the determinate counsel and foreknowledge of God, ye have taken, and by wicked hands have crucified and slain: Whom God hath raised up, having loosed the pains of death: because it was not possible that he should be holden of it. For David speaketh concerning him, I foresaw the Lord always before my face, for he is on my right hand, that I should not be moved: Therefore did my heart rejoice, and my tongue was glad; moreover also my flesh shall rest in hope: Because thou wilt not leave my soul in hell, neither wilt thou suffer thine Holy One to see corruption. Thou hast made known to me the ways of life; thou shalt make me full of joy with thy countenance.

Men *and* brethren, let me freely speak unto you of the patriarch David, that he is both dead and buried, and his sepulchre is with us unto this day. Therefore being a prophet, and knowing that God had sworn with an oath to him, that of the fruit of his loins, according to the flesh, he would raise up Christ to sit on his throne; He seeing this before spake of the resurrection of Christ, that his soul was not left in hell, neither his flesh did see corruption. This Jesus hath God raised up, whereof we all are witnesses. Therefore being by the right hand of God exalted, and having received of the Father the promise of the Holy Ghost, he hath shed forth this, which ye now see and hear. For David is not ascended into the heavens: but he saith himself, The LORD said unto my Lord, Sit thou on my right hand, Until I make thy foes thy footstool.

Therefore let all the house of Israel know assuredly, that God hath made that same Jesus, whom ye have crucified, both Lord and Christ.

Now when they heard *this*, they were pricked in their heart, and said unto Peter and to the rest of the apostles, Men *and* brethren, what shall we do?

Then Peter said unto them, Repent, and be baptized every one of you in the name of Jesus Christ for the remission of sins, and ye shall receive the gift of the Holy Ghost. For the promise is unto you, and to your children, and to all that are afar off, *even* as many as the Lord our God shall call.

And with many other words did he testify and exhort, saying, Save yourselves from this untoward generation. Then they that gladly received his word were baptized: and the same day there were added *unto them* about three thousand souls.   ACTS 2:1–41 ⚷

The thread from here back to where we started is undeniable. The church was born out of a supernatural movement of the Holy Ghost. The Holy Ghost was given to the followers of Jesus. Jesus the Messiah, long promised to the Jewish nation, was born through a lineage that traced back to Abraham. Abraham believed God's original promise to make of him a great nation, and it was upon his faith that the seeds of the church were planted.

EXPANSION

Jesus' commission to the first disciples in AD 30 was to spread the good news and to build his church beyond Jerusalem to all of Judea and Samaria and ultimately, to the ends of the earth. The book of Acts records the fulfillment of that mission by chronicling the miraculous journey and exponential development of the church community. The story of the expansion of the church beyond Jerusalem comes on the heels of the stoning of the disciple Stephen for his bold faith amid a hostile crowd of Jews.

As you read the following story from Acts 8 about the expansion of the church, note some of the events that show the transformation of a small group of Jesus' Jewish followers into a universal Christian church.

And at that time there was a great persecution against the church which was at Jerusalem; and they were all scattered abroad throughout the regions of Judaea and Samaria, except the apostles. And devout men carried Stephen *to his burial*, and made great lamentation over him. As for Saul, he made havock of the church, entering into every house, and haling men and women committed *them* to prison.

Therefore they that were scattered abroad went every where preaching the word. Then Philip went down to the city of Samaria, and preached Christ unto them. And the people with one accord gave heed unto those things which Philip spake, hearing and seeing the miracles which he did. For unclean spirits, crying with loud voice, came out of many that were possessed *with them*: and many taken with palsies, and that were lame, were healed. And there was great joy in that city. ACTS 8:1–8

Now when the apostles which were at Jerusalem heard that Samaria had received the word of God, they sent unto them Peter and John: Who, when they were come down, prayed for them, that they might receive the Holy Ghost: (For as yet he was fallen upon none of them: only they were baptized in the name of the Lord Jesus.) Then laid they *their* hands on them, and they received the Holy Ghost. ACTS 8:14–17

And they, when they had testified and preached the word of the Lord, returned to Jerusalem, and preached the gospel in many villages of the Samaritans. ACTS 8:25

Then had the churches rest throughout all Judaea and Galilee and Samaria, and were edified; and walking in the fear of the Lord, and in the comfort of the Holy Ghost, were multiplied.

ACTS 9:31

Identify some of the ways in which persecution helped the early church in its mission to share the gospel.

Just as Peter had used the "keys of the kingdom" on the day of Pentecost to announce to the Jews in Jerusalem that the door of the kingdom had been unlocked, he also used those keys to open the door to the Gentiles. God supernaturally led Peter and a Roman centurion named Cornelius to meet each other. When Peter told Cornelius and his relatives and close friends the good news about Jesus, they believed, were filled with the Holy Ghost and were baptized.

And the apostles and brethren that were in Judaea heard that the Gentiles had also received the word of God. And when Peter was come up to Jerusalem, they that were of the circumcision contended with him, Saying, Thou wentest in to men uncircumcised, and didst eat with them.

But Peter rehearsed *the matter* from the beginning, and expounded *it* by order unto them, saying, I was in the city of Joppa praying: and in a trance I saw a vision, A certain vessel descend, as it had been a great sheet, let down from heaven by four corners; and it came even to me: Upon the which when I had fastened mine eyes, I considered, and saw fourfooted beasts of the earth, and wild beasts, and creeping things, and fowls of the air. And I heard a voice saying unto me, Arise, Peter; slay and eat.

But I said, Not so, Lord: for nothing common or unclean hath at any time entered into my mouth.

But the voice answered me again from heaven, What God hath cleansed, *that* call not thou common. And this was done three times: and all were drawn up again into heaven.

And, behold, immediately there were three men already come unto the house where I was, sent from Caesarea unto me. And the Spirit bade me go with them, nothing doubting. Moreover these six brethren accompanied me, and we entered into the man's house: And he shewed us how he had seen an angel in his house, which stood and said unto him, Send men to Joppa, and call for Simon, whose surname is Peter; Who shall tell thee words, whereby thou and all thy house shall be saved.

And as I began to speak, the Holy Ghost fell on them, as on us at the beginning. Then remembered I the word of the Lord, how that he said, John indeed baptized with water; but ye shall be baptized with the Holy Ghost. Forasmuch then as God gave them the like gift as *he did* unto us, who believed on the Lord Jesus Christ; what was I, that I could withstand God?

When they heard these things, they held their peace, and glorified God, saying, Then hath God also to the Gentiles granted repentance unto life.   Acts 11:1–18

In an unlikely turn of events, the persecution of the church caused it to spread. Believers fled from Jerusalem where they were in danger, taking refuge in far-flung cities in the Gentile world. And as improbable as it sounds, it is Saul, one of the chief persecutors of the church, who God would use to take the gospel and the church to the Gentiles. Around AD 35, Saul personally encountered the risen Jesus in a vision while on the road to Damascus. Saul surrendered his life to Christ and devoted the rest of his days on earth to building Christ's church. His home base was the church at Antioch.

Now they which were scattered abroad upon the persecution that arose about Stephen travelled as far as Phenice, and Cyprus, and Antioch, preaching the word to none but unto the Jews only. And some of them were men of Cyprus and Cyrene, which, when they were come to Antioch, spake unto the Grecians, preaching the Lord Jesus. And the hand of the Lord was with them: and a great number believed, and turned unto the Lord.

Then tidings of these things came unto the ears of the church which was in Jerusalem: and they sent forth Barnabas, that he should go as far as Antioch. Who, when he came, and had seen the grace of God, was glad, and exhorted them all, that with purpose of heart they would cleave unto the Lord. For he was a good man, and full of the Holy Ghost and of faith: and much people was added unto the Lord.

Then departed Barnabas to Tarsus, for to seek Saul: And when he had found him, he brought him unto Antioch. And it came to pass, that a whole year they assembled themselves with the church, and taught much people. And the disciples were called Christians first in Antioch.   ACTS 11:19–26

Now there were in the church that was at Antioch certain prophets and teachers; as Barnabas, and Simeon that was called Niger, and Lucius of Cyrene, and Manaen, which had been brought up with Herod the tetrarch, and Saul. As they ministered to the Lord, and fasted, the Holy Ghost said, Separate me Barnabas and Saul for the work whereunto I have called them. And when they had fasted and prayed, and laid *their* hands on them, they sent *them* away.   ACTS 13:1–3

Saul, soon to be known as Paul, for approximately the next 20 years, would embark on numerous journeys to spread the gospel and strengthen and build the church as it stretched toward the ends of the earth, just as Jesus had envisioned. Paul's first missionary trip began around AD 46, and in each city he visited, he used a skillful blend of history, theology and philosophy to declare the good news to both Jews and Gentiles, who responded and joined the expanding church.

When Paul and his companions came to Antioch, Paul stood up in the synagogue to a predominantly Jewish audience and gave a powerful sermon similar to Peter's on the day of Pentecost. He told them the story of the Jews in chronological order beginning with Israel of the Old Testament. We pick up at the end of his message, where Paul boldly extends an invitation to them to receive this good news. Notice then the shift in focus away from the Jews, based on their rejection.

Be it known unto you therefore, men *and* brethren, that through this man is preached unto you the forgiveness of

sins: And by him all that believe are justified from all things, from which ye could not be justified by the law of Moses. Beware therefore, lest that come upon you, which is spoken of in the prophets; Behold, ye despisers, and wonder, and perish: for I work a work in your days, a work which ye shall in no wise believe, though a man declare it unto you.

And when the Jews were gone out of the synagogue, the Gentiles besought that these words might be preached to them the next sabbath. Now when the congregation was broken up, many of the Jews and religious proselytes followed Paul and Barnabas: who, speaking to them, persuaded them to continue in the grace of God.

And the next sabbath day came almost the whole city together to hear the word of God. But when the Jews saw the multitudes, they were filled with envy, and spake against those things which were spoken by Paul, contradicting and blaspheming.

Then Paul and Barnabas waxed bold, and said, It was necessary that the word of God should first have been spoken to you: but seeing ye put it from you, and judge yourselves unworthy of everlasting life, lo, we turn to the Gentiles. For so hath the Lord commanded us, *saying*, I have set thee to be a light of the Gentiles, that thou shouldest be for salvation unto the ends of the earth.

And when the Gentiles heard this, they were glad, and glorified the word of the Lord: and as many as were ordained to eternal life believed.

And the word of the Lord was published throughout all the region. But the Jews stirred up the devout and honourable women, and the chief men of the city, and raised persecution against Paul and Barnabas, and expelled them out of their coasts. But they shook off the dust of their feet against them, and came unto Iconium. And the disciples were filled with joy, and with the Holy Ghost.   ACTS 13:38–52

Paul's attention turned to spreading the gospel and building the church in a world dominated by Gentiles. One of the churches dear to Paul's heart was at Ephesus. During his third missionary journey, he spent between two and three years there building the church and its leadership. A couple of years later, around AD 57, Paul was in a hurry to get to Jerusalem before Pentecost. Concerned that he might never return to Ephesus, he called for the elders of the church to meet him on his way to Jerusalem. He wanted to have one last meeting with them to build them up and stabilize the fledgling church he had sacrificed so much to launch.

And from Miletus he sent to Ephesus, and called the elders of the church. And when they were come to him, he said unto them, Ye know, from the first day that I came into Asia, after what manner I have been with you at all seasons, Serving the Lord with all humility of mind, and with many tears, and temptations, which befell me by the lying in wait of the Jews: *And* how I kept back nothing that was profitable *unto you*, but have shewed you, and have taught you publickly, and from house to house, Testifying both to the Jews, and also to the Greeks, repentance toward God, and faith toward our Lord Jesus Christ.

And now, behold, I go bound in the spirit unto Jerusalem, not knowing the things that shall befall me there: Save that the Holy Ghost witnesseth in every city, saying that bonds and afflictions abide me. **But none of these things move me, neither count I my life dear unto myself, so that I might finish my course with joy, and the ministry, which I have received of the Lord Jesus, to testify the gospel of the grace of God.**

And now, behold, I know that ye all, among whom I have gone preaching the kingdom of God, shall see my face no more. Wherefore I take you to record this day, that I *am* pure from the blood of all *men*. For I have not shunned to declare unto you all the counsel of God. **Take heed therefore unto yourselves, and to all the flock, over the which the Holy Ghost hath made you overseers, to feed the church of God, which he hath purchased with his own blood.** For I know this, that after my departing shall grievous wolves enter in among you, not sparing the flock. Also of your own selves shall men arise, speaking perverse things, to draw away disciples after them. Therefore watch, and remember, that by the space of three years I ceased not to warn every one night and day with tears.

And now, brethren, I commend you to God, and to the word

of his grace, which is able to build you up, and to give you an inheritance among all them which are sanctified. I have coveted no man's silver, or gold, or apparel. Yea, ye yourselves know, that these hands have ministered unto my necessities, and to them that were with me. I have shewed you all things, how that so labouring ye ought to support the weak, and to remember the words of the Lord Jesus, how he said, It is more blessed to give than to receive.

And when he had thus spoken, he kneeled down, and prayed with them all. And they all wept sore, and fell on Paul's neck, and kissed him, Sorrowing most of all for the words which he spake, that they should see his face no more. And they accompanied him unto the ship.

And it came to pass, that after we were gotten from them, and had launched, we came with a straight course unto Coos.

ACTS 20:17—21:1

PLAN AND PURPOSE

As Paul had anticipated, prison and hardships awaited him when he arrived in Jerusalem. While under house arrest in Rome a few years later, around AD 60, Paul penned a letter to the church of Ephesus. Paul explained God's great plan for the church, the new community of Christ. Along with reconciling individuals to himself, God has reconciled them to one another. Through his death, Christ has broken down the barriers, uniting believers in one body—the church. The church community is now invited to live up to the calling they have in Jesus Christ.

As you read the passages below from Ephesians 4 and Revelation 2, identify the key phrases that define the purpose of the Christian church in the world.

I therefore, the prisoner of the Lord, beseech you that ye walk worthy of the vocation wherewith ye are called, With all lowliness and meekness, with longsuffering, forbearing one another in love; Endeavouring to keep the unity of the Spirit in the bond of peace. *There is* one body, and one Spirit, even as ye are called in one hope of your calling; One Lord, one faith, one baptism, One God and Father of all, who *is* above all, and through all, and in you all.

But unto every one of us is given grace according to the measure of the gift of Christ. Wherefore he saith, When he ascended up on high, he led captivity captive, and gave gifts unto men. (Now that he ascended, what is it but that he also descended first into the lower parts of the earth? He that descended is the same also that ascended up far above all heavens, that he might fill all things.) And he gave some, apostles; and some, prophets; and some, evangelists; and some, pastors and teachers; For the perfecting of the saints, for the work of the ministry, for the edifying of the body of Christ: Till we all come in the unity of the faith, and of the knowledge of the Son of God, unto a perfect man, unto the measure of the stature of the fulness of Christ:

That we *henceforth* be no more children, tossed to and fro, and carried about with every wind of doctrine, by the sleight of men, *and* cunning craftiness, whereby they lie in wait to deceive; But speaking the truth in love, may grow up into him in all things, which is the head, *even* Christ: From whom the whole body fitly joined together and compacted by that which every joint supplieth, according to the effectual working in the measure of every part, maketh increase of the body unto the edifying of itself in love.

Ephesians 4:1–16

Near the end of the first century, around AD 95, the apostle John received amazing visions from God that are contained in the book of Revelation. He addresses the book to seven churches in the Roman province of Asia (in modern-day Turkey); one of them was the church of Ephesus. As part of the book, John records letters from the risen Christ to those seven churches, in which he typically issues words of commendation, complaint and correction. Some 45 years after Paul penned his letter to the church of Ephesus, Christ's message to them represents a report card on their progress. It is both a word of encouragement and a challenge to the church today.

Unto the angel of the church of Ephesus write; These things saith he that holdeth the seven stars in his right hand, who walketh in the midst of the seven golden candlesticks; I know thy works, and thy labour, and thy patience, and how thou canst not bear them which are evil: and thou hast tried them which say they are apostles, and are not, and hast found them liars: And hast borne, and hast patience, and for my name's sake hast laboured, and hast not fainted.

Nevertheless I have *somewhat* against thee, because thou hast left thy first love. Remember therefore from whence thou art fallen, and repent, and do the first works; or else I will come unto thee quickly, and will remove thy candlestick out of his place, except thou repent. But this thou hast, that thou hatest the deeds of the Nicolaitanes, which I also hate.

He that hath an ear, let him hear what the Spirit saith unto the churches; To him that overcometh will I give to eat of the tree of life, which is in the midst of the paradise of God.   REVELATION 2:1–7

WHAT WE BELIEVE

God used both Israel and the church to accomplish his grand plan to redeem and restore us to a right relationship with him. God's plan for Israel was to bring us Jesus, who would provide the only way back to God. It took a little more than 2,000 years for this divine plan to be fulfilled.

After Jesus' resurrection and ascension back to the Father, God created the church. Empowered by the Holy Ghost, the church has existed for approximately 2,000 years. God's primary plan for the church is to spread the good news of Jesus Christ to all nations until Jesus comes again. Today there are an estimated 2.2 billion Christians in the world. If you have received and accepted the grace of Christ, then you are a member of the body of Christ. And remember you are an integral part of his plan — God wants you to be fully vested in his church to accomplish his great and wonderful purposes!

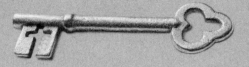

CHAPTER

7

Humanity

—— KEY QUESTION ——

How does God see us?

—— KEY IDEA ——

I believe all people are loved by God
and need Jesus Christ as their Savior.

—— KEY VERSE ——

For God so loved the world,
that he gave his only begotten Son,
that whosoever believeth in him should not perish,
but have everlasting life.

John 3:16

OUR MAP

God created everything, but the pinnacle of creation was the making of human beings—creatures crafted in the image of God. Humanity is special, and the Bible is the record of the love story between Creator and created, between God and humans. From the very beginning of time to the era of the modern-day church, God has loved and pursued his people in order to restore his image within and among them.

In this chapter we will read Scripture passages on:

- Origins
- The Devastating Human Condition
- God's Love
- All and Whosoever
- Seeing People as God Sees Them

This chapter will come to a close with Scripture that invites us to embrace every believer as a precious family member.

ORIGINS

God is the origin of all life.

In the beginning God created the heaven and the earth. And the earth was without form, and void; and darkness *was* upon the face of the deep. And the Spirit of God moved upon the face of the waters.

And God said, Let there be light: and there was light. And God saw the light, that *it was* good: and God divided the light from the darkness. And God called the light Day, and the darkness he called Night. And the evening and the morning were the first day.

And God said, Let there be a firmament in the midst of the waters, and let it divide the waters from the waters. And God made the firmament, and divided the waters which *were* under the firmament from the waters which *were* above the firmament: and it was so. And God called the firmament Heaven. And the evening and the morning were the second day.

And God said, Let the waters under the heaven be gathered together unto one place, and let the dry *land* appear: and it was so.

And God called the dry *land* Earth; and the gathering together of the waters called he Seas: and God saw that *it was* good.

And God said, Let the earth bring forth grass, the herb yielding seed, *and* the fruit tree yielding fruit after his kind, whose seed *is* in itself, upon the earth: and it was so. And the earth brought forth grass, *and* herb yielding seed after his kind, and the tree yielding fruit, whose seed *was* in itself, after his kind: and God saw that *it was* good. And the evening and the morning were the third day.

And God said, Let there be lights in the firmament of the heaven to divide the day from the night; and let them be for signs, and for seasons, and for days, and years: And let them be for lights in the firmament of the heaven to give light upon the earth: and it was so. And God made two great lights; the greater light to rule the day, and the lesser light to rule the night: *he made* the stars also. And God set them in the firmament of the heaven to give light upon the earth, And to rule over the day and over the night, and to divide the light from the darkness: and God saw that *it was* good. And the evening and the morning were the fourth day.

And God said, Let the waters bring forth abundantly the moving creature that hath life, and fowl *that* may fly above the earth in the open firmament of heaven. And God created great whales, and every living creature that moveth, which the waters brought forth abundantly, after their kind, and every winged fowl after his kind: and God saw that *it was* good. And God blessed them, saying, Be fruitful, and multiply, and fill the waters in the seas, and let fowl multiply in the earth. And the evening and the morning were the fifth day.

And God said, Let the earth bring forth the living creature after his kind, cattle, and creeping thing, and beast of the earth after his kind: and it was so. And God made the beast of the earth after his kind, and cattle after their kind, and every thing that creepeth upon the earth after his kind: and God saw that *it was* good.

And God said, Let us make man in our image, after our likeness: and let them have dominion over the fish of the sea, and over the fowl of the air, and over the cattle, and over all the earth, and over every creeping thing that creepeth upon the earth.

So God created man in his *own* image, in the image of God created he him; male and female created he them.

And God blessed them, and God said unto them, Be fruitful, and multiply, and replenish the earth, and subdue it: and have dominion over the fish of the sea, and over the fowl of the air, and over every living thing that moveth upon the earth.

And God said, Behold, I have given you every herb bearing seed, which *is* upon the face of all the earth, and every tree, in the which *is* the fruit of a tree yielding seed; to you it shall be for meat. And to every beast of the earth, and to every fowl of the air, and to every thing that creepeth upon the earth, wherein *there is* life, *I have given* every green herb for meat: and it was so.

And God saw every thing that he had made, and, behold, *it was* very good. And the evening and the morning were the sixth day.

GENESIS 1:1–31

Describe in your own words God's original intent
for the human race.

THE DEVASTATING HUMAN CONDITION

God created the cosmos and everything in it. He created the earth so that he could be with the people he created. Unfortunately, the first two people—Adam and Eve—rejected God's vision for his creation, causing sin to enter into their nature and thereby making them unfit for community with a holy God. The greatest pandemic ever experienced by humanity is the transference of this sin "DNA" to every generation.

What are some of the results of human sin reflected below
in the story of Cain and Abel in Genesis 4?

And Adam knew Eve his wife; and she conceived, and bare Cain, and said, I have gotten a man from the LORD. And she again bare his brother Abel.

And Abel was a keeper of sheep, but Cain was a tiller of the ground. And in process of time it came to pass, that Cain brought of the fruit of the ground an offering unto the Lord. And Abel, he also brought of the firstlings of his flock and of the fat thereof. And the Lord had respect unto Abel and to his offering: But unto Cain and to his offering he had not respect. And Cain was very wroth, and his countenance fell. Genesis 4:1–5 🔑

> Here we see the results of Adam and Eve's choices. We know from other Scriptures that God rejected Cain's offering and accepted Abel's offering because of what he saw in the faith of the two men. The Bible doesn't explicitly tell us why God rejected Cain's offering, but it involved Cain's attitude toward God.
>
> Abel brought the best of his flock, while Cain brought only some of the fruit of the ground. We learn throughout the Old Testament that it pleases God when we bring him our first and best, not our leftovers.

And the Lord said unto Cain, Why art thou wroth? and why is thy countenance fallen? If thou doest well, shalt thou not be accepted? and if thou doest not well, sin lieth at the door. And unto thee *shall be* his desire, and thou shalt rule over him.

And Cain talked with Abel his brother: and it came to pass, when they were in the field, that Cain rose up against Abel his brother, and slew him.

And the Lord said unto Cain, Where *is* Abel thy brother? And he said, I know not: *Am* I my brother's keeper?

And he said, What hast thou done? the voice of thy brother's blood crieth unto me from the ground. And now *art* thou cursed from the earth, which hath opened her mouth to receive thy brother's blood from thy hand; When thou tillest the ground, it shall not henceforth yield unto thee her strength; a fugitive and a vagabond shalt thou be in the earth.

And Cain said unto the Lord, My punishment *is* greater than I can bear. Behold, thou hast driven me out this day from the face of the earth; and from thy face shall I be hid; and I shall be a fugitive and a vagabond in the earth; and it shall come to pass, *that* every one that findeth me shall slay me.

And the Lord said unto him, Therefore whosoever slayeth Cain, vengeance shall be taken on him sevenfold. And the Lord set a mark upon Cain, lest any finding him should kill him. And Cain went out from the presence of the LORD, and dwelt in the land of Nod, on the east of Eden. GENESIS 4:6–16

Adam and Eve had more children, but their offspring continued inheriting and passing on a fallen, sinful nature. In the New Testament era, Jude, who was both a half brother and a follower of Jesus, wrote a letter to warn Christians about false teachers who were trying to convince believers that salvation by grace gave them license to sin. Jude notes that these dangerous teachers had "gone in the way of Cain," meaning the way of selfishness and greed—demonstrated by Cain's careless, thoughtless offering—and the way of hatred and murder—demonstrated by Cain's slaying of Abel.

Jude, the servant of Jesus Christ, and brother of James, to them that are sanctified by God the Father, and preserved in Jesus Christ, *and* called: Mercy unto you, and peace, and love, be multiplied.

Beloved, when I gave all diligence to write unto you of the common salvation, it was needful for me to write unto you, and exhort *you* that ye should earnestly contend for the faith which was once delivered unto the saints. For there are certain men crept in unawares, who were before of old ordained to this condemnation, ungodly men, turning the grace of our God into lasciviousness, and denying the only Lord God, and our Lord Jesus Christ.

I will therefore put you in remembrance, though ye once knew this, how that the Lord, having saved the people out of the land of Egypt, afterward destroyed them that believed not. And the angels which kept not their first estate, but left their own habitation, he hath reserved in everlasting chains under darkness unto the judgment of the great day. Even as Sodom and Gomorrha, and the cities about them in like manner, giving themselves over to fornication, and going after strange flesh, are set forth for an example, suffering the vengeance of eternal fire.

Likewise also these *filthy* dreamers defile the flesh, despise dominion, and speak evil of dignities. Yet Michael the archangel, when contending with the devil he disputed about the body of

Moses, durst not bring against him a railing accusation, but said, The Lord rebuke thee. But these speak evil of those things which they know not: but what they know naturally, as brute beasts, in those things they corrupt themselves.

Woe unto them! for they have gone in the way of Cain, and ran greedily after the error of Balaam for reward, and perished in the gainsaying of Core.

These are spots in your feasts of charity, when they feast with you, feeding themselves without fear: clouds *they are* without water, carried about of winds; trees whose fruit withereth, without fruit, twice dead, plucked up by the roots; Raging waves of the sea, foaming out their own shame; wandering stars, to whom is reserved the blackness of darkness for ever.

And Enoch also, the seventh from Adam, prophesied of these, saying, Behold, the Lord cometh with ten thousands of his saints, To execute judgment upon all, and to convince all that are ungodly among them of all their ungodly deeds which they have ungodly committed, and of all their hard *speeches* which ungodly sinners have spoken against him. These are murmurers, complainers, walking after their own lusts; and their mouth speaketh great swelling *words*, having men's persons in admiration because of advantage.

JUDE 1–16

Paul's letter to the Christians in Rome contains a chilling declaration of the extent and consequences of the sin nature that has permeated the entire human race, beginning with Adam and Eve and their offspring. First, Paul indicts the sinfulness of the Gentiles and then, perhaps surprising his readers, shows the sinfulness of the Jews. He makes it clear that no one is righteous.

For the wrath of God is revealed from heaven against all ungodliness and unrighteousness of men, who hold the truth in unrighteousness; Because that which may be known of God is manifest in them; for God hath shewed *it* unto them. For the invisible things of him from the creation of the world are clearly seen, being understood by the things that are made, *even* his eternal power and Godhead; so that they are without excuse:

Because that, when they knew God, they glorified *him* not as

God, neither were thankful; but became vain in their imaginations, and their foolish heart was darkened. Professing themselves to be wise, they became fools, And changed the glory of the uncorruptible God into an image made like to corruptible man, and to birds, and fourfooted beasts, and creeping things.

Wherefore God also gave them up to uncleanness through the lusts of their own hearts, to dishonour their own bodies between themselves: Who changed the truth of God into a lie, and worshipped and served the creature more than the Creator, who is blessed for ever. Amen.

For this cause God gave them up unto vile affections: for even their women did change the natural use into that which is against nature: And likewise also the men, leaving the natural use of the woman, burned in their lust one toward another; men with men working that which is unseemly, and receiving in themselves that recompence of their error which was meet.

And even as they did not like to retain God in *their* knowledge, God gave them over to a reprobate mind, to do those things which are not convenient; Being filled with all unrighteousness, fornication, wickedness, covetousness, maliciousness; full of envy, murder, debate, deceit, malignity; whisperers, Backbiters, haters of God, despiteful, proud, boasters, inventors of evil things, disobedient to parents, Without understanding, covenant breakers, without natural affection, implacable, unmerciful: Who knowing the judgment of God, that they which commit such things are worthy of death, not only do the same, but have pleasure in them that do them.   Romans 1:18–32

Behold, thou art called a Jew, and restest in the law, and makest thy boast of God, And knowest *his* will, and approvest the things that are more excellent, being instructed out of the law; And art confident that thou thyself art a guide of the blind, a light of them which are in darkness, An instructor of the foolish, a teacher of babes, which hast the form of knowledge and of the truth in the law. Thou therefore which teachest another, teachest thou not thyself? thou that preachest a man should not steal, dost thou steal? Thou that sayest a man should not commit adultery, dost thou commit adultery? thou that abhorrest idols, dost thou commit

sacrilege? Thou that makest thy boast of the law, through breaking the law dishonourest thou God? For the name of God is blasphemed among the Gentiles through you, as it is written.

ROMANS 2:17–24

What then? are we better *than they*? No, in no wise: for we have
before proved both Jews and Gentiles, that they are all under sin;
As it is written, **There is none righteous, no, not one: There is
none that understandeth, there is none that seeketh after God.**
They are all gone out of the way, they are together become unprofitable; there is none that doeth good, no, not one. Their throat *is*
an open sepulchre; with their tongues they have used deceit; the
poison of asps *is* under their lips: Whose mouth *is* full of cursing and bitterness: Their feet *are* swift to shed blood: Destruction
and misery *are* in their ways: And the way of peace have they not
known: There is no fear of God before their eyes.

Now we know that what things soever the law saith, it saith to
them who are under the law: that every mouth may be stopped,
and all the world may become guilty before God. Therefore by the
deeds of the law there shall no flesh be justified in his sight: for by
the law *is* the knowledge of sin. ROMANS 3:9–20

How is God our best defense against false teachers?

GOD'S LOVE

*Despite the sin that has permeated his creation, God remains
faithful to his people. In the Old Testament, God modeled his
love for humankind through his special relationship with Israel.
God used a profound and unusual object lesson to illustrate
how much he loved the Israelites despite their unfaithfulness.
He asked Hosea, a prophet to the northern kingdom of Israel, to
marry an immoral woman named Gomer. Hosea would play the
part of God; Gomer would play the part of Israel.*

The word of the LORD that came unto Hosea, the son of Beeri,
in the days of Uzziah, Jotham, Ahaz, *and* Hezekiah, kings of Judah,
and in the days of Jeroboam the son of Joash, king of Israel.

The beginning of the word of the LORD by Hosea. And the LORD said to Hosea, Go, take unto thee a wife of whoredoms and children of whoredoms: for the land hath committed great whoredom, *departing* from the LORD. So he went and took Gomer the daughter of Diblaim; which conceived, and bare him a son.

HOSEA 1:1–3

Hosea provided Gomer with a wonderful life of love and provision. But she chose to spurn his love; Gomer left Hosea and returned to her immoral lifestyle. Evidently she became a slave. God told Hosea to track down his wife, purchase her, take her back in and love her. What Hosea did for Gomer, God did for the Israelites.

Then said the LORD unto me, Go yet, love a woman beloved of *her* friend, yet an adulteress, according to the love of the LORD toward the children of Israel, who look to other gods, and love flagons of wine.

So I bought her to me for fifteen *pieces* of silver, and *for* an homer of barley, and an half homer of barley: And I said unto her, Thou shalt abide for me many days; thou shalt not play the harlot, and thou shalt not be for *another* man: so *will* I also *be* for thee.

HOSEA 3:1–3

In the book of Hosea, God reflected on his relationship with Israel in terms of a wayward son as well as an unfaithful wife. He intervened for the Israelites even when they didn't recognize his presence. Out of love he had rescued them from slavery in Egypt. Now Israel, referred to as Ephraim after Israel's largest tribe, was about to go into slavery again. This time the mighty nation of Assyria was going to take the people captive. They would experience the blows of God's discipline for walking away from him, but he declared yet again that he would redeem them. This is the same kind of unending, undeserved love God has for us.

When Israel *was* a child, then I loved him, and called my son out of Egypt. *As* they called them, so they went from them: they sacrificed unto Baalim, and burned incense to graven images. I taught Ephraim also to go, taking them by their arms; but they knew not that I healed them. I drew them with cords of a man, with bands of love: and I was to them as they that take off the yoke on their jaws, and I laid meat unto them.

He shall not return into the land of Egypt, but the Assyrian shall be his king, because they refused to return. And the sword shall abide on his cities, and shall consume his branches, and devour *them*, because of their own counsels. And my people are bent to backsliding from me: though they called them to the most High, none at all would exalt *him*.

How shall I give thee up, Ephraim? *how* **shall I deliver thee, Israel? how shall I make thee as Admah?** *how* **shall I set thee as Zeboim? mine heart is turned within me, my repentings are kindled together. I will not execute the fierceness of mine anger,** I will not return to destroy Ephraim: for I *am* God, and not man; the Holy One in the midst of thee: and I will not enter into the city. They shall walk after the LORD: he shall roar like a lion: when he shall roar, then the children shall tremble from the west. They shall tremble as a bird out of Egypt, and as a dove out of the land of Assyria: and I will place them in their houses, saith the LORD.

HOSEA 11:1–11

How does the book of Hosea show God's discipline
and punishment as well as his compassion and redemption?
How do you see his discipline and punishment fitting in
with your concept of God as a God of love?

ALL AND WHOSOEVER

One of the special assignments John took on in his Gospel was to share that Jesus' offer of forgiveness and restoration to God for eternity is for everyone. As you read this collection of powerful declarations, keep in mind that we are included in every statement; therefore God extends his offer of love to us. He "so loves us."

In [the Word, Jesus Christ] was life; and the life was the light of men.

JOHN 1:4

The same came for a witness, to bear witness of the Light, that all *men* through him might believe.　　　　JOHN 1:7

[The Word, Jesus Christ] came unto his own, and his own received him not. But as many as received him, to them gave he power to become the sons of God, *even* to them that believe on his name.　　　　JOHN 1:11–12

For God so loved the world, that he gave his only begotten Son, that whosoever believeth in him should not perish, but have everlasting life.　　　　JOHN 3:16

He that believeth on the Son hath everlasting life: and he that believeth not the Son shall not see life; but the wrath of God abideth on him.　　　　JOHN 3:36

But whosoever drinketh of the water that I shall give him shall never thirst; but the water that I shall give him shall be in him a well of water springing up into everlasting life.　　　　JOHN 4:14

Verily, verily, I say unto you, He that heareth my word, and believeth on him that sent me, hath everlasting life, and shall not come into condemnation; but is passed from death unto life.　　　　JOHN 5:24

And Jesus said unto them, I am the bread of life: he that cometh to me shall never hunger; and he that believeth on me shall never thirst.　　　　JOHN 6:35

All that the Father giveth me shall come to me; and him that cometh to me I will in no wise cast out.　　　　JOHN 6:37

I am the living bread which came down from heaven: if any man eat of this bread, he shall live for ever: and the bread that I will give is my flesh, which I will give for the life of the world.　　　　JOHN 6:51

Whoso eateth my flesh, and drinketh my blood, hath eternal life; and I will raise him up at the last day.　　　　JOHN 6:54

He that believeth on me, as the scripture hath said, out of his belly shall flow rivers of living water.

JOHN 7:38

Then spake Jesus again unto them, saying, I am the light of the world: he that followeth me shall not walk in darkness, but shall have the light of life.

JOHN 8:12

Verily, verily, I say unto you, If a man keep my saying, he shall never see death.

JOHN 8:51

I am the door: by me if any man enter in, he shall be saved, and shall go in and out, and find pasture.

JOHN 10:9

And whosoever liveth and believeth in me shall never die. Believest thou this?

JOHN 11:26

Now is the judgment of this world: now shall the prince of this world be cast out. And I, if I be lifted up from the earth, will draw all *men* unto me.

JOHN 12:31–32

SEEING PEOPLE AS GOD SEES THEM

As the parable of the wandering sheep illustrates, God loves us deeply. He also wants us to follow his example in how we treat one another.

At the same time came the disciples unto Jesus, saying, Who is the greatest in the kingdom of heaven?

And Jesus called a little child unto him, and set him in the midst of them, And said, Verily I say unto you, Except ye be converted, and become as little children, ye shall not enter into the kingdom of heaven. Whosoever therefore shall humble himself as this little child, the same is greatest in the kingdom of heaven. And whoso shall receive one such little child in my name receiveth me.

But whoso shall offend one of these little ones which believe in me, it were better for him that a millstone were hanged about his neck, and *that* he were drowned in the depth of the sea. Woe unto the world because of offences! for it must needs be that offences come; but woe to that man by whom the offence cometh!

Wherefore if thy hand or thy foot offend thee, cut them off, and cast *them* from thee: it is better for thee to enter into life halt or maimed, rather than having two hands or two feet to be cast into everlasting fire. And if thine eye offend thee, pluck it out, and cast *it* from thee: it is better for thee to enter into life with one eye, rather than having two eyes to be cast into hell fire.

Take heed that ye despise not one of these little ones; for I say unto you, That in heaven their angels do always behold the face of my Father which is in heaven. For the Son of man is come to save that which was lost.

How think ye? if a man have an hundred sheep, and one of them be gone astray, doth he not leave the ninety and nine, and goeth into the mountains, and seeketh that which is gone astray? And if so be that he find it, verily I say unto you, he rejoiceth more of that *sheep*, than of the ninety and nine which went not astray. Even so it is not the will of your Father which is in heaven, that one of these little ones should perish.   MATTHEW 18:1–14

> *In the early season of his ministry, Jesus spoke to a large crowd of people who gathered to be healed by him and to hear what he had to say. Jesus taught that we are to see and treat people the way God sees and treats us. Our heavenly Father provides the supreme example that we are to follow.*

But I say unto you which hear, Love your enemies, do good to them which hate you, Bless them that curse you, and pray for them which despitefully use you. And unto him that smiteth thee on the *one* cheek offer also the other; and him that taketh away thy cloak forbid not *to take thy* coat also. Give to every man that asketh of thee; and of him that taketh away thy goods ask *them* not again. And as ye would that men should do to you, do ye also to them likewise.

For if ye love them which love you, what thank have ye? for sinners also love those that love them. And if ye do good to them which do good to you, what thank have ye? for sinners also do even the same. And if ye lend *to them* of whom ye hope to receive, what thank have ye? for sinners also lend to sinners, to receive as much again. **But love ye your enemies, and do good, and lend, hoping**

**for nothing again; and your reward shall be great, and ye shall
be the children of the Highest: for he is kind unto the unthankful and *to* the evil. Be ye therefore merciful, as your Father also
is merciful.** LUKE 6:27–36

*The new reality in Christ is this: There is no more division between
Jews and Gentiles, men and women, masters and slaves. We all
belong to Christ equally. The apostle Paul had a grand opportunity to demonstrate this in the latter years of his life. His good
friend Philemon had a slave — Onesimus — who may have stolen from Philemon and then ran away (a crime punishable by
death). Amazingly, while Paul was in Rome he met Onesimus,
and Onesimus became a Christian. Paul wrote Philemon a letter with the personal appeal to welcome Onesimus back, not as
a slave but as a brother in Christ. God lays before us today the
same challenge — to embrace every believer as a precious family
member.*

Paul, a prisoner of Jesus Christ, and Timothy *our* brother, unto
Philemon our dearly beloved, and fellowlabourer, And to *our* beloved Apphia, and Archippus our fellowsoldier, and to the church
in thy house:

Grace to you, and peace, from God our Father and the Lord
Jesus Christ.

I thank my God, making mention of thee always in my prayers,
Hearing of thy love and faith, which thou hast toward the Lord
Jesus, and toward all saints; That the communication of thy faith
may become effectual by the acknowledging of every good thing
which is in you in Christ Jesus. For we have great joy and consolation in thy love, because the bowels of the saints are refreshed by
thee, brother.

Wherefore, though I might be much bold in Christ to enjoin
thee that which is convenient, Yet for love's sake I rather beseech
thee, being such an one as Paul the aged, and now also a prisoner
of Jesus Christ. I beseech thee for my son Onesimus, whom I have
begotten in my bonds: Which in time past was to thee unprofitable, but now profitable to thee and to me:

Whom I have sent again: thou therefore receive him, that is, mine own bowels: Whom I would have retained with me, that in thy stead he might have ministered unto me in the bonds of the gospel: But without thy mind would I do nothing; that thy benefit should not be as it were of necessity, but willingly. **For perhaps he therefore departed for a season, that thou shouldest receive him for ever; Not now as a servant, but above a servant, a brother beloved, specially to me, but how much more unto thee, both in the flesh, and in the Lord?**

If thou count me therefore a partner, receive him as myself. If he hath wronged thee, or oweth *thee* ought, put that on mine account; I Paul have written *it* with mine own hand, I will repay *it*: albeit I do not say to thee how thou owest unto me even thine own self besides. Yea, brother, let me have joy of thee in the Lord: refresh my bowels in the Lord. Having confidence in thy obedience I wrote unto thee, knowing that thou wilt also do more than I say.

But withal prepare me also a lodging: for I trust that through your prayers I shall be given unto you.

There salute thee Epaphras, my fellowprisoner in Christ Jesus; Marcus, Aristarchus, Demas, Lucas, my fellowlabourers.

The grace of our Lord Jesus Christ *be* with your spirit. Amen.

PHILEMON 1–25

How do the stories in this chapter highlight
God's persistence and compassion in bringing
people into a right relationship with one another?
Which phrases speak to you personally?

WHAT WE BELIEVE

It cannot be denied. We are the crowning achievement of God's creation. We were made in the very image of God with the express purpose of living in perfect community with God on earth. But the first two people rejected God's vision, introducing death and separation from God into the human race. We see clearly in the story of Cain and Abel, throughout human history and even in our own stories that this sin nature has been passed down and all people fall victim to it. But God loves us and wants us back. Like Hosea pursued his unfaithful wife, Gomer, so God pursues us. All of his "repentings are kindled together" (see Hosea 11:8) when he thinks of us. God's love knows no boundaries. Forgiveness and salvation are available to everyone who will receive them in Christ Jesus. God calls all Christians to see people the same way he does. What would happen in our world if we would do just that?

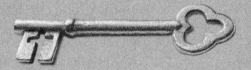

CHAPTER

8

Compassion

—— KEY QUESTION ——

What about the poor and injustice?

—— KEY IDEA ——

I believe God calls all Christians to show
compassion to people in need.

—— KEY VERSE ——

Defend the poor and fatherless:
do justice to the afflicted and needy.
Deliver the poor and needy:
rid *them* out of the hand of the wicked.
Psalm 82:3 – 4

OUR MAP

All human beings are valuable to God, and he calls us to see people as he sees them. Compassion goes a step further by compelling us to feel their pain. Compassion literally means "suffer with." God calls us to come alongside people who are suffering. It doesn't mean we can fix their problems, but it does mean we can enter into their pain. Before we act or practice this belief, we must believe it is God's call on the life of all Christ followers. When we believe this in our hearts, we will show compassion to all people, especially to those in need. This is not a "do as I say, not as I do" command from the Lord. God himself is merciful and full of compassion. This is where our journey into compassion starts.

In this chapter we will read about:

- God: Full of Justice and Compassion
- Israel: Called to Compassion
- Jesus: Model of Compassion
- Believers: The Ongoing Call to Compassion

GOD: FULL OF JUSTICE AND COMPASSION

Throughout their history, the Israelites struggled to stay true to God. Sometimes they followed God, but those periods of faithfulness were followed by times of sin and rebellion. But God's love for his people was always evident. His compassion was constant as he offered the people relief from the misery caused by their sin. In this passage, the Israelites are back in the promised land after suffering years of exile and hardship. The Levites invited the people to stand to their feet as they rehearsed together the history of God's compassion toward them, from the very beginning of time until that very moment.

As you read this account from Nehemiah 9, look for some of the ways God showed compassion and justice to the Israelites.

Now in the twenty and fourth day of this month the children of Israel were assembled with fasting, and with sackclothes, and earth upon them. And the seed of Israel separated themselves from all strangers, and stood and confessed their sins, and the iniquities of their fathers. And they stood up in their place, and read in the book of the law of the LORD their God *one* fourth part of the day; and *another* fourth part they confessed, and worshipped the LORD their God. Then stood up upon the stairs, of the Levites, Jeshua, and Bani, Kadmiel, Shebaniah, Bunni, Sherebiah, Bani, *and* Chenani, and cried with a loud voice unto the LORD their God. Then the Levites, Jeshua, and Kadmiel, Bani, Hashabniah, Sherebiah, Hodijah, Shebaniah, *and* Pethahiah, said, Stand up *and* bless the LORD your God for ever and ever: and blessed be thy glorious name, which is exalted above all blessing and praise.

Thou, *even* thou, *art* LORD alone; thou hast made heaven, the heaven of heavens, with all their host, the earth, and all *things* that *are* therein, the seas, and all that *is* therein, and thou preservest them all; and the host of heaven worshippeth thee.

Thou *art* the LORD the God, who didst choose Abram, and broughtest him forth out of Ur of the Chaldees, and gavest him the name of Abraham; And foundest his heart faithful before thee, and madest a covenant with him to give the land of the Canaanites, the Hittites, the Amorites, and the Perizzites, and the Jebusites, and the Girgashites, to give *it, I say*, to his seed, and hast performed thy words; for thou *art* righteous:

And didst see the affliction of our fathers in Egypt, and heardest their cry by the Red sea; And shewedst signs and wonders upon Pharaoh, and on all his servants, and on all the people of his land: for thou knewest that they dealt proudly against them. So didst thou get thee a name, as *it is* this day. And thou didst divide the sea before them, so that they went through the midst of the sea on the dry land; and their persecutors thou threwest into the deeps, as a stone into the mighty waters. Moreover thou leddest them in the day by a cloudy pillar; and in the night by a pillar of fire, to give them light in the way wherein they should go.

Thou camest down also upon mount Sinai, and spakest with them from heaven, and gavest them right judgments, and true laws, good statutes and commandments: And madest known unto them thy holy sabbath, and commandedst them precepts, statutes, and laws, by the hand of Moses thy servant: And gavest them bread from heaven for their hunger, and broughtest forth water for them out of the rock for their thirst, and promisedst them that they should go in to possess the land which thou hadst sworn to give them.

But they and our fathers dealt proudly, and hardened their necks, and hearkened not to thy commandments, And refused to obey, neither were mindful of thy wonders that thou didst among them; but hardened their necks, and in their rebellion appointed a captain to return to their bondage: **but thou** *art* **a God ready to pardon, gracious and merciful, slow to anger, and of great kindness,** and forsookest them not. Yea, when they had made them a molten calf, and said, This *is* thy God that brought thee up out of Egypt, and had wrought great provocations;

Yet thou in thy manifold mercies forsookest them not in the wilderness: the pillar of the cloud departed not from them by day, to lead them in the way; neither the pillar of fire by night, to shew them light, and the way wherein they should go. Thou gavest also thy good spirit to instruct them, and withheldest not thy manna from their mouth, and gavest them water for their thirst. Yea, forty years didst thou sustain them in the wilderness, *so that* they lacked nothing; their clothes waxed not old, and their feet swelled not.

Moreover thou gavest them kingdoms and nations, and didst divide them into corners: so they possessed the land of Sihon, and the land of the king of Heshbon, and the land of Og king of Bashan. Their children also multipliedst thou as the stars of heaven, and broughtest them into the land, concerning which thou hadst promised to their fathers, that they should go in to possess *it*. So the children went in and possessed the land, and thou subduedst before them the inhabitants of the land, the Canaanites, and gavest them into their hands, with their kings, and the people of the land, that they might do with them as they would. And they took strong cities, and a fat land, and possessed houses full of all goods, wells digged, vineyards, and oliveyards, and fruit trees in abundance: so they did eat, and were filled, and became fat, and delighted themselves in thy great goodness.

Nevertheless they were disobedient, and rebelled against thee, and cast thy law behind their backs, and slew thy prophets which testified against them to turn them to thee, and they wrought great provocations. Therefore thou deliveredst them into the hand of their enemies, who vexed them: and in the time of their trouble, when they cried unto thee, **thou heardest *them* from heaven; and according to thy manifold mercies thou gavest them saviours, who saved them out of the hand of their enemies.**

But after they had rest, they did evil again before thee: therefore leftest thou them in the hand of their enemies, so that they had the dominion over them: **yet when they returned, and cried unto thee, thou heardest *them* from heaven; and many times didst thou deliver them according to thy mercies;**

And testifiedst against them, that thou mightest bring them again unto thy law: yet they dealt proudly, and hearkened not unto thy commandments, but sinned against thy judgments, (which if a man do, he shall live in them;) and withdrew the shoulder, and hardened their neck, and would not hear. Yet many years didst thou forbear them, and testifiedst against them by thy spirit in thy prophets: yet would they not give ear: therefore gavest thou them into the hand of the people of the lands. **Nevertheless for thy great mercies' sake thou didst not utterly consume them, nor forsake them; for thou *art* a gracious and merciful God.**

Now therefore, our God, the great, the mighty, and the terrible God, who keepest covenant and mercy, let not all the trouble seem little before thee, that hath come upon us, on our kings, on our princes, and on our priests, and on our prophets, and on our fathers, and on all thy people, since the time of the kings of Assyria unto this day. Howbeit thou *art* just in all that is brought upon us; for thou hast done right, but we have done wickedly: Neither have our kings, our princes, our priests, nor our fathers, kept thy law, nor hearkened unto thy commandments and thy testimonies, wherewith thou didst testify against them. For they have not served thee in their kingdom, and in thy great goodness that thou gavest them, and in the large and fat land which thou gavest before them, neither turned they from their wicked works.

Behold, we *are* servants this day, and *for* the land that thou gavest unto our fathers to eat the fruit thereof and the good thereof, behold, we *are* servants in it: And it yieldeth much increase unto the kings whom thou hast set over us because of our sins: also they have dominion over our bodies, and over our cattle, at their pleasure, and we *are* in great distress.

And because of all this we make a sure *covenant*, and write *it*; and our princes, Levites, *and* priests, seal *unto it*.   Nehemiah 9:1–38

From the beginning God has graciously shown compassion for his people, with the ultimate demonstration being the sacrifice of his only Son, Jesus Christ. Because the only just response to the sins of humankind was death, our just God, according to his righteousness, issued the death penalty on us. Then, out of his limitless compassion, he offered Jesus as a "substitutionary atonement"—that is, Jesus took humanity's place. Through this act God demonstrated his complete compassion without budging an inch on his complete justice. We who are guilty are made righteous by the sacrifice of the only person who was completely righteous.

But now the righteousness of God without the law is manifested, being witnessed by the law and the prophets; Even the righteousness of God *which is* by faith of Jesus Christ unto all and upon all them that believe: for there is no difference: For all have sinned, and come short of the glory of God; **Being justified freely by his grace through the redemption that is in Christ Jesus: Whom God hath set forth *to be* a propitiation through faith in his blood, to declare his righteousness for the remission of sins that are past, through the forbearance of God; To declare, I say, at this time his righteousness: that he might be just, and the justifier of him which believeth in Jesus.**

Romans 3:21–26

Beloved, let us love one another: for love is of God; and every one that loveth is born of God, and knoweth God. He that loveth not knoweth not God; for God is love. In this was manifested the love of God toward us, because that God sent his only begotten Son into the world, that we might live through him. **Herein is love, not that we loved God, but that he loved us, and sent his Son *to be* the propitiation for our sins.**   1 John 4:7–10

ISRAEL: CALLED TO COMPASSION

Compassion was an important aspect of the testimony of the people of Israel to the world. When God set up the foundational laws for his people, he revealed through Moses specific guidelines for helping the poor and those in need.

As you read the selected passages below from Deuteronomy 24 and 25, look for some of the principles behind the laws Moses gave to govern how the Israelites were to treat others.

When thou dost lend thy brother any thing, thou shalt not go into his house to fetch his pledge. Thou shalt stand abroad, and the man to whom thou dost lend shall bring out the pledge abroad unto thee. And if the man *be* poor, thou shalt not sleep with his pledge: In any case thou shalt deliver him the pledge again when the sun goeth down, that he may sleep in his own raiment, and bless thee: and it shall be righteousness unto thee before the LORD thy God.

Thou shalt not oppress an hired servant *that is* poor and needy, *whether he be* of thy brethren, or of thy strangers that *are* in thy land within thy gates: At his day thou shalt give *him* his hire, neither shall the sun go down upon it; for he *is* poor, and setteth his heart upon it: lest he cry against thee unto the LORD, and it be sin unto thee. DEUTERONOMY 24:10–15

Thou shalt not pervert the judgment of the stranger, *nor* of the fatherless; nor take a widow's raiment to pledge: But thou shalt remember that thou wast a bondman in Egypt, and the LORD thy God redeemed thee thence: therefore I command thee to do this thing.

When thou cuttest down thine harvest in thy field, and hast forgot a sheaf in the field, thou shalt not go again to fetch it: it shall be for the stranger, for the fatherless, and for the widow: that the LORD thy God may bless thee in all the work of thine hands. When thou beatest thine olive tree, thou shalt not go over the boughs again: it shall be for the stranger, for the fatherless, and for the widow. When thou gatherest the grapes of thy vineyard, thou shalt not glean *it* afterward: it shall be for the stranger, for the fatherless, and for the widow. And thou shalt remember that thou wast a bondman in the land of Egypt: therefore I command thee to do this thing.   DEUTERONOMY 24:17–22

> In the promised land, the continuity of each family and its allot-
> ment of land was of considerable importance. Though it may
> seem strange to us today, God led Moses to lay out for Israel
> the custom known as "levirate marriage," by which a brother (or
> nearest relative by marriage) would marry a widow without chil-
> dren and produce descendants in the dead relative's name. This
> ensured a lineage and inheritance for that family. Although the
> brother-in-law (or more distantly related kinsman) wasn't strictly
> obligated to marry his brother's wife, social shame would have
> discouraged him from failing to do so.

If brethren dwell together, and one of them die, and have no child, the wife of the dead shall not marry without unto a stranger: her husband's brother shall go in unto her, and take her to him to wife, and perform the duty of an husband's brother unto her. And it shall be, *that* the firstborn which she beareth shall succeed in the name of his brother *which is* dead, that his name be not put out of Israel.

And if the man like not to take his brother's wife, then let his brother's wife go up to the gate unto the elders, and say, My hus-band's brother refuseth to raise up unto his brother a name in Is-rael, he will not perform the duty of my husband's brother. Then the elders of his city shall call him, and speak unto him: and *if* he stand *to it*, and say, I like not to take her; Then shall his brother's wife come unto him in the presence of the elders, and loose his shoe from off his foot, and spit in his face, and shall answer and say, So shall it be done unto that man that will not build up his brother's house. And his name shall be called in Israel, The house of him that hath his shoe loosed.   DEUTERONOMY 25:5–10

> Moses issued the above laws in the 1400s BC while the Israel-
> ites were wandering in the wilderness. A couple of hundred years
> later, during the time of the judges, a beautiful application of

*the principle of levirate marriage unfolded. Because of famine,
Naomi and Elimelech and their two children left for the land of
Moab. While there, the two sons married Moabite women, but
over the years the father and the sons died. Naomi and one of
her daughters-in-law, Ruth, made their way back to Naomi's
hometown of Bethlehem. Without husbands or children, Naomi
and Ruth were forced to live a life of poverty.*

*One day, Ruth decided to go out and glean after the reapers
in order to provide food for herself and Naomi. When Ruth came
home after a successful day of gleaning, her mother-in-law asked
her in whose field she had gleaned. The rest of the story shows
the power and provision of the principle of gleaning and the rule
of a next kinsman Moses put in place years earlier.*

And Naomi had a kinsman of her husband's, a mighty man of
wealth, of the family of Elimelech; and his name *was* Boaz.

And Ruth the Moabitess said unto Naomi, Let me now go to
the field, and glean ears of corn after *him* in whose sight I shall
find grace.

And she said unto her, Go, my daughter. And she went, and
came, and gleaned in the field after the reapers: and her hap was
to light on a part of the field *belonging* unto Boaz, who *was* of the
kindred of Elimelech.

And, behold, Boaz came from Bethlehem, and said unto the
reapers, The LORD *be* with you.

And they answered him, The LORD bless thee.

Then said Boaz unto his servant that was set over the reapers,
Whose damsel *is* this?

And the servant that was set over the reapers answered and
said, It *is* the Moabitish damsel that came back with Naomi out
of the country of Moab: And she said, I pray you, let me glean and
gather after the reapers among the sheaves: so she came, and hath
continued even from the morning until now, that she tarried a little in the house.

Then said Boaz unto Ruth, Hearest thou not, my daughter? Go
not to glean in another field, neither go from hence, but abide here
fast by my maidens: *Let* thine eyes *be* on the field that they do reap,
and go thou after them: have I not charged the young men that

they shall not touch thee? and when thou art athirst, go unto the vessels, and drink of *that* which the young men have drawn.

Then she fell on her face, and bowed herself to the ground, and said unto him, Why have I found grace in thine eyes, that thou shouldest take knowledge of me, seeing I *am* a stranger?

And Boaz answered and said unto her, It hath fully been shewed me, all that thou hast done unto thy mother in law since the death of thine husband: and *how* thou hast left thy father and thy mother, and the land of thy nativity, and art come unto a people which thou knewest not heretofore. The LORD recompense thy work, and a full reward be given thee of the LORD God of Israel, under whose wings thou art come to trust.

Then she said, Let me find favour in thy sight, my lord; for that thou hast comforted me, and for that thou hast spoken friendly unto thine handmaid, though I be not like unto one of thine handmaidens.

And Boaz said unto her, At mealtime come thou hither, and eat of the bread, and dip thy morsel in the vinegar.

And she sat beside the reapers: and he reached her parched *corn*, and she did eat, and was sufficed, and left. And when she was risen up to glean, Boaz commanded his young men, saying, Let her glean even among the sheaves, and reproach her not: And let fall also *some* of the handfuls of purpose for her, and leave *them*, that she may glean *them*, and rebuke her not.

So she gleaned in the field until even, and beat out that she had gleaned: and it was about an ephah of barley. And she took *it* up, and went into the city: and her mother in law saw what she had gleaned: and she brought forth, and gave to her that she had reserved after she was sufficed.

And her mother in law said unto her, Where hast thou gleaned to day? and where wroughtest thou? blessed be he that did take knowledge of thee.

And she shewed her mother in law with whom she had wrought, and said, The man's name with whom I wrought to day *is* Boaz.

And Naomi said unto her daughter in law, Blessed *be* he of the LORD, who hath not left off his kindness to the living and to the dead. And Naomi said unto her, The man *is* near of kin unto us, one of our next kinsmen.

And Ruth the Moabitess said, He said unto me also, Thou shalt keep fast by my young men, until they have ended all my harvest.

And Naomi said unto Ruth her daughter in law, *It is* good, my daughter, that thou go out with his maidens, that they meet thee not in any other field.

So she kept fast by the maidens of Boaz to glean unto the end of barley harvest and of wheat harvest; and dwelt with her mother in law.   RUTH 2:1–23 ⚷

> The principle of gleaning worked. By gathering the extra grain left behind by the reapers (and helped along by the kind protection of Boaz), Ruth's gleaning helped to sustain these two poor women—one an Israelite, the other a foreigner from a group of people who in the past had caused the Israelites much heartache. Yet the extent of Boaz's compassion didn't stop there. Through a series of events he exercised his right and obligation as a next kinsman.

So Boaz took Ruth, and she was his wife: and when he went in unto her, the LORD gave her conception, and she bare a son. And the women said unto Naomi, Blessed *be* the LORD, which hath not left thee this day without a kinsman, that his name may be famous in Israel. And he shall be unto thee a restorer of *thy* life, and a nourisher of thine old age: for thy daughter in law, which loveth thee, which is better to thee than seven sons, hath born him.

And Naomi took the child, and laid it in her bosom, and became nurse unto it. And the women her neighbours gave it a name, saying, There is a son born to Naomi; and they called his name Obed: he *is* the father of Jesse, the father of David.   RUTH 4:13–17

> When Obed came of age he didn't carry on the name of Boaz but of Elimelech, Naomi's deceased husband, and Mahlon, Ruth's deceased husband. In addition, all the land and property Boaz purchased was kept in Naomi's family line when Obed became heir to it. What an amazing story of human compassion! But the blessings did not stop with Naomi and her family. Through Boaz's act of compassion a child was born. From this child would come David and from David would ultimately come Jesus, our Savior. A single act of compassion can live on for generations to come!

How did Boaz express his faith when he helped Ruth and Naomi?
What was the motive behind his acts of compassion?

JESUS: MODEL OF COMPASSION

Jesus, the very model of compassion, told a beautiful story we call the parable of the good Samaritan. The telling of the story was prompted by an exchange that zeroed in on one of two chief laws of the Old Testament: to love our neighbor as ourselves. Through this classic story, Jesus made the startling point that his most mature follower is not necessarily the priest or the pastor but the one who actually lives out the commandment.

And, behold, a certain lawyer stood up, and tempted him, saying, Master, what shall I do to inherit eternal life?

He said unto him, What is written in the law? how readest thou?

And he answering said, Thou shalt love the Lord thy God with all thy heart, and with all thy soul, and with all thy strength, and with all thy mind; and thy neighbour as thyself.

And he said unto him, Thou hast answered right: this do, and thou shalt live.

But he, willing to justify himself, said unto Jesus, And who is my neighbour?

And Jesus answering said, A certain *man* went down from Jerusalem to Jericho, and fell among thieves, which stripped him of his raiment, and wounded *him*, and departed, leaving *him* half dead. And by chance there came down a certain priest that way: and when he saw him, he passed by on the other side. And likewise a Levite, when he was at the place, came and looked *on him*, and passed by on the other side. But a certain Samaritan, as he journeyed, came where he was: and when he saw him, he had compassion *on him*, And went to *him*, and bound up his wounds, pouring in oil and wine, and set him on his own beast, and brought him to an inn, and took care of him. And on the morrow when he departed, he took out two pence, and gave *them* to the host, and said unto him, Take care of him; and whatsoever thou spendest more, when I come again, I will repay thee.

Which now of these three, thinkest thou, was neighbour unto him that fell among the thieves?

And he said, He that shewed mercy on him.

Then said Jesus unto him, Go, and do thou likewise.

LUKE 10:25–37 ⚷

Throughout his teaching ministry, Jesus frequently and master-fully instructed his followers to show compassion to people in need as the ultimate fulfillment of the Law of Moses. Toward the very end of his life on earth, Jesus provided his disciples with divine insight into the ministry of compassion to the poor and needy. He told them their acts of compassion would have eternal consequences. When Jesus returns he will separate the obedient followers from the unbelievers. How we treat others should make it clear into which of the two groups we fall. After all, our behavior has results that reach far beyond our time on this earth.

When the Son of man shall come in his glory, and all the holy angels with him, then shall he sit upon the throne of his glory: And before him shall be gathered all nations: and he shall separate them one from another, as a shepherd divideth *his* sheep from the goats: And he shall set the sheep on his right hand, but the goats on the left.

Then shall the King say unto them on his right hand, Come, ye blessed of my Father, inherit the kingdom prepared for you from the foundation of the world: For I was an hungred, and ye gave me meat: I was thirsty, and ye gave me drink: I was a stranger, and ye took me in: Naked, and ye clothed me: I was sick, and ye visited me: I was in prison, and ye came unto me.

Then shall the righteous answer him, saying, Lord, when saw we thee an hungred, and fed *thee*? or thirsty, and gave *thee* drink? When saw we thee a stranger, and took *thee* in? or naked, and clothed *thee*? Or when saw we thee sick, or in prison, and came unto thee?

And the King shall answer and say unto them, Verily I say unto you, Inasmuch as ye have done *it* unto one of the least of these my brethren, ye have done *it* unto me.

Then shall he say also unto them on the left hand, Depart from me, ye cursed, into everlasting fire, prepared for the devil and his angels: For I was an hungred, and ye gave me no meat: I was thirsty, and ye gave me no drink: I was a stranger, and ye took me not in: naked, and ye clothed me not: sick, and in prison, and ye visited me not.

Then shall they also answer him, saying, Lord, when saw we thee an hungred, or athirst, or a stranger, or naked, or sick, or in prison, and did not minister unto thee?

Then shall he answer them, saying, Verily I say unto you, Inasmuch as ye did *it* not to one of the least of these, ye did *it* not to me.

And these shall go away into everlasting punishment: but the righteous into life eternal.   MATTHEW 25:31–46

In your own words, describe how love for God
and love for others are related.

BELIEVERS: THE ONGOING CALL TO COMPASSION

The same challenge given to the people of Israel to live a life of compassion was also issued to the newly formed Christian church after Jesus' death and resurrection. James, who became the leader of the church in Jerusalem and was likely the half brother of Jesus, wrote what may have been the first book of the New Testament. In his letter, James instructs new believers on the practical how-tos of living this new life in Christ. These same charges apply to believers today.

Wherefore, my beloved brethren, let every man be swift to hear, slow to speak, slow to wrath: For the wrath of man worketh not the righteousness of God. Wherefore lay apart all filthiness and superfluity of naughtiness, and receive with meekness the engrafted word, which is able to save your souls.

But be ye doers of the word, and not hearers only, deceiving your own selves. For if any be a hearer of the word, and not a doer, he is like unto a man beholding his natural face in a glass: For he beholdeth himself, and goeth his way, and straightway forgetteth what manner of man he was. But whoso looketh into the perfect law of liberty, and continueth *therein*, he being not a forgetful hearer, but a doer of the work, this man shall be blessed in his deed.

If any man among you seem to be religious, and bridleth not his tongue, but deceiveth his own heart, this man's religion *is* vain. **Pure religion and undefiled before God and the Father is this, To visit the fatherless and widows in their affliction, *and* to keep himself unspotted from the world.**

My brethren, have not the faith of our Lord Jesus Christ, *the Lord* of glory, with respect of persons. For if there come unto your assembly a man with a gold ring, in goodly apparel, and there come in also a poor man in vile raiment; And ye have respect to him that weareth the gay clothing, and say unto him, Sit thou here in a good place; and say to the poor, Stand thou there, or sit here under my footstool: Are ye not then partial in yourselves, and are become judges of evil thoughts?

Hearken, my beloved brethren, Hath not God chosen the poor of this world rich in faith, and heirs of the kingdom which he hath promised to them that love him? But ye have despised the poor. Do not rich men oppress you, and draw you before the judgment seats? Do not they blaspheme that worthy name by the which ye are called?

If ye fulfil the royal law according to the scripture, Thou shalt love thy neighbour as thyself, ye do well: But if ye have respect to persons, ye commit sin, and are convinced of the law as transgressors. For whosoever shall keep the whole law, and yet offend in one *point*, he is guilty of all. For he that said, Do not commit adultery, said also, Do not kill. Now if thou commit no adultery, yet if thou kill, thou art become a transgressor of the law.

So speak ye, and so do, as they that shall be judged by the law of liberty. For he shall have judgment without mercy, that hath shewed no mercy; and mercy rejoiceth against judgment.

JAMES 1:19—2:13

What are the attitudes that James advocates?
How can you adopt those same attitudes?

WHAT WE BELIEVE

What about the poor and injustice? We begin by taking our cue from God himself. He showed the ultimate compassion toward humanity by sending Jesus as a sacrifice for sin when we did not deserve it. Throughout Israel's history, time and time again, God showed amazing compassion to rescue his people and provide for their needs. When we look back on our own lives, we will see the same pattern.

Israel was given laws to govern them regarding how to show compassion to each other and to strangers. The story of Ruth provides a beautiful example of the spirit of these laws lived out. And Jesus, the ultimate example of one who suffered for our sake, calls believers to a life of compassion, not because the law demands it but because God's love in us compels us. Living such a life begins when we embrace the belief in our heads and our hearts that God calls all Christians to show compassion to those in need.

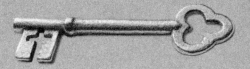

CHAPTER

9

Stewardship

--------- KEY QUESTION ---------

What is God's call on my life?

--------- KEY IDEA ---------

I believe everything I am and
everything I own belong to God.

--------- KEY VERSE ---------

The earth *is* the LORD's, and the fulness thereof;
the world, and they that dwell therein.
For he hath founded it upon the seas,
and established it upon the floods.
Psalm 24:1 – 2

OUR MAP

In Chapter 7 we learned to see humanity the way God does—through eyes of love. Then, in Chapter 8 we were challenged to treat people the way God does—with compassion. And now Chapter 9 declares that everything we are and everything we own belongs to God. The three beliefs are linked together. People devoted to thinking like Jesus believe they are to take the resources they are given, even their very lives, and use them to meet the needs of others. Because we believe the God of the Bible is the one true God who has a good plan revealed in his Word for all people to come into a relationship with him, the church offers a resounding "yes" to this key belief called stewardship.

In this chapter we will learn:

- God Is Owner
- God's People Are Managers
  ... of God's Creation
  ... of Their Children
  ... of Their Money
  ... of Their Homes
  ... of Their Bodies
  ... Over All They Do

GOD IS OWNER

Psalm 24 was a processional psalm used by the ancient Israelites to celebrate the entrance of the ark of the covenant, the symbol of the Lord's presence, into Jerusalem and into God's sanctuary. Whether or not the psalm was written for the occasion when King David brought the ark to Jerusalem, it was likely used at later commemorations of that event. The psalm begins by praising God as the owner of the earth and everything in it—a reality that consequently makes us, in turn, the stewards of the world and its resources.

The earth *is* the LORD's, and the fulness thereof;
 the world, and they that dwell therein.
For he hath founded it upon the seas,
 and established it upon the floods.

Who shall ascend into the hill of the LORD?
   or who shall stand in his holy place?
He that hath clean hands, and a pure heart;
   who hath not lifted up his soul unto vanity,
   nor sworn deceitfully.

He shall receive the blessing from the LORD,
   and righteousness from the God of his salvation.
This *is* the generation of them that seek him,
   that seek thy face, O Jacob.

Lift up your heads, O ye gates;
   and be ye lift up, ye everlasting doors;
   and the King of glory shall come in.
Who *is* this King of glory?
   The LORD strong and mighty,
   the LORD mighty in battle.
Lift up your heads, O ye gates;
   even lift *them* up, ye everlasting doors;
   and the King of glory shall come in.
Who is this King of glory?
   The LORD of hosts,
   he *is* the King of glory.   PSALM 24:1–10

One way that the Lord wanted his people to honor him was through thank offerings, overflowing out of a heart of gratitude for all God has given. But too often the Israelites offered sacrifices but then lived however they wanted, with no sincere thanksgiving behind their actions. They were just going through the motions — like a person today who goes to church on Sunday and then ignores God's commands for living on the other six days of the week. Though God commanded his people to offer sacrifices, and their offerings were pleasing to him, what he was most looking for was their wholehearted obedience in every aspect of their lives.

As you read the passage below from Psalm 50,
ponder this question: if God is self-sufficient, why are
we asked to return a portion of our wealth to him?

The mighty God, *even* the LORD,
>hath spoken, and called the earth
>>from the rising of the sun unto the going down thereof.
Out of Zion, the perfection of beauty,
>God hath shined.
Our God shall come,
>and shall not keep silence:
a fire shall devour before him,
>and it shall be very tempestuous round about him.
He shall call to the heavens from above,
>and to the earth, that he may judge his people.
Gather my saints together unto me;
>>those that have made a covenant with me by sacrifice.
And the heavens shall declare his righteousness:
>for God *is* judge himself.

Hear, O my people, and I will speak;
>O Israel, and I will testify against thee:
I *am* God, *even* thy God.
I will not reprove thee for thy sacrifices
>or thy burnt offerings, *to have been* continually before me.
I will take no bullock out of thy house,
>***nor* he goats out of thy folds.**
For every beast of the forest *is* mine,
>***and* the cattle upon a thousand hills.**
I know all the fowls of the mountains:
>**and the wild beasts of the field *are* mine.**
If I were hungry, I would not tell thee:
>**for the world *is* mine, and the fulness thereof.**
Will I eat the flesh of bulls,
>**or drink the blood of goats?**

Offer unto God thanksgiving;
>and pay thy vows unto the most High:
And call upon me in the day of trouble:
>I will deliver thee, and thou shalt glorify me.

But unto the wicked God saith,
What hast thou to do to declare my statutes,
>or *that* thou shouldest take my covenant in thy mouth?

Seeing thou hatest instruction,
and castest my words behind thee.
When thou sawest a thief, then thou consentedst with him,
and hast been partaker with adulterers.
Thou givest thy mouth to evil,
and thy tongue frameth deceit.
Thou sittest *and* speakest against thy brother;
thou slanderest thine own mother's son.
These *things* hast thou done, and I kept silence;
thou thoughtest that I was altogether *such an one* as
thyself:
but I will reprove thee,
and set *them* in order before thine eyes.

Now consider this, ye that forget God,
lest I tear *you* in pieces, and *there be* none to deliver.
Whoso offereth praise glorifieth me:
and to him that ordereth *his* conversation *aright*
will I shew the salvation of God.   PSALM 50:1–23

GOD'S PEOPLE ARE MANAGERS

Since God created everything, including humans, how do we fit into the created order? What is our role in this reality? The parable below instructs us on the importance of seeing ourselves not as owners but as managers of our lives and gifts. The talents represent any resource God, the master, gives us. He ultimately owns the resource, but we are charged with caring for it and investing it in ways that yield results for the sake of the kingdom of God.

For *the kingdom of heaven is* as a man travelling into a far country, *who* called his own servants, and delivered unto them his goods. And unto one he gave five talents, to another two, and to another one; to every man according to his several ability; and straightway took his journey. Then he that had received the five talents went and traded with the same, and made *them* other five talents. And likewise he that *had received* two, he also gained other two. But he that had received one went and digged in the earth, and hid his lord's money.

After a long time the lord of those servants cometh, and reckoneth with them. And so he that had received five talents came and brought other five talents, saying, Lord, thou deliveredst unto me five talents: behold, I have gained beside them five talents more.

His lord said unto him, Well done, *thou* good and faithful servant: thou hast been faithful over a few things, I will make thee ruler over many things: enter thou into the joy of thy lord.

He also that had received two talents came and said, Lord, thou deliveredst unto me two talents: behold, I have gained two other talents beside them.

His lord said unto him, Well done, good and faithful servant; thou hast been faithful over a few things, I will make thee ruler over many things: enter thou into the joy of thy lord.

Then he which had received the one talent came and said, Lord, I knew thee that thou art an hard man, reaping where thou hast not sown, and gathering where thou hast not strawed: And I was afraid, and went and hid thy talent in the earth: lo, *there* thou hast *that is* thine. His lord answered and said unto him, *Thou* wicked and slothful servant, thou knewest that I reap where I sowed not, and gather where I have not strawed: Thou oughtest therefore to have put my money to the exchangers, and *then* at my coming I should have received mine own with usury.

Take therefore the talent from him, and give *it* unto him which hath ten talents. For unto every one that hath shall be given, and he shall have abundance: but from him that hath not shall be taken away even that which he hath. And cast ye the unprofitable servant into outer darkness: there shall be weeping and gnashing of teeth.

MATTHEW 25:14–30

... OF GOD'S CREATION

God showed great attentiveness in creating the earth, which he entrusted to humankind to care for. Being created in his likeness, we are responsible to be respectful stewards of his precious design and the creatures that are a part of it.

And God said, Let us make man in our image, after our likeness: and let them have dominion over the fish of the sea, and over the fowl of the air, and over the cattle, and over all the earth, and over every creeping thing that creepeth upon the earth. So God created man in his *own* image, in the image of God created he him; male and female created he them.

And God blessed them, and God said unto them, Be fruitful, and multiply, and replenish the earth, and subdue it: and have dominion over the fish of the sea, and over the fowl of the air, and over every living thing that moveth upon the earth.

And God said, Behold, I have given you every herb bearing seed, which *is* upon the face of all the earth, and every tree, in the which *is* the fruit of a tree yielding seed; to you it shall be for meat. And to every beast of the earth, and to every fowl of the air, and to every thing that creepeth upon the earth, wherein *there is* life, *I have given* every green herb for meat: and it was so. Genesis 1:26–30

... of Their Children
The book of 1 Samuel tells the story of a woman named Hannah who could not have children. She pleaded earnestly with the Lord for a child, and he granted her request. Hannah's story highlights that the Lord gives our children to us to raise according to his instructions and purposes, but ultimately, they belong to him.

Now there was a certain man of Ramathaim-zophim, of mount Ephraim, and his name *was* Elkanah, the son of Jeroham, the son of Elihu, the son of Tohu, the son of Zuph, an Ephrathite: And he had two wives; the name of the one *was* Hannah, and the name of the other Peninnah: and Peninnah had children, but Hannah had no children.

And this man went up out of his city yearly to worship and to sacrifice unto the Lord of hosts in Shiloh. And the two sons of Eli, Hophni and Phinehas, the priests of the Lord, *were* there. And when the time was that Elkanah offered, he gave to Peninnah his wife, and to all her sons and her daughters, portions: But unto Hannah he gave a worthy portion; for he loved Hannah: but the Lord had shut up her womb. And her adversary also provoked her sore, for to make her fret, because the Lord had shut up her womb. And *as* he did so year by year, when she went up to the house of the Lord, so she provoked her; therefore she wept, and did not eat. Then said Elkanah her husband to her, Hannah, why weepest thou? and why eatest thou not? and why is thy heart grieved? *am* not I better to thee than ten sons?

So Hannah rose up after they had eaten in Shiloh, and after they had drunk. Now Eli the priest sat upon a seat by a post of the temple of the LORD. And she *was* in bitterness of soul, and prayed unto the LORD, and wept sore. And she vowed a vow, and said, O LORD of hosts, if thou wilt indeed look on the affliction of thine handmaid, and remember me, and not forget thine handmaid, but wilt give unto thine handmaid a man child, then I will give him unto the LORD all the days of his life, and there shall no razor come upon his head.

And it came to pass, as she continued praying before the LORD, that Eli marked her mouth. Now Hannah, she spake in her heart; only her lips moved, but her voice was not heard: therefore Eli thought she had been drunken. And Eli said unto her, How long wilt thou be drunken? put away thy wine from thee.

And Hannah answered and said, No, my lord, I *am* a woman of a sorrowful spirit: I have drunk neither wine nor strong drink, but have poured out my soul before the LORD. Count not thine handmaid for a daughter of Belial: for out of the abundance of my complaint and grief have I spoken hitherto.

Then Eli answered and said, Go in peace: and the God of Israel grant *thee* thy petition that thou hast asked of him.

And she said, Let thine handmaid find grace in thy sight. So the woman went her way, and did eat, and her countenance was no more *sad*.

And they rose up in the morning early, and worshipped before the LORD, and returned, and came to their house to Ramah: and Elkanah knew Hannah his wife; and the LORD remembered her. Wherefore it came to pass, when the time was come about after Hannah had conceived, that she bare a son, and called his name Samuel, *saying*, Because I have asked him of the LORD.

And the man Elkanah, and all his house, went up to offer unto the LORD the yearly sacrifice, and his vow. But Hannah went not up; for she said unto her husband, *I will not go up* until the child be weaned, and *then* I will bring him, that he may appear before the LORD, and there abide for ever.

And Elkanah her husband said unto her, Do what seemeth thee

good; tarry until thou have weaned him; only the LORD establish his word. So the woman abode, and gave her son suck until she weaned him.

And when she had weaned him, she took him up with her, with three bullocks, and one ephah of flour, and a bottle of wine, and brought him unto the house of the LORD in Shiloh: and the child *was* young. **And they slew a bullock, and brought the child to Eli. And she said, Oh my lord,** *as* **thy soul liveth, my lord, I** *am* **the woman that stood by thee here, praying unto the LORD. For this child I prayed; and the LORD hath given me my petition which I asked of him: Therefore also I have lent him to the LORD; as long as he liveth he shall be lent to the LORD. And he worshipped the LORD there.** 1 SAMUEL 1:1–28

But Samuel ministered before the LORD, *being* a child, girded with a linen ephod. Moreover his mother made him a little coat, and brought *it* to him from year to year, when she came up with her husband to offer the yearly sacrifice. And Eli blessed Elkanah and his wife, and said, The LORD give thee seed of this woman for the loan which is lent to the LORD. And they went unto their own home. And the LORD visited Hannah, so that she conceived, and bare three sons and two daughters. And the child Samuel grew before the LORD. 1 SAMUEL 2:18–21

... OF THEIR MONEY

In several places in the Old Testament law, the Israelites were instructed to bring the first portion of the resources and other offerings that God provided back to him. If they did, they would be blessed.

But unto the place which the LORD your God shall choose out of all your tribes to put his name there, *even* unto his habitation shall ye seek, and thither thou shalt come: And thither ye shall bring your burnt offerings, and your sacrifices, and your tithes, and heave offerings of your hand, and your vows, and your freewill offerings, and the firstlings of your herds and of your flocks: And there ye shall eat before the LORD your God, and ye shall rejoice in all that ye put your hand unto, ye and your households, wherein the LORD thy God hath blessed thee. DEUTERONOMY 12:5–7

> *For some people today, money is the hardest thing to let go of. But holding tightly to what we have earned is not just a modern-day problem.*
>
> *During the prophet Malachi's day, at the end of the Old Testament era, the Israelites were failing to follow the requirements for offerings and gifts outlined for them. God, through Malachi, challenged the people to honor him with their material resources as they had been commanded to do.*

For I *am* the LORD, I change not; therefore ye sons of Jacob are not consumed. Even from the days of your fathers ye are gone away from mine ordinances, and have not kept *them*. Return unto me, and I will return unto you, saith the LORD of hosts.

But ye said, Wherein shall we return?

Will a man rob God? Yet ye have robbed me.

But ye say, Wherein have we robbed thee?

In tithes and offerings. Ye *are* cursed with a curse: for ye have robbed me, *even* this whole nation. **Bring ye all the tithes into the storehouse, that there may be meat in mine house, and prove me now herewith, saith the LORD of hosts, if I will not open you the windows of heaven, and pour you out a blessing, that *there shall* not *be room* enough *to receive* it.** And I will rebuke the devourer for your sakes, and he shall not destroy the fruits of your ground; neither shall your vine cast her fruit before the time in the field, saith the LORD of hosts. And all nations shall call you blessed: for ye shall be a delightsome land, saith the LORD of hosts. MALACHI 3:6–12

What are the key identifiers of "good stewardship"? How does God reward good stewardship of his resources?

Because everything we have is ultimately from the Lord, when we fail to return to him a portion of what he has provided for us, we rob him. In a rather unusual parable, Jesus explained a powerful principle regarding how we are to manage the money God has entrusted to us. Money has a lot of power and can be used for good or for evil. We are to look for wise ways to use God's resources, not to help ourselves, but to help others and serve God.

And [Jesus] said also unto his disciples, There was a certain rich man, which had a steward; and the same was accused unto him that he had wasted his goods. And he called him, and said unto him, How is it that I hear this of thee? give an account of thy stewardship; for thou mayest be no longer steward.

Then the steward said within himself, What shall I do? for my lord taketh away from me the stewardship: I cannot dig; to beg I am ashamed. I am resolved what to do, that, when I am put out of the stewardship, they may receive me into their houses.

So he called every one of his lord's debtors *unto him*, and said unto the first, How much owest thou unto my lord?

And he said, An hundred measures of oil.

And he said unto him, Take thy bill, and sit down quickly, and write fifty.

Then said he to another, And how much owest thou?

And he said, An hundred measures of wheat.

And he said unto him, Take thy bill, and write fourscore.

And the lord commended the unjust steward, because he had done wisely: for the children of this world are in their generation wiser than the children of light. And I say unto you, Make to yourselves friends of the mammon of unrighteousness; that, when ye fail, they may receive you into everlasting habitations.

He that is faithful in that which is least is faithful also in much: and he that is unjust in the least is unjust also in much. If therefore ye have not been faithful in the unrighteous mammon, who will commit to your trust the true *riches*? And if ye have not been faithful in that which is another man's, who shall give you that which is your own?

No servant can serve two masters: for either he will hate the one, and love the other; or else he will hold to the one, and despise the other. Ye cannot serve God and mammon.

And the Pharisees also, who were covetous, heard all these things: and they derided him. And he said unto them, Ye are they which justify yourselves before men; but God knoweth your hearts: for that which is highly esteemed among men is abomination in the sight of God.

LUKE 16:1–15

Contrast the lifestyle of someone who loves money
with that of someone who loves God.

In sharp contrast to the Pharisees, one poor widow Jesus encountered outside the temple used the money in her possession, though it was very little, not for herself but for God's kingdom. Unlike many others, she gave not to be noticed but to give back to God.

And Jesus sat over against the treasury, and beheld how the people cast money into the treasury: and many that were rich cast in much. And there came a certain poor widow, and she threw in two mites, which make a farthing.

And he called *unto him* his disciples, and saith unto them, Verily I say unto you, That this poor widow hath cast more in, than all they which have cast into the treasury: For all *they* did cast in of their abundance; but she of her want did cast in all that she had, *even* all her living.

MARK 12:41–44

... OF THEIR HOMES

Hospitality was highly valued during Old Testament times, by the Israelites as well as by other peoples. Elijah was a mighty prophet of God who announced an impending drought in Israel brought on by the spiritual unfaithfulness of the king and the people. God sent Elijah outside Israel's borders, to the home of a destitute Gentile widow, who seemed to be the least likely person to be able to provide hospitality. Their story exemplifies the power of both human hospitality and divine provision.

And Elijah the Tishbite, *who was* of the inhabitants of Gilead, said unto Ahab, As the LORD God of Israel liveth, before whom I stand, there shall not be dew nor rain these years, but according to my word.

And the word of the LORD came unto him, saying, Get thee hence, and turn thee eastward, and hide thyself by the brook Cherith, that *is* before Jordan. And it shall be, *that* thou shalt drink of the brook; and I have commanded the ravens to feed thee there.

So he went and did according unto the word of the LORD: for he went and dwelt by the brook Cherith, that *is* before Jordan. And the ravens brought him bread and flesh in the morning, and bread and flesh in the evening; and he drank of the brook.

And it came to pass after a while, that the brook dried up, because there had been no rain in the land. And the word of the LORD came unto him, saying, Arise, get thee to Zarephath, which *belongeth* to Zidon, and dwell there: behold, I have commanded a widow woman there to sustain thee. So he arose and went to Zarephath. And when he came to the gate of the city, behold, the widow woman *was* there gathering of sticks: and he called to her, and said, Fetch me, I pray thee, a little water in a vessel, that I may drink. And as she was going to fetch *it*, he called to her, and said, Bring me, I pray thee, a morsel of bread in thine hand.

And she said, *As* the LORD thy God liveth, I have not a cake, but an handful of meal in a barrel, and a little oil in a cruse: and, behold, I *am* gathering two sticks, that I may go in and dress it for me and my son, that we may eat it, and die.

And Elijah said unto her, Fear not; go *and* do as thou hast said: but make me thereof a little cake first, and bring *it* unto me, and after make for thee and for thy son. For thus saith the LORD God of Israel, The barrel of meal shall not waste, neither shall the cruse of oil fail, until the day *that* the LORD sendeth rain upon the earth.

And she went and did according to the saying of Elijah: and she, and he, and her house, did eat *many* days. *And* the barrel of meal wasted not, neither did the cruse of oil fail, according to the word of the LORD, which he spake by Elijah.

And it came to pass after these things, *that* the son of the woman, the mistress of the house, fell sick; and his sickness was so sore, that there was no breath left in him. And she said unto Elijah, What have I to do with thee, O thou man of God? art thou come unto me to call my sin to remembrance, and to slay my son?

And he said unto her, Give me thy son. And he took him out of her bosom, and carried him up into a loft, where he abode, and laid him upon his own bed. And he cried unto the LORD, and said, O LORD my God, hast thou also brought evil upon the widow with whom I sojourn, by slaying her son? And he stretched himself upon the child three times, and cried unto the LORD, and said, O LORD my God, I pray thee, let this child's soul come into him again.

And the LORD heard the voice of Elijah; and the soul of the child came into him again, and he revived. And Elijah took the child, and brought him down out of the chamber into the house, and delivered him unto his mother: and Elijah said, See, thy son liveth.

And the woman said to Elijah, Now by this I know that thou *art* a man of God, *and* that the word of the LORD in thy mouth *is* truth.

1 KINGS 17:1–24

Our homes—no matter how large or small, how simple or fancy —belong to God and we can use them to accomplish his purposes. The importance of hospitality portrayed in the Old Testament is intensified in the New Testament, as believers are instructed, commanded and commended in regard to practicing hospitality.

Paul's challenge:

[Be] patient in tribulation; continuing instant in prayer; distributing to the necessity of saints; given to hospitality.   ROMANS 12:12–13

Instruction from the writer of Hebrews:

Be not forgetful to entertain strangers: for thereby some have entertained angels unawares.   HEBREWS 13:2

Peter's charge:

Use hospitality one to another without grudging.   1 PETER 4:9

John's commendation:

Beloved, I wish above all things that thou mayest prosper and be in health, even as thy soul prospereth. For I rejoiced greatly, when the brethren came and testified of the truth that is in thee, even as thou walkest in the truth. I have no greater joy than to hear that my children walk in truth.

Beloved, thou doest faithfully whatsoever thou doest to the brethren, and to strangers; Which have borne witness of thy charity before the church: whom if thou bring forward on their journey after a godly sort, thou shalt do well: Because that for his name's sake they went forth, taking nothing of the Gentiles. **We therefore ought to receive such, that we might be fellowhelpers to the truth.**
3 JOHN 2–8

Why are we encouraged to practice hospitality?
Why is hospitality important to God?

... OF THEIR BODIES

Paul challenged the members of the church at Corinth to honor God with their bodies. Why? Because, like our resources, our bodies belong to God. We are mere caretakers.

All things are lawful unto me, but all things are not expedient: all things are lawful for me, but I will not be brought under the power of any. Meats for the belly, and the belly for meats: but God shall destroy both it and them. Now the body *is* not for fornication, but for the Lord; and the Lord for the body. And God hath both raised up the Lord, and will also raise up us by his own power. Know ye not that your bodies are the members of Christ? shall I then take the members of Christ, and make *them* the members of an harlot? God forbid. What? know ye not that he which is joined to an harlot is one body? for two, saith he, shall be one flesh. But he that is joined unto the Lord is one spirit.

Flee fornication. Every sin that a man doeth is without the body; but he that committeth fornication sinneth against his own body. **What? know ye not that your body is the temple of the Holy Ghost *which* is in you, which ye have of God, and ye are not your own? For ye are bought with a price: therefore glorify God in your body, and in your spirit, which are God's.**
1 CORINTHIANS 6:12–20

... OVER ALL THEY DO

Paul brings us full circle by quoting from Psalm 24, which declares God's ownership over everything. We, however, are not owners, but managers—of the earth, our families, our money, our homes and our bodies. Everything we do, we are to do for his glory.

All things are lawful for me, but all things are not expedient: all things are lawful for me, but all things edify not. Let no man seek his own, but every man another's *wealth.*

Whatsoever is sold in the shambles, *that* eat, asking no question for conscience sake: For the earth *is* the Lord's, and the fulness thereof.

If any of them that believe not bid you *to a feast*, and ye be disposed to go; whatsoever is set before you, eat, asking no question for conscience sake. But if any man say unto you, This is offered in sacrifice unto idols, eat not for his sake that shewed it, and for conscience sake: for the earth *is* the Lord's, and the fulness thereof: Conscience, I say, not thine own, but of the other: for why is my liberty judged of another *man's* conscience? For if I by grace be a partaker, why am I evil spoken of for that for which I give thanks?

Whether therefore ye eat, or drink, or whatsoever ye do, do all to the glory of God. Give none offence, neither to the Jews, nor to the Gentiles, nor to the church of God: Even as I please all *men* in all *things*, not seeking mine own profit, but the *profit* of many, that they may be saved. Be ye followers of me, even as I also *am* of Christ.

1 CORINTHIANS 10:23—11:1

List some of the things God has entrusted to you to manage. How are you doing in each of these areas? How can you improve your stewardship of them?

Stewardship can make a major difference in our lives when we move from simply understanding it in our heads to fully embracing it in our hearts. God is the owner of everything we have and everything we are. When we come to faith in Christ, we turn over the "deed" of everything—our children, our money, our homes, our bodies, our very breath—to him. God then turns to us and invites us to manage all these things according to his purposes. When we do, we are freed from the hassles of ownership and enter into a life of reward and blessing.

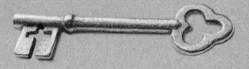

THINK

CHAPTER

10

Eternity

--- KEY QUESTION ---

What happens next?

--- KEY IDEA ---

I believe there is a heaven and a hell and that Jesus will return to judge all people and to establish his eternal kingdom.

--- KEY VERSE ---

Let not your heart be troubled: ye believe in God, believe also in me. In my Father's house are many mansions: if *it were* not *so*, I would have told you. I go to prepare a place for you.
John 14:1 – 2

OUR MAP

Embracing the first nine beliefs of the Christian faith in our minds and hearts dramatically enhances our own quality of life, as well as the quality of life for the community around us. But there is something more—and it is huge. There is life after death. Eternal life with God. God wants to restore his original vision of life with us in the garden. The only way back into the garden (which can be called heaven or God's kingdom) is through faith in Jesus Christ. Those who embrace Christ in this life are reconciled to God and become a new creation with a new identity. For the Christian, not only can life be abundant today, but anticipating what is in store for us when we are reunited with God in the new heaven and new earth is simply breathtaking.

The Scripture in this chapter will unfold the journey to that place:

- The Ending of a Life
- The Intermediate State
- The Resurrection
- The Return of Christ
- A New Heaven and a New Earth

THE ENDING OF A LIFE

While the Old Testament writers don't address the afterlife in as much detail as the New Testament writers, the Old Testament does contain the magnificent description of the prophet Elijah being taken up to heaven without dying. Elijah is one of only three people taken to heaven in bodily form, the other two being Enoch (you can read about him in Genesis 5:21–24) and, of course, Jesus. While our experience will be quite different at the end of our lives in these bodies, we bask in the promise of what awaits us on the other side.

And it came to pass, when the LORD would take up Elijah into heaven by a whirlwind, that Elijah went with Elisha from Gilgal. And Elijah said unto Elisha, Tarry here, I pray thee; for the LORD hath sent me to Beth-el.

And Elisha said *unto him*, As the LORD liveth, and *as* thy soul liveth, I will not leave thee. So they went down to Beth-el.

And the sons of the prophets that *were* at Beth-el came forth to Elisha, and said unto him, Knowest thou that the LORD will take away thy master from thy head to day?

And he said, Yea, I know *it*; hold ye your peace.

And Elijah said unto him, Elisha, tarry here, I pray thee; for the LORD hath sent me to Jericho.

And he said, *As* the LORD liveth, and *as* thy soul liveth, I will not leave thee. So they came to Jericho.

And the sons of the prophets that *were* at Jericho came to Elisha, and said unto him, Knowest thou that the LORD will take away thy master from thy head to day?

And he answered, Yea, I know *it*; hold ye your peace.

And Elijah said unto him, Tarry, I pray thee, here; for the LORD hath sent me to Jordan.

And he said, *As* the LORD liveth, and *as* thy soul liveth, I will not leave thee. And they two went on.

And fifty men of the sons of the prophets went, and stood to view afar off: and they two stood by Jordan. And Elijah took his mantle, and wrapped *it* together, and smote the waters, and they were divided hither and thither, so that they two went over on dry ground.

And it came to pass, when they were gone over, that Elijah said unto Elisha, Ask what I shall do for thee, before I be taken away from thee.

And Elisha said, I pray thee, let a double portion of thy spirit be upon me.

And he said, Thou hast asked a hard thing: *nevertheless*, if thou see me *when I am* taken from thee, it shall be so unto thee; but if not, it shall not be *so*.

And it came to pass, as they still went on, and talked, that, behold, *there appeared* a chariot of fire, and horses of fire, and parted them both asunder; and Elijah went up by a whirlwind into heaven. And Elisha saw *it*, and he cried, My father, my father, the chariot of Israel, and the horsemen thereof. And he saw him no more: and he took hold of his own clothes, and rent them in two pieces.

He took up also the mantle of Elijah that fell from him, and went back, and stood by the bank of Jordan; And he took the mantle of Elijah that fell from him, and smote the waters, and said,

Where *is* the LORD God of Elijah? and when he also had smitten the waters, they parted hither and thither: and Elisha went over.

And when the sons of the prophets which *were* to view at Jericho saw him, they said, The spirit of Elijah doth rest on Elisha. And they came to meet him, and bowed themselves to the ground before him. And they said unto him, Behold now, there be with thy servants fifty strong men; let them go, we pray thee, and seek thy master: lest peradventure the Spirit of the LORD hath taken him up, and cast him upon some mountain, or into some valley.

And he said, Ye shall not send.

And when they urged him till he was ashamed, he said, Send. They sent therefore fifty men; and they sought three days, but found him not. And when they came again to him, (for he tarried at Jericho,) he said unto them, Did I not say unto you, Go not?

2 KINGS 2:1–18

Given that the afterlife was not talked about much in the Old Testament, why do you think the prophets insisted on looking for Elijah? How would you have responded if you were there?

THE INTERMEDIATE STATE

What happens when we die? The New Testament indicates that people experience an "intermediate state," which refers to a person's existence between their time of death and the promised resurrection of their new body. Their earthly body goes into the grave; their spirit lives on in one of two places—in God's presence where they enjoy a time of peace until they receive their resurrected bodies or in a place of torment where they await final judgment. Jesus talked about this vividly in the story about a rich man and Lazarus (not the Lazarus Jesus raised from the dead). Jesus described the place of blessedness for the righteous as Abraham's bosom and the place of torment for the wicked as hell.

There was a certain rich man, which was clothed in purple and fine linen, and fared sumptuously every day: And there was a certain beggar named Lazarus, which was laid at his gate, full of sores, And desiring to be fed with the crumbs which fell from the rich man's table: moreover the dogs came and licked his sores.

And it came to pass, that the beggar died, and was carried by the angels into Abraham's bosom: the rich man also died, and was buried; And in hell he lift up his eyes, being in torments, and seeth Abraham afar off, and Lazarus in his bosom. And he cried and said, Father Abraham, have mercy on me, and send Lazarus, that he may dip the tip of his finger in water, and cool my tongue; for I am tormented in this flame.

But Abraham said, Son, remember that thou in thy lifetime receivedst thy good things, and likewise Lazarus evil things: but now he is comforted, and thou art tormented. And beside all this, between us and you there is a great gulf fixed: so that they which would pass from hence to you cannot; neither can they pass to us, that *would come* from thence.

Then he said, I pray thee therefore, father, that thou wouldest send him to my father's house: For I have five brethren; that he may testify unto them, lest they also come into this place of torment.

Abraham saith unto him, They have Moses and the prophets; let them hear them.

And he said, Nay, father Abraham: but if one went unto them from the dead, they will repent.

And he said unto him, If they hear not Moses and the prophets, neither will they be persuaded, though one rose from the dead.

LUKE 16:19–31

Having a person come back from the dead to tell you what they experienced on the other side would seem rather compelling. Why did Abraham disagree?

THE RESURRECTION

There is more to come after we die than our spirits going to be with God while our bodies remain in the grave. The grand promise of God and the ultimate hope for all Christians is the resurrection. Just as Christ was raised from the dead and received an incorruptible body, so will all those who believe in Christ. Paul, writing to the church at Corinth, details this major truth.

Moreover, brethren, I declare unto you the gospel which I preached unto you, which also ye have received, and wherein ye stand; By which also ye are saved, if ye keep in memory what I preached unto you, unless ye have believed in vain.

For I delivered unto you first of all that which I also received, how that Christ died for our sins according to the scriptures; And that he was buried, and that he rose again the third day according to the scriptures: And that he was seen of Cephas, then of the twelve: After that, he was seen of above five hundred brethren at once; of whom the greater part remain unto this present, but some are fallen asleep. After that, he was seen of James; then of all the apostles. And last of all he was seen of me also, as of one born out of due time.

For I am the least of the apostles, that am not meet to be called an apostle, because I persecuted the church of God. But by the grace of God I am what I am: and his grace which *was bestowed* upon me was not in vain; but I laboured more abundantly than they all: yet not I, but the grace of God which was with me. Therefore whether *it were* I or they, so we preach, and so ye believed.

Now if Christ be preached that he rose from the dead, how say some among you that there is no resurrection of the dead? But if there be no resurrection of the dead, then is Christ not risen: And if Christ be not risen, then *is* our preaching vain, and your faith *is* also vain. Yea, and we are found false witnesses of God; because we have testified of God that he raised up Christ: whom he raised not up, if so be that the dead rise not. For if the dead rise not, then is not Christ raised: And if Christ be not raised, your faith *is* vain; ye are yet in your sins. Then they also which are fallen asleep in Christ are perished. If in this life only we have hope in Christ, we are of all men most miserable.

But now is Christ risen from the dead, *and* become the first-fruits of them that slept. For since by man *came* death, by man *came* also the resurrection of the dead. For as in Adam all die, even so in Christ shall all be made alive. But every man in his own order: Christ the firstfruits; afterward they that are Christ's at his coming. Then *cometh* the end, when he shall have delivered up the kingdom to God, even the Father; when he shall have put down all rule and all authority and power. For he must reign, till he hath put all enemies under his feet. The last enemy *that* shall be destroyed *is* death. For he hath put all things under his feet. But when he saith all things are put under *him, it is* manifest that he is excepted, which did put all things under him. And when all things shall be subdued unto him, then shall the Son also himself be subject unto him that put all things under him, that God may be all in all.

1 CORINTHIANS 15:1–28

But some *man* will say, How are the dead raised up? and with what body do they come? *Thou* fool, that which thou sowest is not quickened, except it die: And that which thou sowest, thou sowest not that body that shall be, but bare grain, it may chance of wheat, or of some other *grain*: But God giveth it a body as it hath pleased him, and to every seed his own body. All flesh *is* not the same flesh: but *there is* one *kind of* flesh of men, another flesh of beasts, another of fishes, *and* another of birds. *There are* also celestial bodies, and bodies terrestrial: but the glory of the celestial *is* one, and the *glory* of the terrestrial *is* another. *There is* one glory of the sun, and another glory of the moon, and another glory of the stars: for *one* star differeth from *another* star in glory.

So also *is* the resurrection of the dead. It is sown in corruption; it is raised in incorruption: It is sown in dishonour; it is raised in glory: it is sown in weakness; it is raised in power: It is sown a natural body; it is raised a spiritual body.
There is a natural body, and there is a spiritual body. And so it is written, The first man Adam was made a living soul; the last Adam *was made* a quickening spirit. Howbeit that *was* not first which is spiritual, but that which is natural; and afterward that which is spiritual. The first man *is* of the earth, earthy: the second man *is* the Lord from heaven. As *is* the earthy, such *are* they also that are earthy: and as *is* the heavenly, such *are* they also that are heavenly. And as we have borne the image of the earthy, we shall also bear the image of the heavenly.
Now this I say, brethren, that flesh and blood cannot inherit the kingdom of God; neither doth corruption inherit incorruption. **Behold, I shew you a mystery; We shall not all sleep, but we shall all be changed, In a moment, in the twinkling of an eye, at the last trump: for the trumpet shall sound, and the dead shall be raised incorruptible, and we shall be changed.** For this

corruptible must put on incorruption, and this mortal *must* put on immortality. So when this corruptible shall have put on incorruption, and this mortal shall have put on immortality, then shall be brought to pass the saying that is written, Death is swallowed up in victory. O death, where *is* thy sting? O grave, where *is* thy victory? The sting of death *is* sin; and the strength of sin *is* the law. But thanks *be* to God, which giveth us the victory through our Lord Jesus Christ.

Therefore, my beloved brethren, be ye stedfast, unmoveable, always abounding in the work of the Lord, forasmuch as ye know that your labour is not in vain in the Lord.   1 CORINTHIANS 15:35–58

How will our resurrected bodies be different from our earthly bodies? How does what the Bible says compare with some of our culture's popular notions of what we'll be like in heaven?

THE RETURN OF CHRIST

The event that will trigger this promised resurrection is the second coming of Christ. There are varied beliefs about the details leading up to this momentous occasion, but all followers of Jesus embrace its truth and significance. Often the Bible refers to the return of Christ as the "day of the Lord." Paul uses this phrase in an important letter addressed to the church at Thessalonica. Some of the believers there thought all Christians would be alive at the return of Christ, causing the Thessalonians to be concerned about fellow believers who had died. Paul explains that on the great day of Christ's return, God will resurrect those who have died. Then all believers will be brought together and will be with the Lord Jesus forever.

As you read the passages below from 1 Thessalonians 4–5 and 2 Peter 3, look for ways we are encouraged to live our lives today considering Christ's imminent return.

But I would not have you to be ignorant, brethren, concerning them which are asleep, that ye sorrow not, even as others which have no hope. For if we believe that Jesus died and rose again, even so them also which sleep in Jesus will God bring with him. For this we say unto you by the word of the Lord, that we which are alive *and* remain unto the coming of the Lord shall not prevent them which are asleep. **For the Lord himself shall descend from heaven with a shout, with the voice of the archangel, and with the trump of God: and the dead in Christ shall rise first: Then we which are alive *and* remain shall be caught up together with them in the clouds, to meet the Lord in the air: and so shall we ever be with the Lord. Wherefore comfort one another with these words.**

But of the times and the seasons, brethren, ye have no need that I write unto you. For yourselves know perfectly that the day of the Lord so cometh as a thief in the night. For when they shall say, Peace and safety; then sudden destruction cometh upon them, as travail upon a woman with child; and they shall not escape.

But ye, brethren, are not in darkness, that that day should over-take you as a thief. Ye are all the children of light, and the children of the day: we are not of the night, nor of darkness. Therefore let us not sleep, as *do* others; but let us watch and be sober. For they that sleep sleep in the night; and they that be drunken are drunken in the night. But let us, who are of the day, be sober, putting on the breastplate of faith and love; and for an helmet, the hope of salva-tion. For God hath not appointed us to wrath, but to obtain salva-tion by our Lord Jesus Christ, Who died for us, that, whether we wake or sleep, we should live together with him. Wherefore com-fort yourselves together, and edify one another, even as also ye do.

1 THESSALONIANS 4:13—5:11

The apostle Peter also writes in great detail about "the day of the Lord," adding further clarification and admonition regarding how believers should live their lives in light of this future reality.

This second epistle, beloved, I now write unto you; in *both* which I stir up your pure minds by way of remembrance: That ye may be mindful of the words which were spoken before by the holy prophets, and of the commandment of us the apostles of the Lord and Saviour:

Knowing this first, that there shall come in the last days scoffers, walking after their own lusts, And saying, Where is the promise of his coming? for since the fathers fell asleep, all things continue as *they were* from the beginning of the creation. For this they willingly are ignorant of, that by the word of God the heavens were of old, and the earth standing out of the water and in the water: Whereby the world that then was, being overflowed with water, perished: But the heavens and the earth, which are now, by the same word are kept in store, reserved unto fire against the day of judgment and perdition of ungodly men.

But, beloved, be not ignorant of this one thing, that one day *is* with the Lord as a thousand years, and a thousand years as one day. The Lord is not slack concerning his promise, as some men count slackness; but is longsuffering to us-ward, not willing that any should perish, but that all should come to repentance.

But the day of the Lord will come as a thief in the night; in the which the heavens shall pass away with a great noise, and the elements shall melt with fervent heat, the earth also and the works that are therein shall be burned up.

Seeing then *that* all these things shall be dissolved, what manner *of persons* ought ye to be in *all* holy conversation and godliness, Looking for and hasting unto the coming of the day of God, wherein the heavens being on fire shall be dissolved, and the elements shall melt with fervent heat? Nevertheless we, according to his promise, look for new heavens and a new earth, wherein dwelleth righteousness.

Wherefore, beloved, seeing that ye look for such things, be diligent that ye may be found of him in peace, without spot, and blameless. And account *that* the longsuffering of our Lord *is* salvation; even as our beloved brother Paul also according to the wisdom given unto him hath written unto you; As also in all *his* epistles, speaking in them of these things; in which are some things hard to be understood, which they that are unlearned and unstable wrest, as *they do* also the other scriptures, unto their own destruction.

Ye therefore, beloved, seeing ye know *these things* before, beware lest ye also, being led away with the error of the wicked, fall from your own stedfastness. But grow in grace, and *in* the knowledge of our Lord and Saviour Jesus Christ. To him *be* glory both now and for ever. Amen.

2 PETER 3:1–18

A NEW HEAVEN AND A NEW EARTH

After Jesus returns and we are resurrected into our incorruptible bodies, there will be a final judgment by God of every nation. John saw and recorded a vision from God about what will happen at this time of judgment. John wrote down the final movement in God's grand story—the restoration of what was lost in the beginning. What we read in the opening creation story of Genesis we see again in Revelation, a re-creation, but on a grander scale to accommodate all the people over the centuries who have embraced Christ and received eternal life.

And I saw a great white throne, and him that sat on it, from whose face the earth and the heaven fled away; and there was found no place for them. And I saw the dead, small and great, stand before God; and the books were opened: and another book was opened, which is *the book* of life: and the dead were judged out of those things which were written in the books, according to their works. And the sea gave up the dead which were in it; and death and hell delivered up the dead which were in them: and they were judged every man according to their works. And death and hell were cast into the lake of fire. This is the second death. And whosoever was not found written in the book of life was cast into the lake of fire.

And I saw a new heaven and a new earth: for the first heaven and the first earth were passed away; and there was no more sea. And I John saw the holy city, new Jerusalem, coming down from God out of heaven, prepared as a bride adorned for her husband. And I heard a great voice out of heaven saying, Behold, the tabernacle of God *is* with men, and he will dwell with them, and they shall be his people, and God himself shall be with them, *and be* their God. And God shall wipe away all tears from their eyes; and there shall be no more death, neither sorrow, nor crying, neither shall there be any more pain: for the former things are passed away.

And he that sat upon the throne said, Behold, I make all things new. And he said unto me, Write: for these words are true and faithful.

And he said unto me, It is done. I am Alpha and Omega, the beginning and the end. I will give unto him that is athirst of the fountain of the water of life freely. He that overcometh shall inherit all things; and I will be his God, and he shall be my son. But the fearful, and unbelieving, and the abominable, and murderers, and whoremongers, and sorcerers, and idolaters, and all liars, shall have their part in the lake which burneth with fire and brimstone: which is the second death.

And there came unto me one of the seven angels which had the seven vials full of the seven last plagues, and talked with me, saying, Come hither, I will shew thee the bride, the Lamb's wife. And he carried me away in the spirit to a great and high mountain, and shewed me that great city, the holy Jerusalem, descending out of heaven from God, Having the glory of God: and her light *was* like unto a stone most precious, even like a jasper stone, clear as crystal; And had a wall great and high, *and* had twelve gates, and at the gates twelve angels, and names written thereon, which are *the names* of the twelve tribes of the children of Israel: On the east three gates; on the north three gates; on the south three gates; and on the west three gates. And the wall of the city had twelve foundations, and in them the names of the twelve apostles of the Lamb

And he that talked with me had a golden reed to measure the city, and the gates thereof, and the wall thereof. And the city lieth foursquare, and the length is as large as the breadth: and he measured the city with the reed, twelve thousand furlongs. The length and the breadth and the height of it are equal. And he measured the wall thereof, an hundred *and* forty *and* four cubits, *according to* the measure of a man, that is, of the angel. And the building of the wall of it was *of* jasper: and the city *was* pure gold, like unto clear glass. And the foundations of the wall of the city *were* garnished with all manner of precious stones. The first foundation *was* jasper; the second, sapphire; the third, a chalcedony; the fourth, an emerald; The fifth, sardonyx; the sixth, sardius; the seventh, chrysolyte; the eighth, beryl; the ninth, a topaz; the tenth, a chrysoprasus; the eleventh, a jacinth; the twelfth, an amethyst.

And the twelve gates *were* twelve pearls; every several gate was of one pearl: and the street of the city *was* pure gold, as it were transparent glass.

And I saw no temple therein: for the Lord God Almighty and the Lamb are the temple of it. And the city had no need of the sun, neither of the moon, to shine in it: for the glory of God did lighten it, and the Lamb *is* the light thereof. And the nations of them which are saved shall walk in the light of it: and the kings of the earth do bring their glory and honour into it. And the gates of it shall not be shut at all by day: for there shall be no night there. And they shall bring the glory and honour of the nations into it. And there shall in no wise enter into it any thing that defileth, neither *whatsoever* worketh abomination, or *maketh* a lie: but they which are written in the Lamb's book of life.

And he shewed me a pure river of water of life, clear as crystal, proceeding out of the throne of God and of the Lamb. In the midst of the street of it, and on either side of the river, *was there* the tree of life, which bare twelve *manner of* fruits, *and* yielded her fruit every month: and the leaves of the tree *were* for the healing of the nations. And there shall be no more curse: but the throne of God and of the Lamb shall be in it; and his servants shall serve him: And they shall see his face; and his name *shall be* in their foreheads. And there shall be no night there; and they need no candle, neither light of the sun; for the Lord God giveth them light: and they shall reign for ever and ever.

And he said unto me, These sayings *are* faithful and true: and the Lord God of the holy prophets sent his angel to shew unto his servants the things which must shortly be done.

Behold, I come quickly: blessed *is* he that keepeth the sayings of the prophecy of this book.

And I John saw these things, and heard *them*. And when I had heard and seen, I fell down to worship before the feet of the angel which shewed me these things. Then saith he unto me, See *thou do it* not: for I am thy fellowservant, and of thy brethren the prophets, and of them which keep the sayings of this book: worship God.

And he saith unto me, Seal not the sayings of the prophecy of this book: for the time is at hand. He that is unjust, let him be unjust still: and he which is filthy, let him be filthy still: and he that is righteous, let him be righteous still: and he that is holy, let him be holy still.

And, behold, I come quickly; and my reward *is* with me, to give every man according as his work shall be. I am Alpha and Omega, the beginning and the end, the first and the last.

Blessed *are* they that do his commandments, that they may have right to the tree of life, and may enter in through the gates into the city. For without *are* dogs, and sorcerers, and whoremongers, and murderers, and idolaters, and whosoever loveth and maketh a lie.

I Jesus have sent mine angel to testify unto you these things in the churches. I am the root and the offspring of David, *and* the bright and morning star.

And the Spirit and the bride say, Come. And let him that heareth say, Come. And let him that is athirst come. And whosoever will, let him take the water of life freely.

For I testify unto every man that heareth the words of the prophecy of this book, If any man shall add unto these things, God shall add unto him the plagues that are written in this book: And if any man shall take away from the words of the book of this prophecy, God shall take away his part out of the book of life, and out of the holy city, and *from* the things which are written in this book.

He which testifieth these things saith, Surely I come quickly. Amen. Even so, come, Lord Jesus.

The grace of our Lord Jesus Christ *be* with you all. Amen.

REVELATION 20:11—22:21

In Jesus' last week on earth before he returned to the Father, he comforted the disciples concerning the future. He informed them that he was leaving, but he also promised that he would be overseeing the construction of a place for each of them in heaven — the new Jerusalem that John saw and described. As you read these words, please know that Jesus' message to the disciples applies to you as well. He has prepared an eternal home for all those who believe.

Let not your heart be troubled: ye believe in God, believe also in me. In my Father's house are many mansions: if *it were* not *so*,

I would have told you. I go to prepare a place for you. **And if I go and prepare a place for you, I will come again, and receive you unto myself; that where I am,** *there* **ye may be also.** And whither I go ye know, and the way ye know.

Thomas saith unto him, Lord, we know not whither thou goest; and how can we know the way?

Jesus saith unto him, I am the way, the truth, and the life: no man cometh unto the Father, but by me. If ye had known me, ye should have known my Father also: and from henceforth ye know him, and have seen him.

John 14:1–7

As you ponder eternal life in the garden on the new earth without the presence of sin, hatred, strife, war or death, what do you most look forward to?

WHAT WE BELIEVE

When we die our bodies go into the ground and our spirits go to be with the Lord as we await the return of Christ. When he comes to establish the new heaven and the new earth, our spirits will receive the tent of a new, incorruptible, resurrected body just as Jesus did. In these bodies we will live forever in the new garden with God and all those who believed in Jesus. And it is with this exciting reality that we conclude our journey through the ten key beliefs of the Christian life. As followers of God we are invited to ponder and understand these profound concepts in our minds. Yet, to really think like Jesus and experience the full life Christ has given us, we must embrace these beliefs in our hearts—where real decisions are made. So how do we move these fantastic ideas from simply being the right answer to a way of life? We do so through the ten key practices of the Christian life, which are highlighted in the next section. Engaging in these activities (in partnership with God) will enable you to express your beliefs while reinforcing them in your heart. Turn the page with the anticipation of actually becoming more like Jesus!

What Should I Do?

Know ye not that they which run in a race run all, but one
receiveth the prize? So run, that ye may obtain. And every man
that striveth for the mastery is temperate in all things. Now they
do it to obtain a corruptible crown; but we an incorruptible.
I therefore so run, not as uncertainly; so fight I, not as one
that beateth the air: But I keep under my body, and bring *it*
into subjection: lest that by any means, when I have preached
to others, I myself should be a castaway.
1 Corinthians 9:24–27

When you study the life of Jesus you will notice a distinct pattern. Jesus faithfully lived in a purposeful way. Once again,
Jesus was modeling for us the Christian life. We would do well to
simply follow his pattern — to *act* like Jesus.

The following ten chapters are going to introduce you to the key
spiritual practices of Christian life. You will encounter axioms to
guide you and real-life stories to inspire you.

As you read each chapter and come to understand what God
wants you to do, prayerfully ask yourself, "Will I do what God is
inviting me to do?" In the passage above, the apostle Paul invites
us to think of the Christian life like an athlete. If an Olympic run-
ner wants to cross the finish line first, they must commit to a life of
strict training. Essentially, Paul is saying that if we want to win at
life, we too need to be disciplined in the way we approach each day.

If you resolve to practice what you are about to learn, remember
you will not be alone. God's Spirit can give you the internal strength,
silence the voices of dissenters and blow wind at your back.

These practices will not only aid you in understanding the key
beliefs, they will also catalyze you in fulfilling your mission to love
God and to let his love flow through you to your neighbors, so all
people will know God and know you are his disciple.

On your mark ... get set ... GO!

CHAPTER

11

Worship

KEY QUESTION

How do I honor God in the way he deserves?

KEY IDEA

I worship God for who he is
and what he has done for me.

KEY VERSE

O come, let us sing unto the LORD:
let us make a joyful noise to the rock of our salvation.
Let us come before his presence with thanksgiving,
and make a joyful noise unto him with psalms.
Psalm 95:1 – 2

As we read in Chapter 1, the first key belief in the Christian life begins with God. It is only logical that the first key practice in the Christian life is worshipping God. When we worship we are taking the revelation about the one true God—Father, Son and Holy Ghost—and reaffirming our belief that he is involved in our lives and wants to be in a relationship with us. As we do this, the amazing truths about God move from concepts in our heads to cries of our hearts. When we worship God for who he is and what he has done for us, it not only cements our confidence in God as we approach each day and each situation, but it also enables us to receive his love. When we receive God's love in our hearts, we begin to see the world differently—as people made in God's image.

So we can read this chapter with great anticipation as we explore the different aspects of worship, including:

- *The Heart's Intent*
- *Unashamed Worshippers*
- *Worshipping Together*

THE HEART'S INTENT

Worshipping God for who he is and what he has done for us can be expressed in many different forms and diverse environments, but it's what we believe in our hearts that matters to God. Throughout Scripture we see how God's people worshipped him on towering mountaintops, inside homes with dirt floors, at a lavishly adorned temple and in dark prisons. They demonstrated their devotion to God with singing, dancing, sacrifices and public and private prayer. What's most important to God is not the way that we choose to worship him, but the motivation that directs our actions.

What does the following passage from Psalm 95 tell us about how and why we should worship God?

O come, let us sing unto the LORD:
let us make a joyful noise to the rock of our salvation.

Let us come before his presence with thanksgiving,
and make a joyful noise unto him with psalms.
For the LORD *is* a great God,
and a great King above all gods.
In his hand *are* the deep places of the earth:
the strength of the hills *is* his also.
The sea *is* his, and he made it:
and his hands formed the dry *land.*

O come, let us worship and bow down:
let us kneel before the LORD our maker.
For he *is* our God;
and we *are* the people of his pasture,
and the sheep of his hand.
                                                                    PSALM 95:1–7

During Old Testament times, worship involved animal sacrifices. Instead of leaving his people with no recourse except to face their punishment for sin, God, in his mercy, allowed his people to sacrifice the best animals from their herd as a payment for their disobedience. The animal had to be without defect, since a defective sacrifice could not be a substitute for a defective people. This practice was intended to be accompanied by repentance. The worshipper confessed their sin and laid hands on the animal; then the sin was symbolically transferred away from the sinner to the sacrifice.

Unfortunately, over time the Israelites' sacrifices became meaningless rituals. God was angry and heartbroken. The people brought him an abundance of sacrifices, yet their character and conduct were anything but pleasing to him. God doesn't want us to simply go through the motions; he wants us to change in our hearts.

To what purpose *is* the multitude of your sacrifices unto me? saith the LORD: I am full of the burnt offerings of rams, and the fat of fed beasts; and I delight not in the blood of bullocks, or of lambs, or of he goats. When ye come to appear before me, who hath required this at your hand, to tread my courts? Bring no more vain oblations; incense is an abomination unto me; the new moons and sabbaths, the calling of assemblies, I cannot away with; *it is* iniquity, even the solemn meeting. Your new moons and your appointed feasts my soul hateth: they are a trouble unto me; I am weary to bear *them*. And when ye spread forth your hands, I will hide mine eyes from you: yea, when ye make many prayers, I will not hear:

Your hands are full of blood. Wash you, make you clean; put away the evil of your doings from before mine eyes; cease to do evil;

Learn to do well; seek judgment, relieve the oppressed, judge the fatherless, plead for the widow.

Come now, and let us reason together, saith the LORD: though your sins be as scarlet, they shall be as white as snow; though they be red like crimson, they shall be as wool. If ye be willing and obedient, ye shall eat the good of the land: But if ye refuse and rebel, ye shall be devoured with the sword: for the mouth of the LORD hath spoken *it*.   ISAIAH 1:11–20

Despite knowing better, God's people throughout history failed him in their worship practices. In the New Testament, those who neglected to worship and honor God properly received some harsh words from Jesus. This was especially true for the religious leaders whose layers of religious exercises and rituals hid a weak and shallow faith. As a crowd gathered to listen to Jesus as he taught, he warned them about the influence of these hollow religious leaders.

As you read the passage below from Matthew 23, ponder this question: With what behaviors and attitudes of the Pharisees did Jesus take issue? (Hint: Jesus introduced each one with "woe unto you.")

Then spake Jesus to the multitude, and to his disciples, Saying, The scribes and the Pharisees sit in Moses' seat: All therefore whatsoever they bid you observe, *that* observe and do; but do not ye after their works: for they say, and do not. For they bind heavy burdens and grievous to be borne, and lay *them* on men's shoulders; but they *themselves* will not move them with one of their fingers.

But all their works they do for to be seen of men: they make broad their phylacteries, and enlarge the borders of their garments,

And love the uppermost rooms at feasts, and the chief seats in the synagogues, And greetings in the markets, and to be called of men, Rabbi, Rabbi.

But be not ye called Rabbi: for one is your Master, *even* Christ; and all ye are brethren. And call no *man* your father upon the earth: for one is your Father, which is in heaven. Neither be ye called masters: for one is your Master, *even* Christ. But he that is greatest among you shall be your servant. And whosoever shall exalt himself shall be abased; and he that shall humble himself shall be exalted.

But **woe unto you**, scribes and Pharisees, hypocrites! for ye shut up the kingdom of heaven against men: for ye neither go in *yourselves*, neither suffer ye them that are entering to go in.

Woe unto you, scribes and Pharisees, hypocrites! for ye devour widows' houses, and for a pretence make long prayer: therefore ye shall receive the greater damnation.

Woe unto you, scribes and Pharisees, hypocrites! for ye compass sea and land to make one proselyte, and when he is made, ye make him twofold more the child of hell than yourselves.

Woe unto you, *ye* blind guides, which say, Whosoever shall swear by the temple, it is nothing; but whosoever shall swear by the gold of the temple, he is a debtor! *Ye* fools and blind: for whether is greater, the gold, or the temple that sanctifieth the gold? And, Whosoever shall swear by the altar, it is nothing; but whosoever sweareth by the gift that is upon it, he is guilty. *Ye* fools and blind: for whether *is* greater, the gift, or the altar that sanctifieth the gift? Whoso therefore shall swear by the altar, sweareth by it, and by all things thereon. And whoso shall swear by the temple, sweareth by it, and by him that dwelleth therein. And he that shall swear by heaven, sweareth by the throne of God, and by him that sitteth thereon.

Woe unto you, scribes and Pharisees, hypocrites! for ye pay tithe of mint and anise and cummin, and have omitted the weightier *matters* of the law, judgment, mercy, and faith: these ought ye to have done, and not to leave the other undone. *Ye* blind guides, which strain at a gnat, and swallow a camel.

Woe unto you, scribes and Pharisees, hypocrites! for ye make clean the outside of the cup and of the platter, but within they are full of extortion and excess. *Thou* blind Pharisee, cleanse first that *which is* within the cup and platter, that the outside of them may be clean also.

Woe unto you, scribes and Pharisees, hypocrites! for ye are like unto whited sepulchres, which indeed appear beautiful outward, but are within full of dead *men's* bones, and of all uncleanness. Even so ye also outwardly appear righteous unto men, but within ye are full of hypocrisy and iniquity.   MATTHEW 23:1–28

UNASHAMED WORSHIPPERS

When God calls us to love him with all our hearts, souls, minds and strength, he is demanding that we hold nothing back from him. A commitment to worship God is a vow to be bold and unashamed of our love and devotion to him. With great power, God rescued the Israelites when the army of Egypt had them backed against the Red Sea. After their escape, Moses and his sister, Miriam, led the Israelites in an unapologetic song of celebration and blessing, praising God for who he is and what he had done for them.

Then sang Moses and the children of Israel this song unto the LORD, and spake, saying, I will sing unto the LORD, for he hath triumphed gloriously: the horse and his rider hath he thrown into the sea.

The LORD *is* my strength and song, and he is become my salvation: he *is* my God, and I will prepare him an habitation; my father's God, and I will exalt him. The LORD *is* a man of war: the LORD *is* his name. Pharaoh's chariots and his host hath he cast into the sea: his chosen captains also are drowned in the Red sea. The depths have covered them: they sank into the bottom as a stone. Thy right hand, O LORD, is become glorious in power: thy right hand, O LORD, hath dashed in pieces the enemy.

And in the greatness of thine excellency thou hast overthrown them that rose up against thee: thou sentest forth thy wrath, *which* consumed them as stubble. And with the blast of thy nostrils the waters were gathered together, the floods stood upright as an heap, *and* the depths were congealed in the heart of the sea. The enemy said, I will pursue, I will overtake, I will divide the spoil; my lust shall be satisfied upon them; I will draw my sword, my hand shall destroy them. Thou didst blow with thy wind, the sea covered them: they sank as lead in the mighty waters. Who *is* like unto thee, O Lord, among the gods? who *is* like thee, glorious in holiness, fearful *in* praises, doing wonders?

Thou stretchedst out thy right hand, the earth swallowed them. Thou in thy mercy hast led forth the people *which* thou hast redeemed: thou hast guided *them* in thy strength unto thy holy habitation. The people shall hear, *and* be afraid: sorrow shall take hold on the inhabitants of Palestina. Then the dukes of Edom shall be amazed; the mighty men of Moab, trembling shall take hold upon them; all the inhabitants of Canaan shall melt away. Fear and dread shall fall upon them; by the greatness of thine arm they shall be *as* still as a stone; till thy people pass over, O Lord, till the people pass over, *which* thou hast purchased. Thou shalt bring them in, and plant them in the mountain of thine inheritance, *in* the place, O Lord, *which* thou hast made for thee to dwell in, *in* the Sanctuary, O Lord, *which* thy hands have established.

The Lord shall reign for ever and ever.

For the horse of Pharaoh went in with his chariots and with his horsemen into the sea, and the Lord brought again the waters of the sea upon them; but the children of Israel went on dry *land* in the midst of the sea. And Miriam the prophetess, the sister of Aaron, took a timbrel in her hand; and all the women went out after her with timbrels and with dances. And Miriam answered them, Sing ye to the Lord, for he hath triumphed gloriously; the horse and his rider hath he thrown into the sea.   Exodus 15:1–21

While Moses and Miriam expressed their praise vocally, bold worship can also be displayed with very few words. Take Daniel, for example. His quiet refusal to worship anyone or anything but the one true God was risky because King Darius dealt harshly with disobedience in his kingdom. Unlike the songs of Moses and Miriam, it was Daniel's actions that did all the talking.

It pleased Darius to set over the kingdom an hundred and twenty princes, which should be over the whole kingdom; And over these three presidents; of whom Daniel *was* first: that the princes might give accounts unto them, and the king should have no damage.

Then this Daniel was preferred above the presidents and princes, because an excellent spirit *was* in him; and the king thought to set him over the whole realm. Then the presidents and princes sought to find occasion against Daniel concerning the kingdom; but they could find none occasion nor fault; forasmuch as he *was* faithful, neither was there any error or fault found in him. Then said these men, We shall not find any occasion against this Daniel, except we find *it* against him concerning the law of his God.

Then these presidents and princes assembled together to the king, and said thus unto him, King Darius, live for ever. All the presidents of the kingdom, the governors, and the princes, the counsellors, and the captains, have consulted together to establish a royal statute, and to make a firm decree, that whosoever shall ask a petition of any God or man for thirty days, save of thee, O king, he shall be cast into the den of lions. Now, O king, establish the decree, and sign the writing, that it be not changed, according to the law of the Medes and Persians, which altereth not. Wherefore king Darius signed the writing and the decree.

Now when Daniel knew that the writing was signed, he went into his house; and his windows being open in his chamber toward Jerusalem, he kneeled upon his knees three times a day, and prayed, and gave thanks before his God, as he did aforetime. Then these men assembled, and found Daniel praying and making supplication before his God. Then they came near, and spake before the king concerning the king's decree; Hast thou not signed a decree, that every man that shall ask *a petition* of any God or man within thirty days, save of thee, O king, shall be cast into the den of lions?

The king answered and said, The thing *is* true, according to the law of the Medes and Persians, which altereth not.

Then answered they and said before the king, That Daniel, which *is* of the children of the captivity of Judah, regardeth not thee, O king, nor the decree that thou hast signed, but maketh his petition three times a day. Then the king, when he heard *these* words, was sore displeased with himself, and set *his* heart on Daniel to deliver him: and he laboured till the going down of the sun to deliver him.

Then these men assembled unto the king, and said unto the

king, Know, O king, that the law of the Medes and Persians *is*, That no decree nor statute which the king establisheth may be changed.

Then the king commanded, and they brought Daniel, and cast *him* into the den of lions. *Now* the king spake and said unto Daniel, Thy God whom thou servest continually, he will deliver thee.

And a stone was brought, and laid upon the mouth of the den; and the king sealed it with his own signet, and with the signet of his lords; that the purpose might not be changed concerning Daniel. Then the king went to his palace, and passed the night fasting: neither were instruments of musick brought before him: and his sleep went from him.

Then the king arose very early in the morning, and went in haste unto the den of lions. And when he came to the den, he cried with a lamentable voice unto Daniel: *and* the king spake and said to Daniel, O Daniel, servant of the living God, is thy God, whom thou servest continually, able to deliver thee from the lions?

Then said Daniel unto the king, O king, live for ever. My God hath sent his angel, and hath shut the lions' mouths, that they have not hurt me: forasmuch as before him innocency was found in me; and also before thee, O king, have I done no hurt.

Then was the king exceedingly glad for him, and commanded that they should take Daniel up out of the den. So Daniel was taken up out of the den, and no manner of hurt was found upon him, because he believed in his God.

And the king commanded, and they brought those men which had accused Daniel, and they cast *them* into the den of lions, them, their children, and their wives; and the lions had the mastery of them, and brake all their bones in pieces or ever they came at the bottom of the den.

Then king Darius wrote unto all people, nations, and languages, that dwell in all the earth; Peace be multiplied unto you. I make a decree, That in every dominion of my kingdom men tremble and fear before the God of Daniel: for he *is* the living God, and stedfast for ever, and his kingdom *that* which shall not be destroyed, and his dominion *shall be even* unto the end. He delivereth and rescueth, and he worketh signs and wonders in heaven and in earth, who hath delivered Daniel from the power of the lions.

DANIEL 6:1–27

What effect did Daniel's bold worship have on
the unbelieving King Darius? In what ways do you think our
modern-day worship could have that same effect?

*God's rescue of Daniel from the lions is just one example of his
power and greatness.*

*God's signs and wonders are undeniably awe-inspiring. In the
book of Acts, Paul's and Silas's boldness got them thrown into
jail; then as they prayed and sang hymns of worship during the
night, a sudden earthquake resulted in their release.*

⚷ And it came to pass, as we went to prayer, a certain damsel
possessed with a spirit of divination met us, which brought her
masters much gain by soothsaying: The same followed Paul and
us, and cried, saying, These men are the servants of the most high
God, which shew unto us the way of salvation. And this did she
many days. But Paul, being grieved, turned and said to the spirit,
I command thee in the name of Jesus Christ to come out of her.
And he came out the same hour.

And when her masters saw that the hope of their gains was
gone, they caught Paul and Silas, and drew *them* into the market-
place unto the rulers, And brought them to the magistrates, saying, These men, being Jews, do exceedingly trouble our city, And
teach customs, which are not lawful for us to receive, neither to
observe, being Romans.

And the multitude rose up together against them: and the magistrates rent off their clothes, and commanded to beat *them*. And
when they had laid many stripes upon them, they cast *them* into
prison, charging the jailor to keep them safely: Who, having received such a charge, thrust them into the inner prison, and made
their feet fast in the stocks.

**And at midnight Paul and Silas prayed, and sang praises
unto God: and the prisoners heard them. And suddenly there
was a great earthquake, so that the foundations of the prison
were shaken: and immediately all the doors were opened, and
every one's bands were loosed.** And the keeper of the prison
awaking out of his sleep, and seeing the prison doors open, he

drew out his sword, and would have killed himself, supposing that the prisoners had been fled. But Paul cried with a loud voice, saying, Do thyself no harm: for we are all here.

Then he called for a light, and sprang in, and came trembling, and fell down before Paul and Silas, And brought them out, and said, Sirs, what must I do to be saved?

And they said, Believe on the Lord Jesus Christ, and thou shalt be saved, and thy house. And they spake unto him the word of the Lord, and to all that were in his house. And he took them the same hour of the night, and washed *their* stripes; and was baptized, he and all his, straightway. And when he had brought them into his house, he set meat before them, and rejoiced, believing in God with all his house.

And when it was day, the magistrates sent the serjeants, saying, Let those men go. ACTS 16:16–35 🔑

Why do you think God desires that we worship him when we are in a difficult situation? When was the last time you worshipped God when it might not have immediately made sense to do so?

WORSHIPPING TOGETHER

A relationship with God can be a private and personal experience, but much of worship is meant to be practiced in community. God is a community within himself (Father, Son and Holy Ghost), and his Word encourages us to gather with other believers to encourage one another, pray together and remember God's love for us. Since the crucifixion, death and resurrection of Jesus, the dynamics of communal worship have changed drastically. Animal sacrifices are no longer required to restore a relationship with God. Instead, through Jesus' blood, shed as a voluntary sacrifice, those who repent and accept Jesus as their Savior will have their sins forgiven.

For the law having a shadow of good things to come, *and* not the very image of the things, can never with those sacrifices which they offered year by year continually make the comers thereunto perfect. For then would they not have ceased to be offered? because that the worshippers once purged should have had no more conscience of sins. But in those *sacrifices there is* a remembrance again *made* of sins every year. For *it is* not possible that the blood of bulls and of goats should take away sins.

Wherefore when he cometh into the world, he saith, Sacrifice and offering thou wouldest not, but a body hast thou prepared me: In burnt offerings and *sacrifices* for sin thou hast had no pleasure. Then said I, Lo, I come (in the volume of the book it is written of me,) to do thy will, O God.

Above when he said, Sacrifice and offering and burnt offerings and *offering* for sin thou wouldest not, neither hadst pleasure *therein*; which are offered by the law; Then said he, Lo, I come to do thy will, O God. He taketh away the first, that he may establish the second. By the which will we are sanctified through the offering of the body of Jesus Christ once *for all.*

And every priest standeth daily ministering and offering oftentimes the same sacrifices, which can never take away sins: But this man, after he had offered one sacrifice for sins for ever, sat down on the right hand of God; From henceforth expecting till his enemies be made his footstool. For by one offering he hath perfected for ever them that are sanctified.

Whereof the Holy Ghost also is a witness to us: for after that he had said before, This *is* the covenant that I will make with them after those days, saith the Lord, I will put my laws into their hearts, and in their minds will I write them; And their sins and iniquities will I remember no more. Now where remission of these *is, there is* no more offering for sin.

Having therefore, brethren, boldness to enter into the holiest by the blood of Jesus, By a new and living way, which he hath consecrated for us, through the veil, that is to say, his flesh; And *having* an high priest over the house of God; Let us draw near with a true heart in full assurance of faith, having our hearts sprinkled from an evil conscience, and our bodies washed with pure water. Let us hold fast the profession of *our* faith without wavering; (for he *is* faithful that promised;) And let us consider one another to provoke unto love and to good works: Not forsaking the assembling of ourselves together, as the manner of some *is*; but exhorting *one another*: and so much the more, as ye see the day approaching. Hebrews 10:1–25

The Lord's Supper essentially replaced the practice of animal sacrifice for sin in the New Testament church. When believers gather to pray, sing and learn, they break bread and share a cup of wine as a way of remembering Christ's love for them. Jesus introduced this new practice to his disciples the night before his crucifixion.

Then came the day of unleavened bread, when the passover must be killed. And he sent Peter and John, saying, Go and prepare us the passover, that we may eat.

And they said unto him, Where wilt thou that we prepare?

And he said unto them, Behold, when ye are entered into the city, there shall a man meet you, bearing a pitcher of water; follow him into the house where he entereth in. And ye shall say unto the goodman of the house, The Master saith unto thee, Where is the guestchamber, where I shall eat the passover with my disciples? And he shall shew you a large upper room furnished: there make ready.

And they went, and found as he had said unto them: and they made ready the passover.

And when the hour was come, he sat down, and the twelve apostles with him. And he said unto them, With desire I have desired to eat this passover with you before I suffer: For I say unto you, I will not any more eat thereof, until it be fulfilled in the kingdom of God.

And he took the cup, and gave thanks, and said, Take this, and divide *it* among yourselves: For I say unto you, I will not drink of the fruit of the vine, until the kingdom of God shall come.

And he took bread, and gave thanks, and brake *it*, and gave unto them, saying, This is my body which is given for you: this do in remembrance of me.

Likewise also the cup after supper, saying, This cup *is* the new testament in my blood, which is shed for you. But, behold, the hand of him that betrayeth me *is* with me on the table. And truly the Son of man goeth, as it was determined: but woe unto that man by whom he is betrayed! And they began to enquire among themselves, which of them it was that should do this thing.

And there was also a strife among them, which of them should be accounted the greatest. And he said unto them, The kings of the Gentiles exercise lordship over them; and they that exercise authority upon them are called benefactors. But ye *shall* not *be* so: but he that is greatest among you, let him be as the younger; and he that is chief, as he that doth serve. For whether *is* greater, he that sitteth at meat, or he that serveth? *is* not he that sitteth at meat? but I am among you as he that serveth. Ye are they which have continued with me in my temptations. And I appoint unto you a kingdom, as my Father hath appointed unto me; That ye may eat and drink at my table in my kingdom, and sit on thrones judging the twelve tribes of Israel.   LUKE 22:7–30

Of course, believers can also honor Jesus' sacrifice every day in the way that they choose to live. No one emphasized this more consistently than the apostle Paul. While under house arrest in Rome, Paul wrote to the Christians in the city of Colosse. He encouraged them to throw off their old, self-centered way of living and commit to live solely for the purpose of worshipping and serving God. Paul's instructions were not addressed to individual worshipers, but to the worship community as a whole.

If ye then be risen with Christ, seek those things which are above, where Christ sitteth on the right hand of God. Set your affection on things above, not on things on the earth. For ye are dead, and your life is hid with Christ in God. When Christ, *who is* our life, shall appear, then shall ye also appear with him in glory.

Mortify therefore your members which are upon the earth; fornication, uncleanness, inordinate affection, evil concupiscence, and covetousness, which is idolatry: For which things' sake the wrath of God cometh on the children of disobedience: In the which ye also walked some time, when ye lived in them. But now ye also put off all these; anger, wrath, malice, blasphemy, filthy communication out of your mouth. Lie not one to another, seeing that ye have put off the old man with his deeds; And have put on the new *man*, which is renewed in knowledge after the image of him that created him: Where there is neither Greek nor Jew, circumcision nor uncircumcision, Barbarian, Scythian, bond *nor* free: but Christ *is* all, and in all.

Put on therefore, as the elect of God, holy and beloved, bowels of mercies, kindness, humbleness of mind, meekness, longsuffering; Forbearing one another, and forgiving one another, if any man have a quarrel against any: even as Christ forgave you, so also *do* ye. And above all these things *put on* charity, which is the bond of perfectness.

And let the peace of God rule in your hearts, to the which also ye are called in one body; and be ye thankful. Let the word of Christ dwell in you richly in all wisdom; teaching and admonishing one another in psalms and hymns and spiritual songs, singing with grace in your hearts to the Lord. And whatsoever ye do in word or deed, *do* all in the name of the Lord Jesus, giving thanks to God and the Father by him.

Colossians 3:1–17

According to the apostle Paul, what was the centerpiece of New Testament worship? What attitudes and actions constituted proper worship?

WHAT WE BELIEVE

Throughout Scripture, believers in God are instructed to worship him. We are not called to merely go through the motions but instead we are encouraged to authentically worship God from our very hearts — as broken as they may be. While worshipping God for who he is and what he has done for us can be a private and personal practice, we can also feel free to share our worship of the one true God with the world. Finally, the practice of worship should also be expressed in community with others. This pleases God and encourages us. We can worship God from our hearts through every single breath, expression, thought and activity of our lives. Doing this habitually will surely lead us closer to the great and gracious God of the universe. So, "O come, let us sing unto the LORD: let us make a joyful noise to the rock of our salvation. Let us come before his presence with thanksgiving, and make a joyful noise unto him with psalms" (Psalm 95:1–2).

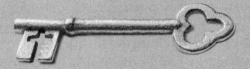

CHAPTER

12

Prayer

——— KEY QUESTION ———

How do I grow by communicating with God?

——— KEY IDEA ———

I pray to God to know him, to find direction for my life
and to lay my requests before him.

——— KEY VERSE ———

If I regard iniquity in my heart, the Lord will not hear *me*:
But verily God hath heard *me*;
he hath attended to the voice of my prayer.
Blessed *be* God, which hath not turned away
my prayer, nor his mercy from me.
Psalm 66:18 – 20

OUR MAP

The key beliefs of the Christian faith we studied in the first ten chapters emphasize that the one true God is a personal God who desires a real relationship with us. He provided the only way to this relationship through the sacrifice of his Son, Jesus Christ. When we embrace and receive Christ's forgiveness, we become children of God and gain access to him. He is not a distant, cosmic being, but a good Father who longs to interact with his children. Prayer is the spiritual practice through which we take God up on his "open door" policy. Prayer is a conversation between God and his people. What an amazing privilege!

In this chapter we will find examples of those who model a vibrant prayer life, as well as information about how to use prayer to make the most of our relationship with God:

- *The Model Prayer Life*
- *A Way to Know God*
- *A Way to Find the Direction We Need*
- *A Way to Lay Our Requests Before God*

We serve a God who is not threatened by our questions and doubts. We don't have to put on a false persona to please him. He permits us to be honest about our fears, our feelings of isolation and our disappointments. When we rehearse our story before him, we see his personal involvement in our lives.

Come *and* hear, all ye that fear God,
    and I will declare what he hath done for my soul.
I cried unto him with my mouth,
    and he was extolled with my tongue.
If I regard iniquity in my heart,
    the Lord will not hear *me*:
But verily God hath heard *me*;
    he hath attended to the voice of my prayer.
Blessed *be* God,
    which hath not turned away my prayer,
    nor his mercy from me.   Psalm 66:16–20

THE MODEL PRAYER LIFE

Scripture contains many examples of men and women who demonstrated a dynamic prayer life, but there is a no more perfect model than Jesus. Spending time in prayer with the Father gave him the strength and guidance he needed to fulfill his purpose in coming to earth. Jesus consistently sought direction and support from his Father, as we see on two occasions from early in his ministry.

Notice how Jesus prayed before and after
each major event in his life. What can we learn
from this pattern of prayer Jesus
demonstrated throughout his life?

And at even, when the sun did set, they brought unto [Jesus] all that were diseased, and them that were possessed with devils. And all the city was gathered together at the door. And he healed many that were sick of divers diseases, and cast out many devils; and suffered not the devils to speak, because they knew him. **And in the morning, rising up a great while before day, [Jesus] went out, and departed into a solitary place, and there prayed.**   MARK 1:32–35

And also …

[Jesus] went out into a mountain to pray, and continued all night in prayer to God. And when it was day, he called *unto him* his disciples: and of them he chose twelve, whom also he named apostles; Simon, (whom he also named Peter,) and Andrew his brother, James and John, Philip and Bartholomew, Matthew and Thomas, James the *son* of Alphaeus, and Simon called Zelotes, And Judas *the brother* of James, and Judas Iscariot, which also was the traitor.   LUKE 6:12–16

Sometime after choosing his disciples, Jesus received news that Herod had cruelly beheaded Jesus' cousin John the Baptist. Upon hearing the news and to avoid the threat of Herod, Jesus went by boat with his disciples to a solitary place. However, thousands of followers got ahead of the group and met them when they landed on shore. Despite the interruption to his plans, Jesus took pity on the people and taught them about the kingdom of God. At the end of the day, when the people were hungry, the disciples told Jesus to send them away. But Jesus miraculously turned five loaves and two fishes into a meal that would feed five thousand people. After the emotion of losing his cousin John and a long day of ministering, Jesus retreated to a secluded place to spend time with the Father.

And [Jesus] commanded [the disciples] to make all sit down by companies upon the green grass. And they sat down in ranks, by hundreds, and by fifties. And when he had taken the five loaves and the two fishes, he looked up to heaven, and blessed, and brake the loaves, and gave *them* to his disciples to set before them; and the two fishes divided he among them all. And they did all eat, and were filled. And they took up twelve baskets full of the fragments, and of the fishes. And they that did eat of the loaves were about five thousand men.

And straightway he constrained his disciples to get into the ship, and to go to the other side before unto Bethsaida, while he sent away the people. And when he had sent them away, he departed into a mountain to pray.   MARK 6:39–46

Prayer never ceased to be part of Jesus' life. As Jesus approached the conclusion of his ministry, he knew it would culminate on a cross, which typically meant a slow and excruciatingly painful death. Knowing what he was about to endure, Jesus took refuge in an extended time of prayer. He appealed to God for a way around the torture, though he remained unflinching in his resolve to accomplish his Father's will.

Then cometh Jesus with them unto a place called Gethsemane, and saith unto the disciples, Sit ye here, while I go and pray yonder. And he took with him Peter and the two sons of Zebedee, and began to be sorrowful and very heavy. Then saith he unto them, My soul is exceeding sorrowful, even unto death: tarry ye here, and watch with me.

And he went a little farther, and fell on his face, and prayed, saying, O my Father, if it be possible, let this cup pass from me: nevertheless not as I will, but as thou *wilt*.

And he cometh unto the disciples, and findeth them asleep, and saith unto Peter, What, could ye not watch with me one hour? Watch and pray, that ye enter not into temptation: the spirit indeed *is* willing, but the flesh *is* weak.

He went away again the second time, and prayed, saying, O my Father, if this cup may not pass away from me, except I drink it, thy will be done.

And he came and found them asleep again: for their eyes were heavy. **And he left them, and went away again, and prayed the third time, saying the same words.**

Then cometh he to his disciples, and saith unto them, Sleep on now, and take *your* rest: behold, the hour is at hand, and the Son of man is betrayed into the hands of sinners. Rise, let us be going: behold, he is at hand that doth betray me.   MATTHEW 26:36–46

A WAY TO KNOW GOD

As Jesus modeled, prayer is the best way to become closer to God. The authors of the psalms seemed to understand this. The prayers in this book reveal that people in Bible times were very much like people today: they had hopes, fears, joy and pain. These writers spilled out to the powerful God of the universe what was on their hearts. They believed God wanted to know what they were experiencing and feeling. God longs to hear from us today as well.

I cried unto God with my voice,
even unto God with my voice;
and he gave ear unto me.
In the day of my trouble I sought the Lord:
my sore ran in the night, and ceased not:
my soul refused to be comforted.

I remembered God, and was troubled:
I complained, and my spirit was overwhelmed.
Thou holdest mine eyes waking:
I am so troubled that I cannot speak.

I have considered the days of old,
 the years of ancient times.
I call to remembrance my song in the night:
 I commune with mine own heart:
 and my spirit made diligent search.

Will the Lord cast off for ever?
 and will he be favourable no more?
Is his mercy clean gone for ever?
 doth *his* promise fail for evermore?
Hath God forgotten to be gracious?
 hath he in anger shut up his tender mercies?

And I said, This *is* my infirmity: *but I will remember*
 the years of the right hand of the most High.
I will remember the works of the LORD:
 surely I will remember thy wonders of old.
I will meditate also of all thy work,
 and talk of thy doings.

Thy way, O God, *is* in the sanctuary:
 who *is so* great a God as *our* God?
Thou *art* the God that doest wonders:
 thou hast declared thy strength among the people.
Thou hast with *thine* arm redeemed thy people,
 the sons of Jacob and Joseph.

The waters saw thee, O God,
 the waters saw thee; they were afraid:
 the depths also were troubled.
The clouds poured out water:
 the skies sent out a sound:
 thine arrows also went abroad.
The voice of thy thunder *was* in the heaven:
 the lightnings lightened the world:
 the earth trembled and shook.
Thy way *is* in the sea,
 and thy path in the great waters,
 and thy footsteps are not known.

> Thou leddest thy people like a flock
> by the hand of Moses and Aaron.   PSALM 77:1–20

It's possible that Solomon was familiar with the psalmist's lyrics that ended with "thou leddest thy people like a flock." The imagery of a flock of sheep who know the shepherd's voice is a repeated theme in Scripture. Perhaps that's why Solomon wrote in the next passage that we should approach prayer with a priority to listen. Like a shepherd, God makes himself accessible, but we should not approach him with hollow words, rote prayers, or promises made lightly. Prayer is an intimate conversation with God and should be treated as such.

Keep thy foot when thou goest to the house of God, and be more ready to hear, than to give the sacrifice of fools: for they consider not that they do evil.
Be not rash with thy mouth, and let not thine heart be hasty to utter *any* thing before God: for God *is* in heaven, and thou upon earth: therefore let thy words be few. For a dream cometh through the multitude of business; and a fool's voice *is known* by multitude of words.   ECCLESIASTES 5:1–3

What can we learn about prayer from
the psalmist and Solomon?

A WAY TO FIND THE DIRECTION WE NEED

Like a needle on a compass, prayer helps us navigate life's toughest obstacles. Heroes of the faith from the beginning to the end of the Bible used prayer to determine their actions. Often the directions they received seemed a bit odd. For example, Gideon, who was by no means fearless, was asked to lead the Israelites into battle against an army that greatly outnumbered his own. God's clear directions allowed him to triumph. But before he set out, Gideon asked God to give him clarity on this overwhelming assignment. This is a good practice for all of us today. When we take our concerns and questions to God, he will provide the clarity we need.

⚷ And the children of Israel did evil in the sight of the LORD: and the LORD delivered them into the hand of Midian seven years. And the hand of Midian prevailed against Israel: *and* because of the Midianites the children of Israel made them the dens which *are* in the mountains, and caves, and strong holds. And *so* it was, when Israel had sown, that the Midianites came up, and the Amalekites, and the children of the east, even they came up against them; And they encamped against them, and destroyed the increase of the earth, till thou come unto Gaza, and left no sustenance for Israel, neither sheep, nor ox, nor ass. For they came up with their cattle and their tents, and they came as grasshoppers for multitude; *for* both they and their camels were without number: and they entered into the land to destroy it. And Israel was greatly impoverished because of the Midianites; and the children of Israel cried unto the LORD.

And it came to pass, when the children of Israel cried unto the LORD because of the Midianites, That the LORD sent a prophet unto the children of Israel, which said unto them, Thus saith the LORD God of Israel, I brought you up from Egypt, and brought you forth out of the house of bondage; And I delivered you out of the hand of the Egyptians, and out of the hand of all that oppressed you, and drave them out from before you, and gave you their land; And I said unto you, I *am* the LORD your God; fear not the gods of the Amorites, in whose land ye dwell: but ye have not obeyed my voice.

And there came an angel of the LORD, and sat under an oak which *was* in Ophrah, that *pertained* unto Joash the Abiezrite: and his son Gideon threshed wheat by the winepress, to hide *it* from the Midianites. And the angel of the LORD appeared unto him, and said unto him, The LORD *is* with thee, thou mighty man of valour.

And Gideon said unto him, Oh my Lord, if the LORD be with us, why then is all this befallen us? and where *be* all his miracles which our fathers told us of, saying, Did not the LORD bring us up from Egypt? but now the LORD hath forsaken us, and delivered us into the hands of the Midianites.

And the LORD looked upon him, and said, Go in this thy might, and thou shalt save Israel from the hand of the Midianites: have not I sent thee?

And he said unto him, Oh my Lord, wherewith shall I save Israel? behold, my family *is* poor in Manasseh, and I *am* the least in my father's house.

And the LORD said unto him, Surely I will be with thee, and thou shalt smite the Midianites as one man.

And he said unto him, If now I have found grace in thy sight, then shew me a sign that thou talkest with me. Depart not hence, I pray thee, until I come unto thee, and bring forth my present, and set *it* before thee.

And he said, I will tarry until thou come again.

And Gideon went in, and made ready a kid, and unleavened cakes of an ephah of flour: the flesh he put in a basket, and he put the broth in a pot, and brought *it* out unto him under the oak, and presented *it*.

And the angel of God said unto him, Take the flesh and the unleavened cakes, and lay *them* upon this rock, and pour out the broth. And he did so. Then the angel of the LORD put forth the end of the staff that *was* in his hand, and touched the flesh and the unleavened cakes; and there rose up fire out of the rock, and consumed the flesh and the unleavened cakes. Then the angel of the LORD departed out of his sight. And when Gideon perceived that he *was* an angel of the LORD, Gideon said, Alas, O Lord GOD! for because I have seen an angel of the LORD face to face.

And the LORD said unto him, Peace *be* unto thee; fear not: thou shalt not die.

Then Gideon built an altar there unto the LORD, and called it Jehovah-shalom: unto this day it *is* yet in Ophrah of the Abiezrites.

And it came to pass the same night, that the LORD said unto him, Take thy father's young bullock, even the second bullock of seven years old, and throw down the altar of Baal that thy father hath, and cut down the grove that *is* by it: And build an altar unto the LORD thy God upon the top of this rock, in the ordered place, and take the second bullock, and offer a burnt sacrifice with the wood of the grove which thou shalt cut down.

Then Gideon took ten men of his servants, and did as the LORD had said unto him: and *so* it was, because he feared his father's household, and the men of the city, that he could not do *it* by day, that he did *it* by night.

And when the men of the city arose early in the morning, behold, the altar of Baal was cast down, and the grove was cut down that *was* by it, and the second bullock was offered upon the altar *that was* built.

And they said one to another, Who hath done this thing?

And when they enquired and asked, they said, Gideon the son of Joash hath done this thing.

Then the men of the city said unto Joash, Bring out thy son, that he may die: because he hath cast down the altar of Baal, and because he hath cut down the grove that *was* by it.

And Joash said unto all that stood against him, Will ye plead for Baal? will ye save him? he that will plead for him, let him be put to death whilst *it is yet* morning: if he *be* a god, let him plead for himself, because *one* hath cast down his altar. Therefore on that day he called him Jerub-baal, saying, Let Baal plead against him, because he hath thrown down his altar.

Then all the Midianites and the Amalekites and the children of the east were gathered together, and went over, and pitched in the valley of Jezreel. But the Spirit of the LORD came upon Gideon, and he blew a trumpet; and Abiezer was gathered after him. And he sent messengers throughout all Manasseh; who also was gathered after him: and he sent messengers unto Asher, and unto Zebulun, and unto Naphtali; and they came up to meet them.

And Gideon said unto God, If thou wilt save Israel by mine hand, as thou hast said, Behold, I will put a fleece of wool in the floor; *and* if the dew be on the fleece only, and *it be* dry upon all the earth *beside*, then shall I know that thou wilt save Israel by mine hand, as thou hast said. And it was so: for he rose up early on the morrow, and thrust the fleece together, and wringed the dew out of the fleece, a bowl full of water.

And Gideon said unto God, Let not thine anger be hot against me, and I will speak but this once: let me prove, I pray thee, but this once with the fleece; let it now be dry only upon the fleece, and upon all the ground let there be dew. And God did so that night: for it was dry upon the fleece only, and there was dew on all the ground.

Then Jerub-baal, who *is* Gideon, and all the people that *were* with him, rose up early, and pitched beside the well of Harod: so that the host of the Midianites were on the north side of them, by the hill of Moreh, in the valley. And the LORD said unto Gideon, The people that *are* with thee *are* too many for me to give the Midianites into their hands, lest Israel vaunt themselves against me, saying, Mine own hand hath saved me. Now therefore go to, proclaim in the ears of the people, saying, Whosoever *is* fearful and afraid, let him return and depart early from mount Gilead. And there returned of the people twenty and two thousand; and there remained ten thousand.

And the LORD said unto Gideon, The people *are* yet *too* many; bring them down unto the water, and I will try them for thee there: and it shall be, *that* of whom I say unto thee, This shall go with thee, the same shall go with thee; and of whomsoever I say unto thee, This shall not go with thee, the same shall not go.

So he brought down the people unto the water: and the LORD said unto Gideon, Every one that lappeth of the water with his tongue, as a dog lappeth, him shalt thou set by himself; likewise every one that boweth down upon his knees to drink. And the number of them that lapped, *putting* their hand to their mouth, were three hundred men: but all the rest of the people bowed down upon their knees to drink water.

And the LORD said unto Gideon, By the three hundred men that lapped will I save you, and deliver the Midianites into thine hand: and let all the *other* people go every man unto his place. So the people took victuals in their hand, and their trumpets: and he sent all *the rest of* Israel every man unto his tent, and retained those three hundred men: and the host of Midian was beneath him in the valley.

And it came to pass the same night, that the LORD said unto him, Arise, get thee down unto the host; for I have delivered it into thine hand. But if thou fear to go down, go thou with Phurah thy servant down to the host: And thou shalt hear what they say; and afterward shall thine hands be strengthened to go down unto the host. Then went he down with Phurah his servant unto the outside of the armed men that *were* in the host. And the Midianites and the Amalekites and all the children of the east lay along in the valley like grasshoppers for multitude; and their camels *were* without number, as the sand by the sea side for multitude.

And when Gideon was come, behold, *there was* a man that told a dream unto his fellow, and said, Behold, I dreamed a dream, and, lo, a cake of barley bread tumbled into the host of Midian, and came unto a tent, and smote it that it fell, and overturned it, that the tent lay along.

And his fellow answered and said, This *is* nothing else save the sword of Gideon the son of Joash, a man of Israel: *for* into his hand hath God delivered Midian, and all the host.

And it was *so*, when Gideon heard the telling of the dream, and the interpretation thereof, that he worshipped, and returned into the host of Israel, and said, Arise; for the LORD hath delivered into your hand the host of Midian. And he divided the three hundred men *into* three companies, and he put a trumpet in every man's hand, with empty pitchers, and lamps within the pitchers.

And he said unto them, Look on me, and do likewise: and, behold, when I come to the outside of the camp, it shall be *that*, as I do, so shall ye do. When I blow with a trumpet, I and all that *are* with me, then blow ye the trumpets also on every side of all the camp, and say, *The sword* of the LORD, and of Gideon.

So Gideon, and the hundred men that *were* with him, came unto the outside of the camp in the beginning of the middle watch; and they had but newly set the watch: and they blew the trumpets, and brake the pitchers that *were* in their hands. And the three companies blew the trumpets, and brake the pitchers, and held the lamps in their left hands, and the trumpets in their right hands to blow *withal*: and they cried, The sword of the LORD, and of Gideon. And they stood every man in his place round about the camp: and all the host ran, and cried, and fled.

And the three hundred blew the trumpets, and the LORD set every man's sword against his fellow, even throughout all the host.

JUDGES 6:1—7:22

What do Gideon's interactions
with God teach us about
God's character?

Like Gideon, shepherd-turned-king David experienced God's leading throughout his life. Psalm 25 captures David's passion for his Lord. Notice how David sought to know God personally by truthfully laying out his requests and seeking God's direction.

Unto thee, O Lord,
  do I lift up my soul.
O my God, I trust in thee:
  let me not be ashamed,
  let not mine enemies triumph over me.
Yea, let none that wait on thee
  be ashamed:
let them be ashamed
  which transgress without cause.

Shew me thy ways, O Lord;
  teach me thy paths.
Lead me in thy truth, and teach me:
  for thou *art* the God of my salvation;
  on thee do I wait all the day.
Remember, O Lord, thy tender mercies and thy
      lovingkindnesses;
  for they *have been* ever of old.
Remember not the sins of my youth,
  nor my transgressions:
according to thy mercy remember thou me
  for thy goodness' sake, O Lord.

Good and upright *is* the Lord:
  therefore will he teach sinners in the way.
The meek will he guide in judgment:
  and the meek will he teach his way.
All the paths of the Lord *are* mercy and truth
  unto such as keep his covenant and his testimonies.
For thy name's sake, O Lord,
  pardon mine iniquity; for it *is* great.

What man *is* he that feareth the Lord?
  him shall he teach in the way *that* he shall choose.

His soul shall dwell at ease;
and his seed shall inherit the earth.
The secret of the LORD *is* with them that fear him;
and he will shew them his covenant.
Mine eyes *are* ever toward the LORD;
for he shall pluck my feet out of the net. PSALM 25:1–15

A WAY TO LAY OUR REQUESTS BEFORE GOD

Because we are God's most prized creations, he wants to know the desires of our hearts. Scripture encourages us to lay our requests before him without hesitation. The Bible includes many stories in which God's people express their needs, wants and desires to God. For example, after God issued the order to destroy the sin-filled cities of Sodom and Gomorrah, where Abraham's nephew Lot and his family lived, Abraham engaged in a conversation with God that displays the freedom we have to talk honestly with him.

And the LORD said, Because the cry of Sodom and Gomorrah is great, and because their sin is very grievous; I will go down now, and see whether they have done altogether according to the cry of it, which is come unto me; and if not, I will know.

And the men turned their faces from thence, and went toward Sodom: but Abraham stood yet before the LORD. And Abraham drew near, and said, Wilt thou also destroy the righteous with the wicked? Peradventure there be fifty righteous within the city: wilt thou also destroy and not spare the place for the fifty righteous that *are* therein? That be far from thee to do after this manner, to slay the righteous with the wicked: and that the righteous should be as the wicked, that be far from thee: Shall not the Judge of all the earth do right?

And the LORD said, If I find in Sodom fifty righteous within the city, then I will spare all the place for their sakes.

And Abraham answered and said, Behold now, I have taken upon me to speak unto the Lord, which *am but* dust and ashes: Peradventure there shall lack five of the fifty righteous: wilt thou destroy all the city for *lack of* five?

And he said, If I find there forty and five, I will not destroy *it*.

And he spake unto him yet again, and said, Peradventure there shall be forty found there.

And he said, I will not do *it* for forty's sake.

And he said *unto him*, Oh let not the Lord be angry, and I will speak: Peradventure there shall thirty be found there.

And he said, I will not do *it*, if I find thirty there.

And he said, Behold now, I have taken upon me to speak unto the Lord: Peradventure there shall be twenty found there.

And he said, I will not destroy *it* for twenty's sake.

And he said, Oh let not the Lord be angry, and I will speak yet but this once: Peradventure ten shall be found there.

And he said, I will not destroy *it* for ten's sake.

And the LORD went his way, as soon as he had left communing with Abraham: and Abraham returned unto his place.

GENESIS 18:20–33

King Hezekiah is another ancient leader who had the boldness to speak honestly before the Lord. Hezekiah was one of the few good kings in Judah during the era of the divided kingdom. He laid a daring personal request before God, and God answered with a powerful "yes."

In those days was Hezekiah sick unto death. And the prophet Isaiah the son of Amoz came to him, and said unto him, Thus saith the LORD, Set thine house in order; for thou shalt die, and not live.

Then he turned his face to the wall, and prayed unto the LORD, saying, I beseech thee, O LORD, remember now how I have walked before thee in truth and with a perfect heart, and have done *that which is* good in thy sight. And Hezekiah wept sore.

And it came to pass, afore Isaiah was gone out into the middle court, that the word of the LORD came to him, saying, Turn again, and tell Hezekiah the captain of my people, Thus saith the LORD, the God of David thy father, I have heard thy prayer, I have seen thy tears: behold, I will heal thee: on the third day thou shalt go up unto the house of the LORD. And I will add unto thy days fifteen years; and I will deliver thee and this city out of the hand of the king of Assyria; and I will defend this city for mine own sake, and for my servant David's sake.

And Isaiah said, Take a lump of figs. And they took and laid *it* on the boil, and he recovered.

And Hezekiah said unto Isaiah, What *shall be* the sign that the LORD will heal me, and that I shall go up into the house of the LORD the third day?

And Isaiah said, This sign shalt thou have of the LORD, that the LORD will do the thing that he hath spoken: shall the shadow go forward ten degrees, or go back ten degrees?

And Hezekiah answered, It is a light thing for the shadow to go down ten degrees: nay, but let the shadow return backward ten degrees.

And Isaiah the prophet cried unto the LORD: and he brought the shadow ten degrees backward, by which it had gone down in the dial of Ahaz.   2 KINGS 20:1–11

Our ultimate prayer model, Jesus, using tangible illustrations, encouraged his followers to be bold in their prayers.

In the following passage from Luke 11, what are the main points of Jesus' teaching about prayer?

And it came to pass, that, as [Jesus] was praying in a certain place, when he ceased, one of his disciples said unto him, Lord, teach us to pray, as John also taught his disciples.

And he said unto them, When ye pray, say, Our Father which art in heaven, Hallowed be thy name. Thy kingdom come. Thy will be done, as in heaven, so in earth. Give us day by day our daily bread. And forgive us our sins; for we also forgive every one that is indebted to us. And lead us not into temptation; but deliver us from evil.

And he said unto them, Which of you shall have a friend, and shall go unto him at midnight, and say unto him, Friend, lend me three loaves; For a friend of mine in his journey is come to me, and I have nothing to set before him? And he from within shall answer and say, Trouble me not: the door is now shut, and my children are with me in bed; I cannot rise and give thee. I say unto you, Though he will not rise and give him, because he is his friend, yet because of his importunity he will rise and give him as many as he needeth.

And I say unto you, Ask, and it shall be given you; seek, and ye shall find; knock, and it shall be opened unto you.For every one that asketh receiveth; and he that seeketh findeth; and to him that knocketh it shall be opened.

If a son shall ask bread of any of you that is a father, will he give him a stone? or if *he ask* a fish, will he for a fish give him a serpent? Or if he shall ask an egg, will he offer him a scorpion? If ye then, being evil, know how to give good gifts unto your children: how much more shall *your* heavenly Father give the Holy Spirit to them that ask him? LUKE 11:1–13

The result of prayerfully laying our requests before God is peace. The apostle Paul experienced this firsthand. He endured incredible hardships, including religious persecution, wrongful imprisonment and a catastrophic shipwreck. Yet in the letters he wrote to the churches he had started throughout the Mediterranean (letters to the Galatians, Ephesians, Philippians, Colossians, etc.), he encouraged the people to do something he was obviously modeling himself: despite circumstances, finding peace in God through prayer.

Be careful for nothing; but in every thing by prayer and supplication with thanksgiving let your requests be made known unto God. And the peace of God, which passeth all understanding, shall keep your hearts and minds through Christ Jesus.

Finally, brethren, whatsoever things are true, whatsoever things *are* honest, whatsoever things *are* just, whatsoever things *are* pure, whatsoever things *are* lovely, whatsoever things *are* of good report; if *there be* any virtue, and if *there be* any praise, think on these things. Those things, which ye have both learned, and received, and heard, and seen in me, do: and the God of peace shall be with you. PHILIPPIANS 4:6–9

How do Paul's words about prayer encourage you?
How do they challenge you?

WHAT WE BELIEVE

Prayer is not only a practice; it is a privilege! To have direct access to the one true God 24/7 proves he is a personal God who wants to be in a relationship with us. Each time we pray we affirm our identity as children of God. He not only gives us the right to come to him, but he also longs for us to come to him. Jesus modeled the life of prayer during his stay on earth. Prayer (talking, listening and resting in God's presence) is an effective way to know him better and find direction for our lives. Why carry life's burdens alone when God invites us to lay them before him? When we do, we find a peace that "passeth" all understanding.

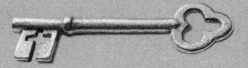

CHAPTER

13

Bible Study

———— KEY QUESTION ————

How do I study God's Word?

———— KEY IDEA ————

I study the Bible to know God and his truth
and to find direction for my daily life.

———— KEY VERSE ————

For the word of God *is* quick, and powerful, and sharper
than any twoedged sword, piercing even to the dividing
asunder of soul and spirit, and of the joints and marrow, and
is a discerner of the thoughts and intents of the heart.
Hebrews 4:12

OUR MAP

The key idea highlighted in Chapter 4—the Bible is the Word of God and has the right to command our beliefs and actions—is a key belief for every Christian. Over many years God superintended the process to bring us his Word, his revelation. It is through the Bible that we learn how to think, act and become like Jesus. The ancient stories and words are "quick" and "powerful" and totally capable of leading us along the right path. But like a trustworthy map, it must be used for it to be effective. Making Bible study a key practice can help us get to where God wants to take us.

In this chapter we will be reading about:

- The First Scriptures
- The Road Map for Living
- Aids to Understanding
- A Transformed Life

Each of these topics, supported with text from the Bible, is crafted to inspire and guide us to access the Bible for ourselves. So we read with great eagerness to learn from God's good Word and apply it to our lives!

THE FIRST SCRIPTURES

Both Jews and Christians have traditionally regarded Moses as the author of the first five books of the Old Testament. Until the time of Moses, the words of God and the stories of his people were communicated orally from generation to generation. And even after Moses wrote these first portions of Scripture, the people didn't have access to their own complete copy. Before Moses died, the Lord led him to deliver farewell messages to the people, which are recorded in Deuteronomy. Parents were charged with the responsibility to share with their children God's principles and commandments. Moses also made a provision to ensure that everyone living in Israel would regularly and faithfully hear God's Word.

Thou shalt fear the Lord thy God, and serve him, and shalt swear by his name. Ye shall not go after other gods, of the gods of the people which *are* round about you; (For the Lord thy God *is* a jealous God among you) lest the anger of the LORD thy God be kindled against thee, and destroy thee from off the face of the earth. Ye shall not tempt the LORD your God, as ye tempted *him* in Massah. Ye shall diligently keep the commandments of the LORD your God, and his testimonies, and his statutes, which he hath commanded thee. And thou shalt do *that which is* right and good in the sight of the LORD: that it may be well with thee, and that thou mayest go in and possess the good land which the LORD sware unto thy fathers, To cast out all thine enemies from before thee, as the LORD hath spoken.

And when thy son asketh thee in time to come, saying, What *mean* the testimonies, and the statutes, and the judgments, which the LORD our God hath commanded you? Then thou shalt say unto thy son, We were Pharaoh's bondmen in Egypt; and the LORD brought us out of Egypt with a mighty hand: And the LORD shewed signs and wonders, great and sore, upon Egypt, upon Pharaoh, and upon all his household, before our eyes: And he brought us out from thence, that he might bring us in, to give us the land which he sware unto our fathers. And the LORD commanded us to do all these statutes, to fear the LORD our God, for our good always, that he might preserve us alive, as *it is* at this day. And it shall be our righteousness, if we observe to do all these commandments before the LORD our God, as he hath commanded us.   DEUTERONOMY 6:13–25

And Moses wrote this law, and delivered it unto the priests the sons of Levi, which bare the ark of the covenant of the LORD, and unto all the elders of Israel. **And Moses commanded them, saying, At the end of *every* seven years, in the solemnity of the year of release, in the feast of tabernacles, When all Israel is come to appear before the LORD thy God in the place which he shall choose, thou shalt read this law before all Israel in their hearing. Gather the people together, men, and women, and children, and thy stranger that *is* within thy gates, that they may hear, and that they may learn, and fear the LORD your God, and observe to do all the words of this law: And *that* their children, which have not known *any thing*, may hear, and learn to fear the LORD your God, as long as ye live in the land whither ye go over Jordan to possess it.**   DEUTERONOMY 31:9–13

After Moses' death, the mantle of leadership was passed to Joshua. God visited Joshua to remind him of the importance of following God's laws and commands.

Now after the death of Moses the servant of the LORD it came to pass, that the LORD spake unto Joshua the son of Nun, Moses' minister, saying, Moses my servant is dead; now therefore arise, go over this Jordan, thou, and all this people, unto the land which I do give to them, *even* to the children of Israel. Every place that the sole of your foot shall tread upon, that have I given unto you, as I said unto Moses. From the wilderness and this Lebanon even unto the great river, the river Euphrates, all the land of the Hittites, and unto the great sea toward the going down of the sun, shall be your coast. There shall not any man be able to stand before thee all the days of thy life: as I was with Moses, *so* I will be with thee: I will not fail thee, nor forsake thee.

Be strong and of a good courage: for unto this people shalt thou divide for an inheritance the land, which I sware unto their fathers to give them. Only be thou strong and very courageous, that thou mayest observe to do according to all the law, which Moses my servant commanded thee: turn not from it *to* the right hand or *to* the left, that thou mayest prosper whithersoever thou goest. **This book of the law shall not depart out of thy mouth; but thou shalt meditate therein day and night, that thou mayest observe to do according to all that is written therein: for then thou shalt make thy way prosperous, and then thou shalt have good success.** Have not I commanded thee? Be strong and of a good courage; be not afraid, neither be thou dismayed: for the LORD thy God *is* with thee whithersoever thou goest.   JOSHUA 1:1–9

The value of reflecting on God's words was not lost on God's people. In 586 BC, Jerusalem was destroyed and the people of Judah went into exile in Babylon. In 537, the Jews began returning home. In 444, the restored community came together in Jerusalem to hear the reading of the book of the law of God. Revival broke out as the people were filled with great emotion and resolve. With an insatiable appetite for Scripture, they discovered the Lord's desire for them to observe the feast of tabernacles.

The great joy with which the people celebrated had not been seen since the days of Joshua nearly a thousand years earlier.

Below you will read a touching account of Israel's return to God's Word from Nehemiah 7–9. In light of this and your own experiences, what are the benefits of studying God's Word in community?

So the priests, and the Levites, and the porters, and the singers, and *some* of the people, and the Nethinims, and all Israel, dwelt in their cities; and when the seventh month came, the children of Israel *were* in their cities. And all the people gathered themselves together as one man into the street that *was* before the water gate; and they spake unto Ezra the scribe to bring the book of the law of Moses, which the LORD had commanded to Israel.

And Ezra the priest brought the law before the congregation both of men and women, and all that could hear with understanding, upon the first day of the seventh month. And he read therein before the street that *was* before the water gate from the morning until midday, before the men and the women, and those that could understand; and the ears of all the people *were attentive* unto the book of the law.

And Ezra the scribe stood upon a pulpit of wood, which they had made for the purpose; and beside him stood Mattithiah, and Shema, and Anaiah, and Urijah, and Hilkiah, and Maaseiah, on his right hand; and on his left hand, Pedaiah, and Mishael, and Malchiah, and Hashum, and Hashbadana, Zechariah, *and* Meshullam.

And Ezra opened the book in the sight of all the people; (for he was above all the people;) and when he opened it, all the people stood up: And Ezra blessed the LORD, the great God. And all the people answered, Amen, Amen, with lifting up their hands: and they bowed their heads, and worshipped the LORD with *their* faces to the ground.

Also Jeshua, and Bani, and Sherebiah, Jamin, Akkub, Shabbethai, Hodijah, Maaseiah, Kelita, Azariah, Jozabad, Hanan, Pelaiah, and the Levites, caused the people to understand the law: and the people *stood* in their place. **So they read in the book in**

the law of God distinctly, and gave the sense, and caused *them* **to understand the reading.**

And Nehemiah, which *is* the Tirshatha, and Ezra the priest the scribe, and the Levites that taught the people, said unto all the people, This day *is* holy unto the LORD your God; mourn not, nor weep. For all the people wept, when they heard the words of the law.

Then he said unto them, Go your way, eat the fat, and drink the sweet, and send portions unto them for whom nothing is prepared: for *this* day *is* holy unto our Lord: neither be ye sorry; for the joy of the LORD is your strength.

So the Levites stilled all the people, saying, Hold your peace, for the day *is* holy; neither be ye grieved.

And all the people went their way to eat, and to drink, and to send portions, and to make great mirth, because they had understood the words that were declared unto them.

And on the second day were gathered together the chief of the fathers of all the people, the priests, and the Levites, unto Ezra the scribe, even to understand the words of the law. And they found written in the law which the LORD had commanded by Moses, that the children of Israel should dwell in booths in the feast of the seventh month: And that they should publish and proclaim in all their cities, and in Jerusalem, saying, Go forth unto the mount, and fetch olive branches, and pine branches, and myrtle branches, and palm branches, and branches of thick trees, to make booths, as *it is* written.

So the people went forth, and brought *them*, and made themselves booths, every one upon the roof of his house, and in their courts, and in the courts of the house of God, and in the street of the water gate, and in the street of the gate of Ephraim. And all the congregation of them that were come again out of the captivity made booths, and sat under the booths: for since the days of Jeshua the son of Nun unto that day had not the children of Israel done so. And there was very great gladness.

Also day by day, from the first day unto the last day, he read in the book of the law of God. And they kept the feast seven days; and on the eighth day *was* a solemn assembly, according unto the manner.

Now in the twenty and fourth day of this month the children of Israel were assembled with fasting, and with sackclothes, and earth upon them. And the seed of Israel separated themselves from all strangers, and stood and confessed their sins, and the iniquities of their fathers. And they stood up in their place, and read in the book of the law of the LORD their God *one* fourth part of the day; and *another* fourth part they confessed, and worshipped the LORD their God. NEHEMIAH 7:73—9:3

THE ROAD MAP FOR LIVING

Judging by their reaction when they heard God's Word again after a long hiatus, the Israelites were lost without their road map for living. But there are other examples in the Bible of those who never seemed to lose sight of God's Word. For instance, the author of Psalm 19 relied on it to guide him, to help him in crisis, to gain understanding in confusing times, and to refresh him and give him joy.

> The law of the LORD *is* perfect,
>   converting the soul:
> the testimony of the LORD *is* sure,
>   making wise the simple.
> The statutes of the LORD *are* right,
>   rejoicing the heart:
> the commandment of the LORD *is* pure,
>   enlightening the eyes.
> The fear of the LORD *is* clean,
>   enduring for ever:
> the judgments of the LORD *are* true
>   *and* righteous altogether.
>
> More to be desired *are they* than gold,
>   yea, than much fine gold:
> sweeter also than honey
>   and the honeycomb.
> Moreover by them is thy servant warned:
>   *and* in keeping of them *there is* great reward.
> Who can understand *his* errors?
>   cleanse thou me from secret *faults*.

Keep back thy servant also from presumptuous *sins*;
>   let them not have dominion over me:
then shall I be upright,
>   and I shall be innocent from the great transgression.

Let the words of my mouth, and the meditation of my
**   heart,**
>   **be acceptable in thy sight,**
>   **O LORD, my strength, and my redeemer.**   PSALM 19:7–14

The value of reading and studying the Word of our strength and redeemer is emphasized vividly throughout Psalm 119, the longest chapter in the Bible. In these portions, the passion the psalmist has for the Holy Scriptures is strikingly obvious.

Wherewithal shall a young man cleanse his way?
>   by taking heed *thereto* according to thy word.
With my whole heart have I sought thee:
>   O let me not wander from thy commandments.
Thy word have I hid in mine heart,
>   **that I might not sin against thee.**
Blessed *art* thou, O LORD:
>   teach me thy statutes.
With my lips have I declared
>   all the judgments of thy mouth.
I have rejoiced in the way of thy testimonies,
>   as *much as* in all riches.
I will meditate in thy precepts,
>   and have respect unto thy ways.
I will delight myself in thy statutes:
>   I will not forget thy word.

Deal bountifully with thy servant, *that* I may live,
>   and keep thy word.
Open thou mine eyes, that I may behold
>   wondrous things out of thy law.
I *am* a stranger in the earth:
>   hide not thy commandments from me.

My soul breaketh for the longing *that it hath*
   unto thy judgments at all times.
Thou hast rebuked the proud *that are* cursed,
   which do err from thy commandments.
Remove from me reproach and contempt;
   for I have kept thy testimonies.
Princes also did sit *and* speak against me:
   but thy servant did meditate in thy statutes.
Thy testimonies also *are* my delight
   and my counsellors.   PSALM 119:9–24

Teach me, O LORD, the way of thy statutes;
   and I shall keep it *unto* the end.
Give me understanding, and I shall keep thy law;
   yea, I shall observe it with *my* whole heart.
Make me to go in the path of thy commandments;
   for therein do I delight.
Incline my heart unto thy testimonies,
   and not to covetousness.
Turn away mine eyes from beholding vanity;
   and quicken thou me in thy way.
Stablish thy word unto thy servant,
   who *is devoted* to thy fear.
Turn away my reproach which I fear:
   for thy judgments *are* good.
Behold, I have longed after thy precepts:
   quicken me in thy righteousness.   PSALM 119:33–40

O how love I thy law!
   it *is* my meditation all the day.
Thou through thy commandments hast made me
   wiser than mine enemies: for they *are* ever with me.
I have more understanding than all my teachers:
   for thy testimonies *are* my meditation.
I understand more than the ancients,
   because I keep thy precepts.
I have refrained my feet from every evil way,
   that I might keep thy word.

I have not departed from thy judgments:
>for thou hast taught me.
How sweet are thy words unto my taste!
>*yea*, *sweeter* than honey to my mouth!
Through thy precepts I get understanding:
>therefore I hate every false way.

Thy word *is* a lamp unto my feet,
>**and a light unto my path.**
I have sworn, and I will perform *it*,
>that I will keep thy righteous judgments.
I am afflicted very much:
>quicken me, O LORD, according unto thy word.
Accept, I beseech thee, the freewill offerings of my mouth,
>O LORD,
>and teach me thy judgments.
My soul *is* continually in my hand:
>yet do I not forget thy law.
The wicked have laid a snare for me:
>yet I erred not from thy precepts.
Thy testimonies have I taken as an heritage for ever:
>for they *are* the rejoicing of my heart.
I have inclined mine heart to perform thy statutes alway,
>*even unto* the end. PSALM 119:97–112

What is the difference between studying
God's Word and hiding it in our hearts?
What is the difference between reading God's Word
and meditating on it day and night?

AIDS TO UNDERSTANDING

As you have probably observed, the Bible is unlike any other narrative. It is God's story, chock-full of amazing depth and application for our lives. Jesus reminds us that the condition of our heart is important when we hear or read God's Word. If we are open and receptive to God's words, they will take root in our lives and transform us.

In the passage below, Jesus refers to four types of soil
on which the seed of his Word falls. Which type
best describes you right now? Was there a time when
you would have answered differently?

The same day went Jesus out of the house, and sat by the sea side. And great multitudes were gathered together unto him, so that he went into a ship, and sat; and the whole multitude stood on the shore. And he spake many things unto them in parables, saying, Behold, a sower went forth to sow; And when he sowed, some *seeds* fell by the way side, and the fowls came and devoured them up: Some fell upon stony places, where they had not much earth: and forthwith they sprung up, because they had no deepness of earth: And when the sun was up, they were scorched; and because they had no root, they withered away. And some fell among thorns; and the thorns sprung up, and choked them: But other fell into good ground, and brought forth fruit, some an hundredfold, some sixtyfold, some thirtyfold. Who hath ears to hear, let him hear.

And the disciples came, and said unto him, Why speakest thou unto them in parables?

He answered and said unto them, Because it is given unto you to know the mysteries of the kingdom of heaven, but to them it is not given. For whosoever hath, to him shall be given, and he shall have more abundance: but whosoever hath not, from him shall be taken away even that he hath. Therefore speak I to them in parables: because they seeing see not; and hearing they hear not, neither do they understand. And in them is fulfilled the prophecy of Esaias, which saith, By hearing ye shall hear, and shall not understand; and seeing ye shall see, and shall not perceive: For this people's heart is waxed gross, and *their* ears are dull of hearing, and their eyes they have closed; lest at any time they should see with *their* eyes, and hear with *their* ears, and should understand with *their* heart, and should be converted, and I should heal them. But blessed *are* your eyes, for they see: and your ears, for they hear. For verily I say unto you, That many prophets and righteous *men* have desired to see *those things* which ye see, and have not seen *them*; and to hear *those things* which ye hear, and have not heard *them*.

Hear ye therefore the parable of the sower. When any one heareth the word of the kingdom, and understandeth *it* not, then cometh the wicked *one*, and catcheth away that which was sown in his heart. This is he which received seed by the way side. But he that received the seed into stony places, the same is he that heareth the word, and anon with joy receiveth it; Yet hath he not root in himself, but dureth for a while: for when tribulation or persecution ariseth because of the word, by and by he is offended. He also that received seed among the thorns is he that heareth the word; and the care of this world, and the deceitfulness of riches, choke the word, and he becometh unfruitful. **But he that received seed into the good ground is he that heareth the word, and understandeth *it*; which also beareth fruit, and bringeth forth, some an hundredfold, some sixty, some thirty.** Matthew 13:1–23 ⚿

But how do our hearts open up to God in order to be receptive to his words? Jesus told his disciples that after he returned to heaven, the Holy Ghost, whom Jesus also called the Spirit of truth, would come to reside in them and to remind them of everything he had said. This same Spirit lives in all believers today.

As you read the following passages from John 14 and 1 Corinthians 2, look for ways in which the Holy Ghost helps us understand Scripture.

If ye love me, keep my commandments. And I will pray the Father, and he shall give you another Comforter, that he may abide with you for ever; *Even* the Spirit of truth; whom the world cannot receive, because it seeth him not, neither knoweth him: but ye know him; for he dwelleth with you, and shall be in you. I will not leave you comfortless: I will come to you. Yet a little while, and the world seeth me no more; but ye see me: because I live, ye shall live also. At that day ye shall know that I *am* in my Father, and ye in me, and I in you. He that hath my commandments, and keepeth them, he it is that loveth me: and he that loveth me shall be loved of my Father, and I will love him, and will manifest myself to him.

Judas saith unto him, not Iscariot, Lord, how is it that thou wilt manifest thyself unto us, and not unto the world?

Jesus answered and said unto him, If a man love me, he will keep my words: and my Father will love him, and we will come unto him, and make our abode with him. He that loveth me not keepeth not my sayings: and the word which ye hear is not mine, but the Father's which sent me.

These things have I spoken unto you, being *yet* present with you. But the Comforter, *which* is the Holy Ghost, whom the Father will send in my name, he shall teach you all things, and bring all things to your remembrance, whatsoever I have said unto you. Peace I leave with you, my peace I give unto you: not as the world giveth, give I unto you. Let not your heart be troubled, neither let it be afraid. JOHN 14:15–27

The early church was devoted to the Word of God. However, at that time people did not have their own personal copies of the books of the Bible, so they had to rely heavily on the public reading of Scripture during their meetings. As promised by Jesus, the Holy Ghost came down to indwell believers.

One of the roles of the Holy Ghost is to illuminate the message of Scripture. It is through the Holy Ghost that we are able to understand the Bible's full meaning, accept it in our hearts and know how to apply it to our lives. The apostle Paul informed the church at Corinth of this truth.

And I, brethren, when I came to you, came not with excellency of speech or of wisdom, declaring unto you the testimony of God. For I determined not to know any thing among you, save Jesus Christ, and him crucified. And I was with you in weakness, and in fear, and in much trembling. And my speech and my preaching *was* not with enticing words of man's wisdom, but in demonstration of the Spirit and of power: That your faith should not stand in the wisdom of men, but in the power of God.

Howbeit we speak wisdom among them that are perfect: yet not the wisdom of this world, nor of the princes of this world, that come to nought: But we speak the wisdom of God in a mystery, *even* the hidden *wisdom*, which God ordained before the world unto our glory: Which none of the princes of this world knew: for had they known *it*, they would not have crucified the Lord of glory. But as it is written, Eye hath not seen, nor ear heard, neither have entered into the heart of man, the things which God hath prepared for them that love him. But God hath revealed *them* unto us by his Spirit: for the Spirit searcheth all things, yea, the deep things of God.

For what man knoweth the things of a man, save the spirit of man which is in him? even so the things of God knoweth no man, but the Spirit of God. **Now we have received, not the spirit of the world, but the spirit which is of God; that we might know the things that are freely given to us of God.** Which things also we speak, not in the words which man's wisdom teacheth, but which the Holy Ghost teacheth; comparing spiritual things with spiritual. But the natural man receiveth not the things of the Spirit of God: for they are foolishness unto him: neither can he know *them*, because they are spiritually discerned. But he that is spiritual judgeth all things, yet he himself is judged of no man. For who hath known the mind of the Lord, that he may instruct him? But we have the mind of Christ.   1 Corinthians 2:1–16

Anchoring our beliefs in the truth of God's Word is critical for the believer. Because of this, teachers of God's Word have a special calling to deliver the teachings of God's Word correctly, to call out false teachings and to model the message before the congregation and community.

Now the Spirit speaketh expressly, that in the latter times some shall depart from the faith, giving heed to seducing spirits, and doctrines of devils; Speaking lies in hypocrisy; having their conscience seared with a hot iron; Forbidding to marry, *and commanding* to abstain from meats, which God hath created to be received with thanksgiving of them which believe and know the truth. For every creature of God *is* good, and nothing to be refused, if it be received with thanksgiving: For it is sanctified by the word of God and prayer.

If thou put the brethren in remembrance of these things, thou shalt be a good minister of Jesus Christ, nourished up in the words of faith and of good doctrine, whereunto thou hast attained. But refuse profane and old wives' fables, and exercise thyself *rather* unto godliness. For bodily exercise profiteth little: but godliness is profitable unto all things, having promise of the life that now is, and of that which is to come. This *is* a faithful saying and worthy of all acceptation. For therefore we both labour and suffer reproach, because we trust in the living God, who is the Saviour of all men, specially of those that believe.

These things command and teach. Let no man despise thy youth; but be thou an example of the believers, in word, in conversation, in charity, in spirit, in faith, in purity. Till I come, give attendance to reading, to exhortation, to doctrine. Neglect not the gift that is in thee, which was given thee by prophecy, with the laying on of the hands of the presbytery.

Meditate upon these things; give thyself wholly to them; that thy profiting may appear to all. Take heed unto thyself, and unto the doctrine; continue in them: for in doing this thou shalt both save thyself, and them that hear thee.   1 TIMOTHY 4:1–16

Of these things put *them* in remembrance, charging *them* before the Lord that they strive not about words to no profit, *but* to the subverting of the hearers. **Study to shew thyself approved unto God, a workman that needeth not to be ashamed, rightly dividing the word of truth.** But shun profane *and* vain babblings: for they will increase unto more ungodliness.   2 TIMOTHY 2:14–16

A TRANSFORMED LIFE
The desired outcome of studying God's truth is transformation. It guides us along a path of maturity in Christ. We get into the Bible and the Bible turns around and gets into us and changes us for the good.

And being made perfect, [Christ] became the author of eternal salvation unto all them that obey him; Called of God an high priest after the order of Melchisedec. Of whom we have many things to say, and hard to be uttered, seeing ye are dull of hearing. For when for the time ye ought to be teachers, ye have need that one teach you again which *be* the first principles of the oracles of God; and are become such as have need of milk, and not of strong meat. For every one that useth milk *is* unskilful in the word of righteousness: for he is a babe. **But strong meat belongeth to them that are of full age, *even* those who by reason of use have their senses exercised to discern both good and evil.**

Therefore leaving the principles of the doctrine of Christ, let us go on unto perfection; not laying again the foundation of repentance from dead works, and of faith toward God, Of the doctrine of baptisms, and of laying on of hands, and of resurrection of the dead, and of eternal judgment. And this will we do, if God permit.

HEBREWS 5:9—6:3

Reflect on the key verse at the beginning of this chapter. According to the author, the Word of God is like a twoedged sword; it gets under our skins and speaks directly to our hearts. In what ways have you experienced this?

WHAT WE BELIEVE

If we believe the Bible is the Word of God and can be trusted to guide us in the best and right direction, we must gain the skill and discipline to read, study, meditate on and apply it to our lives. God told Joshua that if he did this, he would be successful. God makes the same offer to us. When we open up God's Word, we learn more about the one true God who knows and loves us. The more we know about God's nature, character and movements, the easier it is to discern his will and direction for our lives. But the Bible can be a bit overwhelming, can't it? Remember, you are not alone. You have the Spirit of God within you and a community of believers around you to help you. So please don't give up. Keep reading!

CHAPTER

14

Single-Mindedness

―――――― KEY QUESTION ――――――

How do I keep my focus on Jesus
amidst distractions?

―――――――― KEY IDEA ――――――――

I focus on God and his priorities for my life.

――――――――― KEY VERSE ―――――――――

But seek ye first the kingdom of God,
and his righteousness;
and all these things shall be added unto you.
Matthew 6:33

OUR MAP

To be single-minded means to have one desire that trumps all others. One goal. One focus. From the beginning God made clear that he should be his people's main focus. But this is challenging in a hectic, fast-paced world. It's easy for days, months and even years to get away from us. The spiritual practice of single-mindedness is all about determining our priorities to ensure we are practicing our faith, living out our beliefs and accomplishing God's will for our lives.

In this chapter we will be reading Scripture that addresses:

- Principles of Single-Mindedness
- Profiles of Single-Mindedness
- Product of Single-Mindedness

PRINCIPLES OF SINGLE-MINDEDNESS

I *am* the LORD thy God, which have brought thee out of the land of Egypt, out of the house of bondage. Thou shalt have no other gods before me.

EXODUS 20:2–3

In the first of the Ten Commandments, God commanded the Israelites to serve him exclusively because he was worthy of their trust, as he had proved by delivering them from Egypt. Later, just before Moses died and the Israelites entered the promised land, God inspired Moses to remind the people of their single-minded calling.

We read this passage in Chapter 1 to reinforce that the God of the Bible is the one true God. Now we will read this powerful text again and hear the call to prioritize our lives around God.

As you read the passage below from Deuteronomy 6, look for what God promised to the Israelites if they obeyed the first commandment and kept their covenant with him.

Now these are the commandments, the statutes, and the judgments, which the LORD your God commanded to teach you, that ye might do *them* in the land whither ye go to possess it: That thou mightest fear the LORD thy God, to keep all his statutes and his commandments, which I command thee, thou, and thy son, and thy son's son, all the days of thy life; and that thy days may be prolonged. Hear therefore, O Israel, and observe to do *it*; that it may be well with thee, and that ye may increase mightily, as the LORD God of thy fathers hath promised thee, in the land that floweth with milk and honey.

Hear, O Israel: The LORD our God *is* one LORD: And thou shalt love the LORD thy God with all thine heart, and with all thy soul, and with all thy might. **And these words, which I command thee this day, shall be in thine heart: And thou shalt teach them diligently unto thy children, and shalt talk of them when thou sittest in thine house, and when thou walkest by the way, and when thou liest down, and when thou risest up. And thou shalt bind them for a sign upon thine hand, and they shall be as frontlets between thine eyes. And thou shalt write them upon the posts of thy house, and on thy gates.** DEUTERONOMY 6:1–9

God's people were given the first commandment because they needed to submit fully to his authority and look to him and him only to provide all they needed. In the New Testament, Jesus described the "other gods" we might have in a way that hits close to home.

Lay not up for yourselves treasures upon earth, where moth and rust doth corrupt, and where thieves break through and steal: But lay up for yourselves treasures in heaven, where neither moth nor rust doth corrupt, and where thieves do not break through nor steal: For where your treasure is, there will your heart be also.

The light of the body is the eye: if therefore thine eye be single, thy whole body shall be full of light. But if thine eye be evil, thy whole body shall be full of darkness. If therefore the light that is in thee be darkness, how great *is* that darkness!

No man can serve two masters: for either he will hate the one, and love the other; or else he will hold to the one, and despise the other. Ye cannot serve God and mammon.

MATTHEW 6:19–24

What kind of "treasure" keeps us from being single-minded?
How can "evil eyes" keep us from being single-minded?
Why isn't it possible to serve two masters?

Seeking first God's kingdom was the apostle Paul's message as he traveled from city to city teaching people about the gift of salvation and how believers could single-mindedly follow Christ. In many cases, a combative group of religious leaders approached the new churches after Paul had left and tried to undermine his authority and teaching. They boasted about their religious credentials and weighed down Paul's message with Jewish laws and traditions. This infuriated Paul, who then urged the believers to follow his example in keeping their focus steadfastly on Jesus alone.

Finally, my brethren, rejoice in the Lord. To write the same things to you, to me indeed *is* not grievous, but for you *it is* safe. Beware of dogs, beware of evil workers, beware of the concision. For we are the circumcision, which worship God in the spirit, and rejoice in Christ Jesus, and have no confidence in the flesh. Though I might also have confidence in the flesh.

If any other man thinketh that he hath whereof he might trust in the flesh, I more: Circumcised the eighth day, of the stock of Israel, *of* the tribe of Benjamin, an Hebrew of the Hebrews; as touching the law, a Pharisee; Concerning zeal, persecuting the church; touching the righteousness which is in the law, blameless.

But what things were gain to me, those I counted loss for Christ. Yea doubtless, and I count all things *but* loss for the excellency of the knowledge of Christ Jesus my Lord: for whom I have suffered the loss of all things, and do count them *but* dung, that I may win Christ, And be found in him, not having mine own righteousness, which is of the law, but that which is through the faith of Christ, the righteousness which is of God by faith: That I may know him, and the power of his resurrection, and the fellowship of his sufferings, being made conformable unto his death; If by any means I might attain unto the resurrection of the dead.

Not as though I had already attained, either were already

perfect: but I follow after, if that I may apprehend that for which also I am apprehended of Christ Jesus. Brethren, I count not myself to have apprehended: **but *this* one thing *I do*, forgetting those things which are behind, and reaching forth unto those things which are before, I press toward the mark for the prize of the high calling of God in Christ Jesus.** PHILIPPIANS 3:1–14

PROFILES OF SINGLE-MINDEDNESS

King Jehoshaphat of the southern kingdom of Judah faced a tremendous challenge. His land was threatened by a hostile army. Rather than being overcome by fear, Jehoshaphat led the people to turn to the Lord with single-minded and wholehearted trust.

In the following passage from 2 Chronicles 20, identify the key beliefs in which Jehoshaphat anchors his prayer. How can these key beliefs instill confidence in God's provision and guide our decisions?

The children of Moab, and the children of Ammon, and with them *other* beside the Ammonites, came against Jehoshaphat to battle.

Then there came some that told Jehoshaphat, saying, There cometh a great multitude against thee from beyond the sea on this side Syria; and, behold, they *be* in Hazazon-tamar, which is En-gedi. And Jehoshaphat feared, and set himself to seek the LORD, and proclaimed a fast throughout all Judah. And Judah gathered themselves together, to ask *help* of the LORD: even out of all the cities of Judah they came to seek the LORD.

And Jehoshaphat stood in the congregation of Judah and Jerusalem, in the house of the LORD, before the new court, And said, O LORD God of our fathers, *art* not thou God in heaven? and rulest *not* thou over all the kingdoms of the heathen? and in thine hand *is there not* power and might, so that none is able to withstand thee? *Art* not thou our God, *who* didst drive out the inhabitants of this land before thy people Israel, and gavest it to the seed of Abraham thy friend for ever? And they dwelt therein, and have built thee a sanctuary therein for thy name, saying, If, *when* evil cometh upon us, *as* the sword, judgment, or pestilence, or famine, we stand before this house, and in thy presence, (for thy name *is* in this house,) and cry unto thee in our affliction, then thou wilt hear and help.

And now, behold, the children of Ammon and Moab and mount Seir, whom thou wouldest not let Israel invade, when they came out of the land of Egypt, but they turned from them, and destroyed them not; Behold, *I say, how* they reward us, to come to cast us out of thy possession, which thou hast given us to inherit. O our God, wilt thou not judge them? for we have no might against this great company that cometh against us; **neither know we what to do: but our eyes** *are* **upon thee.**

And all Judah stood before the LORD, with their little ones, their wives, and their children.

Then upon Jahaziel the son of Zechariah, the son of Benaiah, the son of Jeiel, the son of Mattaniah, a Levite of the sons of Asaph, came the Spirit of the LORD in the midst of the congregation;

And he said, Hearken ye, all Judah, and ye inhabitants of Jerusalem, and thou king Jehoshaphat, Thus saith the LORD unto you, Be not afraid nor dismayed by reason of this great multitude; for the battle *is* not yours, but God's. To morrow go ye down against them: behold, they come up by the cliff of Ziz; and ye shall find them at the end of the brook, before the wilderness of Jeruel. **Ye shall not** *need* **to fight in this** *battle*: **set yourselves, stand ye** *still*, **and see the salvation of the LORD with you, O Judah and Jerusalem: fear not, nor be dismayed; to morrow go out against them: for the LORD** *will be* **with you.**

And Jehoshaphat bowed his head with *his* face to the ground: and all Judah and the inhabitants of Jerusalem fell before the LORD, worshipping the LORD. And the Levites, of the children of the Kohathites, and of the children of the Korhites, stood up to praise the LORD God of Israel with a loud voice on high.

And they rose early in the morning, and went forth into the wilderness of Tekoa: and as they went forth, Jehoshaphat stood and said, Hear me, O Judah, and ye inhabitants of Jerusalem; Believe in the LORD your God, so shall ye be established; believe his prophets, so shall ye prosper. And when he had consulted with the people, he appointed singers unto the LORD, and that should praise the beauty of holiness, as they went out before the army, and to say, Praise the LORD; for his mercy *endureth* for ever.

And when they began to sing and to praise, the LORD set ambushments against the children of Ammon, Moab, and mount Seir, which were come against Judah; and they were smitten. For the children of Ammon and Moab stood up against the inhabitants of mount Seir, utterly to slay and destroy *them*: and when they had made an end of the inhabitants of Seir, every one helped to destroy another.

And when Judah came toward the watch tower in the wilderness, they looked unto the multitude, and, behold, they *were* dead bodies fallen to the earth, and none escaped. And when Jehoshaphat and his people came to take away the spoil of them, they found among them in abundance both riches with the dead bodies, and precious jewels, which they stripped off for themselves, more than they could carry away: and they were three days in gathering of the spoil, it was so much. And on the fourth day they assembled themselves in the valley of Berachah; for there they blessed the LORD: therefore the name of the same place was called, The valley of Berachah, unto this day.

Then they returned, every man of Judah and Jerusalem, and Jehoshaphat in the forefront of them, to go again to Jerusalem with joy; for the LORD had made them to rejoice over their enemies. And they came to Jerusalem with psalteries and harps and trumpets unto the house of the LORD.

And the fear of God was on all the kingdoms of *those* countries, when they had heard that the LORD fought against the enemies of Israel. So the realm of Jehoshaphat was quiet: for his God gave him rest round about.   2 CHRONICLES 20:1–30 🔑

> *While Jehoshaphat certainly proved that his focus was on God, Jesus serves as an exemplary model for the type of single-mindedness God had in mind when he announced in the first of his Ten Commandments: "Thou shalt have no other gods before me." Living out this ancient command, Jesus didn't make choices based on his desires or anyone else's expectations. His sole goal was to live according to his Father's will.*

Then spake Jesus again unto them, saying, I am the light of the world: he that followeth me shall not walk in darkness, but shall have the light of life.

The Pharisees therefore said unto him, Thou bearest record of thyself; thy record is not true.

Jesus answered and said unto them, Though I bear record of myself, *yet* my record is true: for I know whence I came, and whither I go; but ye cannot tell whence I come, and whither I go. Ye judge after the flesh; I judge no man. And yet if I judge, my judgment is true: for I am not alone, but I and the Father that sent me. It is also written in your law, that the testimony of two men is true. I am one that bear witness of myself, and the Father that sent me beareth witness of me.

Then said they unto him, Where is thy Father?

Jesus answered, Ye neither know me, nor my Father: if ye had known me, ye should have known my Father also. These words spake Jesus in the treasury, as he taught in the temple: and no man laid hands on him; for his hour was not yet come.

Then said Jesus again unto them, I go my way, and ye shall seek me, and shall die in your sins: whither I go, ye cannot come.

Then said the Jews, Will he kill himself? because he saith, Whither I go, ye cannot come.

And he said unto them, Ye are from beneath; I am from above: ye are of this world; I am not of this world. I said therefore unto you, that ye shall die in your sins: for if ye believe not that I am *he*, ye shall die in your sins.

Then said they unto him, Who art thou?

And Jesus saith unto them, Even *the same* that I said unto you from the beginning. I have many things to say and to judge of you: but he that sent me is true; and I speak to the world those things which I have heard of him.

They understood not that he spake to them of the Father. **Then said Jesus unto them, When ye have lifted up the Son of man, then shall ye know that I am *he*, and *that* I do nothing of myself; but as my Father hath taught me, I speak these things. And he that sent me is with me: the Father hath not left me alone; for I do always those things that please him.** As he spake these words, many believed on him. JOHN 8:12–30

Unfortunately, Jesus' disciple Peter had a bit more trouble retaining his single-minded focus when he was distracted. Peter's experience is a good reminder of how we are to think about Jesus, and keep our eyes on him, even when our thoughts get sidetracked or we feel frightened.

Jesus constrained his disciples to get into a ship, and to go before him unto the other side, while he sent the multitudes away. And when he had sent the multitudes away, he went up into a mountain apart to pray: and when the evening was come, he was there alone. But the ship was now in the midst of the sea, tossed with waves: for the wind was contrary.

And in the fourth watch of the night Jesus went unto them, walking on the sea. And when the disciples saw him walking on the sea, they were troubled, saying, It is a spirit; and they cried out for fear.

But straightway Jesus spake unto them, saying, Be of good cheer; it is I; be not afraid.

And Peter answered him and said, Lord, if it be thou, bid me come unto thee on the water.

And he said, Come.

And when Peter was come down out of the ship, he walked on the water, to go to Jesus. But when he saw the wind boisterous, he was afraid; and beginning to sink, he cried, saying, Lord, save me.

And immediately Jesus stretched forth *his* hand, and caught him, and said unto him, O thou of little faith, wherefore didst thou doubt?

And when they were come into the ship, the wind ceased. Then they that were in the ship came and worshipped him, saying, Of a truth thou art the Son of God.   MATTHEW 14:22–33

Can you list some of the things that distract you from putting God first in your life? What can you do to become more focused on God?

Ultimately, the disciples adopted Jesus' bold and unwavering devotion to God and his purposes.

And by the hands of the apostles were many signs and wonders wrought among the people; (and they were all with one accord in Solomon's porch. And of the rest durst no man join himself to them: but the people magnified them. And believers were the more added to the Lord, multitudes both of men and women.) Insomuch that they brought forth the sick into the streets, and laid *them* on beds and couches, that at the least the shadow of Peter passing by might overshadow some of them. There came also a multitude *out* of the cities round about unto Jerusalem, bringing sick folks, and them which were vexed with unclean spirits: and they were healed every one.

Then the high priest rose up, and all they that were with him, (which is the sect of the Sadducees,) and were filled with indignation, And laid their hands on the apostles, and put them in the common prison. But the angel of the Lord by night opened the prison doors, and brought them forth, and said, Go, stand and speak in the temple to the people all the words of this life.

And when they heard *that*, they entered into the temple early in the morning, and taught.

But the high priest came, and they that were with him, and called the council together, and all the senate of the children of Israel, and sent to the prison to have them brought. But when the officers came, and found them not in the prison, they returned, and told, Saying, The prison truly found we shut with all safety, and the keepers standing without before the doors: but when we had opened, we found no man within. Now when the high priest and the captain of the temple and the chief priests heard these things, they doubted of them whereunto this would grow.

Then came one and told them, saying, Behold, the men whom ye put in prison are standing in the temple, and teaching the people. Then went the captain with the officers, and brought them without violence: for they feared the people, lest they should have been stoned.

And when they had brought them, they set *them* before the council: and the high priest asked them, Saying, Did not we straitly command you that ye should not teach in this name? and, behold, ye have filled Jerusalem with your doctrine, and intend to bring this man's blood upon us.

Then Peter and the *other* apostles answered and said, We ought to obey God rather than men. The God of our fathers raised up Jesus, whom ye slew and hanged on a tree. Him hath God exalted with his right hand *to be* a Prince and a Saviour, for to give repentance to Israel, and forgiveness of sins. And we are his witnesses of these things; and *so is* also the Holy Ghost, whom God hath given to them that obey him.

When they heard *that*, they were cut *to the heart*, and took counsel to slay them. Then stood there up one in the council, a Pharisee, named Gamaliel, a doctor of the law, had in reputation among all the people, and commanded to put the apostles forth a little space; And said unto them, Ye men of Israel, take heed to yourselves what ye intend to do as touching these men. For before these days rose up Theudas, boasting himself to be somebody; to whom a number of men, about four hundred, joined themselves: who was slain; and all, as many as obeyed him, were scattered, and brought to nought. After this man rose up Judas of Galilee in the days of the taxing, and drew away much people after him: he also perished; and all, *even* as many as obeyed him, were dispersed. **And now I say unto you, Refrain from these men, and let them alone: for if this counsel or this work be of men, it will come to nought: But if it be of God, ye cannot overthrow it; lest haply ye be found even to fight against God.**

And to him they agreed: and when they had called the apostles, and beaten *them*, they commanded that they should not speak in the name of Jesus, and let them go.

And they departed from the presence of the council, rejoicing that they were counted worthy to suffer shame for his name. **And daily in the temple, and in every house, they ceased not to teach and preach Jesus Christ.**   Acts 5:12–42

PRODUCT OF SINGLE-MINDEDNESS

Near the end of the book of Deuteronomy—and Moses' life—the Lord called the Israelites to make a choice: trust and obey his commands or go their own way. Speaking through Moses, God gave this message to his people. And what was the result of the people's decision? Because they chose obedience, the following seven years were the most fruitful years in Israel's history—the glory days!

(For ye know how we have dwelt in the land of Egypt; and how we came through the nations which ye passed by; And ye have seen their abominations, and their idols, wood and stone, silver and gold, which *were* among them:) Lest there should be among you man, or woman, or family, or tribe, whose heart turneth away this day from the LORD our God, to go *and* serve the gods of these nations; lest there should be among you a root that beareth gall and wormwood;

And it come to pass, when he heareth the words of this curse, that he bless himself in his heart, saying, I shall have peace, though I walk in the imagination of mine heart, to add drunkenness to thirst: The LORD will not spare him, but then the anger of the LORD and his jealousy shall smoke against that man, and all the curses that are written in this book shall lie upon him, and theLORD shall blot out his name from under heaven. And the LORD shall separate him unto evil out of all the tribes of Israel, according to all the curses of the covenant that are written in this book of the law:

So that the generation to come of your children that shall rise up after you, and the stranger that shall come from a far land, shall say, when they see the plagues of that land, and the sicknesses which the LORD hath laid upon it; *And that* the whole land thereof *is* brimstone, and salt, *and* burning, *that* it is not sown, nor beareth, nor any grass groweth therein, like the overthrow of Sodom, and Gomorrah, Admah, and Zeboim, which the LORD overthrew in his anger, and in his wrath: Even all nations shall say, Wherefore hath the LORD done thus unto this land? what *meaneth* the heat of this great anger?

Then men shall say, Because they have forsaken the covenant of the LORD God of their fathers, which he made with them when he brought them forth out of the land of Egypt: For they went and served other gods, and worshipped them, gods whom they knew not, and *whom* he had not given unto them: And the anger of the LORD was kindled against this land, to bring upon it all the curses that are written in this book: And the LORD rooted them out of their land in anger, and in wrath, and in great indignation, and cast them into another land, as *it is* this day.

The secret *things belong* unto the LORD our God: but those

things which are revealed ***belong*** **unto us and to our children**
for ever, that *we* may do all the words of this law.

And it shall come to pass, when all these things are come upon
thee, the blessing and the curse, which I have set before thee, and
thou shalt call *them* to mind among all the nations, whither the
Lord thy God hath driven thee, And shalt return unto the Lord
thy God, and shalt obey his voice according to all that I command
thee this day, thou and thy children, with all thine heart, and with
all thy soul; That then the Lord thy God will turn thy captivity, and have compassion upon thee, and will return and gather
thee from all the nations, whither the Lord thy God hath scattered thee. If *any* of thine be driven out unto the outmost *parts* of
heaven, from thence will the Lord thy God gather thee, and from
thence will he fetch thee: And the Lord thy God will bring thee
into the land which thy fathers possessed, and thou shalt possess it;
and he will do thee good, and multiply thee above thy fathers. **And**
the Lord thy God will circumcise thine heart, and the heart
of thy seed, to love the Lord thy God with all thine heart, and
with all thy soul, that thou mayest live. And the Lord thy God
will put all these curses upon thine enemies, and on them that
hate thee, which persecuted thee. And thou shalt return and obey
the voice of the Lord, and do all his commandments which I command thee this day. And the Lord thy God will make thee plenteous in every work of thine hand, in the fruit of thy body, and in
the fruit of thy cattle, and in the fruit of thy land, for good: for the
Lord will again rejoice over thee for good, as he rejoiced over thy
fathers: If thou shalt hearken unto the voice of the Lord thy God,
to keep his commandments and his statutes which are written in
this book of the law, *and* if thou turn unto the Lord thy God with
all thine heart, and with all thy soul.

For this commandment which I command thee this day, it *is*
not hidden from thee, neither *is* it far off. It *is* not in heaven, that
thou shouldest say, Who shall go up for us to heaven, and bring it
unto us, that we may hear it, and do it? Neither *is* it beyond the sea,
that thou shouldest say, Who shall go over the sea for us, and bring
it unto us, that we may hear it, and do it? But the word *is* very nigh
unto thee, in thy mouth, and in thy heart, that thou mayest do it.

See, I have set before thee this day life and good, and death and evil; In that I command thee this day to love the LORD thy God, to walk in his ways, and to keep his commandments and his statutes and his judgments, that thou mayest live and multiply: and the LORD thy God shall bless thee in the land whither thou goest to possess it.

But if thine heart turn away, so that thou wilt not hear, but shalt be drawn away, and worship other gods, and serve them; I denounce unto you this day, that ye shall surely perish, *and that* ye shall not prolong *your* days upon the land, whither thou passest over Jordan to go to possess it.

I call heaven and earth to record this day against you, *that* I have set before you life and death, blessing and cursing: therefore choose life, that both thou and thy seed may live: That thou mayest love the LORD thy God, *and* that thou mayest obey his voice, and that thou mayest cleave unto him: for he *is* thy life, and the length of thy days: that thou mayest dwell in the land which the Lord sware unto thy fathers, to Abraham, to Isaac, and to Jacob, to give them. DEUTERONOMY 29:16—30:20

In the New Testament, the apostle Paul also challenged believers to establish a single-minded commitment to God. And with his exhortations came encouraging promises about the fruitful results of such devotion. As it was for the Israelites, so it is with us today: if we single-mindedly focus on Christ and his will for our lives, we will experience our own glory days!

I beseech you therefore, brethren, by the mercies of God, that ye present your bodies a living sacrifice, holy, acceptable unto God, *which is* your reasonable service. **And be not conformed to this world: but be ye transformed by the renewing of your mind, that ye may prove what *is* that good, and acceptable, and perfect, will of God.** ROMANS 12:1–2

If ye then be risen with Christ, seek those things which are above, where Christ sitteth on the right hand of God. **Set your affection on things above, not on things on the earth.** For ye are dead, and your life is hid with Christ in God. When Christ, *who is* our life, shall appear, then shall ye also appear with him in glory. COLOSSIANS 3:1–4

And let the peace of God rule in your hearts, to the which also ye are called in one body; and be ye thankful. Let the word of Christ dwell in you richly in all wisdom; teaching and admonishing one another in psalms and hymns and spiritual songs, singing with grace in your hearts to the Lord. **And whatsoever ye do in word or deed, *do* all in the name of the Lord Jesus, giving thanks to God and the Father by him.**   COLOSSIANS 3:15–17

Paul writes, "Whatsoever ye do in word or deed,
do all in the name of the Lord Jesus."
What does this admonishment mean to you?
Does it change how you prioritize things in your life?

WHAT WE BELIEVE

The practice of single-mindedness is about setting priorities. This involves putting our past decisions and actions behind us and focusing on God's kingdom with help from the Holy Ghost. The Bible presents us with many inspiring profiles of people who have displayed tremendous single-mindedness for God, including King Jehoshaphat in the Old Testament and Jesus in the New Testament. During his early years Peter struggled to "fix his eyes" on Jesus, but later he and the disciples declared with great conviction in the face of persecution, "We ought to obey God rather than men" (Acts 5:29). The product of a life of single-minded determination and focus is an untouchable peace from the hand of the one true God who loves us deeply. Seek first God's kingdom!

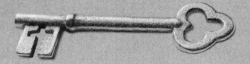

CHAPTER

15

Total Surrender

─────── KEY QUESTION ───────

How do I cultivate a life of sacrificial service?

─────── KEY IDEA ───────

I dedicate my life to God's purposes.

─────── KEY VERSE ───────

I beseech you therefore, brethren,
by the mercies of God, that ye present your bodies
a living sacrifice, holy, acceptable unto God,
which is your reasonable service.
Romans 12:1

OUR MAP

A genuine decision to follow and obey God is a decision of total surrender. We leave nothing off the negotiation table. We are "all in" as a reasonable response to God being "all in" for us. When God the Father offered up his Son for our redemption, he revealed how valuable we are to him. The gift of salvation was an act of total surrender by our Savior. Are you willing to return the gesture? Are you prepared to surrender your life for his purposes?

Total surrender does not occur without some sacrifice, which is illustrated poignantly through the people and stories of the Bible:

- *The Expectation: What God Wants From Us*
- *Profiles of Total Surrender*
- *The Cost of Total Surrender*
- *The Inspiration of Martyrs*

Reflect on the key verse. What do you think it means to offer ourselves as "living sacrifices"? Recalling our study of the practice of worship in Chapter 11, why do you think offering ourselves as a living sacrifice is the reasonable way to serve God?

THE EXPECTATION: WHAT GOD WANTS FROM US

God is often referred to in the Old Testament as "jealous." This passionate description comes out of the language of love, similar to that of a marriage. God is totally committed to us. He, in turn, asks us to be totally committed to him. He will not share our allegiance with anyone or anything else. He made this very clear to the Israelites when he etched the Ten Commandments on the stone tablets. The first three commandments clearly communicate the exclusivity of our relationship with God.

And God spake all these words, saying,

I *am* the LORD thy God, which have brought thee out of the land of Egypt, out of the house of bondage.

Thou shalt have no other gods before me.

Thou shalt not make unto thee any graven image, or any likeness *of any thing* that *is* in heaven above, or that *is* in the earth beneath, or that *is* in the water under the earth: **Thou shalt not bow down thyself to them, nor serve them: for I the L**ORD **thy God** *am* **a jealous God, visiting the iniquity of the fathers upon the children unto the third and fourth** *generation* **of them that hate me; And shewing mercy unto thousands of them that love me, and keep my commandments.**

Thou shalt not take the name of the LORD thy God in vain; for the LORD will not hold him guiltless that taketh his name in vain.

EXODUS 20:1–7

The first three of the Ten Commandments govern our relationship with God. Why do you think it is important to get in a right relationship with God in order to keep the rest of God's commandments?

PROFILES OF TOTAL SURRENDER

Despite having God's expectations written in stone, the Israelites failed to remain faithful. After many years of disobedience, the people suffered when God removed his protection. The northern kingdom of Israel was destroyed by the Assyrians, and the southern kingdom of Judah was conquered by the Babylonians. Before Judah was captured, some of the people were carried off in deportations. Along with Daniel, a small group of bright young men—Shadrach, Meshach and Abed-nego—were selected from the captives to be trained to serve the king. While in captivity, they were forced to make a crucial choice: worship the one true God or compromise and save their lives. They chose total surrender.

Nebuchadnezzar the king made an image of gold, whose height *was* threescore cubits, *and* the breadth thereof six cubits: he set it up in the plain of Dura, in the province of Babylon. Then Nebuchadnezzar the king sent to gather together the princes, the governors, and the captains, the judges, the treasurers, the counsellors, the sheriffs, and all the rulers of the provinces, to come to the dedication of the image which Nebuchadnezzar the king had set up. Then the princes, the governors, and captains, the judges, the treasurers, the counsellors, the sheriffs, and all the rulers of the provinces, were gathered together unto the dedication of the image that Nebuchadnezzar the king had set up; and they stood before the image that Nebuchadnezzar had set up.

Then an herald cried aloud, To you it is commanded, O people, nations, and languages, *That* at what time ye hear the sound of the cornet, flute, harp, sackbut, psaltery, dulcimer, and all kinds of musick, ye fall down and worship the golden image that Nebuchadnezzar the king hath set up: And whoso falleth not down and worshippeth shall the same hour be cast into the midst of a burning fiery furnace.

Therefore at that time, when all the people heard the sound of the cornet, flute, harp, sackbut, psaltery, and all kinds of musick, all the people, the nations, and the languages, fell down *and* worshipped the golden image that Nebuchadnezzar the king had set up.

Wherefore at that time certain Chaldeans came near, and accused the Jews. They spake and said to the king Nebuchadnezzar, O king, live for ever. Thou, O king, hast made a decree, that every man that shall hear the sound of the cornet, flute, harp, sackbut, psaltery, and dulcimer, and all kinds of musick, shall fall down and worship the golden image: And whoso falleth not down and worshippeth, *that* he should be cast into the midst of a burning fiery furnace. There are certain Jews whom thou hast set over the affairs of the province of Babylon, Shadrach, Meshach, and Abednego; these men, O king, have not regarded thee: they serve not thy gods, nor worship the golden image which thou hast set up.

Then Nebuchadnezzar in *his* rage and fury commanded to bring Shadrach, Meshach, and Abed-nego. Then they brought these men before the king. Nebuchadnezzar spake and said unto them, *Is it* true, O Shadrach, Meshach, and Abed-nego, do not ye serve my gods, nor worship the golden image which I have set up? Now if ye be ready that at what time ye hear the sound of the cornet, flute, harp, sackbut, psaltery, and dulcimer, and all kinds of musick, ye fall down and worship the image which I have made; *well*: but if ye worship not, ye shall be cast the same hour into the midst of a burning fiery furnace; and who *is* that God that shall deliver you out of my hands?

Shadrach, Meshach, and Abed-nego, answered and said to the king, O Nebuchadnezzar, we *are* not careful to answer thee in this matter. If it be *so*, our God whom we serve is able to deliver us from the burning fiery furnace, and he will deliver *us* out of thine hand, O king. But if not, be it known unto thee, O king, that we will not serve thy gods, nor worship the golden image which thou hast set up.

Then was Nebuchadnezzar full of fury, and the form of his visage was changed against Shadrach, Meshach, and Abed-nego: *therefore* he spake, and commanded that they should heat the furnace one seven times more than it was wont to be heated. And he commanded the most mighty men that *were* in his army to bind Shadrach, Meshach, and Abed-nego, *and* to cast *them* into the burning fiery furnace. Then these men were bound in their coats, their hosen, and their hats, and their *other* garments, and were cast into the midst of the burning fiery furnace. Therefore because the king's commandment was urgent, and the furnace exceeding hot, the flame of the fire slew those men that took up Shadrach, Meshach, and Abed-nego. And these three men, Shadrach, Meshach, and Abed-nego, fell down bound into the midst of the burning fiery furnace.

Then Nebuchadnezzar the king was astonied, and rose up in haste, *and* spake, and said unto his counsellors, Did not we cast three men bound into the midst of the fire?

They answered and said unto the king, True, O king.

He answered and said, Lo, I see four men loose, walking in the midst of the fire, and they have no hurt; and the form of the fourth is like the Son of God.

Then Nebuchadnezzar came near to the mouth of the burning fiery furnace, *and* spake, and said, Shadrach, Meshach, and Abed-nego, ye servants of the most high God, come forth, and come *hither*.

Then Shadrach, Meshach, and Abed-nego, came forth of the midst of the fire. And the princes, governors, and captains, and the king's counsellors, being gathered together, saw these men, upon whose bodies the fire had no power, nor was an hair of their head singed, neither were their coats changed, nor the smell of fire had passed on them.

Then Nebuchadnezzar spake, and said, Blessed *be* the God of Shadrach, Meshach, and Abed-nego, who hath sent his angel, and delivered his servants that trusted in him, and have changed the king's word, and yielded their bodies, that they might not serve nor worship any god, except their own God.   DANIEL 3:1–28 🔑

About 70 years after the first deportation of Jews to Babylon, the Babylonians were conquered by the Persians. Although King Cyrus of Persia decreed in 538 BC that the Jews could return to Judah, many of them chose not to go home. We know that Esther and her cousin Mordecai stayed in Shushan under the rule of the Persian king, Ahasuerus. When the reigning queen was removed from power, Esther (who kept her Jewish heritage a secret) was selected to replace her. Haman, the king's highest official, hated Mordecai because Mordecai refused to bow down and honor him. As revenge, Haman made plans to kill Mordecai and all the rest of the Jews in Ahasuerus's kingdom. Like Shadrach, Meshach and Abed-nego, Esther had a difficult decision to make: protect her people or protect her position as queen—and perhaps her own life. She chose total surrender.

After these things did king Ahasuerus promote Haman the son of Hammedatha the Agagite, and advanced him, and set his seat above all the princes that *were* with him. And all the king's servants, that *were* in the king's gate, bowed, and reverenced Haman: for the king had so commanded concerning him. But Mordecai bowed not, nor did *him* reverence.

Then the king's servants, which *were* in the king's gate, said unto Mordecai, Why transgressest thou the king's commandment? Now it came to pass, when they spake daily unto him, and he hearkened not unto them, that they told Haman, to see whether Mordecai's matters would stand: for he had told them that he *was* a Jew.

And when Haman saw that Mordecai bowed not, nor did him reverence, then was Haman full of wrath. And he thought scorn to lay hands on Mordecai alone; for they had shewed him the people of Mordecai: wherefore Haman sought to destroy all the Jews that *were* throughout the whole kingdom of Ahasuerus, *even* the people of Mordecai.

In the first month, that *is*, the month Nisan, in the twelfth year of king Ahasuerus, they cast Pur, that *is*, the lot, before Haman from day to day, and from month to month, *to* the twelfth *month*, that *is*, the month Adar.

And Haman said unto king Ahasuerus, There is a certain people scattered abroad and dispersed among the people in all the provinces of thy kingdom; and their laws *are* diverse from all people; neither keep they the king's laws: therefore it *is* not for the king's profit to suffer them. If it please the king, let it be written that they may be destroyed: and I will pay ten thousand talents of silver to the hands of those that have the charge of the business, to bring *it* into the king's treasuries.

And the king took his ring from his hand, and gave it unto Haman the son of Hammedatha the Agagite, the Jews' enemy. And the king said unto Haman, The silver *is* given to thee, the people also, to do with them as it seemeth good to thee.

Then were the king's scribes called on the thirteenth day of the first month, and there was written according to all that Haman had commanded unto the king's lieutenants, and to the governors that *were* over every province, and to the rulers of every people of every province according to the writing thereof, and *to* every people after their language; in the name of king Ahasuerus was it written, and sealed with the king's ring. And the letters were sent by posts into all the king's provinces, to destroy, to kill, and to cause to perish, all Jews, both young and old, little children and women, in one day, *even* upon the thirteenth *day* of the twelfth month, which *is* the month Adar, and *to take* the spoil of them for a prey. The copy of the writing for a commandment to be given in every province was published unto all people, that they should be ready against that day.

The posts went out, being hastened by the king's commandment, and the decree was given in Shushan the palace. And the king and Haman sat down to drink; but the city Shushan was perplexed.

When Mordecai perceived all that was done, Mordecai rent his clothes, and put on sackcloth with ashes, and went out into the midst of the city, and cried with a loud and a bitter cry; And came even before the king's gate: for none *might* enter into the king's gate clothed with sackcloth. And in every province, whithersoever the king's commandment and his decree came, *there was* great mourning among the Jews, and fasting, and weeping, and wailing; and many lay in sackcloth and ashes.

So Esther's maids and her chamberlains came and told *it* her. Then was the queen exceedingly grieved; and she sent raiment to clothe Mordecai, and to take away his sackcloth from him: but he received *it* not. Then called Esther for Hatach, *one* of the king's chamberlains, whom he had appointed to attend upon her, and gave him a commandment to Mordecai, to know what it *was*, and why it *was*.

So Hatach went forth to Mordecai unto the street of the city, which *was* before the king's gate. And Mordecai told him of all that had happened unto him, and of the sum of the money that Haman had promised to pay to the king's treasuries for the Jews, to destroy them. Also he gave him the copy of the writing of the decree that was given at Shushan to destroy them, to shew *it* unto Esther, and to declare *it* unto her, and to charge her that she should go in unto the king, to make supplication unto him, and to make request before him for her people.

And Hatach came and told Esther the words of Mordecai. Again Esther spake unto Hatach, and gave him commandment unto Mordecai; All the king's servants, and the people of the king's provinces, do know, that whosoever, whether man or woman, shall come unto the king into the inner court, who is not called, *there is* one law of his to put *him* to death, except such to whom the king shall hold out the golden sceptre, that he may live: but I have not been called to come in unto the king these thirty days.

And they told to Mordecai Esther's words. Then Mordecai commanded to answer Esther, Think not with thyself that thou shalt escape in the king's house, more than all the Jews. For if thou altogether holdest thy peace at this time, *then* shall there enlargement and deliverance arise to the Jews from another place; but thou and thy father's house shall be destroyed: and who knoweth whether thou art come to the kingdom for *such* a time as this?

Then Esther bade *them* return Mordecai *this answer*, **Go, gather together all the Jews that are present in Shushan, and fast ye for me, and neither eat nor drink three days, night or day: I also and my maidens will fast likewise; and so will I go in unto the king, which *is* not according to the law: and if I perish, I perish.** ESTHER 3:1—4:16

THE COST OF TOTAL SURRENDER

A commitment to surrender completely to God's purposes is easy to say but hard to do. Jesus made this clear to his disciples and never masked the harsh reality they would encounter or the impact it would have on their lives. He also never shied away from difficult conversations, as is obvious from his interactions with Peter regarding the disciple's betrayal before Jesus' death. Through Peter's story, we learn that the cost of total surrender can sometimes feel like it's too much to bear.

And [Jesus] said to *them* all, If any *man* will come after me, let him deny himself, and take up his cross daily, and follow me. For whosoever will save his life shall lose it: but whosoever will lose his life for my sake, the same shall save it. For what is a man advantaged, if he gain the whole world, and lose himself, or be cast away? For whosoever shall be ashamed of me and of my words, of him shall the Son of man be ashamed, when he shall come in his own glory, and *in his* Father's, and of the holy angels. LUKE 9:23–26

And there was also a strife among them, which of them should be accounted the greatest. And he said unto them, The kings of the Gentiles exercise lordship over them; and they that exercise authority upon them are called benefactors. But ye *shall* not *be* so: but he that is greatest among you, let him be as the younger; and he that is chief, as he that doth serve. For whether *is* greater, he that sitteth at meat, or he that serveth? *is* not he that sitteth at meat? but I am among you as he that serveth. Ye are they which have continued with me in my temptations. And I appoint unto you a kingdom, as my Father hath appointed unto me; That ye may eat and drink at my table in my kingdom, and sit on thrones judging the twelve tribes of Israel.

And the Lord said, Simon, Simon, behold, Satan hath desired *to have* you, that he may sift *you* as wheat: But I have prayed for thee, that thy faith fail not: and when thou art converted, strengthen thy brethren.

And he said unto him, Lord, I am ready to go with thee, both into prison, and to death.

And he said, I tell thee, Peter, the cock shall not crow this day, before that thou shalt thrice deny that thou knowest me.

And he said unto them, When I sent you without purse, and scrip, and shoes, lacked ye any thing?

And they said, Nothing.

Then said he unto them, But now, he that hath a purse, let him take *it*, and likewise *his* scrip: and he that hath no sword, let him sell his garment, and buy one. For I say unto you, that this that is written must yet be accomplished in me, And he was reckoned among the transgressors: for the things concerning me have an end.

And they said, Lord, behold, here *are* two swords.

And he said unto them, It is enough.

And he came out, and went, as he was wont, to the mount of Olives; and his disciples also followed him. And when he was at the place, he said unto them, Pray that ye enter not into temptation. And he was withdrawn from them about a stone's cast, and kneeled down, and prayed, Saying, Father, if thou be willing, remove this cup from me: nevertheless not my will, but thine, be done. And there appeared an angel unto him from heaven, strengthening him. And being in an agony he prayed more earnestly: and his sweat was as it were great drops of blood falling down to the ground.

And when he rose up from prayer, and was come to his disciples, he found them sleeping for sorrow, And said unto them, Why sleep ye? rise and pray, lest ye enter into temptation.

And while he yet spake, behold a multitude, and he that was called Judas, one of the twelve, went before them, and drew near unto Jesus to kiss him. But Jesus said unto him, Judas, betrayest thou the Son of man with a kiss?

When they which were about him saw what would follow, they said unto him, Lord, shall we smite with the sword? And one of them smote the servant of the high priest, and cut off his right ear.

And Jesus answered and said, Suffer ye thus far. And he touched his ear, and healed him.

Then Jesus said unto the chief priests, and captains of the temple, and the elders, which were come to him, Be ye come out, as against a thief, with swords and staves? When I was daily with you in the temple, ye stretched forth no hands against me: but this is your hour, and the power of darkness.

Then took they him, and led *him*, and brought him into the high priest's house. And Peter followed afar off. And when they had kindled a fire in the midst of the hall, and were set down together, Peter sat down among them. But a certain maid beheld him as he sat by the fire, and earnestly looked upon him, and said, This man was also with him.

And he denied him, saying, Woman, I know him not.

And after a little while another saw him, and said, Thou art also of them.

And Peter said, Man, I am not.

And about the space of one hour after another confidently affirmed, saying, Of a truth this *fellow* also was with him: for he is a Galilaean.

And Peter said, Man, I know not what thou sayest. And immediately, while he yet spake, the cock crew. And the Lord turned, and looked upon Peter. And Peter remembered the word of the Lord, how he had said unto him, Before the cock crow, thou shalt deny me thrice. And Peter went out, and wept bitterly. LUKE 22:24–62

What did Jesus mean when he instructed the disciples to "take up their cross daily"? Why does Jesus say this is a wise decision to make?

THE INSPIRATION OF MARTYRS

Despite his betrayal, Peter was graciously given a second chance to prove he was totally surrendered to God's purposes. After Jesus' resurrection, Jesus forgave and reinstated Peter to a leadership position. Peter boldly lived out his faith and later in his life, according to ancient tradition, was crucified upside down—perhaps because he didn't feel worthy of dying as Christ had.

Stephen, however, was the first martyr of the Christian church. Although he was not an apostle, he played an important role in the early church by ministering to the widows in Jerusalem and by being a powerful witness for Jesus. His death triggered a tidal wave of persecution in the first century. Stephen was brought before the Sanhedrin where he courageously put his total surrender to God on display.

And Stephen, full of faith and power, did great wonders and miracles among the people. Then there arose certain of the synagogue, which is called *the synagogue* of the Libertines, and Cyrenians, and Alexandrians, and of them of Cilicia and of Asia, disputing with Stephen. And they were not able to resist the wisdom and the spirit by which he spake.

Then they suborned men, which said, We have heard him speak blasphemous words against Moses, and *against* God.

And they stirred up the people, and the elders, and the scribes, and came upon *him*, and caught him, and brought *him* to the council, And set up false witnesses, which said, This man ceaseth not to speak blasphemous words against this holy place, and the law: For we have heard him say, that this Jesus of Nazareth shall destroy this place, and shall change the customs which Moses delivered us.

And all that sat in the council, looking stedfastly on him, saw his face as it had been the face of an angel.

Then said the high priest, Are these things so?

And he said, Men, brethren, and fathers, hearken; The God of glory appeared unto our father Abraham, when he was in Mesopotamia, before he dwelt in Charran, And said unto him, Get thee out of thy country, and from thy kindred, and come into the land which I shall shew thee.

Then came he out of the land of the Chaldeans, and dwelt in Charran: and from thence, when his father was dead, he removed him into this land, wherein ye now dwell. And he gave him none inheritance in it, no, not *so much as* to set his foot on: yet he promised that he would give it to him for a possession, and to his seed after him, when *as yet* he had no child. And God spake on this wise, That his seed should sojourn in a strange land; and that they should bring them into bondage, and entreat *them* evil four hundred years. And the nation to whom they shall be in bondage will I judge, said God: and after that shall they come forth, and serve me in this place. And he gave him the covenant of circumcision: and so *Abraham* begat Isaac, and circumcised him the eighth day; and Isaac *begat* Jacob; and Jacob *begat* the twelve patriarchs.

And the patriarchs, moved with envy, sold Joseph into Egypt: but God was with him, And delivered him out of all his afflictions, and gave him favour and wisdom in the sight of Pharaoh king of Egypt; and he made him governor over Egypt and all his house.

Now there came a dearth over all the land of Egypt and Chanaan, and great affliction: and our fathers found no sustenance. But when Jacob heard that there was corn in Egypt, he sent out our fathers first. And at the second *time* Joseph was made known to his brethren; and Joseph's kindred was made known unto Pharaoh. Then sent Joseph, and called his father Jacob to *him*, and all his kindred, threescore and fifteen souls. So Jacob went down into Egypt, and died, he, and our fathers, And were carried over into Sychem, and laid in the sepulchre that Abraham bought for a sum of money of the sons of Emmor *the father* of Sychem.

But when the time of the promise drew nigh, which God had sworn to Abraham, the people grew and multiplied in Egypt, Till another king arose, which knew not Joseph. The same dealt subtilly with our kindred, and evil entreated our fathers, so that they cast out their young children, to the end they might not live.

In which time Moses was born, and was exceeding fair, and nourished up in his father's house three months: And when he was cast out, Pharaoh's daughter took him up, and nourished him for her own son. And Moses was learned in all the wisdom of the Egyptians, and was mighty in words and in deeds.

And when he was full forty years old, it came into his heart to visit his brethren the children of Israel. And seeing one *of them* suffer wrong, he defended *him*, and avenged him that was oppressed, and smote the Egyptian: For he supposed his brethren would have understood how that God by his hand would deliver them: but they understood not. And the next day he shewed himself unto them as they strove, and would have set them at one again, saying, Sirs, ye are brethren; why do ye wrong one to another?

But he that did his neighbour wrong thrust him away, saying, Who made thee a ruler and a judge over us? Wilt thou kill me, as thou diddest the Egyptian yesterday? Then fled Moses at this saying, and was a stranger in the land of Madian, where he begat two sons.

And when forty years were expired, there appeared to him in the wilderness of mount Sina an angel of the Lord in a flame of fire in a bush. When Moses saw *it*, he wondered at the sight: and as he drew near to behold *it*, the voice of the Lord came unto him, *Saying*, I *am* the God of thy fathers, the God of Abraham, and the God of Isaac, and the God of Jacob. Then Moses trembled, and durst not behold.

Then said the Lord to him, Put off thy shoes from thy feet: for the place where thou standest is holy ground. I have seen, I have seen the affliction of my people which is in Egypt, and I have heard their groaning, and am come down to deliver them. And now come, I will send thee into Egypt.

This Moses whom they refused, saying, Who made thee a ruler and a judge? the same did God send *to be* a ruler and a deliverer by the hand of the angel which appeared to him in the bush. He brought them out, after that he had shewed wonders and signs in the land of Egypt, and in the Red sea, and in the wilderness forty years.

This is that Moses, which said unto the children of Israel, A prophet shall the Lord your God raise up unto you of your brethren, like unto me; him shall ye hear. This is he, that was in the church in the wilderness with the angel which spake to him in the mount Sina, and *with* our fathers: who received the lively oracles to give unto us:

To whom our fathers would not obey, but thrust *him* from them, and in their hearts turned back again into Egypt, Saying unto Aaron, Make us gods to go before us: for *as for* this Moses, which brought us out of the land of Egypt, we wot not what is become of him. And they made a calf in those days, and offered sacrifice unto the idol, and rejoiced in the works of their own hands. Then God turned, and gave them up to worship the host of heaven; as it is written in the book of the prophets, O ye house of Israel, have ye offered to me slain beasts and sacrifices *by the space of* forty years in the wilderness? Yea, ye took up the tabernacle of Moloch, and the star of your god Remphan, figures which ye made to worship them: and I will carry you away beyond Babylon.

Our fathers had the tabernacle of witness in the wilderness, as he had appointed, speaking unto Moses, that he should make it according to the fashion that he had seen. Which also our fathers that came after brought in with Jesus into the possession of the Gentiles, whom God drave out before the face of our fathers, unto the days of David; Who found favour before God, and desired to find a tabernacle for the God of Jacob. But Solomon built him an house.

Howbeit the most High dwelleth not in temples made with hands; as saith the prophet, Heaven *is* my throne, and earth *is* my footstool: what house will ye build me? saith the Lord: or what *is* the place of my rest? Hath not my hand made all these things?

Ye stiffnecked and uncircumcised in heart and ears, ye do always resist the Holy Ghost: as your fathers *did*, so *do* ye. Which of the prophets have not your fathers persecuted? and they have slain them which shewed before of the coming of the Just One; of whom ye have been now the betrayers and murderers: Who have received the law by the disposition of angels, and have not kept *it*.

When they heard these things, they were cut to the heart, and they gnashed on him with *their* teeth. But he, being full of the Holy Ghost, looked up stedfastly into heaven, and saw the glory of God, and Jesus standing on the right hand of God, And said, Behold, I see the heavens opened, and the Son of man standing on the right hand of God.

Then they cried out with a loud voice, and stopped their ears, and ran upon him with one accord, And cast *him* out of the city, and stoned *him*: and the witnesses laid down their clothes at a young man's feet, whose name was Saul.

And they stoned Stephen, calling upon *God*, and saying, Lord Jesus, receive my spirit. And he kneeled down, and cried with a loud voice, Lord, lay not this sin to their charge. And when he had said this, he fell asleep. ACTS 6:8—7:60

Compare and contrast Stephen's story with the story of
Shadrach, Meshach and Abed-nego. Compare Stephen's death
with the death of Christ. Which detail of each story
best exemplifies total surrender?

Another martyr of the early church was the apostle Paul. While traveling throughout the Roman Empire on numerous missionary journeys, Paul formed countless close friendships and made some serious enemies. Knowing that severe hardship was in his future, he met with many believers for what he assumed would be one last time.

And finding disciples, we tarried there seven days: who said to Paul through the Spirit, that he should not go up to Jerusalem. And when we had accomplished those days, we departed and went our way; and they all brought us on our way, with wives and children, till *we were* out of the city: and we kneeled down on the shore, and prayed. And when we had taken our leave one of another, we took ship; and they returned home again.

And when we had finished *our* course from Tyre, we came to Ptolemais, and saluted the brethren, and abode with them one day. And the next *day* we that were of Paul's company departed, and came unto Caesarea: and we entered into the house of Philip the evangelist, which was *one* of the seven; and abode with him. And the same man had four daughters, virgins, which did prophesy.

And as we tarried *there* many days, there came down from Judaea a certain prophet, named Agabus. And when he was come unto us, he took Paul's girdle, and bound his own hands and feet, and said, Thus saith the Holy Ghost, So shall the Jews at Jerusalem bind the man that owneth this girdle, and shall deliver *him* into the hands of the Gentiles.

And when we heard these things, both we, and they of that place, besought him not to go up to Jerusalem. **Then Paul answered, What mean ye to weep and to break mine heart? for I am ready not to be bound only, but also to die at Jerusalem for the name of the Lord Jesus. And when he would not be persuaded, we ceased, saying, The will of the Lord be done.**

ACTS 21:4–14

The predictions made by Agabus were correct. Paul was arrested in Jerusalem and spent a couple of years imprisoned in Caesarea before finally being shipped to Rome, where he remained under house arrest for a couple more years. Jesus promised that when we lose our life we will truly find it. Surrendering his life for God's purposes was Paul's ultimate goal. Will you make it yours?

But I would ye should understand, brethren, that the things *which happened* unto me have fallen out rather unto the furtherance of the gospel; So that my bonds in Christ are manifest in all the palace, and in all other *places*; And many of the brethren in the Lord, waxing confident by my bonds, are much more bold to speak the word without fear.

Some indeed preach Christ even of envy and strife; and some also of good will: The one preach Christ of contention, not sincerely, supposing to add affliction to my bonds: But the other of love, knowing that I am set for the defence of the gospel. What then? notwithstanding, every way, whether in pretence, or in truth, Christ is preached; and I therein do rejoice, yea, and will rejoice.

For I know that this shall turn to my salvation through your prayer, and the supply of the Spirit of Jesus Christ, **According to my earnest expectation and *my* hope, that in nothing I shall be ashamed, but *that* with all boldness, as always, *so* now also Christ shall be magnified in my body, whether *it be* by life, or by death. For to me to live *is* Christ, and to die *is* gain.**

PHILIPPIANS 1:12–21

Which of the stories you've read
inspires you the most? Why?

WHAT WE BELIEVE

The decision to dedicate our lives to God's purposes is a daily practice. Jesus instructed his disciples to take up their cross daily and follow him. God expects this kind of dedication from us as well. Part of this dedication includes being a "living sacrifice," which requires a daily decision to crawl up on the altar. Thankfully, we can find inspiration from the stories of many courageous and faithful followers of God, including Shadrach, Meshach, Abed-nego, Esther, Stephen and Paul. We can also find comfort from the life of Peter, who denied Jesus three times in some of the most critical moments of Jesus' life. Because of the unconditional love he had for him, Jesus restored Peter. And he will do the same for us!

CHAPTER

16

Biblical Community

―――――― KEY QUESTION ――――――

How do I develop healthy relationships with others?

―――――――― KEY IDEA ――――――――

I fellowship with Christians to accomplish God's purposes
in my life, in the lives of others and in the world.

――――――――― KEY VERSE ―――――――――

And all that believed were together, and had all things common;
And sold their possessions and goods, and parted them to all
men, as every man had need. And they, continuing daily with
one accord in the temple, and breaking bread from house to
house, did eat their meat with gladness and singleness of heart,
Praising God, and having favour with all the people. And the
Lord added to the church daily such as should be saved.

Acts 2:44 – 47

We are at the halfway point in our study of the ten key practices. The first five deepen our relationship with God: worship, prayer, Bible study, single-mindedness and total surrender. Now we shift to those that bless our relationships with people around us. The first of these is Biblical community.

We believe the one true God wants to be in a relationship with us for eternity. To make that possible, God provided the way to restore our relationship with him—through the sacrifice of his Son, Jesus Christ. All those who believe receive a new identity and come together to form a new community called the church. It is through the church that God will accomplish his primary purposes on earth.

Biblical community is essential to the Christian life and a vital aspect of the church. As we engage in this new family under God's leadership, we not only achieve God's purposes in our lives, in the lives of others and in the world, but we also reinforce our belief in God and his church.

Here are the big ideas we will be exploring in this chapter:

- *Created for Community*
- *The Presence of God*
- *The New Community*
- *Marks of Biblical Community*

CREATED FOR COMMUNITY

From the creation account in previous chapters we learned about the Trinity and the origin of sin. Both are necessary to revisit as we talk about how we were created for community. From the beginning, God designed and hardwired us for community. Biblical community is both vertical and horizontal, between God and us, and between us and others. When God planted the garden in Eden, he established one rule that would guard Adam's ability to be in unbroken community with him—to eat from any tree but the tree of the knowledge of good and evil. Then he created Eve, so that Adam, like God, would not be alone but would have a being out of his own essence with whom to be in community.

These *are* the generations of the heavens and of the earth when they were created, in the day that the LORD God made the earth and the heavens,

And every plant of the field before it was in the earth, and every herb of the field before it grew: for the LORD God had not caused it to rain upon the earth, and *there was* not a man to till the ground. But there went up a mist from the earth, and watered the whole face of the ground. And the LORD God formed man *of* the dust of the ground, and breathed into his nostrils the breath of life; and man became a living soul.

And the LORD God planted a garden eastward in Eden; and there he put the man whom he had formed. And out of the ground made the LORD God to grow every tree that is pleasant to the sight, and good for food; the tree of life also in the midst of the garden, and the tree of knowledge of good and evil.

And a river went out of Eden to water the garden; and from thence it was parted, and became into four heads. The name of the first *is* Pison: that *is* it which compasseth the whole land of Havilah, where *there is* gold; And the gold of that land *is* good: there *is* bdellium and the onyx stone. And the name of the second river *is* Gihon: the same *is* it that compasseth the whole land of Ethiopia. And the name of the third river *is* Hiddekel: that *is* it which goeth toward the east of Assyria. And the fourth river *is* Euphrates.

And the LORD God took the man, and put him into the garden of Eden to dress it and to keep it. And the LORD God commanded the man, saying, Of every tree of the garden thou mayest freely eat: But of the tree of the knowledge of good and evil, thou shalt not eat of it: for in the day that thou eatest thereof thou shalt surely die.

And the LORD God said, *It is* not good that the man should be alone; I will make him an help meet for him.

And out of the ground the LORD God formed every beast of the field, and every fowl of the air; and brought *them* unto Adam to see what he would call them: and whatsoever Adam called every living creature, that *was* the name thereof. And Adam gave names to all cattle, and to the fowl of the air, and to every beast of the field; **but for Adam there was not found an help meet for him.**

And the LORD God caused a deep sleep to fall upon Adam, and he slept: and he took one of his ribs, and closed up the flesh instead thereof; And the rib, which the LORD God had taken from man, made he a woman, and brought her unto the man.

And Adam said, This *is* now bone of my bones, and flesh of my flesh: she shall be called Woman, because she was taken out of Man. Therefore shall a man leave his father and his mother, and shall cleave unto his wife: and they shall be one flesh.

And they were both naked, the man and his wife, and were not ashamed. GENESIS 2:4–25

Community is not a "nice-to-have" addition, but an essential experience for living a godly and healthy life. God intended for humans to have rich, life-giving relationships with each other; relationships energized and motivated by the actual presence of God among them. Adam and Eve experienced this perfect ideal in the garden. But their rejection of God's vision for their life together caused them to be escorted from the garden and out of community with God. This separation from God and the presence of sin in every human being's nature is a perpetual challenge to creating strong community. But it is clear from God's Word that people were not meant for separation from him and isolation from one another.

There is one *alone*, and there is not a second; yea, he hath neither child nor brother: yet *is there* no end of all his labour; neither is his eye satisfied with riches; neither *saith he*, For whom do I labour, and bereave my soul of good? This *is* also vanity, yea, it *is* a sore travail.

Two *are* better than one; because they have a good reward for their labour. For if they fall, the one will lift up his fellow: but woe to him *that is* alone when he falleth; for *he hath* not another to help him up. Again, if two lie together, then they have heat: but how can one be warm *alone*? And if one prevail against him, two shall withstand him; and a threefold cord is not quickly broken. ECCLESIASTES 4:8–12

The passage above from Ecclesiastes 4 describes a relationship
between two people. Why, then, does the Preacher say
"a threefold cord" is not quickly broken?

THE PRESENCE OF GOD

*In order to sustain life-giving community, God must be at the
center of it. But Adam and Eve rejected him in the garden, so
community with God and with each other was difficult to recapture. But God never gave up on us, and the narrative of the Bible
traces God's efforts to get back into community with us. After
delivering Israel from bondage in Egypt, the Lord informed
Moses of his intent to be with his people in a tent known as the
tabernacle.*

And the LORD spake unto Moses, saying, Speak unto the children of Israel, that they bring me an offering: of every man that
giveth it willingly with his heart ye shall take my offering. And
this *is* the offering which ye shall take of them; gold, and silver, and
brass, And blue, and purple, and scarlet, and fine linen, and goats'
hair, And rams' skins dyed red, and badgers' skins, and shittim
wood, Oil for the light, spices for anointing oil, and for sweet incense, Onyx stones, and stones to be set in the ephod, and in the
breastplate.

**And let them make me a sanctuary; that I may dwell among
them. According to all that I shew thee, *after* the pattern of the
tabernacle, and the pattern of all the instruments thereof, even
so shall ye make *it*.**   EXODUS 25:1–9

*God's presence would be represented by the ark of the testimony—an elaborate box containing the Ten Commandments
tablets, a gold jar filled with manna, and Aaron's staff. The ark
was placed in a special room in the tabernacle called the holy
place, which was sectioned off by a thick curtain or "vail." While
Moses and the Israelites were camped at the foot of Mount Sinai,
they finished the building and preparation necessary to set up
the tabernacle.*

And the LORD spake unto Moses, saying, On the first day of the first month shalt thou set up the tabernacle of the tent of the congregation. And thou shalt put therein the ark of the testimony, and cover the ark with the vail. And thou shalt bring in the table, and set in order the things that are to be set in order upon it; and thou shalt bring in the candlestick, and light the lamps thereof. And thou shalt set the altar of gold for the incense before the ark of the testimony, and put the hanging of the door to the tabernacle.

And thou shalt set the altar of the burnt offering before the door of the tabernacle of the tent of the congregation. And thou shalt set the laver between the tent of the congregation and the altar, and shalt put water therein. And thou shalt set up the court round about, and hang up the hanging at the court gate.

And thou shalt take the anointing oil, and anoint the tabernacle, and all that *is* therein, and shalt hallow it, and all the vessels thereof: and it shall be holy. And thou shalt anoint the altar of the burnt offering, and all his vessels, and sanctify the altar: and it shall be an altar most holy. And thou shalt anoint the laver and his foot, and sanctify it.

And thou shalt bring Aaron and his sons unto the door of the tabernacle of the congregation, and wash them with water. And thou shalt put upon Aaron the holy garments, and anoint him, and sanctify him; that he may minister unto me in the priest's office. And thou shalt bring his sons, and clothe them with coats: And thou shalt anoint them, as thou didst anoint their father, that they may minister unto me in the priest's office: for their anointing shall surely be an everlasting priesthood throughout their generations. Thus did Moses: according to all that the LORD commanded him, so did he. And it came to pass in the first month in the second year, on the first *day* of the month, *that* the tabernacle was reared up.   Exodus 40:1–17

Then a cloud covered the tent of the congregation, and the glory of the LORD filled the tabernacle. And Moses was not able to enter into the tent of the congregation, because the cloud abode thereon, and the glory of the LORD filled the tabernacle.

Exodus 40:34–35

The cloud, symbolic of God's glory that had led the Israelites after their escape from Egypt, covered and filled the newly established tabernacle. About 500 years later, the Israelites built a temple in Jerusalem to replace the tabernacle with a permanent place where they could meet with God. Then God's glory came down after King Solomon's prayer at the dedication of that temple.

Now when Solomon had made an end of praying, the fire came down from heaven, and consumed the burnt offering and the sacrifices; and the glory of the LORD filled the house. And the priests could not enter into the house of the LORD, because the glory of the LORD had filled the LORD's house. And when all the children of Israel saw how the fire came down, and the glory of the LORD upon the house, they bowed themselves with their faces to the ground upon the pavement, and worshipped, and praised the LORD, *saying*, For *he is* good; for his mercy *endureth* for ever.

2 CHRONICLES 7:1–3

In the New Testament, God's presence among his people changed to a new location. Simultaneous with the death of Jesus on the cross, the heavy vail hanging in front of the holy place that quarantined God's people from God's presence was torn from top to bottom. God's presence was no longer isolated to this small room in the temple. Forgiveness of sins was now available to all. Paul instructs us on the new "temple" for God's presence.

As you read the passage below from Ephesians 2, look for the differences between the two dwelling places for God: the temple and the New Testament church. What barriers are there in each of the two places? Who is allowed into each place? What is the cornerstone of each place?

Wherefore remember, that ye *being* in time past Gentiles in the flesh, who are called Uncircumcision by that which is called the Circumcision in the flesh made by hands; That at that time ye were without Christ, being aliens from the commonwealth of

Israel, and strangers from the covenants of promise, having no hope, and without God in the world: But now in Christ Jesus ye who sometimes were far off are made nigh by the blood of Christ.

For he is our peace, who hath made both one, and hath broken down the middle wall of partition *between us*; Having abolished in his flesh the enmity, *even* the law of commandments *contained* in ordinances; for to make in himself of twain one new man, *so* making peace; And that he might reconcile both unto God in one body by the cross, having slain the enmity thereby: And came and preached peace to you which were afar off, and to them that were nigh. For through him we both have access by one Spirit unto the Father.

Now therefore ye are no more strangers and foreigners, but fellowcitizens with the saints, and of the household of God; And are built upon the foundation of the apostles and prophets, Jesus Christ himself being the chief corner *stone*; In whom all the building fitly framed together groweth unto an holy temple in the Lord: In whom ye also are builded together for an habitation of God through the Spirit. EPHESIANS 2:11–22

THE NEW COMMUNITY

After the resurrection of Jesus and before his ascension back to the Father, Jesus told the disciples to wait in Jerusalem for the indwelling of the Holy Ghost. As promised, the actual presence of God descended on the believers in Jesus Christ—the new "temple." We read about the arrival of the Holy Ghost on the day of Pentecost when we studied the birth of the church. Now we read further to discover that with God's presence dwelling in the hearts of believers, their potential for vibrant community with each other escalated.

And when the day of Pentecost was fully come, they were all with one accord in one place. And suddenly there came a sound from heaven as of a rushing mighty wind, and it filled all the house where they were sitting. And there appeared unto them cloven tongues like as of fire, and it sat upon each of them. And they were all filled with the Holy Ghost, and began to speak with other tongues, as the Spirit gave them utterance. ACTS 2:1–4

And they continued stedfastly in the apostles' doctrine and fellowship, and in breaking of bread, and in prayers. And fear came upon every soul: and many wonders and signs were done by the apostles. **And all that believed were together, and had all things common;** And sold their possessions and goods, and parted them to all *men*, as every man had need. And they, continuing daily with one accord in the temple, and breaking bread from house to house, did eat their meat with gladness and singleness of heart, Praising God, and having favour with all the people. And the Lord added to the church daily such as should be saved. ACTS 2:42–47

And the multitude of them that believed were of one heart and of one soul: neither said any *of them* that ought of the things which he possessed was his own; but they had all things common. And with great power gave the apostles witness of the resurrection of the Lord Jesus: and great grace was upon them all. Neither was there any among them that lacked: for as many as were possessors of lands or houses sold them, and brought the prices of the things that were sold, And laid *them* down at the apostles' feet: and distribution was made unto every man according as he had need.

And Joses, who by the apostles was surnamed Barnabas, (which is, being interpreted, The son of consolation,) a Levite, *and* of the country of Cyprus, Having land, sold *it*, and brought the money, and laid *it* at the apostles' feet. ACTS 4:32–37 ⚷

Imagine what it would have been like to be a member of the early church after Pentecost. Would you have wanted to be a part of that community? Why or why not? In what ways should the early church be a model for churches today?

During the first century, it proved difficult for many Jewish converts to overcome the pressure and persecution they received from other family members who remained in Judaism. The author of Hebrews wrote a letter to these believers to convince them of the superiority of Christ over the law and to encourage them to lean heavily into their new community of faith in order to persevere.

Having therefore, brethren, boldness to enter into the holiest by the blood of Jesus, By a new and living way, which he hath consecrated for us, through the veil, that is to say, his flesh; And *having* an high priest over the house of God; Let us draw near with a true heart in full assurance of faith, having our hearts sprinkled from an evil conscience, and our bodies washed with pure water. Let us hold fast the profession of *our* faith without wavering; (for he *is* faithful that promised;) **And let us consider one another to provoke unto love and to good works: Not forsaking the assembling of ourselves together, as the manner of some *is*; but exhorting *one another*: and so much the more, as ye see the day approaching.** HEBREWS 10:19–25

It doesn't take hundreds of people to gather to make a difference and accomplish God's purposes. Jesus said it just takes a few who are committed to gathering around a common purpose.

For where two or three are gathered together in my name, there am I in the midst of them. MATTHEW 18:20

MARKS OF BIBLICAL COMMUNITY

Biblical community engages all its members to use their gifts, resources and time in unison to accomplish a task important to the plan of God. The Israelites returned from 70 years of captivity and were rebuilding their lives under the reign of God. Nehemiah returned to spearhead the rebuilding of the wall around the city to protect them from bullying from the surrounding nations. Everyone, including children, was called to help. As you read this story, you might be tempted to quickly skim over the many names. To help you, imagine that your family's name was recorded in connection with this important community project.

So I [Nehemiah] came to Jerusalem, and was there three days. And I arose in the night, I and some few men with me; neither told I *any* man what my God had put in my heart to do at Jerusalem: neither *was there any* beast with me, save the beast that I rode upon.

And I went out by night by the gate of the valley, even before the dragon well, and to the dung port, and viewed the walls of Jerusalem, which were broken down, and the gates thereof were consumed with fire. Then I went on to the gate of the fountain, and to the king's pool: but *there was* no place for the beast *that was* under me to pass. Then went I up in the night by the brook, and viewed the wall, and turned back, and entered by the gate of the valley, and *so* returned. And the rulers knew not whither I went, or what I did; neither had I as yet told *it* to the Jews, nor to the priests, nor to the nobles, nor to the rulers, nor to the rest that did the work.

Then said I unto them, Ye see the distress that we *are* in, how Jerusalem *lieth* waste, and the gates thereof are burned with fire: come, and let us build up the wall of Jerusalem, that we be no more a reproach. Then I told them of the hand of my God which was good upon me; as also the king's words that he had spoken unto me.

And they said, Let us rise up and build. So they strengthened their hands for *this* good *work*.

But when Sanballat the Horonite, and Tobiah the servant, the Ammonite, and Geshem the Arabian, heard *it*, they laughed us to scorn, and despised us, and said, What *is* this thing that ye do? will ye rebel against the king?

Then answered I them, and said unto them, The God of heaven, he will prosper us; therefore we his servants will arise and build: but ye have no portion, nor right, nor memorial, in Jerusalem.

Then Eliashib the high priest rose up with his brethren the priests, and they builded the sheep gate; they sanctified it, and set up the doors of it; even unto the tower of Meah they sanctified it, unto the tower of Hananeel. And next unto him builded the men of Jericho. And next to them builded Zaccur the son of Imri.

But the fish gate did the sons of Hassenaah build, who *also* laid the beams thereof, and set up the doors thereof, the locks thereof, and the bars thereof. And next unto them repaired Meremoth the son of Urijah, the son of Koz. And next unto them repaired Meshullam the son of Berechiah, the son of Meshezabeel. And next unto them repaired Zadok the son of Baana. And next unto them the Tekoites repaired; but their nobles put not their necks to the work of their Lord.

Moreover the old gate repaired Jehoiada the son of Paseah, and Meshullam the son of Besodeiah; they laid the beams thereof, and set up the doors thereof, and the locks thereof, and the bars thereof. And next unto them repaired Melatiah the Gibeonite, and Jadon the Meronothite, the men of Gibeon, and of Mizpah, unto the throne of the governor on this side the river. Next unto him repaired Uzziel the son of Harhaiah, of the goldsmiths. Next unto him also repaired Hananiah the son of *one of* the apothecaries, and they fortified Jerusalem unto the broad wall. And next unto them repaired Rephaiah the son of Hur, the ruler of the half part of Jerusalem. And next unto them repaired Jedaiah the son of Harumaph, even over against his house. And next unto him repaired Hattush the son of Hashabniah. Malchijah the son of Harim, and Hashub the son of Pahath-moab, repaired the other piece, and the tower of the furnaces. And next unto him repaired Shallum the son of Halohesh, the ruler of the half part of Jerusalem, he and his daughters.

The valley gate repaired Hanun, and the inhabitants of Zanoah; they built it, and set up the doors thereof, the locks thereof, and the bars thereof, and a thousand cubits on the wall unto the dung gate.

But the dung gate repaired Malchiah the son of Rechab, the ruler of part of Beth-haccerem; he built it, and set up the doors thereof, the locks thereof, and the bars thereof.

But the gate of the fountain repaired Shallun the son of Colhozeh, the ruler of part of Mizpah; he built it, and covered it, and set up the doors thereof, the locks thereof, and the bars thereof, and the wall of the pool of Siloah by the king's garden, and unto the stairs that go down from the city of David. After him repaired Nehemiah the son of Azbuk, the ruler of the half part of Beth-zur, unto *the place* over against the sepulchres of David, and to the pool that was made, and unto the house of the mighty.

After him repaired the Levites, Rehum the son of Bani. Next unto him repaired Hashabiah, the ruler of the half part of Keilah, in his part. After him repaired their brethren, Bavai the son of Henadad, the ruler of the half part of Keilah. And next to him repaired Ezer the son of Jeshua, the ruler of Mizpah, another piece over against the going up to the armoury at the turning *of the wall*. After him Baruch the son of Zabbai earnestly repaired the other piece, from the turning *of the wall* unto the door of the house of Eliashib the high priest. After him repaired Meremoth the son of Urijah the son of Koz another piece, from the door of the house of Eliashib even to the end of the house of Eliashib.

And after him repaired the priests, the men of the plain. After him repaired Benjamin and Hashub over against their house. After him repaired Azariah the son of Maaseiah the son of Ananiah by his house. After him repaired Binnui the son of Henadad another piece, from the house of Azariah unto the turning *of the wall*, even unto the corner. Palal the son of Uzai, over against the turning *of the wall*, and the tower which lieth out from the king's high house, that *was* by the court of the prison. After him Pedaiah the son of Parosh. Moreover the Nethinims dwelt in Ophel, unto *the place* over against the water gate toward the east, and the tower that lieth out. After them the Tekoites repaired another piece, over against the great tower that lieth out, even unto the wall of Ophel.

From above the horse gate repaired the priests, every one over against his house. After them repaired Zadok the son of Immer over against his house. After him repaired also Shemaiah the son of Shechaniah, the keeper of the east gate. After him repaired Hananiah the son of Shelemiah, and Hanun the sixth son of Zalaph, another piece. After him repaired Meshullam the son of Berechiah over against his chamber. After him repaired Malchiah the goldsmith's son unto the place of the Nethinims, and of the merchants, over against the gate Miphkad, and to the going up of the corner. And between the going up of the corner unto the sheep gate repaired the goldsmiths and the merchants. Nehemiah 2:11—3:32

So the wall was finished in the twenty and fifth *day* of *the month* Elul, in fifty and two days. Nehemiah 6:15 ⟨○—ᴴ

One of the marked differences between the church and the rest of society is the call to live for others. Throughout the New Testament, Jesus' followers were urged to look out for "one another." When the early Christians did this in faith, it irresistibly attracted outsiders to belong to the family of God. The practice of looking out for one another is a hallmark of true Biblical community.

For as we have many members in one body, and all members have not the same office: So we, *being* many, are one body in Christ, and every one members one of another.   Romans 12:4–5

Be kindly affectioned one to another with brotherly love; in honour preferring one another.   Romans 12:10

Owe no man any thing, but to **love one another**: for he that loveth another hath fulfilled the law.   Romans 13:8

Now the God of patience and consolation grant you to be like-minded one toward another according to Christ Jesus: That ye may with one mind *and* one mouth glorify God, even the Father of our Lord Jesus Christ.

Wherefore **receive ye one another**, as Christ also received us to the glory of God.   Romans 15:5–7

And I myself also am persuaded of you, my brethren, that ye also are full of goodness, filled with all knowledge, able also to **admonish one another.**   Romans 15:14

For, brethren, ye have been called unto liberty; only *use* not liberty for an occasion to the flesh, but by love **serve one another**.   Galatians 5:13

Bear ye one another's burdens, and so fulfil the law of Christ.   Galatians 6:2

Walk worthy of the vocation wherewith ye are called, With all lowliness and meekness, with longsuffering, **forbearing one another** in love.   Ephesians 4:1–2

[Submit] yourselves one to another in the fear of God.   Ephesians 5:21

For God hath not appointed us to wrath, but to obtain salvation by our Lord Jesus Christ, Who died for us, that, whether we wake or sleep, we should live together with him. Wherefore **comfort yourselves together**, and edify one another, even as also ye do.

1 Thessalonians 5:9–11

The calling among the early church to care for one another was also demonstrated through simple hospitality. This mandate to show love and demonstrate an open door policy greatly enhanced the quality of community and always left room for new people to belong, regardless of their stations in life.

As you read the passages below from Hebrews 13; Acts 18;
1 Corinthians 16; Romans 16 and 1 John 1–3, ponder
the emphasis and importance placed on hospitality.
Why do you think it was so important to the early church?
Is it still important today? Why or why not?

Let brotherly love continue. **Be not forgetful to entertain strangers: for thereby some have entertained angels unawares.** Remember them that are in bonds, as bound with them; *and* them which suffer adversity, as being yourselves also in the body.

HEBREWS 13:1–3

By him [Jesus] therefore let us offer the sacrifice of praise to God continually, that is, the fruit of *our* lips giving thanks to his name. **But to do good and to communicate forget not: for with such sacrifices God is well pleased.** HEBREWS 13:15–16

A couple named Priscilla and Aquila serve as a beautiful example of how to be hospitable. In the first century, inns were not commonplace, and the early church didn't own buildings. For Biblical community to be experienced, people who owned homes had to open them up for the church to meet in. Paul was on his second missionary journey when he first encountered this warm-hearted couple, who invited him to stay with them.

After these things Paul departed from Athens, and came to Corinth; And found a certain Jew named Aquila, born in Pontus, lately come from Italy, with his wife Priscilla; (because that Claudius had commanded all Jews to depart from Rome:) and came unto them. And because he was of the same craft, he abode with them, and wrought: for by their occupation they were tentmakers.

ACTS 18:1–3

And Paul *after this* tarried *there* yet a good while, and then took his leave of the brethren, and sailed thence into Syria, and with him Priscilla and Aquila; having shorn *his* head in Cenchrea: for he had a vow. And he came to Ephesus, and left them there.

ACTS 18:18–19

And a certain Jew named Apollos, born at Alexandria, an eloquent man, *and* mighty in the scriptures, came to Ephesus. This man was instructed in the way of the Lord; and being fervent in the spirit, he spake and taught diligently the things of the Lord, knowing only the baptism of John. **And he began to speak boldly in the synagogue: whom when Aquila and Priscilla had heard [Apollos], they took him unto *them*, and expounded unto him the way of God more perfectly.** ACTS 18:24–26

Paul's admiration for Priscilla and Aquila can be found throughout his letters. Paul wrote 1 Corinthians when he was in Ephesus. He sent greetings on behalf of Aquila and Priscilla, who were hosting the church in their home.

The churches of Asia salute you. Aquila and Priscilla salute you much in the Lord, with the church that is in their house.

1 CORINTHIANS 16:19

A couple years later when Paul penned the letter to the Romans, he expressed his gratitude to Priscilla and Aquila, who were now in Rome.

Greet Priscilla and Aquila my helpers in Christ Jesus: Who have for my life laid down their own necks: unto whom not only I give thanks, but also all the churches of the Gentiles. ROMANS 16:3–4

In order for the church to accomplish its mission, all believers, looking to the example of Priscilla and Aquila, need to use the gifts God has given them to serve others. In 1 John, the apostle John emphasized the value of Christian fellowship. If we practice this quality and depth of fellowship with other Christians, we will accomplish God's purposes in our lives, in the lives of others and in the world.

That which was from the beginning, which we have heard, which we have seen with our eyes, which we have looked upon, and our hands have handled, of the Word of life; (For the life was manifested, and we have seen *it*, and bear witness, and shew unto you that eternal life, which was with the Father, and was manifested unto us;) That which we have seen and heard declare we unto you, that ye also may have fellowship with us: and truly our fellowship *is* with the Father, and with his Son Jesus Christ. And these things write we unto you, that your joy may be full.

This then is the message which we have heard of him, and declare unto you, that God is light, and in him is no darkness at all. If we say that we have fellowship with him, and walk in darkness, we lie, and do not the truth: **But if we walk in the light, as he is in the light, we have fellowship one with another, and the blood of Jesus Christ his Son cleanseth us from all sin.** 1 JOHN 1:1–7

Brethren, I write no new commandment unto you, but an old commandment which ye had from the beginning. The old commandment is the word which ye have heard from the beginning. Again, a new commandment I write unto you, which thing is true in him and in you: because the darkness is past, and the true light now shineth.

He that saith he is in the light, and hateth his brother, is in darkness even until now. He that loveth his brother abideth in the light, and there is none occasion of stumbling in him. But he that hateth his brother is in darkness, and walketh in darkness, and knoweth not whither he goeth, because that darkness hath blinded his eyes. 1 JOHN 2:7–11

Hereby perceive we the love *of God,* because he laid down his life for us: and we ought to lay down *our* lives for the brethren. But whoso hath this world's good, and seeth his brother have need, and shutteth up his bowels *of compassion* from him, how dwelleth the love of God in him? My little children, let us not love in word, neither in tongue; but in deed and in truth. 1 JOHN 3:16–18

God's Word places a high value on Christian fellowship.
How important is fellowship to you right now?
What difference is it making in your life?

WHAT WE BELIEVE

We were created by God for community. Given our sinful nature, it is essential for God to be at the center of that community. He was in the garden with Adam and Eve; he dwelled in the tabernacle and temple with Israel; he literally walked among the first disciples for more than 30 years. From the inception of the church until now, God has dwelt not in a temple built by human hands, but in a new temple — the lives of his followers. As we yield to the presence of God's Spirit in and among us, we grow in true Biblical community, marked by caring for one another and open hospitality. As we fellowship with other Christians, it not only becomes the rich experience we were created for, but it also emits an "aroma" that draws others in. So we must make Biblical community a priority in order to accomplish God's purposes in our lives, in the lives of others and in the world.

CHAPTER

17

Spiritual Gifts

---------- KEY QUESTION ----------

What gifts and skills has God given me to serve others?

---------- KEY IDEA ----------

I know my spiritual gifts and
use them to fulfill God's purposes.

---------- KEY VERSE ----------

For as we have many members in one body, and
all members have not the same office: so we,
being many, are one body in Christ, and every one
members one of another. Having then gifts
differing according to the grace that is given to us.

Romans 12:4–6

OUR MAP

God has used two primary communities to accomplish his grand purpose to redeem humanity and restore his vision of being with them forever. In the Old Testament that community was Israel. In the New Testament that community was (and continues to be) the church. God equipped the individual members of these communities with the skills and gifts needed to accomplish his purpose and plan. It is up to each individual to acknowledge and use their gifts for God's intended purposes. Then, collectively, the community must decide to work together in unity. When this happens, amazing things are accomplished. Miracles. Life change.

In this chapter we will be reading Scripture that will help us understand more about spiritual gifts, including:

- Spiritual Gifts in the Old Testament
- The Promised Gift of the Holy Ghost
- The Purpose and Function of Spiritual Gifts
- Stewardship of Our Gifts

SPIRITUAL GIFTS IN THE OLD TESTAMENT

Although the term "spiritual gift" isn't found in the Old Testament, we see clear evidence of the Holy Spirit working through people during this time. The unique empowering of the Spirit was given to individuals (often only temporarily) primarily to enable them to carry out the special responsibilities God had given them. When the Israelites were in the wilderness following the exodus from Egypt, God instructed Moses to build a tabernacle that would be used for God's dwelling place from that day forward. It would take the special gifts and skills of many people to carry out God's intricate plan for building his new sanctuary.

And Moses said unto the children of Israel, See, the LORD hath called by name Bezaleel the son of Uri, the son of Hur, of the tribe of Judah; And he hath filled him with the spirit of God, in wisdom, in understanding, and in knowledge, and in all manner of workmanship; And to devise curious works, to work in gold, and in silver, and in brass, And in the cutting of stones, to set *them*, and in carving of wood, to make any manner of cunning work. And he hath put in his heart that he may teach, *both* he, and Aholiab, the son of Ahisamach, of the tribe of Dan. Them hath he filled with wisdom of heart, to work all manner of work, of the engraver, and of the cunning workman, and of the embroiderer, in blue, and in purple, in scarlet, and in fine linen, and of the weaver, *even* of them that do any work, and of those that devise cunning work.

Then wrought Bezaleel and Aholiab, and every wise hearted man, in whom the LORD put wisdom and understanding to know how to work all manner of work for the service of the sanctuary, according to all that the LORD had commanded.   EXODUS 35:30—36:1

> *God instills in his people the skills needed to accomplish his purposes. This includes not only the work of the priest or pastor but also the swinging of the hammer of the construction worker and the reading of the blueprints of the project manager.*
>
> *Occasionally in the Old Testament, spiritual gifts were used for the sake of outsiders. In these situations, God used miraculous signs to reveal himself as the one true God. For instance, while the Israelites were living in exile in Babylon, God empowered Daniel with the ability to interpret a complex dream for King Nebuchadnezzar.*

And in the second year of the reign of Nebuchadnezzar Nebuchadnezzar dreamed dreams, wherewith his spirit was troubled, and his sleep brake from him. Then the king commanded to call the magicians, and the astrologers, and the sorcerers, and the Chaldeans, for to shew the king his dreams. So they came and stood before the king. And the king said unto them, I have dreamed a dream, and my spirit was troubled to know the dream.

Then spake the Chaldeans to the king in Syriack, O king, live for ever: tell thy servants the dream, and we will shew the interpretation.

The king answered and said to the Chaldeans, The thing is gone from me: if ye will not make known unto me the dream, with the interpretation thereof, ye shall be cut in pieces, and your houses shall be made a dunghill. But if ye shew the dream, and the interpretation thereof, ye shall receive of me gifts and rewards and great honour: therefore shew me the dream, and the interpretation thereof.

They answered again and said, Let the king tell his servants the dream, and we will shew the interpretation of it.

The king answered and said, I know of certainty that ye would gain the time, because ye see the thing is gone from me. But if ye will not make known unto me the dream, *there is but* one decree for you: for ye have prepared lying and corrupt words to speak before me, till the time be changed: therefore tell me the dream, and I shall know that ye can shew me the interpretation thereof.

The Chaldeans answered before the king, and said, There is not a man upon the earth that can shew the king's matter: therefore *there is* no king, lord, nor ruler, *that* asked such things at any magician, or astrologer, or Chaldean. And *it is* a rare thing that the king requireth, and there is none other that can shew it before the king, except the gods, whose dwelling is not with flesh.

For this cause the king was angry and very furious, and commanded to destroy all the wise *men* of Babylon. And the decree went forth that the wise *men* should be slain; and they sought Daniel and his fellows to be slain.

Then Daniel answered with counsel and wisdom to Arioch the captain of the king's guard, which was gone forth to slay the wise *men* of Babylon: He answered and said to Arioch the king's captain, Why *is* the decree *so* hasty from the king? Then Arioch made the thing known to Daniel. Then Daniel went in, and desired of the king that he would give him time, and that he would shew the king the interpretation.

Then Daniel went to his house, and made the thing known to Hananiah, Mishael, and Azariah, his companions: That they would desire mercies of the God of heaven concerning this secret; that Daniel and his fellows should not perish with the rest of the wise *men* of Babylon. Then was the secret revealed unto Daniel in a night vision. Then Daniel blessed the God of heaven. Daniel answered and said, Blessed be the name of God for ever and ever: for wisdom and might are his: And he changeth the times and the seasons: he removeth kings, and setteth up kings: he giveth wisdom unto the wise, and knowledge to them that know understanding: He revealeth the deep and secret things: he knoweth what *is* in the darkness, and the light dwelleth with him. I thank thee, and praise thee, O thou God of my fathers, who hast given me wisdom and might, and hast made known unto me now what we desired of thee: for thou hast *now* made known unto us the king's matter.

Therefore Daniel went in unto Arioch, whom the king had ordained to destroy the wise *men* of Babylon: he went and said thus unto him; Destroy not the wise *men* of Babylon: bring me in before the king, and I will shew unto the king the interpretation.

Then Arioch brought in Daniel before the king in haste, and said thus unto him, I have found a man of the captives of Judah, that will make known unto the king the interpretation.

The king answered and said to Daniel, whose name *was* Belteshazzar, Art thou able to make known unto me the dream which I have seen, and the interpretation thereof?

Daniel answered in the presence of the king, and said, The secret which the king hath demanded cannot the wise *men*, the astrologers, the magicians, the soothsayers, shew unto the king; But there is a God in heaven that revealeth secrets, and maketh known to the king Nebuchadnezzar what shall be in the latter days. Thy dream, and the visions of thy head upon thy bed, are these;

As for thee, O king, thy thoughts came *into thy mind* upon thy bed, what should come to pass hereafter: and he that revealeth secrets maketh known to thee what shall come to pass. But as for me, this secret is not revealed to me for *any* wisdom that I have more than any living, but for *their* sakes that shall make known the interpretation to the king, and that thou mightest know the thoughts of thy heart.

Thou, O king, sawest, and behold a great image. This great image, whose brightness *was* excellent, stood before thee; and the form thereof *was* terrible. This image's head *was* of fine gold, his breast and his arms of silver, his belly and his thighs of brass, His legs of iron, his feet part of iron and part of clay. Thou sawest till that a stone was cut out without hands, which smote the image upon his feet *that were* of iron and clay, and brake them to pieces. Then was the iron, the clay, the brass, the silver, and the gold, broken to pieces together, and became like the chaff of the summer threshingfloors; and the wind carried them away, that no place was found for them: and the stone that smote the image became a great mountain, and filled the whole earth.

This *is* the dream; and we will tell the interpretation thereof before the king. Thou, O king, *art* a king of kings: for the God of heaven hath given thee a kingdom, power, and strength, and glory. And wheresoever the children of men dwell, the beasts of the field and the fowls of the heaven hath he given into thine hand, and hath made thee ruler over them all. Thou *art* this head of gold.

And after thee shall arise another kingdom inferior to thee, and another third kingdom of brass, which shall bear rule over all the earth. And the fourth kingdom shall be strong as iron: forasmuch as iron breaketh in pieces and subdueth all *things*: and as iron that breaketh all these, shall it break in pieces and bruise. And whereas thou sawest the feet and toes, part of potters' clay, and part of iron, the kingdom shall be divided; but there shall be in it of the strength of the iron, forasmuch as thou sawest the iron mixed with miry clay. And *as* the toes of the feet *were* part of iron, and part of clay, *so* the kingdom shall be partly strong, and partly broken. And whereas thou sawest iron mixed with miry clay, they shall mingle themselves with the seed of men: but they shall not cleave one to another, even as iron is not mixed with clay.

And in the days of these kings shall the God of heaven set up a kingdom, which shall never be destroyed: and the kingdom shall not be left to other people, *but* it shall break in pieces and consume all these kingdoms, and it shall stand for ever. Forasmuch as thou sawest that the stone was cut out of the mountain without hands, and that it brake in pieces the iron, the brass, the clay, the silver, and the gold.

The great God hath made known to the king what shall come to pass hereafter: and the dream *is* certain, and the interpretation thereof sure.

Then the king Nebuchadnezzar fell upon his face, and worshipped Daniel, and commanded that they should offer an oblation and sweet odours unto him. **The king answered unto Daniel, and said, Of a truth *it is*, that your God *is* a God of gods, and a Lord of kings, and a revealer of secrets, seeing thou couldest reveal this secret.** DANIEL 2:1–47 ⚷

What was Daniel's spiritual gift? Why was it important that Daniel acknowledge his gift was from the Lord?

THE PROMISED GIFT OF THE HOLY GHOST

In the New Testament, when Jesus ate the Last Supper with his disciples, he knew he would soon be put to death. Wanting them to be encouraged and prepared for life without him beside them, Jesus promised to send the gift of the Holy Ghost, who would empower them with hope and guidance and the ability to get through the difficult days ahead.

If ye love me, keep my commandments. And I will pray the Father, and he shall give you another Comforter, that he may abide with you for ever; *Even* the Spirit of truth; whom the world cannot receive, because it seeth him not, neither knoweth him: but ye know him; for he dwelleth with you, and shall be in you. I will not leave you comfortless: I will come to you. Yet a little while, and the world seeth me no more; but ye see me: because I live, ye shall live also. At that day ye shall know that I *am* in my Father, and ye in me, and I in you. He that hath my commandments, and keepeth them, he it is that loveth me: and he that loveth me shall be loved of my Father, and I will love him, and will manifest myself to him.

Judas saith unto him, not Iscariot, Lord, how is it that thou wilt manifest thyself unto us, and not unto the world?

Jesus answered and said unto him, If a man love me, he will keep my words: and my Father will love him, and we will come unto him, and make our abode with him. He that loveth me not keepeth not my sayings: and the word which ye hear is not mine, but the Father's which sent me.

These things have I spoken unto you, being *yet* present with you. But the Comforter, *which is* the Holy Ghost, whom the Father will send in my name, he shall teach you all things, and bring all things to your remembrance, whatsoever I have said unto you. Peace I leave with you, my peace I give unto you: not as the world giveth, give I unto you. Let not your heart be troubled, neither let it be afraid.

Ye have heard how I said unto you, I go away, and come *again* unto you. If ye loved me, ye would rejoice, because I said, I go unto the Father: for my Father is greater than I. And now I have told you before it come to pass, that, when it is come to pass, ye might believe. Hereafter I will not talk much with you: for the prince of this world cometh, and hath nothing in me. But that the world may know that I love the Father; and as the Father gave me commandment, even so I do. Arise, let us go hence. JOHN 14:15–31

Later, Jesus' last words to his disciples before he ascended to heaven instructed them to wait in Jerusalem for the promised gift of the Holy Ghost. Ten days later, on the Jewish celebration of Pentecost (i.e., 50 days after Passover), the Holy Ghost arrived and the disciples were filled with incredible boldness. The church was born. Jews use this celebration to commemorate the giving of the law. Christians use this day to commemorate the giving of the Holy Ghost.

And when the day of Pentecost was fully come, they were all with one accord in one place. And suddenly there came a sound from heaven as of a rushing mighty wind, and it filled all the house where they were sitting. And there appeared unto them cloven tongues like as of fire, and it sat upon each of them. And they were all filled with the Holy Ghost, and began to speak with other tongues, as the Spirit gave them utterance.

And there were dwelling at Jerusalem Jews, devout men, out of every nation under heaven. Now when this was noised abroad, the multitude came together, and were confounded, because that every man heard them speak in his own language. And they were all amazed and marvelled, saying one to another, Behold, are not all these which speak Galilaeans? And how hear we every man in our own tongue, wherein we were born? Parthians, and Medes, and Elamites, and the dwellers in Mesopotamia, and in Judaea, and Cappadocia, in Pontus, and Asia, Phrygia, and Pamphylia, in Egypt, and in the parts of Libya about Cyrene, and strangers of Rome, Jews and proselytes, Cretes and Arabians, we do hear them speak in our tongues the wonderful works of God. And they were all amazed, and were in doubt, saying one to another, What meaneth this?

Others mocking said, These men are full of new wine.

But Peter, standing up with the eleven, lifted up his voice, and said unto them, Ye men of Judaea, and all *ye* that dwell at Jerusalem, be this known unto you, and hearken to my words: For these are not drunken, as ye suppose, seeing it is *but* the third hour of the day. But this is that which was spoken by the prophet Joel; **And it shall come to pass in the last days, saith God, I will pour out of my Spirit upon all flesh:** and your sons and your daughters shall prophesy, and your young men shall see visions, and your old men shall dream dreams: And on my servants and on my handmaidens I will pour out in those days of my Spirit; and they shall prophesy: And I will shew wonders in heaven above, and signs in the earth beneath; blood, and fire, and vapour of smoke: The sun shall be turned into darkness, and the moon into blood, before that great and notable day of the Lord come: And it shall come to pass, *that* whosoever shall call on the name of the Lord shall be saved.

ACTS 2:1–21

The Holy Ghost now takes up residence in all who believe in Jesus. We are the new temple of God. In John 14, Jesus called the Holy Ghost our "Comforter." What do you think that means?

THE PURPOSE AND FUNCTION OF SPIRITUAL GIFTS

Spiritual gifts are given with a purpose. God wants to redeem this broken world, and he has chosen to use us, the church, to do it. Whereas in the Old Testament the Holy Ghost temporarily came upon followers of God to enable them to fulfill specific tasks, the New Testament clearly indicates that the Holy Ghost indwells all believers and that all believers have spiritual gifts. And since the New Testament refers to specific gifts, it seems safe to assume that God wants us to identify our gifts in order to best use them.

As you read the following passages from Romans 12 and 1 Corinthians 12, highlight or write down which gift(s) you believe you possess. Choose a family member or a friend and do the same for them. Let them know what you think their gifts are and how you have been positively impacted by them.

For as we have many members in one body, and all members have not the same office: So we, *being* many, are one body

in Christ, and every one members one of another. Having then gifts differing according to the grace that is given to us, whether prophecy, *let us prophesy* according to the proportion of faith; Or ministry, *let us wait* on *our* ministering: or he that teacheth, on teaching; Or he that exhorteth, on exhortation: he that giveth, *let him do it* with simplicity; he that ruleth, with diligence; he that sheweth mercy, with cheerfulness. ROMANS 12:4–8

Now there are diversities of gifts, but the same Spirit. And there are differences of administrations, but the same Lord. And there are diversities of operations, but it is the same God which worketh all in all.

But the manifestation of the Spirit is given to every man to profit withal. For to one is given by the Spirit the word of wisdom; to another the word of knowledge by the same Spirit; To another faith by the same Spirit; to another the gifts of healing by the same Spirit; To another the working of miracles; to another prophecy; to another discerning of spirits; to another *divers* kinds of tongues; to another the interpretation of tongues: But all these worketh that one and the selfsame Spirit, dividing to every man severally as he will.

For as the body is one, and hath many members, and all the members of that one body, being many, are one body: so also *is* Christ. For by one Spirit are we all baptized into one body, whether *we be* Jews or Gentiles, whether *we be* bond or free; and have been all made to drink into one Spirit. For the body is not one member, but many.

If the foot shall say, Because I am not the hand, I am not of the body; is it therefore not of the body? And if the ear shall say, Because I am not the eye, I am not of the body; is it therefore not of the body? If the whole body *were* an eye, where *were* the hearing? If the whole *were* hearing, where *were* the smelling? But now hath God set the members every one of them in the body, as it hath pleased him. And if they were all one member, where *were* the body? But now *are they* many members, yet but one body.

And the eye cannot say unto the hand, I have no need of thee: nor again the head to the feet, I have no need of you. Nay, much more those members of the body, which seem to be more feeble, are necessary: And those *members* of the body, which we think to be less honourable, upon these we bestow more abundant honour; and our uncomely *parts* have more abundant comeliness. For our comely *parts* have no need: but God hath tempered the body together, having given more abundant honour to that *part* which lacked: That there should be no schism in the body; but *that* the members should have the same care one for another. And whether one member suffer, all the members suffer with it; or one member be honoured, all the members rejoice with it.

Now ye are the body of Christ, and members in particular. And God hath set some in the church, first apostles, secondarily prophets, thirdly teachers, after that miracles, then gifts of healings, helps, governments, diversities of tongues. *Are* all apostles? *are* all prophets? *are* all teachers? *are* all workers of miracles? Have all the gifts of healing? do all speak with tongues? do all interpret? But covet earnestly the best gifts.   1 CORINTHIANS 12:4–31

STEWARDSHIP OF OUR GIFTS

We are meant to use our spiritual gifts to benefit the body of Christ. Jesus used the unit of money called talents to graphically illustrate this principle for his disciples. Like money that should be invested, our spiritual gifts should be used for the good of others, multiplying the blessing as we share them according to God's purposes.

For *the kingdom of heaven is* as a man travelling into a far country, *who* called his own servants, and delivered unto them his goods. And unto one he gave five talents, to another two, and to another one; to every man according to his several ability; and straightway took his journey. Then he that had received the five talents went and traded with the same, and made *them* other five talents. And likewise he that *had received* two, he also gained other two. But he that had received one went and digged in the earth, and hid his lord's money.

After a long time the lord of those servants cometh, and reckoneth with them. And so he that had received five talents came and brought other five talents, saying, Lord, thou deliveredst unto me five talents: behold, I have gained beside them five talents more.

His lord said unto him, Well done, *thou* good and faithful servant: thou hast been faithful over a few things, I will make thee ruler over many things: enter thou into the joy of thy lord.

He also that had received two talents came and said, Lord, thou deliveredst unto me two talents: behold, I have gained two other talents beside them.

His lord said unto him, Well done, good and faithful servant; thou hast been faithful over a few things, I will make thee ruler over many things: enter thou into the joy of thy lord.

Then he which had received the one talent came and said, Lord, I knew thee that thou art an hard man, reaping where thou hast not sown, and gathering where thou hast not strawed: And I was afraid, and went and hid thy talent in the earth: lo, *there* thou hast *that is* thine.

His lord answered and said unto him, *Thou* wicked and slothful servant, thou knewest that I reap where I sowed not, and gather where I have not strawed: Thou oughtest therefore to have put my money to the exchangers, and *then* at my coming I should have received mine own with usury.

Take therefore the talent from him, and give *it* unto him which hath ten talents. For unto every one that hath shall be given, and he shall have abundance: but from him that hath not shall be taken away even that which he hath. And cast ye the unprofitable servant into outer darkness: there shall be weeping and gnashing of teeth.

MATTHEW 25:14–30

Just as a piston engine requires pure gasoline to run smoothly, our gifts must be fueled with loving intentions. Spiritual gifts that are powered by selfish ambition and pride will sputter and fail.

But the end of all things is at hand: be ye therefore sober, and watch unto prayer. And above all things have fervent charity among yourselves: for charity shall cover the multitude of sins. Use hospitality one to another without grudging. **As every man hath received the gift, *even so* minister the same one to another, as good stewards of the manifold grace of God.** If any man speak, *let him speak* as the oracles of God; if any man minister, *let him do* *it* as of the ability which God giveth: that God in all things may be glorified through Jesus Christ.

What happens when spiritual gifts are exercised without love? (Peter cites offering hospitality with grudging as unacceptable.) Why is it so important to be driven by love when using our spiritual gifts?

This final selection from Ephesians 4:1–16 also appeared in Chapter 6 (Church). For the church to accomplish its purpose we must all work together as one unified body. As you reread this passage, note how church leaders are a gift to the church. As they use their spiritual gifts, other believers will be equipped to steward their gifts, resulting in the body of Christ being built up and individual believers becoming mature.

I therefore, the prisoner of the Lord, beseech you that ye walk worthy of the vocation wherewith ye are called, With all lowliness and meekness, with longsuffering, forbearing one another in love; Endeavouring to keep the unity of the Spirit in the bond of peace. *There is* one body, and one Spirit, even as ye are called in one hope of your calling; One Lord, one faith, one baptism, One God and Father of all, who *is* above all, and through all, and in you all.

But unto every one of us is given grace according to the measure of the gift of Christ. Wherefore he saith, When he ascended up on high, he led captivity captive, and gave gifts unto men. (Now that he ascended, what is it but that he also descended first into the lower parts of the earth? He that descended is the same also that ascended up far above all heavens, that he might fill all things.) And he gave some, apostles; and some, prophets; and some, evangelists; and some, pastors and teachers; For the perfecting of the saints, for the work of the ministry, for the edifying of the body of Christ: Till we all come in the unity of the faith, and of the knowledge of the Son of God, unto a perfect man, unto the measure of the stature of the fulness of Christ:

That we *henceforth* be no more children, tossed to and fro, and carried about with every wind of doctrine, by the sleight of men, *and* cunning craftiness, whereby they lie in wait to deceive; But speaking the truth in love, may grow up into him in all things, which is the head, *even* Christ: **From whom the whole body fitly joined together and compacted by that which every joint supplieth, according to the effectual working in the measure of every part, maketh increase of the body unto the edifying of itself in love.**   Ephesians 4:1–16

The Bible compares the church to a body. Collectively, we are the body of Christ. Individual believers are compared to parts of the body that all work together to accomplish what needs to be done. Can you recall a time when one part of your body was injured in some way and how this affected the whole body? How does this analogy work in regard to the church?

WHAT WE BELIEVE

The one true God has partnered with his people to accomplish his purposes on earth. The third person of the Trinity, the Holy Ghost, is the driver of this initiative. In the Old Testament, the Holy Ghost only indwelled select individuals for a period of time to accomplish God's purposes. The spirit of God instilled gifts in artisans, architects, builders, priests and prophets. In the New Testament, Jesus promised the indwelling of the Holy Ghost for all believers. That promise was fulfilled on the day of Pentecost as recorded in Acts 2. The Spirit deposits gifts in every believer for the express purpose of building God's kingdom on earth. We do not all have the same gift. In unity we are to celebrate the giftedness of others and work together to accomplish God's will in our lives and in the world.

ACT

CHAPTER

18

Offering My Time

---- KEY QUESTION ----

How do I best use my time to serve God and others?

---- KEY IDEA ----

I offer my time to fulfill God's purposes.

---- KEY VERSE ----

And whatsoever ye do in word or deed,
do all in the name of the Lord Jesus, giving
thanks to God and the Father by him.
Colossians 3:17

Believe is an action verb. Whatever we believe in our hearts will be expressed in the way we live. Beliefs such as the church, compassion and stewardship naturally lead to the practice of offering our time to God to accomplish his purposes. Every time we act on this key spiritual practice, even if our hearts are not totally committed, it helps to drive these beliefs from our heads to our hearts. So we act out our beliefs in faith.

In this chapter we will be reading Scripture focused on the following key topics:

- *Offering God Our Time*
- *Serving God's Purposes*
- *Managing Our Time*
- *The Rewards of Offering Our Time*

OFFERING GOD OUR TIME

In essence, we cannot talk about "our" time since all time belongs to God. Every moment we have is a gift from him. It is because of this fact that we are called to use that time to honor our Father. The prophet Jonah learned this the hard way. God called Jonah to redirect his time from the popular job of serving Israel to the unpopular assignment of traveling to Nineveh to give Israel's enemy a chance to repent and be saved by God. Needless to say, Jonah was not committed to the call.

Now the word of the LORD came unto Jonah the son of Amittai, saying, Arise, go to Nineveh, that great city, and cry against it; for their wickedness is come up before me.

But Jonah rose up to flee unto Tarshish from the presence of the LORD, and went down to Joppa; and he found a ship going to Tarshish: so he paid the fare thereof, and went down into it, to go with them unto Tarshish from the presence of the LORD.

But the LORD sent out a great wind into the sea, and there was a mighty tempest in the sea, so that the ship was like to be broken. Then the mariners were afraid, and cried every man unto his god, and cast forth the wares that *were* in the ship into the sea, to lighten *it* of them.

But Jonah was gone down into the sides of the ship; and he lay, and was fast asleep. So the shipmaster came to him, and said unto him, What meanest thou, O sleeper? arise, call upon thy God, if so be that God will think upon us, that we perish not.

And they said every one to his fellow, Come, and let us cast lots, that we may know for whose cause this evil *is* upon us. So they cast lots, and the lot fell upon Jonah. Then said they unto him, Tell us, we pray thee, for whose cause this evil *is* upon us; What *is* thine occupation? and whence comest thou? what *is* thy country? and of what people *art* thou?

And he said unto them, I *am* an Hebrew; and I fear the LORD, the God of heaven, which hath made the sea and the dry *land*.

Then were the men exceedingly afraid, and said unto him, Why hast thou done this? For the men knew that he fled from the presence of the LORD, because he had told them.

Then said they unto him, What shall we do unto thee, that the sea may be calm unto us? for the sea wrought, and was tempestuous.

And he said unto them, Take me up, and cast me forth into the sea; so shall the sea be calm unto you: for I know that for my sake this great tempest *is* upon you.

Nevertheless the men rowed hard to bring *it* to the land; but they could not: for the sea wrought, and was tempestuous against them. Wherefore they cried unto the LORD, and said, We beseech thee, O LORD, we beseech thee, let us not perish for this man's life, and lay not upon us innocent blood: for thou, O LORD, hast done as it pleased thee. So they took up Jonah, and cast him forth into the sea: and the sea ceased from her raging. Then the men feared the LORD exceedingly, and offered a sacrifice unto the LORD, and made vows.

Now the LORD had prepared a great fish to swallow up Jonah. And Jonah was in the belly of the fish three days and three nights.

Then Jonah prayed unto the LORD his God out of the fish's belly, And said, I cried by reason of mine affliction unto the LORD, and he heard me; out of the belly of hell cried I, *and* thou heardest my voice. For thou hadst cast me into the deep, in the midst of the seas; and the floods compassed me about: all thy billows and thy waves passed over me. Then I said, I am cast out of thy sight; yet I will look again toward thy holy temple. The waters compassed me about, *even* to the soul: the depth closed me round about, the weeds were wrapped about my head. I went down to the bottoms of the mountains; the earth with her bars *was* about me for ever: yet hast thou brought up my life from corruption, O LORD my God.

When my soul fainted within me I remembered the LORD: and my prayer came in unto thee, into thine holy temple.

They that observe lying vanities forsake their own mercy. But I will sacrifice unto thee with the voice of thanksgiving; I will pay *that* that I have vowed. Salvation *is* of the LORD.

And the LORD spake unto the fish, and it vomited out Jonah upon the dry *land*.   JONAH 1:1—2:10

Do you think God still puts people in predicaments such as "the belly of a fish" when they ignore his call?

SERVING GOD'S PURPOSES

Not only are we to give our time to God, but we are also to use that time to serve his purposes, which can mean many different things. Like Jonah, God's people often needed reminders about this. When the first exiles returned to Judah from captivity in Babylon, one of their first priorities was to rebuild the temple and restore worship to the one true God. In 536 BC, under the leadership of Zerubbabel, the building project began. When opposition from the Samaritans and other neighbors intensified, the people got discouraged and the building came to a complete halt. For ten years the project lay dormant. The prophet Haggai delivered a chilling and effective message from God encouraging the people of God to reconsider how they prioritized their time.

⚷ In the second year of Darius the king, in the sixth month, in the first day of the month, came the word of the LORD by Haggai the prophet unto Zerubbabel the son of Shealtiel, governor of Judah, and to Joshua the son of Josedech, the high priest, saying,

Thus speaketh the LORD of hosts, saying, This people say, The time is not come, the time that the LORD's house should be built.

Then came the word of the LORD by Haggai the prophet, saying, *Is it* time for you, O ye, to dwell in your cieled houses, and this house *lie* waste?

Now therefore thus saith the LORD of hosts; Consider your ways. Ye have sown much, and bring in little; ye eat, but ye have not enough; ye drink, but ye are not filled with drink; ye clothe you, but there is none warm; and he that earneth wages earneth wages to put it into a bag with holes.

Thus saith the LORD of hosts; Consider your ways. Go up to the mountain, and bring wood, and build the house; and I will take pleasure in it, and I will be glorified, saith the LORD. Ye looked for much, and, lo, *it came* to little; and when ye brought *it* home, I did blow upon it. Why? saith the LORD of hosts. Because of mine house that *is* waste, and ye run every man unto his own house. Therefore the heaven over you is stayed from dew, and the earth is stayed *from* her fruit. And I called for a drought upon the land, and upon the mountains, and upon the corn, and upon the new wine, and upon the oil, and upon *that* which the ground bringeth forth, and upon men, and upon cattle, and upon all the labour of the hands.

Then Zerubbabel the son of Shealtiel, and Joshua the son of Josedech, the high priest, with all the remnant of the people, obeyed the voice of the LORD their God, and the words of Haggai the prophet, as the LORD their God had sent him, and the people did fear before the LORD.

Then spake Haggai the LORD's messenger in the LORD's message unto the people, saying, I *am* with you, saith the LORD. And the LORD stirred up the spirit of Zerubbabel the son of Shealtiel, governor of Judah, and the spirit of Joshua the son of Josedech, the high priest, and the spirit of all the remnant of the people; and they came and did work in the house of the LORD of hosts, their God, In the four and twentieth day of the sixth month, in the second year of Darius the king.   HAGGAI 1:1–15 ⚷

In light of what we have learned about the Old Testament temple from previous chapters, why did God want the returning captives to build his house before they built their own?

One person who never needed reminding of the fact that his time was to be dedicated to God was God's Son, Jesus. After attending the feast of the passover with his earthly parents, Jesus made the decision to stay a little longer and spend some time in the house of his heavenly Father. Even at the young age of twelve, Jesus understood how best to use his time.

⊙—ᴴ Now his [Jesus'] parents went to Jerusalem every year at the feast of the passover. And when he was twelve years old, they went up to Jerusalem after the custom of the feast. And when they had fulfilled the days, as they returned, the child Jesus tarried behind in Jerusalem; and Joseph and his mother knew not *of it*. But they, supposing him to have been in the company, went a day's journey; and they sought him among *their* kinsfolk and acquaintance. And when they found him not, they turned back again to Jerusalem, seeking him. And it came to pass, that after three days they found him in the temple, sitting in the midst of the doctors, both hearing them, and asking them questions. And all that heard him were astonished at his understanding and answers. And when they saw him, they were amazed: and his mother said unto him, Son, why hast thou thus dealt with us? behold, thy father and I have sought thee sorrowing.

And he said unto them, How is it that ye sought me? wist ye not that I must be about my Father's business? And they understood not the saying which he spake unto them.

And he went down with them, and came to Nazareth, and was subject unto them: but his mother kept all these sayings in her heart. And Jesus increased in wisdom and stature, and in favour with God and man. LUKE 2:41–52 ⊙—ᴴ

MANAGING OUR TIME

God desires us to be replenished and renewed to best serve him and others. But to experience this, we must manage our time according to God's design for the rhythm and balance of life. In the Old Testament, one of the Ten Commandments instructed God's people to set aside the Sabbath as a day of rest. But before God gave the Israelites the Ten Commandments at Mount Sinai, he gave them a command and a lesson regarding the Sab-

bath and collecting manna. Although Christians today disagree about whether or not Sabbath-keeping is obligatory, God clearly designed people with the need for regular and deliberate rest.

As you read the following passages from Exodus 16; 18 and Proverbs 31, write down any practical principles you find regarding managing time.

And they took their journey from Elim, and all the congregation of the children of Israel came unto the wilderness of Sin, which *is* between Elim and Sinai, on the fifteenth day of the second month after their departing out of the land of Egypt. And the whole congregation of the children of Israel murmured against Moses and Aaron in the wilderness: And the children of Israel said unto them, Would to God we had died by the hand of the LORD in the land of Egypt, when we sat by the flesh pots, *and* when we did eat bread to the full; for ye have brought us forth into this wilderness, to kill this whole assembly with hunger.

Then said the LORD unto Moses, Behold, I will rain bread from heaven for you; and the people shall go out and gather a certain rate every day, that I may prove them, whether they will walk in my law, or no. And it shall come to pass, that on the sixth day they shall prepare *that* which they bring in; and it shall be twice as much as they gather daily.

And Moses and Aaron said unto all the children of Israel, At even, then ye shall know that the LORD hath brought you out from the land of Egypt: And in the morning, then ye shall see the glory of the LORD; for that he heareth your murmurings against the LORD: and what *are* we, that ye murmur against us? And Moses said, *This shall be*, when the LORD shall give you in the evening flesh to eat, and in the morning bread to the full; for that the LORD heareth your murmurings which ye murmur against him: and what *are* we? your murmurings *are* not against us, but against the LORD.

And Moses spake unto Aaron, Say unto all the congregation of the children of Israel, Come near before the LORD: for he hath heard your murmurings.

And it came to pass, as Aaron spake unto the whole congregation of the children of Israel, that they looked toward the wilderness, and, behold, the glory of the LORD appeared in the cloud.

And the LORD spake unto Moses, saying, I have heard the murmurings of the children of Israel: speak unto them, saying, At even ye shall eat flesh, and in the morning ye shall be filled with bread; and ye shall know that I *am* the LORD your God.

And it came to pass, that at even the quails came up, and covered the camp: and in the morning the dew lay round about the host. And when the dew that lay was gone up, behold, upon the face of the wilderness *there lay* a small round thing, *as* small as the hoar frost on the ground. And when the children of Israel saw *it*, they said one to another, It *is* manna: for they wist not what it *was*.

And Moses said unto them, This *is* the bread which the LORD hath given you to eat. This *is* the thing which the LORD hath commanded, Gather of it every man according to his eating, an omer for every man, *according to* the number of your persons; take ye every man for *them* which *are* in his tents.

And the children of Israel did so, and gathered, some more, some less. And when they did mete *it* with an omer, he that gathered much had nothing over, and he that gathered little had no lack; they gathered every man according to his eating.

And Moses said, Let no man leave of it till the morning.

Notwithstanding they hearkened not unto Moses; but some of them left of it until the morning, and it bred worms, and stank: and Moses was wroth with them.

And they gathered it every morning, every man according to his eating: and when the sun waxed hot, it melted. And it came to pass, *that* on the sixth day they gathered twice as much bread, two omers for one *man*: and all the rulers of the congregation came and told Moses. And he said unto them, This *is that* which the LORD hath said, To morrow *is* the rest of the holy sabbath unto the LORD: bake *that* which ye will bake *to day*, and seethe that ye will seethe; and that which remaineth over lay up for you to be kept until the morning.

And they laid it up till the morning, as Moses bade: and it did not stink, neither was there any worm therein. And Moses said, Eat that to day; for to day *is* a sabbath unto the LORD: to day ye shall not find it in the field. Six days ye shall gather it; but on the seventh day, *which is* the sabbath, in it there shall be none.

And it came to pass, *that* there went out *some* of the people on the seventh day for to gather, and they found none. And the LORD said unto Moses, How long refuse ye to keep my commandments and my laws? See, for that the LORD hath given you the sabbath, therefore he giveth you on the sixth day the bread of two days; abide ye every man in his place, let no man go out of his place on the seventh day. So the people rested on the seventh day. EXODUS 16:1–30

Clearly, God's Word, the Bible, contains stories and advice that illustrate healthy and godly time management. For example, the Israelites' needs were daunting after they escaped from Egypt. Living together in the harsh wilderness created conflicts that needed refereeing. As the leader of the community, Moses tried his best to deal with each and every case on his own. Apparently Moses sent his wife, Zipporah, to her father with the news that the Lord had blessed his mission and brought Israel out of Egypt. When his father-in-law came to visit, he was deeply concerned with what he saw and gave Moses a lesson in time management.

And Jethro, Moses' father in law, came with his sons and his wife unto Moses into the wilderness, where he encamped at the mount of God: And he said unto Moses, I thy father in law Jethro am come unto thee, and thy wife, and her two sons with her.

And Moses went out to meet his father in law, and did obeisance, and kissed him; and they asked each other of *their* welfare; and they came into the tent. And Moses told his father in law all that the LORD had done unto Pharaoh and to the Egyptians for Israel's sake, *and* all the travail that had come upon them by the way, and *how* the LORD delivered them.

And Jethro rejoiced for all the goodness which the LORD had done to Israel, whom he had delivered out of the hand of the Egyptians. And Jethro said, Blessed *be* the LORD, who hath delivered you out of the hand of the Egyptians, and out of the hand of Pharaoh, who hath delivered the people from under the hand of the Egyptians. Now I know that the LORD *is* greater than all gods: for in the thing wherein they dealt proudly *he was* above them. And Jethro, Moses' father in law, took a burnt offering and sacrifices for God: and Aaron came, and all the elders of Israel, to eat bread with Moses' father in law before God.

And it came to pass on the morrow, that Moses sat to judge the people: and the people stood by Moses from the morning unto the evening. And when Moses' father in law saw all that he did to the people, he said, What *is* this thing that thou doest to the people? why sittest thou thyself alone, and all the people stand by thee from morning unto even?

And Moses said unto his father in law, Because the people come unto me to enquire of God: When they have a matter, they come unto me; and I judge between one and another, and I do make *them* know the statutes of God, and his laws.

And Moses' father in law said unto him, The thing that thou doest *is* not good. Thou wilt surely wear away, both thou, and this people that *is* with thee: for this thing *is* too heavy for thee; thou art not able to perform it thyself alone. Hearken now unto my voice, I will give thee counsel, and God shall be with thee: Be thou for the people to God-ward, that thou mayest bring the causes unto God: And thou shalt teach them ordinances and laws, and shalt shew them the way wherein they must walk, and the work that they must do. Moreover thou shalt provide out of all the people able men, such as fear God, men of truth, hating covetousness; and place *such* over them, *to be* rulers of thousands, *and* rulers of hundreds, rulers of fifties, and rulers of tens: And let them judge the people at all seasons: and it shall be, *that* every great matter they shall bring unto thee, but every small matter they shall judge: so shall it be easier for thyself, and they shall bear *the burden* with thee. If thou shalt do this thing, and God command thee *so*, then thou shalt be able to endure, and all this people shall also go to their place in peace.

So Moses hearkened to the voice of his father in law, and did all that he had said. And Moses chose able men out of all Israel, and made them heads over the people, rulers of thousands, rulers of hundreds, rulers of fifties, and rulers of tens. And they judged the people at all seasons: the hard causes they brought unto Moses, but every small matter they judged themselves.

And Moses let his father in law depart; and he went his way into his own land.

EXODUS 18:5–27

The book of Proverbs in the Old Testament is a collection of brief words of wisdom loosely bound together to teach the reader skills for living, including time management. The last chapter in the book is unique. In detail, it describes the day-to-day workings of the "virtuous woman," who is, essentially, a personification of wisdom. The way she juggles her responsibilities while keeping God's purposes at the center of them all is an inspiration to every follower of God.

Who can find a virtuous woman?
  for her price *is* far above rubies.
The heart of her husband doth safely trust in her,
  so that he shall have no need of spoil.
She will do him good and not evil
  all the days of her life.
She seeketh wool, and flax,
  and worketh willingly with her hands.
She is like the merchants' ships;
  she bringeth her food from afar.
She riseth also while it is yet night,
  and giveth meat to her household,
  and a portion to her maidens.
She considereth a field, and buyeth it:
  with the fruit of her hands she planteth a vineyard.
She girdeth her loins with strength,
  and strengtheneth her arms.
She perceiveth that her merchandise *is* good:
  her candle goeth not out by night.
She layeth her hands to the spindle,
  and her hands hold the distaff.
She stretcheth out her hand to the poor;
  yea, she reacheth forth her hands to the needy.
She is not afraid of the snow for her household:
  for all her household *are* clothed with scarlet.
She maketh herself coverings of tapestry;
  her clothing *is* silk and purple.

Her husband is known in the gates,
   when he sitteth among the elders of the land.
She maketh fine linen, and selleth *it*;
   and delivereth girdles unto the merchant.
Strength and honour *are* her clothing;
   and she shall rejoice in time to come.
She openeth her mouth with wisdom;
   and in her tongue *is* the law of kindness.
She looketh well to the ways of her household,
   and eateth not the bread of idleness.
Her children arise up, and call her blessed;
   her husband *also*, and he praiseth her.
Many daughters have done virtuously,
   but thou excellest them all.
Favour *is* deceitful, and beauty *is* vain:
   ***but* a woman *that* feareth the LORD, she shall be**
      praised.
Give her of the fruit of her hands;
   and let her own works praise her in the gates.

PROVERBS 31:10–31

Like the virtuous woman, Jesus also kept God as his focus in everything he did, including how he managed his time. When Jesus' ministry was in full swing, the demands on his schedule were intense. At this time in his journey, his brothers did not embrace his position as Messiah. With tongues in cheek they suggested Jesus make his way to Judea in time for a major Jewish feast to expedite his "campaign." Jesus informed them of an important principle of his life—he managed his priorities according to the timing of God the Father.

Jesus walked in Galilee: for he would not walk in Jewry, because the Jews sought to kill him. Now the Jews' feast of tabernacles was at hand. His brethren therefore said unto him, Depart hence, and go into Judaea, that thy disciples also may see the works that thou doest. For *there is* no man *that* doeth any thing in secret, and he himself seeketh to be known openly. If thou do these things, shew thyself to the world. For neither did his brethren believe in him.

Then Jesus said unto them, My time is not yet come: but your time is alway ready. The world cannot hate you; but me it hateth, because I testify of it, that the works thereof are evil. Go ye up unto this feast: I go not up yet unto this feast; for my time is not yet full come. When he had said these words unto them, he abode *still* in Galilee.

But when his brethren were gone up, then went he also up unto the feast, not openly, but as it were in secret. Then the Jews sought him at the feast, and said, Where is he?

And there was much murmuring among the people concerning him: for some said, He is a good man.

Others said, Nay; but he deceiveth the people. Howbeit no man spake openly of him for fear of the Jews.

Now about the midst of the feast Jesus went up into the temple, and taught. And the Jews marvelled, saying, How knoweth this man letters, having never learned?

Jesus answered them, and said, My doctrine is not mine, but his that sent me. JOHN 7:1–16

THE REWARDS OF OFFERING OUR TIME

When we give our time to others in order to serve the purposes of God, particularly to those who cannot reciprocate, God not only takes notice but may also reward us greatly.

As you read the passages below from Matthew 25; Ephesians 5 and Galatians 6, look for the answer to this question: How does God reward those who do what he has asked them to do?

When the Son of man shall come in his glory, and all the holy angels with him, then shall he sit upon the throne of his glory: And before him shall be gathered all nations: and he shall separate them one from another, as a shepherd divideth *his* sheep from the goats: And he shall set the sheep on his right hand, but the goats on the left.

Then shall the King say unto them on his right hand, Come, ye blessed of my Father, inherit the kingdom prepared for you from the foundation of the world: For I was an hungred, and ye gave me meat: I was thirsty, and ye gave me drink: I was a stranger, and ye took me in: Naked, and ye clothed me: I was sick, and ye visited me: I was in prison, and ye came unto me.

Then shall the righteous answer him, saying, Lord, when saw we thee an hungred, and fed *thee*? or thirsty, and gave *thee* drink? When saw we thee a stranger, and took *thee* in? or naked, and clothed *thee*? Or when saw we thee sick, or in prison, and came unto thee?

And the King shall answer and say unto them, Verily I say unto you, Inasmuch as ye have done *it* unto one of the least of these my brethren, ye have done *it* unto me.

Then shall he say also unto them on the left hand, Depart from me, ye cursed, into everlasting fire, prepared for the devil and his angels: For I was an hungred, and ye gave me no meat: I was thirsty, and ye gave me no drink: I was a stranger, and ye took me not in: naked, and ye clothed me not: sick, and in prison, and ye visited me not.

Then shall they also answer him, saying, Lord, when saw we thee an hungred, or athirst, or a stranger, or naked, or sick, or in prison, and did not minister unto thee?

Then shall he answer them, saying, Verily I say unto you, Inasmuch as ye did *it* not to one of the least of these, ye did *it* not to me.

And these shall go away into everlasting punishment: but the righteous into life eternal. MATTHEW 25:31–46

See then that ye walk circumspectly, not as fools, but as wise, Redeeming the time, because the days are evil. Wherefore be ye not unwise, but understanding what the will of the Lord *is*. EPHESIANS 5:15–17

Be not deceived; God is not mocked: for whatsoever a man soweth, that shall he also reap. For he that soweth to his flesh shall of the flesh reap corruption; but he that soweth to the Spirit shall of the Spirit reap life everlasting. **And let us not be weary in well doing: for in due season we shall reap, if we faint not.** As we have therefore opportunity, let us do good unto all *men*, especially unto them who are of the household of faith. GALATIANS 6:7–10

What one thing can you do to improve in the
key practice of offering your time to God?

WHAT WE BELIEVE

Jonah nailed it on the head when confronted by the sailors about the cause of the storm. He answered, "I am an Hebrew; and I fear the LORD, the God of heaven, which hath made the sea and the dry land" (Jonah 1:9). Jonah worshipped the one true God and knew that God made everything and everything belonged to him. This belief drives our obedience in offering God our time to accomplish his purposes. As we seek to serve God, we would do well to keep on our minds God's words through the prophet Haggai: "Consider your ways" (Haggai 1:5). God's Word teaches and encourages us to learn how to manage our time—not for our own sakes, but for the sake of God's kingdom. The goal, reflected in the key verse at the beginning of the chapter, is not only to offer more time to God but to repurpose everything we have, everything we are and everything we do for his glory and honor. The spiritual, physical and relational rewards from God make it worth the effort for those who give themselves faithfully to this godly exercise.

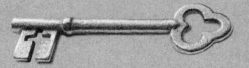

CHAPTER

19

Giving My Resources

---------- KEY QUESTION ----------

How do I best use my resources to serve God and others?

---------- KEY IDEA ----------

I give my resources to fulfill God's purposes.

---------- KEY VERSE ----------

Therefore, as ye abound in every *thing*,
in faith, and utterance, and knowledge,
and *in* all diligence, and *in* your love to us,
see that ye abound in this grace also.
2 Corinthians 8:7

The key beliefs that compel us to offer our time to God to fulfill his purposes—the church, compassion and stewardship—also drive us to give our resources. Everything we have belongs to God, and we have received clear instruction from the Bible to offer our time and give our resources to help those in need. We also recognize that our God is the one true God who loves us and has provided a way into a relationship with him as his children now and forever. Because of this, we surrender what rightfully belongs to him as an act of worship.

In this chapter we will be reading passages from the Old and New Testament that address these topics:

- Giving Tithes and Offerings
- Advice From Wise Men
- Teachings From Jesus on Money and Giving
- Generosity in Action

GIVING TITHES AND OFFERINGS

Throughout the Old Testament, God's people set aside a tenth of their proceeds of land, herds and flocks for God's purposes. This principle is called tithing. Giving a tithe started as a non-religious, political tradition in the ancient world where giving a tribute or tax of a tenth (tithe) to the king was customary. This offering demonstrated allegiance to the monarch's kingdom. When we give the first tenth of our income to God's purposes, we declare our allegiance to God and his kingdom.

Jacob was one of the first followers of God to make a declaration to honor the Lord with a tithe. He was the grandson of Abraham, the son of Isaac and Rebekah, and the twin brother of Esau. Jacob and Esau had a deeply strained relationship. Esau was the firstborn, yet Jacob manipulated him in order to acquire his birthright and then—with the help of his mother—deceived his father in order to receive the firstborn's special blessing. As one might expect, this angered Esau greatly. As a result, Jacob was sent off to live among his relatives in a land far away from Esau.

And Jacob went out from Beer-sheba, and went toward Haran. And he lighted upon a certain place, and tarried there all night, because the sun was set; and he took of the stones of that place, and put *them for* his pillows, and lay down in that place to sleep. And he dreamed, and behold a ladder set up on the earth, and the top of it reached to heaven: and behold the angels of God ascending and descending on it. And, behold, the LORD stood above it, and said, I *am* the LORD God of Abraham thy father, and the God of Isaac: the land whereon thou liest, to thee will I give it, and to thy seed; And thy seed shall be as the dust of the earth, and thou shalt spread abroad to the west, and to the east, and to the north, and to the south: and in thee and in thy seed shall all the families of the earth be blessed. And, behold, I *am* with thee, and will keep thee in all *places* whither thou goest, and will bring thee again into this land; for I will not leave thee, until I have done *that* which I have spoken to thee of.

And Jacob awaked out of his sleep, and he said, Surely the LORD is in this place; and I knew *it* not. And he was afraid, and said, How dreadful *is* this place! this *is* none other but the house of God, and this *is* the gate of heaven.

And Jacob rose up early in the morning, and took the stone that he had put *for* his pillows, and set it up *for* a pillar, and poured oil upon the top of it. And he called the name of that place Beth-el: but the name of that city *was called* Luz at the first.

And Jacob vowed a vow, saying, If God will be with me, and will keep me in this way that I go, and will give me bread to eat, and raiment to put on, So that I come again to my father's house in peace; then shall the LORD be my God: And this stone, which I have set *for* a pillar, shall be God's house: and of all that thou shalt give me I will surely give the tenth unto thee.

GENESIS 28:10–22

It is evident from many examples in the Bible that our offerings to God need not be confined to our money, but can extend to our possessions, skills, labor, creativity and time. Remarkably, at a point in Israel's history when the Israelites were at their most vulnerable, wandering in the wilderness as nomads, they demonstrated their greatest generosity. God asked Moses to build a place called the tabernacle for him to dwell with his people. In order for this to happen, God's people needed to contribute their treasures and talents. Their generous response was so over-whelming that Moses had to tell them to stop bringing their gifts for the tabernacle.

Find all the times the word "willing" is used below in the passages from Exodus 35 and 36. Why is a willing heart so important to God?

⚡ And Moses spake unto all the congregation of the children of Israel, saying, This *is* the thing which the LORD commanded, saying, Take ye from among you an offering unto the LORD: whosoever *is* of a willing heart, let him bring it, an offering of the LORD; gold, and silver, and brass, And blue, and purple, and scarlet, and fine linen, and goats' *hair*, And rams' skins dyed red, and badgers' skins, and shittim wood, And oil for the light, and spices for anointing oil, and for the sweet incense, And onyx stones, and stones to be set for the ephod, and for the breastplate.

And every wise hearted among you shall come, and make all that the LORD hath commanded; The tabernacle, his tent, and his covering, his taches, and his boards, his bars, his pillars, and his sockets, The ark, and the staves thereof, *with* the mercy seat, and the vail of the covering, The table, and his staves, and all his vessels, and the shewbread, The candlestick also for the light, and his furniture, and his lamps, with the oil for the light, And the incense altar, and his staves, and the anointing oil, and the sweet incense, and the hanging for the door at the entering in of the tabernacle, The altar of burnt offering, with his brasen grate, his staves, and all his vessels, the laver and his foot, The hangings of the court, his pillars, and their sockets, and the hanging for the door of the court, The pins of the tabernacle, and the pins of the court, and their cords, The cloths of service, to do service in the holy *place*, the holy garments for Aaron the priest, and the garments of his sons, to minister in the priest's office.

And all the congregation of the children of Israel departed from the presence of Moses. And they came, every one whose heart stirred him up, and every one whom his spirit made willing, *and* they brought the LORD's offering to the work of the tabernacle of the congregation, and for all his service, and for the holy garments. And they came, both men and women, as many as were willing hearted, *and* brought bracelets, and earrings, and rings, and tablets, all jewels of gold: and every man that offered *offered* an offering of gold unto the LORD. And every man, with whom was found blue, and purple, and scarlet, and fine linen, and goats' *hair*, and red skins of rams, and badgers' skins, brought *them*. Every one that did offer an offering of silver and brass brought the LORD's offering: and every man, with whom was found shittim wood for any work of the service, brought *it*. And all the women that were wise hearted did spin with their hands, and brought that which they had spun, *both* of blue, and of purple, *and* of scarlet, and of fine linen. And all the women whose heart stirred them up in wisdom spun goats' *hair*. And the rulers brought onyx stones, and stones to be set, for the ephod, and for the breastplate; And spice, and oil for the light, and for the anointing oil, and for the sweet incense. The children of Israel brought a willing offering unto the LORD, every man and woman, whose heart made them willing to bring for all manner of work, which the LORD had commanded to be made by the hand of Moses. EXODUS 35:4–29

And they [the people] brought yet unto him free offerings every morning. And all the wise men, that wrought all the work of the sanctuary, came every man from his work which they made; And they spake unto Moses, saying, The people bring much more than enough for the service of the work, which the LORD commanded to make.

And Moses gave commandment, and they caused it to be proclaimed throughout the camp, saying, Let neither man nor woman make any more work for the offering of the sanctuary. So the people were restrained from bringing. For the stuff they had was sufficient for all the work to make it, and too much.

EXODUS 36:3–7 ⌗

While the Israelites moved from place to place in the wilderness during the time of Moses, they took the tabernacle with them wherever they relocated. Hundreds of years later, after Israel had occupied the promised land and become a stable nation, the people once again generously gave from their resources, which they acknowledged had come from God, to build a house worthy of God's presence.

Furthermore David the king said unto all the congregation, Solomon my son, whom alone God hath chosen, *is yet* young and tender, and the work *is* great: for the palace *is* not for man, but for the LORD God. Now I have prepared with all my might for the house of my God the gold for *things to be made* of gold, and the silver for *things* of silver, and the brass for *things* of brass, the iron for *things* of iron, and wood for *things* of wood; onyx stones, and *stones* to be set, glistering stones, and of divers colours, and all manner of precious stones, and marble stones in abundance. Moreover, because I have set my affection to the house of my God, I have of mine own proper good, of gold and silver, *which* I have given to the house of my God, over and above all that I have prepared for the holy house, *Even* three thousand talents of gold, of the gold of Ophir, and seven thousand talents of refined silver, to overlay the walls of the houses *withal*: The gold for *things* of gold, and the silver for *things* of silver, and for all manner of work *to be made* by the hands of artificers. And who *then* is willing to consecrate his service this day unto the LORD?

Then the chief of the fathers and princes of the tribes of Israel, and the captains of thousands and of hundreds, with the rulers of the king's work, offered willingly, And gave for the service of the house of God of gold five thousand talents and ten thousand drams, and of silver ten thousand talents, and of brass eighteen thousand talents, and one hundred thousand talents of iron. And they with whom *precious* stones were found gave *them* to the treasure of the house of the LORD, by the hand of Jehiel the Gershonite. Then the people rejoiced, for that they offered willingly, because with perfect heart they offered willingly to the LORD: and David the king also rejoiced with great joy.

Wherefore David blessed the LORD before all the congregation: and David said, Blessed *be* thou, LORD God of Israel our father, for ever and ever. Thine, O LORD, *is* the greatness, and the power, and the glory, and the victory, and the majesty: for all *that is* in the heaven and in the earth *is thine*; thine *is* the kingdom, O LORD, and thou art exalted as head above all. Both riches and honour *come* of thee, and thou reignest over all; and in thine hand *is* power and might; and in thine hand *it is* to make great, and to give strength unto all. Now therefore, our God, we thank thee, and praise thy glorious name.

But who *am* I, and what *is* my people, that we should be able to offer so willingly after this sort? for all things *come* of thee, and of thine own have we given thee. For we *are* strangers before thee, and sojourners, as *were* all our fathers: our days on the earth *are* as a shadow, and *there is* none abiding. O LORD our God, all this store that we have prepared to build thee an house for thine holy name *cometh* of thine hand, and *is* all thine own. I know also, my God, that thou triest the heart, and hast pleasure in uprightness. As for me, in the uprightness of mine heart I have willingly offered all these things: and now have I seen with joy thy people, which are present here, to offer willingly unto thee. O LORD God of Abraham, Isaac, and of Israel, our fathers, keep this for ever in the imagination of the thoughts of the heart of thy people, and prepare their heart unto thee. 1 CHRONICLES 29:1–18

ADVICE FROM WISE MEN

As you read the following passages from Proverbs 3 and 11, identify the one piece of advice that speaks most clearly to you right now.

Giving away our money and resources is beneficial not only for the recipients but also for us. When we make giving to God's purposes part of our regular spending habits, we honor God and keep greed at bay. The writers of Proverbs offered the following words of wisdom regarding how we should handle what God has given us.

Honour the LORD with thy substance,
    and with the firstfruits of all thine increase:
So shall thy barns be filled with plenty,
    and thy presses shall burst out with new wine.

PROVERBS 3:9–10

There is that scattereth, and yet increaseth;
> and *there is* that withholdeth more than is meet,
> but *it tendeth* to poverty.
> **The liberal soul shall be made fat:**
> **and he that watereth shall be watered also himself.**

PROVERBS 11:24–25

He that trusteth in his riches shall fall:
> but the righteous shall flourish as a branch. PROVERBS 11:28

Solomon, one of the writers of Proverbs and the son of King David, accumulated immense wealth during his lifetime. In the book of Ecclesiastes, traditionally considered to be written by Solomon, he reflects on his life and shares his words of wisdom with us regarding the dangers of wealth. Money itself is not evil, but the love of money can lead to sin. More wealth does not mean more satisfaction in life. To avoid falling victim to money's seductive lure, we are to use what we have for the Lord.

He that loveth silver shall not be satisfied with silver; nor he that loveth abundance with increase: this *is* also vanity.

When goods increase, they are increased that eat them: and what good *is there* to the owners thereof, saving the beholding *of them* with their eyes?

The sleep of a labouring man *is* sweet, whether he eat little or much: but the abundance of the rich will not suffer him to sleep.

There is a sore evil *which* I have seen under the sun, *namely,* riches kept for the owners thereof to their hurt. But those riches perish by evil travail: and he begetteth a son, and *there is* nothing in his hand. As he came forth of his mother's womb, naked shall he return to go as he came, and shall take nothing of his labour, which he may carry away in his hand.

And this also *is* a sore evil, *that* in all points as he came, so shall he go: and what profit hath he that hath laboured for the wind? All his days also he eateth in darkness, and *he hath* much sorrow and wrath with his sickness.

Behold *that* which I have seen: *it is* good and comely *for one* to eat and to drink, and to enjoy the good of all his labour that he taketh under the sun all the days of his life, which God giveth him: for it *is* his portion. **Every man also to whom God hath given riches and wealth, and hath given him power to eat thereof, and to take his portion, and to rejoice in his labour; this *is* the gift of God. For he shall not much remember the days of his life; because God answereth *him* in the joy of his heart.**

ECCLESIASTES 5:10–20

> At the birth of Jesus, three men came from afar with gifts to visit him. They were likely astrologers from Persia, southern Arabia or Mesopotamia who had been anticipating the arrival of the "king of the Jews" for some time. Their advice for us doesn't come from their lips as much as from their actions. They gave him months of their time as they traveled to see him. They were honored men, yet they humbled themselves and bowed their knees to worship Jesus. They also gave him costly gifts that were the best they had to give.

Now when Jesus was born in Bethlehem of Judaea in the days of Herod the king, behold, there came wise men from the east to Jerusalem, Saying, Where is he that is born King of the Jews? for we have seen his star in the east, and are come to worship him.

When Herod the king had heard *these things*, he was troubled, and all Jerusalem with him. And when he had gathered all the chief priests and scribes of the people together, he demanded of them where Christ should be born. And they said unto him, In Bethlehem of Judaea: for thus it is written by the prophet, And thou Bethlehem, *in* the land of Juda, art not the least among the princes of Juda: for out of thee shall come a Governor, that shall rule my people Israel.

Then Herod, when he had privily called the wise men, enquired of them diligently what time the star appeared. And he sent them to Bethlehem, and said, Go and search diligently for the young child; and when ye have found *him*, bring me word again, that I may come and worship him also.

When they had heard the king, they departed; and, lo, the star, which they saw in the east, went before them, till it came and stood over where the young child was. When they saw the star, they rejoiced with exceeding great joy. **And when they were come into the house, they saw the young child with Mary his mother, and fell down, and worshipped him: and when they had opened their treasures, they presented unto him gifts; gold, and frankincense, and myrrh.** And being warned of God in a dream that they should not return to Herod, they departed into their own country another way. MATTHEW 2:1–12 🔑

TEACHINGS FROM JESUS ON MONEY AND GIVING

Jesus said more about money than the topics of heaven and hell combined. Our attitudes toward money and personal resources say so much about our lives. Giving should flow from a pure heart that desires to meet a need. There's a subtle trap to avoid in our giving—it should not be a way to draw attention to ourselves. It is important to think beyond our earthly lives and ask how we can share what we've been given to build God's kingdom.

Take heed that ye do not your alms before men, to be seen of them: otherwise ye have no reward of your Father which is in heaven.

Therefore when thou doest *thine* alms, do not sound a trumpet before thee, as the hypocrites do in the synagogues and in the streets, that they may have glory of men. Verily I say unto you, They have their reward. **But when thou doest alms, let not thy left hand know what thy right hand doeth: That thine alms may be in secret: and thy Father which seeth in secret himself shall reward thee openly.** MATTHEW 6:1–4

Lay not up for yourselves treasures upon earth, where moth and rust doth corrupt, and where thieves break through and steal: But lay up for yourselves treasures in heaven, where neither moth nor rust doth corrupt, and where thieves do not break through nor steal: For where your treasure is, there will your heart be also.

The light of the body is the eye: if therefore thine eye be single, thy whole body shall be full of light. But if thine eye be evil, thy whole body shall be full of darkness. If therefore the light that is in thee be darkness, how great *is* that darkness!

No man can serve two masters: for either he will hate the

one, and love the other; or else he will hold to the one, and despise the other. Ye cannot serve God and mammon.

MATTHEW 6:19–24

And one of the company said unto him, Master, speak to my brother, that he divide the inheritance with me.

And he said unto him, Man, who made me a judge or a divider over you? And he said unto them, Take heed, and beware of covetousness: for a man's life consisteth not in the abundance of the things which he possesseth.

And he spake a parable unto them, saying, The ground of a certain rich man brought forth plentifully: And he thought within himself, saying, What shall I do, because I have no room where to bestow my fruits?

And he said, This will I do: I will pull down my barns, and build greater; and there will I bestow all my fruits and my goods. And I will say to my soul, Soul, thou hast much goods laid up for many years; take thine ease, eat, drink, *and* be merry.

But God said unto him, *Thou* fool, this night thy soul shall be required of thee: then whose shall those things be, which thou hast provided?

So *is* he that layeth up treasure for himself, and is not rich toward God.

LUKE 12:13–21

As is evident from the above parable of the rich fool, Jesus had a knack for noticing teachable moments. Everyday encounters with fig trees, water wells and simple dinner parties provided illustrations for Jesus to explain what matters the most to God. In this situation, Jesus was observing the daily activities at the temple when an opportunity arose for Jesus to teach his disciples what type of giving touches God's heart.

And Jesus sat over against the treasury, and beheld how the people cast money into the treasury: and many that were rich cast in much. And there came a certain poor widow, and she threw in two mites, which make a farthing.

And he called *unto him* his disciples, and saith unto them, Verily I say unto you, That this poor widow hath cast more in,

than all they which have cast into the treasury: For all *they* did cast in of their abundance; but she of her want did cast in all that she had, *even* all her living.   MARK 12:41–44

It's easy to give when we know we will receive something in return. Jesus challenges us to remember that true giving has no strings attached.

For if ye love them which love you, what thank have ye? for sinners also love those that love them. And if ye do good to them which do good to you, what thank have ye? for sinners also do even the same. And if ye lend *to them* of whom ye hope to receive, what thank have ye? for sinners also lend to sinners, to receive as much again. But love ye your enemies, and do good, and lend, hoping for nothing again; and your reward shall be great, and ye shall be the children of the Highest: for he is kind unto the unthankful and *to* the evil. Be ye therefore merciful, as your Father also is merciful.

LUKE 6:32–36

If someone asked you to summarize what Jesus taught about money and giving, what would you say?

GENEROSITY IN ACTION

After Jesus' death, resurrection and ascension to heaven, his followers committed to give their money generously to help the needy among them and fulfill God's purposes.

And the multitude of them that believed were of one heart and of one soul: neither said any *of them* that ought of the things which he possessed was his own; but they had all things common. And with great power gave the apostles witness of the resurrection of the Lord Jesus: and great grace was upon them all. Neither was there any among them that lacked: for as many as were possessors of lands or houses sold them, and brought the prices of the things that were sold, And laid *them* down at the apostles' feet: and distribution was made unto every man according as he had need.

And Joses, who by the apostles was surnamed Barnabas, (which is, being interpreted, The son of consolation,) a Levite, *and* of the country of Cyprus, Having land, sold *it*, and brought the money, and laid *it* at the apostles' feet.

ACTS 4:32–37

Evidence of the generosity of the early church can be seen in many circumstances. For instance, Paul encouraged the believers at Corinth to send an offering to their needy fellow believers in Jerusalem, something the Corinthians had intended to do but had not finished.

As you read the Scripture below from 2 Corinthians 8 and 9, look for details concerning how believers can determine what they should give.

Moreover, brethren, we do you to wit of the grace of God bestowed on the churches of Macedonia; How that in a great trial of affliction the abundance of their joy and their deep poverty abounded unto the riches of their liberality. For to *their* power, I bear record, yea, and beyond *their* power *they were* willing of themselves; Praying us with much intreaty that we would receive the gift, and *take upon us* the fellowship of the ministering to the saints. And *this they did*, not as we hoped, but first gave their own selves to the Lord, and unto us by the will of God. Insomuch that we desired Titus, that as he had begun, so he would also finish in you the same grace also. **Therefore, as ye abound in every *thing*, *in* faith, and utterance, and knowledge, and *in* all diligence, and *in* your love to us, *see* that ye abound in this grace also.**

I speak not by commandment, but by occasion of the forwardness of others, and to prove the sincerity of your love. For ye know the grace of our Lord Jesus Christ, that, though he was rich, yet for your sakes he became poor, that ye through his poverty might be rich.

And herein I give *my* advice: for this is expedient for you, who have begun before, not only to do, but also to be forward a year ago. Now therefore perform the doing *of it*; that as *there was* a readiness to will, so *there may be* a performance also out of that which ye have. For if there be first a willing mind, *it is* accepted according to that a man hath, *and* not according to that he hath not.

For *I mean* not that other men be eased, and ye burdened: But by an equality, *that* now at this time your abundance *may be a supply* for their want, that their abundance also may be *a supply* for your want: that there may be equality: As it is written, He that *had gathered* much had nothing over; and he that *had gathered* little had no lack.

But thanks *be* to God, which put the same earnest care into the heart of Titus for you. For indeed he accepted the exhortation; but being more forward, of his own accord he went unto you. And we have sent with him the brother, whose praise *is* in the gospel throughout all the churches; And not *that* only, but who was also chosen of the churches to travel with us with this grace, which is administered by us to the glory of the same Lord, and *declaration of* your ready mind: Avoiding this, that no man should blame us in this abundance which is administered by us: Providing for honest things, not only in the sight of the Lord, but also in the sight of men.

And we have sent with them our brother, whom we have oftentimes proved diligent in many things, but now much more diligent, upon the great confidence which *I have* in you. Whether *any do enquire* of Titus, *he is* my partner and fellowhelper concerning you: or our brethren *be enquired of, they are* the messengers of the churches, *and* the glory of Christ. Wherefore shew ye to them, and before the churches, the proof of your love, and of our boasting on your behalf.

For as touching the ministering to the saints, it is superfluous for me to write to you: For I know the forwardness of your mind, for which I boast of you to them of Macedonia, that Achaia was ready a year ago; and your zeal hath provoked very many. Yet have I sent the brethren, lest our boasting of you should be in vain in this behalf; that, as I said, ye may be ready: Lest haply if they of Macedonia come with me, and find you unprepared, we (that we say not, ye) should be ashamed in this same confident boasting. Therefore I thought it necessary to exhort the brethren, that they would go before unto you, and make up beforehand your bounty, whereof ye had notice before, that the same might be ready, as *a matter of* bounty, and not as *of* covetousness.

But this *I say*, He which soweth sparingly shall reap also sparingly; and he which soweth bountifully shall reap also bountifully. Every man according as he purposeth in his heart, *so let him give*; not grudgingly, or of necessity: for God loveth a cheerful giver. And God *is* able to make all grace abound toward you; that ye, always having all sufficiency in all *things*, may abound to every good work. (As it is written, He hath dispersed abroad; he hath given to the poor: his righteousness remaineth for ever. Now he that ministereth seed to the sower both minister bread for *your* food, and multiply your seed sown, and increase the fruits of your righteousness;) Being enriched in every thing to all bountifulness, which causeth through us thanksgiving to God.

For the administration of this service not only supplieth the want of the saints, but is abundant also by many thanksgivings unto God; Whiles by the experiment of this ministration they glorify God for your professed subjection unto the gospel of Christ, and for *your* liberal distribution unto them, and unto all *men*; And by their prayer for you, which long after you for the exceeding grace of God in you. Thanks *be* unto God for his unspeakable gift.

2 CORINTHIANS 8:1—9:15

On a scale of 1–10, evaluate your level of generosity.
What has helped you become more generous?
What still causes you to hold back?

WHAT WE BELIEVE

Many people see giving as an obligation, but it is really an act of worship from someone who has embraced in their heart the key beliefs of the Christian faith. The one true God is good and has provided the way to eternal salvation. When we accept this gift of life we are given a new identity and called to a new purpose to fulfill God's mission on earth until he returns. We give away our resources with that motivation and purpose in mind. The people of the Old Testament gave the first 10 percent to God as a declaration of their allegiance to him. But they gave beyond the tithe out of a willing heart because of God's great love for them. The words of the wisdom writers and the lives of the wise men who visited the baby Jesus illustrate the importance and benefits of being content and generous with our resources. Jesus reminds us that we should strive to think bigger than our earthly lives and use our resources to strengthen God's kingdom. God is more concerned about the reasons we give than about the size of our gift.

CHAPTER

20

Sharing My Faith

KEY QUESTION

How do I share my faith with those who don't know God?

KEY IDEA

I share my faith with others to fulfill God's purposes.

KEY VERSE

And for me, that utterance may be given unto me,
that I may open my mouth boldly, to make
known the mystery of the gospel,
For which I am an ambassador in bonds:
that therein I may speak boldly, as I ought to speak.
Ephesians 6:19 – 20

OUR MAP

We believe the one true God has unfolded his grand plan to provide salvation through Jesus Christ. We believe God loves all people and extends an invitation to everyone to receive eternal life. We believe there is a heaven and a hell and that Jesus is returning to judge the earth and establish his eternal kingdom. Only those who receive salvation by faith in Christ in this life will be a part of the eternal life to come. We believe God has purposed the church to be the primary ambassador to spread this message, this good news to the world. Because of these values we commit ourselves to sharing our faith. So how do we share our faith with those who don't know God?

In this chapter we will read Scripture passages that answer that question. Here are the main topics of this chapter:

- *The Call to Share Our Faith*
- *Sharing Our Faith Through Our Lives*
- *Sharing Our Faith Through Our Words*
- *Sharing Our Faith With All*

THE CALL TO SHARE OUR FAITH

Catastrophically, the fall of humankind in the Garden of Eden shattered humanity's connection with God—the connection he originally intended when he created people. So God unfolded a plan to provide the way for all people to come back into a relationship with him. His grand plan included the founding of a brand-new nation. Two thousand years before the arrival of Jesus, God called Abram (later renamed Abraham) to start this new nation, eventually known as Israel. People from all nations would come to know God through Abraham's offspring.

Now the LORD had said unto Abram, Get thee out of thy country, and from thy kindred, and from thy father's house, unto a land that I will shew thee: And I will make of thee a great nation, and I will bless thee, and make thy name great; and thou shalt be a blessing: And I will bless them that bless thee, and curse him that curseth thee: **and in thee shall all families of the earth be blessed.**

So Abram departed, as the LORD had spoken unto him; and Lot went with him.   GENESIS 12:1–4

In the 2,000 years that followed, Israel was a living demonstration to the world of the lengths to which God would go to reestablish his relationship with his people. Then, with the ultimate sacrifice of his Son, the reconciliation with God that was formerly confined to Israel now became available to all humankind. What's remarkable is that we can play a pivotal role in God's restoration plan. By responding to the call to share our faith, we partner with God in his divine pursuit of broken souls.

For the love of Christ constraineth us; because we thus judge, that if one died for all, then were all dead: And *that* he died for all, that they which live should not henceforth live unto themselves, but unto him which died for them, and rose again.

Wherefore henceforth know we no man after the flesh: yea, though we have known Christ after the flesh, yet now henceforth know we *him* no more. Therefore if any man *be* in Christ, *he is* a new creature: old things are passed away; behold, all things are become new. And all things *are* of God, who hath reconciled us to himself by Jesus Christ, and hath given to us the ministry of reconciliation; To wit, **that God was in Christ, reconciling the world unto himself, not imputing their trespasses unto them; and hath committed unto us the word of reconciliation. Now then we are ambassadors for Christ, as though God did beseech *you* by us:** we pray *you* in Christ's stead, be ye reconciled to God. For he hath made him *to be* sin for us, who knew no sin; that we might be made the righteousness of God in him.

2 CORINTHIANS 5:14–21

What are some ways in which we can be God's
"ambassadors" to the world?

SHARING OUR FAITH THROUGH OUR LIVES
The most powerful way to share our faith in God is through our lives—being a positive example to all in how we live every day.

When others see the faith, hope and love in our lives, they are drawn to live the same way. After paying attention over time, they will notice our confidence in and relationship with the one true God. In 2 Kings we find a story in which a young girl from Israel who had been taken captive speaks up because of her faith and her noble concern for her master, the captain of the host of Syria—Israel's enemy. The girl's words eventually led to the healing of this foreign soldier and inspired his belief in the one true God.

Now Naaman, captain of the host of the king of Syria, was a great man with his master, and honourable, because by him the LORD had given deliverance unto Syria: he was also a mighty man in valour, *but he was* a leper.

And the Syrians had gone out by companies, and had brought away captive out of the land of Israel a little maid; and she waited on Naaman's wife. And she said unto her mistress, Would God my lord *were* with the prophet that *is* in Samaria! for he would recover him of his leprosy.

And *one* went in, and told his lord, saying, Thus and thus said the maid that *is* of the land of Israel. And the king of Syria said, Go to, go, and I will send a letter unto the king of Israel. And he departed, and took with him ten talents of silver, and six thousand *pieces* of gold, and ten changes of raiment. And he brought the letter to the king of Israel, saying, Now when this letter is come unto thee, behold, I have *therewith* sent Naaman my servant to thee, that thou mayest recover him of his leprosy.

And it came to pass, when the king of Israel had read the letter, that he rent his clothes, and said, *Am* I God, to kill and to make alive, that this man doth send unto me to recover a man of his leprosy? wherefore consider, I pray you, and see how he seeketh a quarrel against me.

And it was *so*, when Elisha the man of God had heard that the king of Israel had rent his clothes, that he sent to the king, saying, Wherefore hast thou rent thy clothes? let him come now to me, and he shall know that there is a prophet in Israel. So Naaman came with his horses and with his chariot, and stood at the door of the house of Elisha. And Elisha sent a messenger unto him, saying,

Go and wash in Jordan seven times, and thy flesh shall come again to thee, and thou shalt be clean.

But Naaman was wroth, and went away, and said, Behold, I thought, He will surely come out to me, and stand, and call on the name of the LORD his God, and strike his hand over the place, and recover the leper. *Are* not Abana and Pharpar, rivers of Damascus, better than all the waters of Israel? may I not wash in them, and be clean? So he turned and went away in a rage.

And his servants came near, and spake unto him, and said, My father, *if* the prophet had bid thee *do some* great thing, wouldest thou not have done *it*? how much rather then, when he saith to thee, Wash, and be clean? Then went he down, and dipped himself seven times in Jordan, according to the saying of the man of God: and his flesh came again like unto the flesh of a little child, and he was clean.

And he [Naaman] returned to the man of God, he and all his company, and came, and stood before him: and he said, Behold, now I know that *there is* no God in all the earth, but in Israel. 2 KINGS 5:1–15

The one true God wants us to be a reflection of his image to the world. In his famous Sermon on the Mount, Jesus used the metaphor of "salt and light" to express the power of a life lived in faith and obedience to God.

Ye are the salt of the earth: but if the salt have lost his savour, wherewith shall it be salted? it is thenceforth good for nothing, but to be cast out, and to be trodden under foot of men.

Ye are the light of the world. A city that is set on an hill cannot be hid. Neither do men light a candle, and put it under a bushel, but on a candlestick; and it giveth light unto all that are in the house. **Let your light so shine before men, that they may see your good works, and glorify your Father which is in heaven.** MATTHEW 5:13–16

Being the light of the world requires the attitude of a humble servant. Sometimes we must adapt our approach in order to meet the needs of the people we are trying to reach with the gospel.

Many new believers in the early church were drawn to the Christian faith by the way the people of the church served one another.

And they continued stedfastly in the apostles' doctrine and fellowship, and in breaking of bread, and in prayers. And fear came upon every soul: and many wonders and signs were done by the apostles. And all that believed were together, and had all things common; And sold their possessions and goods, and parted them to all *men*, as every man had need. **And they, continuing daily with one accord in the temple, and breaking bread from house to house, did eat their meat with gladness and singleness of heart, Praising God, and having favour with all the people. And the Lord added to the church daily such as should be saved.**

ACTS 2:42–47

The apostle Paul was very aware that his life was to be the light of Christ and the good flavor of salt to his world. He consciously did whatever it took to make sure he was putting others' needs before his own so they would have no reason to reject the good news.

For though I be free from all *men*, yet have I made myself servant unto all, that I might gain the more. And unto the Jews I became as a Jew, that I might gain the Jews; to them that are under the law, as under the law, that I might gain them that are under the law; To them that are without law, as without law, (being not without law to God, but under the law to Christ,) that I might gain them that are without law. To the weak became I as weak, that I might gain the weak: **I am made all things to all *men*, that I might by all means save some. And this I do for the gospel's sake, that I might be partaker thereof with *you*.**

1 CORINTHIANS 9:19–23

What does Paul mean when he writes,
"I am made all things to all *men*,
that I might by means save some"?
What do you think this does not mean?

SHARING OUR FAITH THROUGH OUR WORDS

In addition to sharing our faith by the way we live our lives, we are also called to share through our words who God is and what great things he has done for us. David, overwhelmed with God's involvement in his life, was a strong witness through his words to God's character and acts.

I waited patiently for the LORD;
　and he inclined unto me, and heard my cry.
He brought me up also out of an horrible pit,
　out of the miry clay,
and set my feet upon a rock,
　and established my goings.
And he hath put a new song in my mouth,
　even praise unto our God:
many shall see *it*, and fear,
　and shall trust in the LORD.

Blessed *is* that man
　that maketh the LORD his trust,
and respecteth not the proud,
　nor such as turn aside to lies.
Many, O LORD my God,
　are thy wonderful works *which* thou hast done,
　and thy thoughts *which are* to usward:
they cannot be reckoned up in order unto thee:
　if I would declare and speak *of them*,
　they are more than can be numbered.

Sacrifice and offering thou didst not desire;
　mine ears hast thou opened:
　burnt offering and sin offering hast thou not required.
Then said I, Lo, I come:
　in the volume of the book *it is* written of me,
I delight to do thy will, O my God:
　yea, thy law *is* within my heart.

**I have preached righteousness in the great
　congregation:**

**lo, I have not refrained my lips, O LORD,
thou knowest.**
I have not hid thy righteousness within my heart;
I have declared thy faithfulness and thy salvation:
I have not concealed thy lovingkindness
and thy truth from the great congregation. PSALM 40:1–10

The entire early church had a mission to share the truth about God's love and faithfulness, which they accomplished by testifying about the resurrected Christ. Although we may feel we are not as eloquent as David or as knowledgeable as Paul, like the early church members, we all have a mission to share our faith with others. It is through God that we have been given the power to carry out that assignment.

The former treatise have I made, O Theophilus, of all that Jesus began both to do and teach, Until the day in which he was taken up, after that he through the Holy Ghost had given commandments unto the apostles whom he had chosen: To whom also he shewed himself alive after his passion by many infallible proofs, being seen of them forty days, and speaking of the things pertaining to the kingdom of God: And, being assembled together with *them*, commanded them that they should not depart from Jerusalem, but wait for the promise of the Father, which, *saith he*, ye have heard of me. For John truly baptized with water; but ye shall be baptized with the Holy Ghost not many days hence.

When they therefore were come together, they asked of him, saying, Lord, wilt thou at this time restore again the kingdom to Israel?

And he said unto them, It is not for you to know the times or the seasons, which the Father hath put in his own power. **But ye shall receive power, after that the Holy Ghost is come upon you: and ye shall be witnesses unto me both in Jerusalem, and in all Judaea, and in Samaria, and unto the uttermost part of the earth.** ACTS 1:1–8

The people of the early church had a mission to share the truth about God's love and faithfulness, which they accomplished by testifying about the resurrected Christ. But when it comes to actually using words, we may be afraid we won't know what to say. God promised us the Holy Ghost to give us words when we need them, just as Paul prays in the key verse at the beginning of the chapter. As we see with Philip, the Spirit even makes sure we meet people at just the right time—when they are ready to hear the good news.

As you read about Philip's divine encounter with the Ethiopian in Acts 8, identify Philip's effective strategies for sharing his faith that you can emulate.

And at that time there was a great persecution against the church which was at Jerusalem; and they were all scattered abroad throughout the regions of Judaea and Samaria, except the apostles. And devout men carried Stephen *to his burial*, and made great lamentation over him. As for Saul, he made havock of the church, entering into every house, and haling men and women committed *them* to prison.

Therefore they that were scattered abroad went every where preaching the word. Then Philip went down to the city of Samaria, and preached Christ unto them. And the people with one accord gave heed unto those things which Philip spake, hearing and seeing the miracles which he did. For unclean spirits, crying with loud voice, came out of many that were possessed *with them*: and many taken with palsies, and that were lame, were healed. And there was great joy in that city. ACTS 8:1–8

And the angel of the Lord spake unto Philip, saying, Arise, and go toward the south unto the way that goeth down from Jerusalem unto Gaza, which is desert. And he arose and went: and, behold, a man of Ethiopia, an eunuch of great authority under Candace queen of the Ethiopians, who had the charge of all her treasure, and had come to Jerusalem for to worship, Was returning, and sitting in his chariot read Esaias the prophet. Then the Spirit said unto Philip, Go near, and join thyself to this chariot.

And Philip ran thither to *him*, and heard him read the prophet Esaias, and said, Understandest thou what thou readest?

And he said, How can I, except some man should guide me? And he desired Philip that he would come up and sit with him.

The place of the scripture which he read was this, He was led as a sheep to the slaughter; and like a lamb dumb before his shearer, so opened he not his mouth: In his humiliation his judgment was taken away: and who shall declare his generation? for his life is taken from the earth.

And the eunuch answered Philip, and said, I pray thee, of whom speaketh the prophet this? of himself, or of some other man? **Then Philip opened his mouth, and began at the same scripture, and preached unto him Jesus.**

And as they went on *their* way, they came unto a certain water: and the eunuch said, See, *here is* water; what doth hinder me to be baptized? And Philip said, If thou believest with all thine heart, thou mayest. And he answered and said, I believe that Jesus Christ is the Son of God. And he commanded the chariot to stand still: and they went down both into the water, both Philip and the eunuch; and he baptized him. And when they were come up out of the water, the Spirit of the Lord caught away Philip, that the eunuch saw him no more: and he went on his way rejoicing. But Philip was found at Azotus: and passing through he preached in all the cities, till he came to Caesarea. Acts 8:26–40

Like Philip illustrated by following the leading of the Spirit, when we partner with God in his plan to piece together this broken world, we become his ambassadors, his representatives on earth. Being an ambassador of Christ is not easy. The apostle Paul, who suffered greatly for sharing his faith, understood this well. Despite the persecution, he was passionate about spreading the good news. While headed to Jerusalem during his third missionary journey, he requested a meeting with his good friends from Ephesus, since he knew there was a chance he'd never see them again. At the meeting, Paul declared his passion for sharing his faith.

And from Miletus he sent to Ephesus, and called the elders of the church. And when they were come to him, he said unto them, Ye know, from the first day that I came into Asia, after what manner I have been with you at all seasons, Serving the Lord with all humility of mind, and with many tears, and temptations, which befell me by the lying in wait of the Jews: *And* how I kept back nothing that was profitable *unto you*, but have shewed you, and have taught you publickly, and from house to house, Testifying both to the Jews, and also to the Greeks, repentance toward God, and faith toward our Lord Jesus Christ.

And now, behold, I go bound in the spirit unto Jerusalem, not knowing the things that shall befall me there: Save that the Holy Ghost witnesseth in every city, saying that bonds and afflictions abide me. **But none of these things move me, neither count I my life dear unto myself, so that I might finish my course with joy, and the ministry, which I have received of the Lord Jesus, to testify the gospel of the grace of God.**   ACTS 20:17–24

In his letters, Paul asked fellow believers to pray for him as he shared his faith. And he called them to make the most of every opportunity to share the message of the good news. Paul's words are precious to us today as we share our faith with those God brings across our paths.

And [pray] for me, that utterance may be given unto me, that I may open my mouth boldly, to make known the mystery of the gospel, For which I am an ambassador in bonds: that therein I may speak boldly, as I ought to speak.   EPHESIANS 6:19–20

Continue in prayer, and watch in the same with thanksgiving; Withal praying also for us, that God would open unto us a door of utterance, to speak the mystery of Christ, for which I am also in bonds: That I may make it manifest, as I ought to speak. **Walk in wisdom toward them that are without, redeeming the time. Let your speech *be* alway with grace, seasoned with salt, that ye may know how ye ought to answer every man.**   COLOSSIANS 4:2–6

What does it mean to "walk in wisdom toward them that are without"? What does it mean to have our conversation "with grace" and "seasoned with salt"?

SHARING OUR FAITH WITH ALL

From the very beginning God anticipated that all nations and all people would be a part of his plan of redemption and restoration. The Israelites resisted God's call to be the channel of his redemptive purposes for the people of the world. This sentiment was demonstrated in the story of Jonah, whom God called to take his message to the Assyrian people in the great city of Nineveh. The Assyrians, a major enemy of Israel, were wicked people with wicked practices. As we read in Chapter 18 (Offering My Time), when God gave Jonah this assignment, Jonah ran away in the opposite direction; he thought the people in Nineveh were beyond saving. He had time to rethink his decision when God placed him in the belly of a giant fish for three days. After God had the fish vomit Jonah onto dry land, God offered Jonah an opportunity to obey, even though Jonah still did not think the people would respond.

⌐╥ And the word of the LORD came unto Jonah the second time, saying, Arise, go unto Nineveh, that great city, and preach unto it the preaching that I bid thee.

So Jonah arose, and went unto Nineveh, according to the word of the LORD. Now Nineveh was an exceeding great city of three days' journey. And Jonah began to enter into the city a day's journey, and he cried, and said, Yet forty days, and Nineveh shall be overthrown. So the people of Nineveh believed God, and proclaimed a fast, and put on sackcloth, from the greatest of them even to the least of them.

For word came unto the king of Nineveh, and he arose from his throne, and he laid his robe from him, and covered *him* with sackcloth, and sat in ashes. And he caused *it* to be proclaimed and published through Nineveh by the decree of the king and his nobles, saying, Let neither man nor beast, herd nor flock, taste any thing: let them not feed, nor drink water: But let man and beast be covered with sackcloth, and cry mightily unto God: yea, let them turn every one from his evil way, and from the violence that *is* in their hands. Who can tell *if* God will turn and repent, and turn away from his fierce anger, that we perish not?

And God saw their works, that they turned from their evil way;

and God repented of the evil, that he had said that he would do unto them; and he did *it* not.

But it displeased Jonah exceedingly, and he was very angry. And he prayed unto the LORD, and said, I pray thee, O LORD, *was* not this my saying, when I was yet in my country? Therefore I fled before unto Tarshish: for I knew that thou *art* a gracious God, and merciful, slow to anger, and of great kindness, and repentest thee of the evil. Therefore now, O LORD, take, I beseech thee, my life from me; for *it is* better for me to die than to live.

Then said the LORD, Doest thou well to be angry?

So Jonah went out of the city, and sat on the east side of the city, and there made him a booth, and sat under it in the shadow, till he might see what would become of the city. And the LORD God prepared a gourd, and made *it* to come up over Jonah, that it might be a shadow over his head, to deliver him from his grief. So Jonah was exceeding glad of the gourd. But God prepared a worm when the morning rose the next day, and it smote the gourd that it withered. And it came to pass, when the sun did arise, that God prepared a vehement east wind; and the sun beat upon the head of Jonah, that he fainted, and wished in himself to die, and said, *It is* better for me to die than to live.

And God said to Jonah, Doest thou well to be angry for the gourd?

And he said, I do well to be angry, *even* unto death.

Then said the LORD, Thou hast had pity on the gourd, for the which thou hast not laboured, neither madest it grow; which came up in a night, and perished in a night: And should not I spare Nineveh, that great city, wherein are more than sixscore thousand persons that cannot discern between their right hand and their left hand; and *also* much cattle?   JONAH 3:1—4:11 ⚷

The resistance of the Jews to sharing their faith with outsiders carried over into the time of Jesus. The Samaritans were a mixed-blood race resulting from the intermarriage of Israelites who were left behind when the people of the northern kingdom were exiled and Gentiles who were brought into the land by the Assyrians. Resentful hostility existed between Jews and Samaritans in Jesus' day. To avoid these people, who lived in the large region between Judea and Galilee, Jews would often go out of their way to cross over the Jordan River and travel on the east side. Modeling the value of inclusivity to his disciples, Jesus traveled directly through Samaria and went out of his way to talk to a Samaritan woman.

[Jesus] left Judaea, and departed again into Galilee.

And he must needs go through Samaria. Then cometh he to a city of Samaria, which is called Sychar, near to the parcel of ground that Jacob gave to his son Joseph. Now Jacob's well was there. Jesus therefore, being wearied with *his* journey, sat thus on the well: *and* it was about the sixth hour.

There cometh a woman of Samaria to draw water: Jesus saith unto her, Give me to drink. (For his disciples were gone away unto the city to buy meat.)

Then saith the woman of Samaria unto him, How is it that thou, being a Jew, askest drink of me, which am a woman of Samaria? for the Jews have no dealings with the Samaritans.

Jesus answered and said unto her, If thou knewest the gift of God, and who it is that saith to thee, Give me to drink; thou wouldest have asked of him, and he would have given thee living water.

The woman saith unto him, Sir, thou hast nothing to draw with, and the well is deep: from whence then hast thou that living water? Art thou greater than our father Jacob, which gave us the well, and drank thereof himself, and his children, and his cattle?

Jesus answered and said unto her, Whosoever drinketh of this water shall thirst again: But whosoever drinketh of the water that I shall give him shall never thirst; but the water that I shall give him shall be in him a well of water springing up into everlasting life.

The woman saith unto him, Sir, give me this water, that I thirst not, neither come hither to draw.

Jesus saith unto her, Go, call thy husband, and come hither.

The woman answered and said, I have no husband.

Jesus said unto her, Thou hast well said, I have no husband: For thou hast had five husbands; and he whom thou now hast is not thy husband: in that saidst thou truly.

The woman saith unto him, Sir, I perceive that thou art a

prophet. Our fathers worshipped in this mountain; and ye say, that in Jerusalem is the place where men ought to worship.

Jesus saith unto her, Woman, believe me, the hour cometh, when ye shall neither in this mountain, nor yet at Jerusalem, worship the Father. Ye worship ye know not what: we know what we worship: for salvation is of the Jews. But the hour cometh, and now is, when the true worshippers shall worship the Father in spirit and in truth: for the Father seeketh such to worship him. God *is* a Spirit: and they that worship him must worship *him* in spirit and in truth.

The woman saith unto him, I know that Messias cometh, which is called Christ: when he is come, he will tell us all things.

Jesus saith unto her, I that speak unto thee am *he.*

And upon this came his disciples, and marvelled that he talked with the woman: yet no man said, What seekest thou? or, Why talkest thou with her?

The woman then left her waterpot, and went her way into the city, and saith to the men, Come, see a man, which told me all things that ever I did: is not this the Christ? Then they went out of the city, and came unto him.

In the mean while his disciples prayed him, saying, Master, eat.

But he said unto them, I have meat to eat that ye know not of.

Therefore said the disciples one to another, Hath any man brought him *ought* to eat?

Jesus saith unto them, My meat is to do the will of him that sent me, and to finish his work. Say not ye, There are yet four months, and *then* cometh harvest? behold, **I say unto you, Lift up your eyes, and look on the fields; for they are white already to harvest. And he that reapeth receiveth wages, and gathereth fruit unto life eternal: that both he that soweth and he that reapeth may rejoice together. And herein is that saying true, One soweth, and another reapeth. I sent you to reap that whereon ye bestowed no labour: other men laboured, and ye are entered into their labours.**

And many of the Samaritans of that city believed on him for the saying of the woman, which testified, He told me all that ever I did. So when the Samaritans were come unto him, they besought him that he would tarry with them: and he abode there two days. And many more believed because of his own word;

And said unto the woman, Now we believe, not because of thy saying: for we have heard *him* ourselves, and know that this is indeed the Christ, the Saviour of the world.   JOHN 4:3–42

In regard to sharing our faith, what did Jesus mean
that one "soweth" the seed and another "reapeth"
the harvest? Why should we share our faith,
even if we think our message could be rejected?

Although Paul was known as the apostle to the Gentiles, his heart longed for his fellow Jews to respond to the message about Jesus. In his letter to the Romans, Paul declares God's plan and desire for both Jew and Gentile—all people—to hear the gospel and know Jesus as Lord. We also read this passage in Chapter 3 (Salvation). This time read it with our responsibility to share our faith in mind.

Brethren, my heart's desire and prayer to God for Israel is, that they might be saved. For I bear them record that they have a zeal of God, but not according to knowledge. For they being ignorant of God's righteousness, and going about to establish their own righteousness, have not submitted themselves unto the righteousness of God. For Christ *is* the end of the law for righteousness to every one that believeth.

For Moses describeth the righteousness which is of the law, That the man which doeth those things shall live by them. But the righteousness which is of faith speaketh on this wise, Say not in thine heart, Who shall ascend into heaven? (that is, to bring Christ down *from above*:) Or, Who shall descend into the deep? (that is, to bring up Christ again from the dead.) But what saith it? The word is nigh thee, *even* in thy mouth, and in thy heart: that is, the word of faith, which we preach; That if thou shalt confess with thy mouth the Lord Jesus, and shalt believe in thine heart that God hath raised him from the dead, thou shalt be saved. For with the heart man believeth unto righteousness; and with the mouth confession is made unto salvation. For the scripture saith, Whosoever believeth on him shall not be ashamed. For there is no difference between the Jew and the Greek: for the same Lord over all is rich unto all that call upon him. For whosoever shall call upon the name of the Lord shall be saved.

How then shall they call on him in whom they have not believed? and how shall they believe in him of whom they have not heard? and how shall they hear without a preacher? And how shall they preach, except they be sent? as it is written, How beautiful are the feet of them that preach the gospel of peace, and bring glad tidings of good things! ROMANS 10:1–15

WHAT WE BELIEVE

All believers are called to share their faith with others. We have been given the "ministry of reconciliation"; we are God's "ambassadors" in the world. We are called to share our faith through the way we live our lives. We are to be "salt and light" to the people God has placed in our sphere of influence. The mere beauty of how Christians treat each other is an aroma that draws outsiders to want to know God and be in a relationship with him. We are also called to share our faith through our words. Like David, our relationship with God is so meaningful to us that we will have a hard time "refraining our lips." Like Philip, we will look for divine appointments to share the gospel with people who are genuinely seeking. God's grace and love know no boundaries. He desires for all people to come into a saving relationship with him. Therefore, we will share our faith with our enemies, people of different races or religions or sometimes even people in our own family. Let's pray, like Paul, that we "may speak boldly."

Who Am I Becoming?

*I am the vine, ye are the branches: He that abideth
in me, and I in him, the same bringeth forth
much fruit: for without me ye can do nothing.*
John 15:5

In the passage above Jesus compares the Christian life to a vine. He is the vine; we are the branches. If we remain in the vine of Christ, over time we will produce amazing and scrumptious fruit at the end of our branches for all to see and taste.

People love ripe, delicious-tasting fruit but grimace at green, rotten or artificial fruit. Jesus wants to produce in us fruit that brings great joy to us and to others. For this to happen, we must remain in Christ. To remain simply means to "stay put." Becoming like Jesus is a journey. Spiritual growth is compounding. The longer we remain consistent with Christ, the better it gets.

Nurturing the passion and discipline to *think* and *act* like Jesus is our proactive part in remaining in the vine of Christ, but we are not alone. The Father is the gardener. He waters, tills the soil, makes sure we have the proper exposure to the sun and prunes us.

As we remain in Christ and the Gardener does his work, eventually the bud of fruit appears on the end of our branches. With more time the fruit grows and ripens. Mature fruit on the outside gives evidence to the health of the branch on the inside. Mature fruit on the outside ministers to the people God has put in our life. It draws them to us; it nurtures them and gives them refreshment. This pleases God when we "pay forward" the love he first deposited in us.

The final ten chapters lay out the ten key virtues God desires to see developed in your life. As you read, pray, "This is who I want to become!" And with God's help, you will.

I can do all things through Christ which strengtheneth me.
Philippians 4:13

CHAPTER

21

Love

KEY QUESTION

What does it mean to sacrificially,
and unconditionally love others?

KEY IDEA

I am committed to loving God and loving others.

KEY VERSE

Herein is love, not that we loved God, but that he loved us,
and sent his Son *to be* the propitiation for our sins.
Beloved, if God so loved us, we ought also to love one another.
No man hath seen God at any time. If we love one another,
God dwelleth in us, and his love is perfected in us.
1 John 4:10 – 12

OUR MAP

We believe to become. The ten key beliefs of the Christian life are not an end in themselves. They are to be understood in our minds (a renewal from the fall) and then accepted in our hearts by engaging in the ten spiritual practices. We are now moving to the ten key virtues of the Christian life. As the beliefs are embraced and owned in our hearts, "buds" of the virtues, or the fruit of the Spirit, appear on the external branches of our lives for others to see and taste. The ultimate fruit, the essential virtue, the most important expression of being like Jesus, is LOVE. What does it mean to sacrificially and unconditionally love others?

The Scripture passages included in this chapter will provide the answer under the following topics:

- *Love Defined*
- *The Greatest Commandment*
- *A New Command*
- *Loving Examples*

LOVE DEFINED

The Bible is a complex narrative. But what is the big—yet simple—idea behind all the stories and teachings contained in this ancient book? Love. Love dominates God's story. First Corinthians 13 provides us with an earnest description of love—called "charity" in this chapter—that resonates throughout Scripture.

As you read 1 Corinthians 13 below, make two lists.
What are the characteristics of charity in the positive sense
(all that charity is). What characteristics does charity not have?

Though I speak with the tongues of men and of angels, and have not charity, I am become *as* sounding brass, or a tinkling cymbal. And though I have *the gift of* prophecy, and understand all mysteries, and all knowledge; and though I have all faith, so that I could remove mountains, and have not charity, I am nothing. And though I bestow all my goods to feed *the poor,* and though I give my body to be burned, and have not charity, it profiteth me nothing.

Charity suffereth long, *and* is kind; charity envieth not; charity vaunteth not itself, is not puffed up, Doth not behave itself unseemly, seeketh not her own, is not easily provoked, thinketh no evil; Rejoiceth not in iniquity, but rejoiceth in the truth; Beareth all things, believeth all things, hopeth all things, endureth all things.

Charity never faileth: but whether *there be* prophecies, they shall fail; whether *there be* tongues, they shall cease; whether *there be* knowledge, it shall vanish away. For we know in part, and we prophesy in part. But when that which is perfect is come, then that which is in part shall be done away. When I was a child, I spake as a child, I understood as a child, I thought as a child: but when I became a man, I put away childish things. For now we see through a glass, darkly; but then face to face: now I know in part; but then shall I know even as also I am known.

And now abideth faith, hope, charity, these three; but the greatest of these *is* charity.   1 Corinthians 13:1–13

The Greatest Commandment

As the greatest commandment, this "charity," or love, can be found early in God's story with his people. For example, near the end of his life, Moses gathered the Israelites together to remind them of what truly mattered as they readied themselves to enter the promised land. His words, recorded in the book of Deuteronomy, include a passage known as the Shema (Hebrew for "hear"), which later became the Jewish confession of faith, recited twice daily at the morning and evening prayer services. As the Shema beautifully articulates, the love between God and his people has always been the driver behind a life of faith.

Hear, O Israel: The Lord our God *is* one Lord: **And thou shalt love the Lord thy God with all thine heart, and with all thy soul, and with all thy might.** And these words, which I command thee this day, shall be in thine heart: And thou shalt teach them diligently unto thy children, and shalt talk of them when thou sittest in thine house, and when thou walkest by the way, and when thou liest down, and when thou risest up. And thou shalt bind them for a sign upon thine hand, and they shall be as frontlets between thine eyes. And thou shalt write them upon the posts of thy house, and on thy gates.   DEUTERONOMY 6:4–9

Flowing from the priority to love God with our whole hearts, souls and might is the command to love our neighbor as ourselves.

Thou shalt not hate thy brother in thine heart: thou shalt in any wise rebuke thy neighbour, and not suffer sin upon him.

Thou shalt not avenge, nor bear any grudge against the children of thy people, but thou shalt love thy neighbour as thyself: I *am* the LORD.   LEVITICUS 19:17–18

Jesus confirmed these two commands from the Old Testament — love God and love others — as the greatest of all the commandments during an encounter recorded in the New Testament between Jesus and the religious leaders.

And one of the scribes came, and having heard them reasoning together, and perceiving that he had answered them well, asked him, Which is the first commandment of all?

And Jesus answered him, The first of all the commandments *is*, Hear, O Israel; The Lord our God is one Lord: And thou shalt love the Lord thy God with all thy heart, and with all thy soul, and with all thy mind, and with all thy strength: this *is* the first commandment. And the second *is* like, *namely* this, Thou shalt love thy neighbour as thyself. There is none other commandment greater than these.

And the scribe said unto him, Well, Master, thou hast said the truth: for there is one God; and there is none other but he: And to love him with all the heart, and with all the understanding, and with all the soul, and with all the strength, and to love *his* neighbour as himself, is more than all whole burnt offerings and sacrifices.

And when Jesus saw that he answered discreetly, he said unto him, Thou art not far from the kingdom of God. And no man after that durst ask him *any question.*   MARK 12:28–34

Do you love the Lord your God with all your heart, soul, mind and strength? How would you describe the amount of love you show for others? Are you satisfied with your answers?

A NEW COMMAND

Every moral law of the Old Testament fits under one of these two greater commands — love God and love others. The Law was given to express God's high standards for community in his kingdom and to demonstrate legally that people were incapable of keeping God's perfect commands and requirements and needed a savior. Jesus came to fulfill the Law and offered us a new commandment. Interestingly, it was after Judas left the gathering with the disciples at the Last Supper to betray Jesus that Jesus changed the formula for love and issued a new command.

Therefore, when he was gone out, Jesus said, Now is the Son of man glorified, and God is glorified in him. If God be glorified in him, God shall also glorify him in himself, and shall straightway glorify him.

Little children, yet a little while I am with you. Ye shall seek me: and as I said unto the Jews, Whither I go, ye cannot come; so now I say to you.

A new commandment I give unto you, That ye love one another; as I have loved you, that ye also love one another. By this shall all *men* know that ye are my disciples, if ye have love one to another.

JOHN 13:31–35

From this point on the commandment to love is never referred to again in the same way. Instead of us trying hard to love God and others, we receive Christ's love for us and then pass it on to others. This is what Jesus did as our example. He received the love of the Father and passed it on to us. It is God's love in us that gives us the capacity to love others.

Put into your own words what happened in the shift from the Great Commandment of the Old Testament to the new command of Jesus.

Left to our own sinful nature, or flesh, we move away from uncon-
ditional and sacrificial love and instead crave to satisfy our own
wants over the needs and interests of others. Living a life of love
requires the presence of God's love and power within us. When
we yield to this presence in our lives, it produces within us love for
others. The Law provides some instruction regarding how to live
a life of love; the Spirit empowers us to actually do it.

For, brethren, ye have been called unto liberty; only *use* not liberty for an occasion to the flesh, but by love serve one another. For
all the law is fulfilled in one word, *even* in this; Thou shalt love thy
neighbour as thyself. But if ye bite and devour one another, take
heed that ye be not consumed one of another.

This I say then, Walk in the Spirit, and ye shall not fulfil the lust
of the flesh. For the flesh lusteth against the Spirit, and the Spirit
against the flesh: and these are contrary the one to the other: so
that ye cannot do the things that ye would. But if ye be led of the
Spirit, ye are not under the law.

Now the works of the flesh are manifest, which are *these*; Adultery, fornication, uncleanness, lasciviousness, Idolatry, witchcraft,
hatred, variance, emulations, wrath, strife, seditions, heresies,
Envyings, murders, drunkenness, revellings, and such like: of the
which I tell you before, as I have also told *you* in time past, that
they which do such things shall not inherit the kingdom of God.

But the fruit of the Spirit is love, joy, peace, longsuffering,
gentleness, goodness, faith, Meekness, temperance: against
such there is no law. And they that are Christ's have crucified the
flesh with the affections and lusts. If we live in the Spirit, let us
also walk in the Spirit.   GALATIANS 5:13–25

After Paul lists all the qualities of the fruit
of the Spirit, why did he then write,
"Against such there is no law"?

Our capacity to love begins with receiving God's love for us.
From this reservoir we pour out love toward one another. The
presence of God's Spirit in us, working through us to overcome

our passion for self in favor of loving others, is confirmation that
we are, in fact, children of God.

Beloved, let us love one another: for love is of God; and every one that loveth is born of God, and knoweth God. He that loveth not knoweth not God; for God is love. In this was manifested the love of God toward us, because that God sent his only begotten Son into the world, that we might live through him. **Herein is love, not that we loved God, but that he loved us, and sent his Son** *to be* **the propitiation for our sins. Beloved, if God so loved us, we ought also to love one another.** No man hath seen God at any time. If we love one another, God dwelleth in us, and his love is perfected in us.

Hereby know we that we dwell in him, and he in us, because he hath given us of his Spirit. And we have seen and do testify that the Father sent the Son *to be* the Saviour of the world. Whosoever shall confess that Jesus is the Son of God, God dwelleth in him, and he in God. And we have known and believed the love that God hath to us.

God is love; and he that dwelleth in love dwelleth in God, and God in him. Herein is our love made perfect, that we may have boldness in the day of judgment: because as he is, so are we in this world. There is no fear in love; but perfect love casteth out fear: because fear hath torment. He that feareth is not made perfect in love.

We love him, because he first loved us. If a man say, I love God, and hateth his brother, he is a liar: for he that loveth not his brother whom he hath seen, how can he love God whom he hath not seen? And this commandment have we from him, That he who loveth God love his brother also. 1 JOHN 4:7–21

With this increased capacity for God's love to flow in and through
us comes increased expectation. The bar that Jesus and Paul set
is higher than we can achieve on our own. But with God's love in
us, it becomes quite possible.

Ye have heard that it hath been said, Thou shalt love thy neighbour, and hate thine enemy. But I say unto you, Love your enemies, bless them that curse you, do good to them that hate you, and pray for them which despitefully use you, and persecute you; That ye may be the children of your Father which is in heaven: for he maketh his sun to rise on the evil and on the good, and sendeth rain on the just and on the unjust. For if ye love them which love you, what reward have ye? do not even the publicans the same? And if ye salute your brethren only, what do ye more *than others*? do not even the publicans so? Be ye therefore perfect, even as your Father which is in heaven is perfect.   MATTHEW 5:43–48

Owe no man any thing, but to love one another: for he that loveth another hath fulfilled the law. For this, Thou shalt not commit adultery, Thou shalt not kill, Thou shalt not steal, Thou shalt not bear false witness, Thou shalt not covet; and if *there be* any other commandment, it is briefly comprehended in this saying, namely, Thou shalt love thy neighbour as thyself. Love worketh no ill to his neighbour: therefore love *is* the fulfilling of the law.

ROMANS 13:8–10

Although we may love our brother or sister, all relationships have their issues. Unfortunately, dissonance can replace the love when we leave hurts and offenses unresolved. When Peter approached Jesus with a question about forgiveness, Jesus answered the question and followed it up with a poignant parable to illustrate his point. It is forgiveness that keeps relationships connected and prevents bitterness from dividing people.

Then came Peter to him, and said, Lord, how oft shall my brother sin against me, and I forgive him? till seven times?

Jesus saith unto him, I say not unto thee, Until seven times: but, Until seventy times seven.

Therefore is the kingdom of heaven likened unto a certain king, which would take account of his servants. And when he had begun to reckon, one was brought unto him, which owed him ten thousand talents. But forasmuch as he had not to pay, his lord commanded him to be sold, and his wife, and children, and all that he had, and payment to be made.

The servant therefore fell down, and worshipped him, saying, Lord, have patience with me, and I will pay thee all. Then the lord of that servant was moved with compassion, and loosed him, and forgave him the debt.

But the same servant went out, and found one of his fellowservants, which owed him an hundred pence: and he laid hands on him, and took *him* by the throat, saying, Pay me that thou owest.

And his fellowservant fell down at his feet, and besought him, saying, Have patience with me, and I will pay thee all.

And he would not: but went and cast him into prison, till he should pay the debt. So when his fellowservants saw what was done, they were very sorry, and came and told unto their lord all that was done.

Then his lord, after that he had called him, said unto him, O thou wicked servant, I forgave thee all that debt, because thou desiredst me: Shouldest not thou also have had compassion on thy fellowservant, even as I had pity on thee? And his lord was wroth, and delivered him to the tormentors, till he should pay all that was due unto him.

So likewise shall my heavenly Father do also unto you, if ye from your hearts forgive not every one his brother their trespasses.

MATTHEW 18:21–35

LOVING EXAMPLES

Now that we have a clear understanding of love as God intended it to be, it's powerful to look at how that love has been exemplified by God's people in the Bible. One of the most beautiful and inspiring stories of someone loving another as they would themselves is Jonathan and David. Jonathan, the son of King Saul, the first monarch of Israel, was next in line to reign. But when young David emerged into the limelight after killing the Philistine giant Goliath with only a slingshot, it was clear that God had other plans. Jonathan recognized God's hand on David and graciously stepped aside and even protected David. King Saul saw the same thing, but instead became driven by jealousy and insecurity.

As you read the story below from 1 Samuel 18 and 19, write down the ways that Jonathan offered David unconditional and sacrificial love.

And it came to pass, when he had made an end of speaking unto Saul, that the soul of Jonathan was knit with the soul of David, and Jonathan loved him as his own soul. And Saul took him that day, and would let him go no more home to his father's house. **Then Jonathan and David made a covenant, because he loved him as his own soul. And Jonathan stripped himself of the robe that *was* upon him, and gave it to David, and his garments, even to his sword, and to his bow, and to his girdle.** 1 SAMUEL 18:1–4

And Saul spake to Jonathan his son, and to all his servants, that they should kill David. But Jonathan Saul's son delighted much in David: and Jonathan told David, saying, Saul my father seeketh to kill thee: now therefore, I pray thee, take heed to thyself until the morning, and abide in a secret *place*, and hide thyself: And I will go out and stand beside my father in the field where thou *art*, and I will commune with my father of thee; and what I see, that I will tell thee.

And Jonathan spake good of David unto Saul his father, and said unto him, Let not the king sin against his servant, against David; because he hath not sinned against thee, and because his works *have been* to thee-ward very good: For he did put his life in his hand, and slew the Philistine, and the LORD wrought a great salvation for all Israel: thou sawest *it*, and didst rejoice: wherefore then wilt thou sin against innocent blood, to slay David without a cause?

And Saul hearkened unto the voice of Jonathan: and Saul sware, *As* the LORD liveth, he shall not be slain.

And Jonathan called David, and Jonathan shewed him all those things. And Jonathan brought David to Saul, and he was in his presence, as in times past. 1 SAMUEL 19:1–7

Before long, Saul jealously turned against David again and threw a spear at David with the intent of killing him. David escaped and found himself on the run. It appears the purpose of this hardship in David's life was to give him the opportunity to see God's hand in his life and to learn to trust God unreservedly. David eventually found his way safely to Jonathan. David apparently wanted to make one more attempt to come alongside Saul and serve him if Saul would accept him. David and Jonathan agreed on a plan to expose the intent of Saul's heart.

And David fled from Naioth in Ramah, and came and said before Jonathan, What have I done? what *is* mine iniquity? and what *is* my sin before thy father, that he seeketh my life?

And he said unto him, God forbid; thou shalt not die: behold, my father will do nothing either great or small, but that he will shew it me: and why should my father hide this thing from me? it *is* not *so*.

And David sware moreover, and said, Thy father certainly knoweth that I have found grace in thine eyes; and he saith, Let not Jonathan know this, lest he be grieved: but truly *as* the LORD liveth, and *as* thy soul liveth, *there is* but a step between me and death.

Then said Jonathan unto David, Whatsoever thy soul desireth, I will even do *it* for thee.

And David said unto Jonathan, Behold, to morrow *is* the new moon, and I should not fail to sit with the king at meat: but let me go, that I may hide myself in the field unto the third *day* at even. If thy father at all miss me, then say, David earnestly asked *leave* of me that he might run to Beth-lehem his city: for *there is* a yearly sacrifice there for all the family. If he say thus, *It is* well; thy servant shall have peace: but if he be very wroth, *then* be sure that evil is determined by him. Therefore thou shalt deal kindly with thy servant; for thou hast brought thy servant into a covenant of the LORD with thee: notwithstanding, if there be in me iniquity, slay me thyself; for why shouldest thou bring me to thy father?

And Jonathan said, Far be it from thee: for if I knew certainly that evil were determined by my father to come upon thee, then would not I tell it thee?

Then said David to Jonathan, Who shall tell me? or what *if* thy father answer thee roughly?

And Jonathan said unto David, Come, and let us go out into the field. And they went out both of them into the field.

And Jonathan said unto David, O LORD God of Israel, when I have sounded my father about to morrow any time, *or* the third *day*, and, behold, *if there be* good toward David, and I then send not unto thee, and shew it thee; The LORD do so and much more to Jonathan: but if it please my father *to do* thee evil, then I will shew it thee, and send thee away, that thou mayest go in peace: and the LORD be with thee, as he hath been with my father. And thou shalt not only while yet I live shew me the kindness of the LORD, that I die not: But *also* thou shalt not cut off thy kindness from my house for ever: no, not when the LORD hath cut off the enemies of David every one from the face of the earth.

So Jonathan made *a covenant* with the house of David, *saying,* Let the LORD even require *it* at the hand of David's enemies. And Jonathan caused David to swear again, because he loved him: for he loved him as he loved his own soul.

Then Jonathan said to David, To morrow *is* the new moon: and thou shalt be missed, because thy seat will be empty. And *when* thou hast stayed three days, *then* thou shalt go down quickly, and come to the place where thou didst hide thyself when the business was *in hand*, and shalt remain by the stone Ezel. And I will shoot three arrows on the side *thereof,* as though I shot at a mark. And, behold, I will send a lad, *saying,* Go, find out the arrows. If I expressly say unto the lad, Behold, the arrows *are* on this side of thee, take them; then come thou: for *there is* peace to thee, and no hurt; *as* the LORD liveth. But if I say thus unto the young man, Behold, the arrows *are* beyond thee; go thy way: for the LORD hath sent thee away. And *as touching* the matter which thou and I have spoken of, behold, the LORD *be* between thee and me for ever.

So David hid himself in the field: and when the new moon was come, the king sat him down to eat meat. And the king sat upon his seat, as at other times, *even* upon a seat by the wall: and Jonathan arose, and Abner sat by Saul's side, and David's place was empty. Nevertheless Saul spake not any thing that day: for he thought, Something hath befallen him, he *is* not clean; surely he *is* not clean. And it came to pass on the morrow, *which was* the second *day* of the month, that David's place was empty: and Saul said unto Jonathan his son, Wherefore cometh not the son of Jesse to meat, neither yesterday, nor to day?

And Jonathan answered Saul, David earnestly asked *leave* of me *to go* to Beth-lehem: And he said, Let me go, I pray thee; for our family hath a sacrifice in the city; and my brother, he hath commanded me *to be there*: and now, if I have found favour in thine eyes, let me get away, I pray thee, and see my brethren. Therefore he cometh not unto the king's table.

Then Saul's anger was kindled against Jonathan, and he said unto him, Thou son of the perverse rebellious *woman*, do not I know that thou hast chosen the son of Jesse to thine own confusion, and unto the confusion of thy mother's nakedness? For as long as the son of Jesse liveth upon the ground, thou shalt not be established, nor thy kingdom. Wherefore now send and fetch him unto me, for he shall surely die.

And Jonathan answered Saul his father, and said unto him, Wherefore shall he be slain? what hath he done? And Saul cast a javelin at him to smite him: whereby Jonathan knew that it was determined of his father to slay David.

So Jonathan arose from the table in fierce anger, and did eat no meat the second day of the month: for he was grieved for David, because his father had done him shame.

And it came to pass in the morning, that Jonathan went out into the field at the time appointed with David, and a little lad with him. And he said unto his lad, Run, find out now the arrows which I shoot. *And* as the lad ran, he shot an arrow beyond him. And when the lad was come to the place of the arrow which Jonathan had shot, Jonathan cried after the lad, and said, *Is* not the arrow beyond thee? And Jonathan cried after the lad, Make speed, haste, stay not. And Jonathan's lad gathered up the arrows, and came to his master. But the lad knew not any thing: only Jonathan and David knew the matter. And Jonathan gave his artillery unto his lad, and said unto him, Go, carry *them* to the city.

And as soon as the lad was gone, David arose out of *a place* toward the south, and fell on his face to the ground, and bowed himself three times: and they kissed one another, and wept one with another, until David exceeded.

And Jonathan said to David, Go in peace, forasmuch as we have sworn both of us in the name of the LORD, saying, The LORD be between me and thee, and between my seed and thy seed for ever. And he arose and departed: and Jonathan went into the city.

1 SAMUEL 20:1–42

David was a fugitive on the run from King Saul for several years. While David was hiding from Saul, the Philistines — the same enemy David defeated as a young man — attacked and defeated

Israel. Jonathan was killed in battle and Saul took his own life as the enemy closed in on him. A short time later, David was inaugurated as the king of Israel. When David's kingdom was well established, he demonstrated that he hadn't forgotten his promise to show kindness to Jonathan's family by taking care of Jonathan's son Mephibosheth. In his relationship with both Jonathan and Mephibosheth and throughout his reign as king, David demonstrated his commitment to love God and others.

Of course, the ultimate model for a life of love comes from Jesus. He consistently referred to love and grace flowing first from the Father to him and then to us. This is the secret to loving others.

I am the good shepherd, and know my *sheep,* and am known of mine. As the Father knoweth me, even so know I the Father: and I lay down my life for the sheep. And other sheep I have, which are not of this fold: them also I must bring, and they shall hear my voice; and there shall be one fold, *and* one shepherd. Therefore doth my Father love me, because I lay down my life, that I might take it again. No man taketh it from me, but I lay it down of myself. I have power to lay it down, and I have power to take it again. This commandment have I received of my Father.

JOHN 10:14–18

WHAT WE BELIEVE

Love is the ultimate expression of becoming like Jesus. God the Father desires for us to unconditionally and sacrificially love others. Biblical love is defined in 1 Corinthians 13 (where it is called "charity") and declared the Great Commandment in Mark 12. To love God and love our neighbor is the standard of God, which on our own we cannot achieve. But in Christ, a new command is issued. God pours his presence and love within us first. Then, as we receive it, we let his love pass through us to others. Jonathan provides a beautiful example of love in his relationship with David. But no one models it better than Jesus himself. With God's love and presence in us, we can become more and more like Jesus.

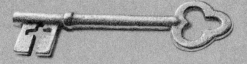

CHAPTER

22

Joy

---------- KEY QUESTION ----------

What gives us true happiness and contentment in life?

---------- KEY IDEA ----------

Despite my circumstances,
I feel inner contentment and understand
my purpose in life.

---------- KEY VERSE ----------

These things have I spoken unto you,
that my joy might remain in you,
and *that* your joy might be full.
John 15:11

A person can have money, all the possessions they desire, health and even good looks, but if they don't have joy, life can be rather challenging. It is easier to find joy when things are going well. Yet some people struggle to experience this virtue even amidst life's most favorable situations. Here is some amazing news! Christ offers us joy, no matter our circumstances. True joy is rooted in the key belief that the one true God is a personal God who is involved in and cares about our daily lives. He loves us and is working out a good plan for us. When we confidently believe this in our hearts, we can rise above our circumstances and find joy in Christ alone. How can this be? We will be exploring the following Biblical concepts in this chapter:

- *Source of Joy*
- *Joyful Celebrations*
- *Joy Despite Our Circumstances*

SOURCE OF JOY

God may shower us with blessings and circumstances that bring joy to our lives, but true joy is found not in those things themselves but in their source. Joy can also be fueled and found in living out God's Word and trusting in the promises God makes to us in his Word. The psalmist declared this truth with great confidence in this song.

> Preserve me, O God:
> for in thee do I put my trust.
>
> *O my soul,* thou hast said unto the LORD, Thou *art* my
> Lord:
> my goodness *extendeth* not to thee;
> *But* to the saints that *are* in the earth,
> and *to* the excellent, in whom *is* all my delight.
> Their sorrows shall be multiplied *that* hasten *after* another
> god:
> their drink offerings of blood will I not offer,
> nor take up their names into my lips.

The L ORD *is* the portion of mine inheritance and of my
    cup:
  thou maintainest my lot.
The lines are fallen unto me in pleasant *places*;
  yea, I have a goodly heritage.
I will bless the L ORD, who hath given me counsel:
  my reins also instruct me in the night seasons.
I have set the L ORD always before me:
  because *he is* at my right hand, I shall not be moved.

Therefore my heart is glad, and my glory rejoiceth:
  my flesh also shall rest in hope.
For thou wilt not leave my soul in hell;
  neither wilt thou suffer thine Holy One to see
    corruption.
Thou wilt shew me the path of life:
  in thy presence *is* fulness of joy;
  at thy right hand *there are* pleasures for evermore.

P SALM 16:1–11

*God's promises find their ultimate fulfillment in his Son Jesus.
Note how his arrival into our world brought joy to everyone
present.*

And it came to pass in those days, that there went out a decree
from Caesar Augustus, that all the world should be taxed. *(And
this taxing was first made when Cyrenius was governor of Syria.)*
And all went to be taxed, every one into his own city.

And Joseph also went up from Galilee, out of the city of Nazareth, into Judaea, unto the city of David, which is called Bethlehem; (because he was of the house and lineage of David:) To be
taxed with Mary his espoused wife, being great with child. And so
it was, that, while they were there, the days were accomplished that
she should be delivered. And she brought forth her firstborn son,
and wrapped him in swaddling clothes, and laid him in a manger;
because there was no room for them in the inn.

And there were in the same country shepherds abiding in the
field, keeping watch over their flock by night. And, lo, the angel of

the Lord came upon them, and the glory of the Lord shone round about them: and they were sore afraid. **And the angel said unto them, Fear not: for, behold, I bring you good tidings of great joy, which shall be to all people. For unto you is born this day in the city of David a Saviour, which is Christ the Lord.** And this *shall be* a sign unto you; Ye shall find the babe wrapped in swaddling clothes, lying in a manger.

And suddenly there was with the angel a multitude of the heavenly host praising God, and saying, Glory to God in the highest, and on earth peace, good will toward men.

And it came to pass, as the angels were gone away from them into heaven, the shepherds said one to another, Let us now go even unto Bethlehem, and see this thing which is come to pass, which the Lord hath made known unto us.

And they came with haste, and found Mary, and Joseph, and the babe lying in a manger. And when they had seen *it*, they made known abroad the saying which was told them concerning this child. And all they that heard *it* wondered at those things which were told them by the shepherds. But Mary kept all these things, and pondered *them* in her heart. And the shepherds returned, glorifying and praising God for all the things that they had heard and seen, as it was told unto them.

And when eight days were accomplished for the circumcising of the child, his name was called JESUS, which was so named of the angel before he was conceived in the womb.   LUKE 2:1–21

> *Jesus taught us that spiritual growth is much like the development of fruit on a vine. He is the vine and we become the branches when we place our faith in him. As we abide in the vine of Christ through obedience to his commands, his nutrients of joy run through our spiritual veins from the inside out and produce the ripe, juicy fruit of joy in and through our lives.*

I am the true vine, and my Father is the husbandman. Every branch in me that beareth not fruit he taketh away: and *every branch* that beareth fruit, he purgeth it, that it may bring forth more fruit. Now ye are clean through the word which I have spoken unto you. Abide in me, and I in you. As the branch cannot bear fruit of itself, except it abide in the vine; no more can ye, except ye abide in me.

I am the vine, ye *are* the branches: He that abideth in me, and I in him, the same bringeth forth much fruit: for without me ye can do nothing. If a man abide not in me, he is cast forth as a branch, and is withered; and men gather them, and cast *them* into the fire, and they are burned. If ye abide in me, and my words abide in you, ye shall ask what ye will, and it shall be done unto you. Herein is my Father glorified, that ye bear much fruit; so shall ye be my disciples.

As the Father hath loved me, so have I loved you: continue ye in my love. If ye keep my commandments, ye shall abide in my love; even as I have kept my Father's commandments, and abide in his love. These things have I spoken unto you, that my joy might remain in you, and *that* your joy might be full.

JOHN 15:1–11

How does keeping God's commandments
produce joy in our lives?

JOYFUL CELEBRATIONS

In the Old Testament, people often responded to God's blessings with joyful celebrations. Coming together intentionally to remember God stimulated joy in the hearts of the people. The annual feast of tabernacles especially provided an opportunity for the Israelites to celebrate God's goodness, since the focus was reminding them that God provided food and shelter during their days in the wilderness. When the people returned from captivity, it had been years since they had gathered for this joy-filled celebration. With great passion they reinstated this tradition, and the results speak for themselves.

And on the second day were gathered together the chief of the fathers of all the people, the priests, and the Levites, unto Ezra the scribe, even to understand the words of the law. And they found written in the law which the LORD had commanded by Moses, that the children of Israel should dwell in booths in the feast of the seventh month: And that they should publish and proclaim in all their cities, and in Jerusalem, saying, Go forth unto the mount, and fetch olive branches, and pine branches, and myrtle branches, and palm branches, and branches of thick trees, to make booths, as *it is* written.

So the people went forth, and brought *them*, and made themselves booths, every one upon the roof of his house, and in their courts, and in the courts of the house of God, and in the street of the water gate, and in the street of the gate of Ephraim. **And all the congregation of them that were come again out of the captivity made booths, and sat under the booths: for since the days of Jeshua the son of Nun unto that day had not the children of Israel done so. And there was very great gladness.**

NEHEMIAH 8:13–17

Another joyful celebration recorded in the Old Testament occurred when David retrieved the ark of the covenant from the Philistines. David understood the power of God's presence at the center of Israelite life and community. After he built a tent in which to store the ark, he wrote a song to celebrate God for who he is and what he had consistently done for Israel. Celebrating God's involvement in our lives evokes joy.

Then on that day David delivered first *this psalm* to thank the LORD into the hand of Asaph and his brethren.

Give thanks unto the LORD, call upon his name, make known his deeds among the people. Sing unto him, sing psalms unto him, talk ye of all his wondrous works. Glory ye in his holy name: let the heart of them rejoice that seek the LORD. Seek the LORD and his strength, seek his face continually.

Remember his marvellous works that he hath done, his wonders, and the judgments of his mouth; O ye seed of Israel his servant, ye children of Jacob, his chosen ones. He *is* the LORD our God; his judgments *are* in all the earth.

Be ye mindful always of his covenant; the word *which* he commanded to a thousand generations; *Even of the covenant* which he made with Abraham, and of his oath unto Isaac; And hath confirmed the same to Jacob for a law, *and* to Israel *for* an everlasting covenant, Saying, Unto thee will I give the land of Canaan, the lot of your inheritance;

When ye were but few, even a few, and strangers in it. And *when* they went from nation to nation, and from *one* kingdom to another people; He suffered no man to do them wrong: yea, he reproved kings for their sakes, *Saying*, Touch not mine anointed, and do my prophets no harm.

Sing unto the LORD, all the earth; shew forth from day to day his salvation. Declare his glory among the heathen; his marvellous works among all nations.

For great *is* the LORD, and greatly to be praised: he also *is* to be feared above all gods. For all the gods of the people *are* idols: but the LORD made the heavens. Glory and honour *are* in his presence; strength and gladness *are* in his place.

Give unto the LORD, ye kindreds of the people, give unto the LORD glory and strength. Give unto the LORD the glory *due* unto his name: bring an offering, and come before him: worship the LORD in the beauty of holiness. Fear before him, all the earth: the world also shall be stable, that it be not moved.

Let the heavens be glad, and let the earth rejoice: and let *men* say among the nations, The LORD reigneth. Let the sea roar, and the fulness thereof: let the fields rejoice, and all that *is* therein. Then shall the trees of the wood sing out at the presence of the LORD, because he cometh to judge the earth.

O give thanks unto the LORD; for *he is* good; for his mercy *endureth* for ever. And say ye, Save us, O God of our salvation, and gather us together, and deliver us from the heathen, that we may give thanks to thy holy name, *and* glory in thy praise. Blessed *be* the LORD God of Israel for ever and ever.

And all the people said, Amen, and praised the LORD.

1 CHRONICLES 16:7–36

How does acknowledging God's involvement
in our lives evoke joy? Israel held annual feasts and
traditions to celebrate God's blessings.
How do Christians accomplish this today?

JOY DESPITE OUR CIRCUMSTANCES

After the reign of David, the divided kingdom fell steadily into a dark season of disobedience. The people were led, almost without interruption, by a succession of evil kings. Habakkuk was a prophet trying desperately to get the people of Judah back on track. He asked God how long he was going to let injustice and wickedness go on before he disciplined the nation. God informed the prophet that he was going to use the Babylonians to deal with Judah's persistent disobedience. Habakkuk struggled with this idea at first but in the end found resolve. Even though God's people were going to go through a difficult season, Habakkuk knew they could retain their joy based on what God had done for them in the past and his promises for the future.

When I heard, my belly trembled; my lips quivered at the voice: rottenness entered into my bones, and I trembled in myself, that I might rest in the day of trouble: when he cometh up unto the people, he will invade them with his troops. **Although the fig tree shall not blossom, neither *shall* fruit *be* in the vines; the labour of the olive shall fail, and the fields shall yield no meat; the flock shall be cut off from the fold, and *there shall be* no herd in the stalls. Yet I will rejoice in the LORD, I will joy in the God of my salvation.**

The LORD God *is* my strength, and he will make my feet like hinds' *feet*, and he will make me to walk upon mine high places.

HABAKKUK 3:16–19

Just as God's people found joy and strength in God's promises amid dark times during Habakkuk's day, Jesus' disciples drew comfort and strength from Jesus' promises as they prepared for his death. A few hours before he was crucified, Jesus sat with them and reassured them that their grief would be short-lived— three days to be exact. After that time something was going to happen to secure their joy in any and all circumstances.

Now before the feast of the passover, when Jesus knew that his hour was come that he should depart out of this world unto the Father, having loved his own which were in the world, he loved them unto the end.

JOHN 13:1

[Jesus said] a little while, and ye shall not see me: and again, a little while, and ye shall see me, because I go to the Father.

Then said *some* of his disciples among themselves, What is this that he saith unto us, A little while, and ye shall not see me: and again, a little while, and ye shall see me: and, Because I go to the Father? They said therefore, What is this that he saith, A little while? we cannot tell what he saith.

Now Jesus knew that they were desirous to ask him, and said unto them, Do ye enquire among yourselves of that I said, A little while, and ye shall not see me: and again, a little while, and ye shall see me? Verily, verily, I say unto you, That ye shall weep and lament, but the world shall rejoice: and ye shall be sorrowful, but your sorrow shall be turned into joy. A woman when she is in travail hath sorrow, because her hour is come: but as soon as she is delivered of the child, she remembereth no more the anguish, for joy that a man is born into the world. **And ye now therefore have sorrow: but I will see you again, and your heart shall rejoice, and your joy no man taketh from you.** And in that day ye shall ask me nothing. Verily, verily, I say unto you, Whatsoever ye shall ask the Father in my name, he will give *it* you. Hitherto have ye asked nothing in my name: ask, and ye shall receive, that your joy may be full.

JOHN 16:16–24

James introduces the book bearing his name with a thought-provoking declaration: not only can we have joy despite our difficult circumstances, but joy can grow through our difficult circumstances.

My brethren, count it all joy when ye fall into divers temptations; Knowing *this*, that the trying of your faith worketh patience. But let patience have *her* perfect work, that ye may be perfect and entire, wanting nothing. If any of you lack wisdom, let him ask of God, that giveth to all *men* liberally, and upbraideth not; and it shall be given him. But let him ask in faith, nothing wavering. For he that wavereth is like a wave of the sea driven with the wind and tossed. For let not that man think that he shall receive any thing of the Lord. A double minded man *is* unstable in all his ways.

Let the brother of low degree rejoice in that he is exalted: But the rich, in that he is made low: because as the flower of the grass he shall pass away. For the sun is no sooner risen with a burning heat, but it withereth the grass, and the flower thereof falleth, and the grace of the fashion of it perisheth: so also shall the rich man fade away in his ways.

Blessed *is* the man that endureth temptation: for when he is tried, he shall receive the crown of life, which the Lord hath promised to them that love him.

Let no man say when he is tempted, I am tempted of God: for God cannot be tempted with evil, neither tempteth he any man: But every man is tempted, when he is drawn away of his own lust, and enticed. Then when lust hath conceived, it bringeth forth sin: and sin, when it is finished, bringeth forth death.

Do not err, my beloved brethren. Every good gift and every perfect gift is from above, and cometh down from the Father of lights, with whom is no variableness, neither shadow of turning.

JAMES 1:2–17

How can difficult circumstances actually produce joy? What role do our attitudes play in being able to experience joy?

One person whose joy seemed to grow despite his circumstances was the apostle Paul, who wrote a joyful treatise of sorts while under house arrest and chained to a Roman guard. In a passionate letter to the church at Philippi, Paul fervently expressed his joy in Christ. Half of the lessons on increasing our joy are "taught" explicitly by Paul. Half of the lessons are "caught" implicitly by observing how Paul found joy despite his circumstances. At the letter's opening, notice how he found joy in the people God had placed in his life. Then we learn that Paul even saw his imprisonment as a blessing, for it helped bring attention to the gospel message.

Paul and Timotheus, the servants of Jesus Christ, to all the saints in Christ Jesus which are at Philippi, with the bishops and deacons: Grace *be* unto you, and peace, from God our Father, and *from* the Lord Jesus Christ.

I thank my God upon every remembrance of you, Always in every prayer of mine for you all making request with joy, For your fellowship in the gospel from the first day until now; Being confident of this very thing, that he which hath begun a good work in you will perform *it* until the day of Jesus Christ:

Even as it is meet for me to think this of you all, because I have you in my heart; inasmuch as both in my bonds, and in the defence and confirmation of the gospel, ye all are partakers of my grace. For God is my record, how greatly I long after you all in the bowels of Jesus Christ.
PHILIPPIANS 1:1–8

But I would ye should understand, brethren, that the things *which happened* unto me have fallen out rather unto the furtherance of the gospel; So that my bonds in Christ are manifest in all the palace, and in all other *places*; And many of the brethren in the Lord, waxing confident by my bonds, are much more bold to speak the word without fear.

Some indeed preach Christ even of envy and strife; and some also of good will: The one preach Christ of contention, not sincerely, supposing to add affliction to my bonds: But the other of love, knowing that I am set for the defence of the gospel. **What then? notwithstanding, every way, whether in pretence, or in truth, Christ is preached; and I therein do rejoice, yea, and will rejoice.**

For I know that this shall turn to my salvation through your prayer, and the supply of the Spirit of Jesus Christ.
PHILIPPIANS 1:12–19

Paul also instructed the Philippian believers how to rise above the fear spurred by those who opposed them. He invited them to remove "murmurings and disputings" from their vocabulary as a means to increase their joy. The ultimate source of joy is in knowing Christ better, so Paul encouraged his readers to put the past behind them and stay focused on the future, giving all their troubles to God and celebrating his blessings continuously.

Do all things without murmurings and disputings: That ye may be blameless and harmless, the sons of God, without rebuke, in the midst of a crooked and perverse nation, among whom ye shine as lights in the world; Holding forth the word of life; that I may rejoice in the day of Christ, that I have not run in vain, neither laboured in vain. Yea, and if I be offered upon the sacrifice and service of your faith, I joy, and rejoice with you all. For the same cause also do ye joy, and rejoice with me.   PHILIPPIANS 2:14–18

Finally, my brethren, rejoice in the Lord. To write the same things to you, to me indeed *is* not grievous, but for you *it is* safe. Beware of dogs, beware of evil workers, beware of the concision. For we are the circumcision, which worship God in the spirit, and rejoice in Christ Jesus, and have no confidence in the flesh. Though I might also have confidence in the flesh.

If any other man thinketh that he hath whereof he might trust in the flesh, I more: Circumcised the eighth day, of the stock of Israel, *of* the tribe of Benjamin, an Hebrew of the Hebrews; as touching the law, a Pharisee; Concerning zeal, persecuting the church; touching the righteousness which is in the law, blameless.

But what things were gain to me, those I counted loss for Christ. Yea doubtless, and I count all things *but* loss for the excellency of the knowledge of Christ Jesus my Lord: for whom I have suffered the loss of all things, and do count them *but* dung, that I may win Christ, And be found in him, not having mine own righteousness, which is of the law, but that which is through the faith of Christ, the righteousness which is of God by faith: That I may know him, and the power of his resurrection, and the fellowship of his sufferings, being made conformable unto his death; If by any means I might attain unto the resurrection of the dead.

Not as though I had already attained, either were already perfect: but I follow after, if that I may apprehend that for which also I am apprehended of Christ Jesus. Brethren, I count not myself to have apprehended: but *this* one thing *I do*, forgetting those things which are behind, and reaching forth unto those things which are before, I press toward the mark for the prize of the high calling of God in Christ Jesus.

Let us therefore, as many as be perfect, be thus minded: and if in any thing ye be otherwise minded, God shall reveal even this unto you. Nevertheless, whereto we have already attained, let us walk by the same rule, let us mind the same thing.

Brethren, be followers together of me, and mark them which walk so as ye have us for an ensample. (For many walk, of whom I have told you often, and now tell you even weeping, *that they are* the enemies of the cross of Christ: Whose end *is* destruction, whose God *is their* belly, and *whose* glory *is* in their shame, who mind earthly things.) For our conversation is in heaven; from whence also we look for the Saviour, the Lord Jesus Christ: Who shall change our vile body, that it may be fashioned like unto his glorious body, according to the working whereby he is able even to subdue all things unto himself. PHILIPPIANS 3:1–21

Therefore, my brethren dearly beloved and longed for, my joy and crown, so stand fast in the Lord, *my* dearly beloved. PHILIPPIANS 4:1

Rejoice in the Lord alway: *and* again I say, Rejoice. PHILIPPIANS 4:4

Paul wrapped up his thoughts by disclosing the secret to contentment despite life's varying circumstances.

But I rejoiced in the Lord greatly, that now at the last your care of me hath flourished again; wherein ye were also careful, but ye lacked opportunity. Not that I speak in respect of want: for I have learned, in whatsoever state I am, *therewith* to be content. **I know both how to be abased, and I know how to abound: every where and in all things I am instructed both to be full and to be hungry, both to abound and to suffer need. I can do all things through Christ which strengtheneth me.** PHILIPPIANS 4:10–13

Paul said he had learned how to be content even when he had plenty. Why is it sometimes difficult for people who have plenty to be content?

Like Paul, the apostle Peter also taught through his letters to the Christians scattered throughout Asia Minor that believers are in a position to experience joy in spite of, and even because of, their difficult circumstances. The same is true for followers of Jesus today.

Blessed *be* the God and Father of our Lord Jesus Christ, which according to his abundant mercy hath begotten us again unto a lively hope by the resurrection of Jesus Christ from the dead, To an inheritance incorruptible, and undefiled, and that fadeth not away, reserved in heaven for you, Who are kept by the power of God through faith unto salvation ready to be revealed in the last time. Wherein ye greatly rejoice, though now for a season, if need be, ye are in heaviness through manifold temptations: That the trial of your faith, being much more precious than of gold that perisheth, though it be tried with fire, might be found unto praise and honour and glory at the appearing of Jesus Christ: **Whom having not seen, ye love; in whom, though now ye see *him* not, yet believing, ye rejoice with joy unspeakable and full of glory: Receiving the end of your faith, *even* the salvation of *your* souls.**

1 PETER 1:3–9

Beloved, think it not strange concerning the fiery trial which is to try you, as though some strange thing happened unto you: **But rejoice, inasmuch as ye are partakers of Christ's sufferings; that, when his glory shall be revealed, ye may be glad also with exceeding joy.** If ye be reproached for the name of Christ, happy *are ye*; for the spirit of glory and of God resteth upon you: on their part he is evil spoken of, but on your part he is glorified. But let none of you suffer as a murderer, or *as* a thief, or *as* an evildoer, or as a busybody in other men's matters. Yet if *any man suffer* as a Christian, let him not be ashamed; but let him glorify God on this behalf.

1 PETER 4:12–16

Humble yourselves therefore under the mighty hand of God, that he may exalt you in due time: Casting all your care upon him; for he careth for you.
Be sober, be vigilant; because your adversary the devil, as a

roaring lion, walketh about, seeking whom he may devour: Whom resist stedfast in the faith, knowing that the same afflictions are accomplished in your brethren that are in the world.

But the God of all grace, who hath called us unto his eternal glory by Christ Jesus, after that ye have suffered a while, make you perfect, stablish, strengthen, settle *you*. To him *be* glory and dominion for ever and ever. Amen.　　　　　　　1 PETER 5:6–11

How often do you joyfully acknowledge God's goodness
in your life? Identify one good thing God has given
to you or done for you in the past week and
take a moment to celebrate that with someone else.

WHAT WE BELIEVE

If we want to experience true joy, we must anchor our lives in the source of that joy—God himself. Saturating our minds in the key beliefs and practices of the Christian faith can help draw us closer to God. The closer we are to him, the more confidence we will have as we face each day. Like the Israelites did, we can celebrate even God's smallest blessings in our lives. Christ offers contentment and happiness not limited by circumstances. Because of God's integrity, faithfulness and promises, we can surmount any circumstances with both smiles on our faces and true joy in our hearts. As Christians, we share the knowledge of this virtue with those God places in our lives so that they too can experience the deep and never-ending well of God's joy.

CHAPTER

23

Peace

———— KEY QUESTION ————

Where do I find strength to battle anxiety and fear?

———— KEY IDEA ————

I am free from anxiety because I have found peace with God,
peace with others and peace with myself.

———— KEY VERSE ————

Be careful for nothing; but in every thing by prayer
and supplication with thanksgiving let your requests
be made known unto God. And the peace of God,
which passeth all understanding, shall keep
your hearts and minds through Christ Jesus.
Philippians 4:6 – 7

OUR MAP

Most of us think of peace as a feeling. We want to trade our anxiety, depression and fear for calm and tranquility. There are many harmful and temporal ways people attempt to achieve this feeling, most notoriously by using alcohol or drugs. Biblical peace, however, starts not with the feeling of peace but with the source of peace, namely a strong and healthy relationship with God and with others. Where does one find the strength to battle anxiety and fear? In right relationships.

In this chapter we will discover how to find:

- Peace With God
- Peace With Others
- Peace With Yourself (Inner Peace)

PEACE WITH GOD

Peace with God is made possible only through the Prince of Peace. When Christ establishes his eternal kingdom, societal peace will be the norm. Around 700 years before Jesus was born, Isaiah foretold of Jesus' arrival on earth and the far-reaching impact of his reign.

For unto us a child is born, unto us a son is given: and the government shall be upon his shoulder: and his name shall be called Wonderful, Counsellor, The mighty God, The everlasting Father, The Prince of Peace. Of the increase of *his* government and peace *there shall be* no end, upon the throne of David, and upon his kingdom, to order it, and to establish it with judgment and with justice from henceforth even for ever. The zeal of the LORD of hosts will perform this.   ISAIAH 9:6–7

Jesus Christ is the Prince of Peace, not only in the future kingdom of heaven, but also in our lives as well. The pouring out of his lifeblood produced the possibility of a life of peace between us and God today.

In the following two passages from Romans 5 and
Ephesians 2, look for all the references to "peace" and
similar terms such as "reconciled," "made nigh"
and "together." How does Jesus Christ establish
peace between us and God and with each other?

**Therefore being justified by faith, we have peace with God
through our Lord Jesus Christ: By whom also we have access
by faith into this grace wherein we stand,** and rejoice in hope
of the glory of God. And not only *so*, but we glory in tribulations
also: knowing that tribulation worketh patience; And patience, experience; and experience, hope: And hope maketh not ashamed;
because the love of God is shed abroad in our hearts by the Holy
Ghost which is given unto us.

For when we were yet without strength, in due time Christ died
for the ungodly. For scarcely for a righteous man will one die: yet
peradventure for a good man some would even dare to die. But
God commendeth his love toward us, in that, while we were yet
sinners, Christ died for us.

Much more then, being now justified by his blood, we shall be
saved from wrath through him. For if, when we were enemies, we
were reconciled to God by the death of his Son, much more, being
reconciled, we shall be saved by his life. And not only *so*, but we
also joy in God through our Lord Jesus Christ, by whom we have
now received the atonement.   ROMANS 5:1–11

*In Paul's day, there were enormous barriers of cultural prejudice
and religious isolation between Jews and Gentiles. The Jews arro-
gantly despised the pagan Gentiles and viewed them contemptu-
ously as the "uncircumcised." Those attitudes went both ways; for
instance, the Greeks divided all people into two classes—Greeks
and barbarians. But these barriers came crashing down because
of Christ. Through the saving work of Jesus' death and resurrection, all believers share citizenship in God's kingdom of peace.*

And you *hath he quickened*, who were dead in trespasses and
sins; Wherein in time past ye walked according to the course of

this world, according to the prince of the power of the air, the spirit that now worketh in the children of disobedience: Among whom also we all had our conversation in times past in the lusts of our flesh, fulfilling the desires of the flesh and of the mind; and were by nature the children of wrath, even as others. But God, who is rich in mercy, for his great love wherewith he loved us, Even when we were dead in sins, hath quickened us together with Christ, (by grace ye are saved;) And hath raised *us* up together, and made *us* sit together in heavenly *places* in Christ Jesus: That in the ages to come he might shew the exceeding riches of his grace in *his* kindness toward us through Christ Jesus. For by grace are ye saved through faith; and that not of yourselves: *it is* the gift of God: Not of works, lest any man should boast. For we are his workmanship, created in Christ Jesus unto good works, which God hath before ordained that we should walk in them.

Wherefore remember, that ye *being* in time past Gentiles in the flesh, who are called Uncircumcision by that which is called the Circumcision in the flesh made by hands; That at that time ye were without Christ, being aliens from the commonwealth of Israel, and strangers from the covenants of promise, having no hope, and without God in the world: But now in Christ Jesus ye who sometimes were far off are made nigh by the blood of Christ.

For he is our peace, who hath made both one, and hath broken down the middle wall of partition *between us*; Having abolished in his flesh the enmity, *even* the law of commandments *contained* in ordinances; for to make in himself of twain one new man, *so* making peace; And that he might reconcile both unto God in one body by the cross, having slain the enmity thereby: And came and preached peace to you which were afar off, and to them that were nigh. For through him we both have access by one Spirit unto the Father.

Now therefore ye are no more strangers and foreigners, but fellowcitizens with the saints, and of the household of God; And are built upon the foundation of the apostles and prophets, Jesus Christ himself being the chief corner *stone*; In whom all the building fitly framed together groweth unto an holy temple in the Lord: In whom ye also are builded together for an habitation of God through the Spirit.

EPHESIANS 2:1–22

PEACE WITH OTHERS

While the Bible is brimming with examples of hostility and fighting, it also contains notable examples of people striving for peace. For instance, in the Old Testament, Abram (later named Abraham) and his wife, Sarai (later named Sarah), and nephew Lot moved to Canaan and lived as nomadic shepherds. When conflict arose between the two men regarding space and land, Abram took the initiative to end their dispute. Although Abram, as the elder, would normally have first pick of the land, he put the peace of the family above his own rights.

And Abram went up out of Egypt, he, and his wife, and all that he had, and Lot with him, into the south. And Abram *was* very rich in cattle, in silver, and in gold.

And he went on his journeys from the south even to Beth-el, unto the place where his tent had been at the beginning, between Beth-el and Hai; Unto the place of the altar, which he had made there at the first: and there Abram called on the name of the LORD.

And Lot also, which went with Abram, had flocks, and herds, and tents. And the land was not able to bear them, that they might dwell together: for their substance was great, so that they could not dwell together. And there was a strife between the herdmen of Abram's cattle and the herdmen of Lot's cattle: and the Canaanite and the Perizzite dwelled then in the land.

And Abram said unto Lot, Let there be no strife, I pray thee, between me and thee, and between my herdmen and thy herdmen; for we *be* brethren. *Is* not the whole land before thee? separate thyself, I pray thee, from me: if *thou wilt take* the left hand, then I will go to the right; or if *thou depart* to the right hand, then I will go to the left.

And Lot lifted up his eyes, and beheld all the plain of Jordan, that it *was* well watered every where, before the LORD destroyed Sodom and Gomorrah, *even* as the garden of the LORD, like the land of Egypt, as thou comest unto Zoar. Then Lot chose him all the plain of Jordan; and Lot journeyed east: and they separated themselves the one from the other. Abram dwelled in the land of Canaan, and Lot dwelled in the cities of the plain, and pitched *his* tent toward Sodom. But the men of Sodom *were* wicked and sinners before the LORD exceedingly.

And the L ORD said unto Abram, after that Lot was separated from him, Lift up now thine eyes, and look from the place where thou art northward, and southward, and eastward, and westward: For all the land which thou seest, to thee will I give it, and to thy seed for ever. And I will make thy seed as the dust of the earth: so that if a man can number the dust of the earth, *then* shall thy seed also be numbered. Arise, walk through the land in the length of it and in the breadth of it; for I will give it unto thee.

Then Abram removed *his* tent, and came and dwelt in the plain of Mamre, which *is* in Hebron, and built there an altar unto the L ORD.

GENESIS 13:1–18

During the early part of his reign, King Solomon had a special encounter with God. His response to that encounter led to greater peace with God and a greater ability to discern right from wrong in his administration. Wise and just ruling resolves conflicts properly and leads to greater peace with others in the long run. The same principles apply to our lives today. (Note: Solomon's obedience to God is found in the shift in the location of his sacrifices to God from where he started on the high place of Gibeon to where he worshipped after his dream.)

And Solomon loved the L ORD, walking in the statutes of David his father: only he sacrificed and burnt incense in high places.

And the king went to Gibeon to sacrifice there; for that *was* the great high place: a thousand burnt offerings did Solomon offer upon that altar. In Gibeon the L ORD appeared to Solomon in a dream by night: and God said, Ask what I shall give thee.

And Solomon said, Thou hast shewed unto thy servant David my father great mercy, according as he walked before thee in truth, and in righteousness, and in uprightness of heart with thee; and thou hast kept for him this great kindness, that thou hast given him a son to sit on his throne, as *it is* this day.

And now, O L ORD my God, thou hast made thy servant king instead of David my father: and I *am but* a little child: I know not *how* to go out or come in. And thy servant *is* in the midst of thy people which thou hast chosen, a great people, that cannot be numbered nor counted for multitude. Give therefore thy servant an understanding heart to judge thy people, that I may discern between good and bad: for who is able to judge this thy so great a people?

And the speech pleased the Lord, that Solomon had asked this thing. And God said unto him, Because thou hast asked this thing, and hast not asked for thyself long life; neither hast asked riches for thyself, nor hast asked the life of thine enemies; but hast asked for thyself understanding to discern judgment; Behold, I have done according to thy words: lo, I have given thee a wise and an understanding heart; so that there was none like thee before thee, neither after thee shall any arise like unto thee. And I have also given thee that which thou hast not asked, both riches, and honour: so that there shall not be any among the kings like unto thee all thy days. And if thou wilt walk in my ways, to keep my statutes and my commandments, as thy father David did walk, then I will lengthen thy days. And Solomon awoke; and, behold, *it was* a dream.

And he came to Jerusalem, and stood before the ark of the covenant of the LORD, and offered up burnt offerings, and offered peace offerings, and made a feast to all his servants.   1 KINGS 3:3–15

> The outcome of Solomon's decision is recorded below. If we want greater peace in our lives, we should first seek to live in obedience to God and then apply his wisdom to find peace in our relationships with others.

Judah and Israel *were* many, as the sand which *is* by the sea in multitude, eating and drinking, and making merry. And Solomon reigned over all kingdoms from the river unto the land of the Philistines, and unto the border of Egypt: they brought presents, and served Solomon all the days of his life.

And Solomon's provision for one day was thirty measures of fine flour, and threescore measures of meal, Ten fat oxen, and twenty oxen out of the pastures, and an hundred sheep, beside harts, and roebucks, and fallowdeer, and fatted fowl. **For he had dominion over all *the region* on this side the river, from Tiphsah even to Azzah, over all the kings on this side the river: and he had peace on all sides round about him. And Judah and**

Israel dwelt safely, every man under his vine and under his fig tree, from Dan even to Beer-Sheba, all the days of Solomon.

1 KINGS 4:20–25 🔑

Another example in the Bible of people striving for peace is found in the life of Jesus. In the Sermon on the Mount, Jesus encourages us to make living at peace with one another one of our top priorities, even above acts of worship. God makes it clear throughout Scripture that he values obedience over sacrifice. So if we are not at peace in our relationships, Jesus urges us not to keep performing acts of worship, but to pursue reconciliation first.

Ye have heard that it was said by them of old time, Thou shalt not kill; and whosoever shall kill shall be in danger of the judgment: But I say unto you, That whosoever is angry with his brother without a cause shall be in danger of the judgment: and whosoever shall say to his brother, Raca, shall be in danger of the council: but whosoever shall say, Thou fool, shall be in danger of hell fire.

Therefore if thou bring thy gift to the altar, and there rememberest that thy brother hath ought against thee; Leave there thy gift before the altar, and go thy way; first be reconciled to thy brother, and then come and offer thy gift.

Agree with thine adversary quickly, whiles thou art in the way with him; lest at any time the adversary deliver thee to the judge, and the judge deliver thee to the officer, and thou be cast into prison. Verily I say unto thee, Thou shalt by no means come out thence, till thou hast paid the uttermost farthing.   MATTHEW 5:21–26

Living at peace, even with fellow followers of Jesus, can be a challenge. We each think and feel differently. Naturally there are bound to be conflicts. The church in New Testament times was made up of both Jews and Gentiles. Many Jewish converts held on to the rituals of the Old Testament Law regarding diet and festivals. Some Jewish followers gladly left these rules behind in favor of their new freedom in Christ. Because the Gentiles had little regard for these traditions, it created tension in their communities. Paul instructed the church in Rome how to experience peace even amid intense disagreement.

Him that is weak in the faith receive ye, *but* not to doubtful disputations. For one believeth that he may eat all things: another, who is weak, eateth herbs. Let not him that eateth despise him that eateth not; and let not him which eateth not judge him that eateth: for God hath received him. Who art thou that judgest another man's servant? to his own master he standeth or falleth. Yea, he shall be holden up: for God is able to make him stand.

One man esteemeth one day above another: another esteemeth every day *alike*. Let every man be fully persuaded in his own mind. He that regardeth the day, regardeth *it* unto the Lord; and he that regardeth not the day, to the Lord he doth not regard *it*. He that eateth, eateth to the Lord, for he giveth God thanks; and he that eateth not, to the Lord he eateth not, and giveth God thanks. For none of us liveth to himself, and no man dieth to himself. For whether we live, we live unto the Lord; and whether we die, we die unto the Lord: whether we live therefore, or die, we are the Lord's. For to this end Christ both died, and rose, and revived, that he might be Lord both of the dead and living.

But why dost thou judge thy brother? or why dost thou set at nought thy brother? for we shall all stand before the judgment seat of Christ. For it is written, *As* I live, saith the Lord, every knee shall bow to me, and every tongue shall confess to God. So then every one of us shall give account of himself to God.

Let us not therefore judge one another any more: but judge this rather, that no man put a stumblingblock or an occasion to fall in *his* brother's way. I know, and am persuaded by the Lord Jesus, that *there is* nothing unclean of itself: but to him that esteemeth any thing to be unclean, to him *it is* unclean. But if thy brother be grieved with *thy* meat, now walkest thou not charitably. Destroy not him with thy meat, for whom Christ died. Let not then your good be evil spoken of: For the kingdom of God is not meat and drink; but righteousness, and peace, and joy in the Holy Ghost. For he that in these things serveth Christ *is* acceptable to God, and approved of men.

Let us therefore follow after the things which make for peace, and things wherewith one may edify another. For meat destroy not the work of God. All things indeed *are* pure; but *it is* evil for that man who eateth with offence. *It is* good neither to eat flesh, nor to drink wine, nor *any thing* whereby thy brother stumbleth, or is offended, or is made weak.

Hast thou faith? have *it* to thyself before God. Happy *is* he that condemneth not himself in that thing which he alloweth. And he that doubteth is damned if he eat, because *he eateth* not of faith: for whatsoever *is* not of faith is sin.

We then that are strong ought to bear the infirmities of the weak, and not to please ourselves. Let every one of us please *his* neighbour for *his* good to edification. For even Christ pleased not himself; but, as it is written, The reproaches of them that reproached thee fell on me. For whatsoever things were written aforetime were written for our learning, that we through patience and comfort of the scriptures might have hope.

Now the God of patience and consolation grant you to be likeminded one toward another according to Christ Jesus: That ye may with one mind *and* one mouth glorify God, even the Father of our Lord Jesus Christ.

Wherefore receive ye one another, as Christ also received us to the glory of God. Now I say that Jesus Christ was a minister of the circumcision for the truth of God, to confirm the promises *made* unto the fathers: And that the Gentiles might glorify God for *his* mercy; as it is written, For this cause I will confess to thee among the Gentiles, and sing unto thy name. And again he saith, Rejoice, ye Gentiles, with his people. And again, Praise the Lord, all ye Gentiles; and laud him, all ye people. And again, Esaias saith, There shall be a root of Jesse, and he that shall rise to reign over the Gentiles; in him shall the Gentiles trust.

Now the God of hope fill you with all joy and peace in believing, that ye may abound in hope, through the power of the Holy Ghost.

ROMANS 14:1—15:13

"Doubtful disputations" are areas where there is more than one acceptable option or opinion, so we must each decide with conviction and yet respect others who choose differently. What are "doubtful disputations" for Christians today?

Many of the New Testament letters helped to resocialize the church to live in God's kingdom—a kingdom of righteousness, peace and joy. Paul offered specific instruction to believers in the various churches regarding how to achieve this divine vision through Christ. Believers were to set their sights on living at peace with everyone to the best of their ability.

If ye then be risen with Christ, seek those things which are above, where Christ sitteth on the right hand of God. Set your affection on things above, not on things on the earth. For ye are dead, and your life is hid with Christ in God. When Christ, *who is* our life, shall appear, then shall ye also appear with him in glory.

Mortify therefore your members which are upon the earth; fornication, uncleanness, inordinate affection, evil concupiscence, and covetousness, which is idolatry: For which things' sake the wrath of God cometh on the children of disobedience: In the which ye also walked some time, when ye lived in them. But now ye also put off all these; anger, wrath, malice, blasphemy, filthy communication out of your mouth. Lie not one to another, seeing that ye have put off the old man with his deeds; And have put on the new *man*, which is renewed in knowledge after the image of him that created him: Where there is neither Greek nor Jew, circumcision nor uncircumcision, Barbarian, Scythian, bond *nor* free: but Christ *is* all, and in all.

Put on therefore, as the elect of God, holy and beloved, bowels of mercies, kindness, humbleness of mind, meekness, longsuffering; Forbearing one another, and forgiving one another, if any man have a quarrel against any: even as Christ forgave you, so also *do* ye. And above all these things *put on* charity, which is the bond of perfectness.

And let the peace of God rule in your hearts, to the which also ye are called in one body; and be ye thankful. Let the word of Christ dwell in you richly in all wisdom; teaching and admonishing one another in psalms and hymns and spiritual songs, singing with grace in your hearts to the Lord. And whatsoever ye do in word or deed, *do* all in the name of the Lord Jesus, giving thanks to God and the Father by him. COLOSSIANS 3:1–17

Recompense to no man evil for evil. Provide things honest in the sight of all men. If it be possible, as much as lieth in you, live peaceably with all men. Dearly beloved, avenge not yourselves, but *rather* give place unto wrath: for it is written, Vengeance *is* mine; I will repay, saith the Lord. Therefore, If thine enemy hunger, feed him; if he thirst, give him drink: for in so doing thou shalt heap coals of fire on his head. Be not overcome of evil, but overcome evil with good.   Romans 12:17–21

After reading Paul's counsel to the churches at Colosse and Rome from Romans 12, how would you describe the principles that promote peace in our relationships with one another?

Paul offered a similar discourse to the church of Ephesus.

I exhort therefore, that, first of all, supplications, prayers, intercessions, *and* giving of thanks, be made for all men; For kings, and *for* all that are in authority; that we may lead a quiet and peaceable life in all godliness and honesty. For this *is* good and acceptable in the sight of God our Saviour; Who will have all men to be saved, and to come unto the knowledge of the truth. For *there is* one God, and one mediator between God and men, the man Christ Jesus; Who gave himself a ransom for all, to be testified in due time. Whereunto I am ordained a preacher, and an apostle, (I speak the truth in Christ, *and* lie not;) a teacher of the Gentiles in faith and verity.

I will therefore that men pray every where, lifting up holy hands, without wrath and doubting.   1 Timothy 2:1–8

How does living at peace with people outside the faith, including government leaders, promote the gospel? How do we achieve this when the government is making decisions and taking actions that conflict with our Christian faith?

Paul penned a letter to his faithful ministry partner Titus while Titus was leading the new believers on the island of Crete in the

Mediterranean Sea. At this time Crete was known as an immoral, dishonest place filled with selfish people—all the ingredients for conflict and strife. Paul gave Titus tangible and practical advice to guide the believers there regarding how to live a life of peace.

Put them in mind to be subject to principalities and powers, to obey magistrates, to be ready to every good work, To speak evil of no man, to be no brawlers, *but* gentle, shewing all meekness unto all men.

For we ourselves also were sometimes foolish, disobedient, deceived, serving divers lusts and pleasures, living in malice and envy, hateful, *and* hating one another. But after that the kindness and love of God our Saviour toward man appeared, Not by works of righteousness which we have done, but according to his mercy he saved us, by the washing of regeneration, and renewing of the Holy Ghost; Which he shed on us abundantly through Jesus Christ our Saviour; That being justified by his grace, we should be made heirs according to the hope of eternal life. *This is* a faithful saying, and these things I will that thou affirm constantly, that they which have believed in God might be careful to maintain good works. These things are good and profitable unto men.

But avoid foolish questions, and genealogies, and contentions, and strivings about the law; for they are unprofitable and vain. A man that is an heretick after the first and second admonition reject; Knowing that he that is such is subverted, and sinneth, being condemned of himself. TITUS 3:1–11

PEACE WITH YOURSELF (INNER PEACE)

Worry is the chief robber of peace in our lives. It prevents us from lying down and sleeping at night. It keeps us on edge during the day. Our Prince of Peace, Jesus, emphasized the immense capacity of God the Father to love and care for his people individually before they let the worries of this life overtake them.

Therefore I say unto you, Take no thought for your life, what ye shall eat, or what ye shall drink; nor yet for your body, what ye shall put on. Is not the life more than meat, and the body than raiment? Behold the fowls of the air: for they sow not, neither do they reap, nor gather into barns; yet your heavenly Father feedeth them. Are ye not much better than they? Which of you by taking thought can add one cubit unto his stature?

And why take ye thought for raiment? Consider the lilies of the field, how they grow; they toil not, neither do they spin: And yet I say unto you, That even Solomon in all his glory was not arrayed like one of these. Wherefore, if God so clothe the grass of the field, which to day is, and to morrow is cast into the oven, *shall he* not much more *clothe* you, O ye of little faith? **Therefore take no thought, saying, What shall we eat? or, What shall we drink? or, Wherewithal shall we be clothed? (For after all these things do the Gentiles seek:) for your heavenly Father knoweth that ye have need of all these things. But seek ye first the kingdom of God, and his righteousness; and all these things shall be added unto you.** Take therefore no thought for the morrow: for the morrow shall take thought for the things of itself. Sufficient unto the day *is* the evil thereof.
MATTHEW 6:25–34

> It's true that each day has enough trouble of its own. As followers of Christ, we must be prepared to deal with these troubles in the strength God provides. It might be tempting to give in to the anxiety but, as Jesus vividly illustrated to his disciples, through our faith we can find peace and remain in control.

And the same day, when the even was come, he saith unto them, Let us pass over unto the other side. And when they had sent away the multitude, they took him even as he was in the ship. And there were also with him other little ships. And there arose a great storm of wind, and the waves beat into the ship, so that it was now full. And he was in the hinder part of the ship, asleep on a pillow: and they awake him, and say unto him, Master, carest thou not that we perish?

And he arose, and rebuked the wind, and said unto the sea, Peace, be still. And the wind ceased, and there was a great calm.

And he said unto them, Why are ye so fearful? how is it that ye have no faith?

And they feared exceedingly, and said one to another, What manner of man is this, that even the wind and the sea obey him?
MARK 4:35–41

As Paul wrapped up his personal letter to the believers at Philippi, he spoke to them directly on how to obtain a peace that "passeth all understanding."

Rejoice in the Lord alway: *and* again I say, Rejoice. Let your moderation be known unto all men. The Lord *is* at hand. **Be careful for nothing; but in every thing by prayer and supplication with thanksgiving let your requests be made known unto God. And the peace of God, which passeth all understanding, shall keep your hearts and minds through Christ Jesus.**

Finally, brethren, whatsoever things are true, whatsoever things *are* honest, whatsoever things *are* just, whatsoever things *are* pure, whatsoever things *are* lovely, whatsoever things *are* of good report; if *there be* any virtue, and if *there be* any praise, think on these things. Those things, which ye have both learned, and received, and heard, and seen in me, do: and the God of peace shall be with you.

PHILIPPIANS 4:4–9

What is Paul's prescription for anxiety and worry?

WHAT WE BELIEVE

The feeling of peace we long for will flow naturally when things are right in our relationships. Of greatest importance is a reconciled relationship with God, made possible through Jesus Christ. When we accept his offer of salvation, the conflict between God and us is forever eliminated. A reconciled relationship with God now becomes the source of peace in our relationships with others. The Scripture passages in this chapter lay out how we do our part to promote peace in our relationships. God's Spirit enables us to achieve this. We are also called to live at peace with ourselves by accepting God's love and forgiveness in our lives. It requires that we take the things that burden and trouble us and give them to God. When we do this we declare that God is bigger than any of our problems and that the "peace of God, which passeth all understanding, shall keep [our] hearts and minds through Christ Jesus" (Philippians 4:7).

CHAPTER

24

Self-Control

———— KEY QUESTION ————

How does God free me from addictions and sinful habits?

———— KEY IDEA ————

I have the power through Christ to control myself.

———— KEY VERSE ————

For the grace of God that bringeth salvation hath appeared
to all men, Teaching us that, denying ungodliness
and worldly lusts, we should live soberly,
righteously, and godly, in this present world; Looking
for that blessed hope, and the glorious appearing
of the great God and our Saviour Jesus Christ.

Titus 2:11 – 13

Self-control refers to the ability to control one's emotions and behavior. Everyone at some point struggles with self-control—it's the presence of the sin nature within us. So how does God help us when we've lost control and let our sinful nature take over? How does he free us from addictions and sinful habits? God's Word contains the answer.

In this chapter we will be reading about:

- *The Call and the Challenge*
- *Models of Self-Control: Bad and Good*
- *The How-Tos*

THE CALL AND THE CHALLENGE

God desires for all of us to demonstrate self-control. However, in the face of external pressures, the battle to keep our sinful nature in check is easier said than done. The writer of Proverbs places options before us, clearly highlighting self-control.

He that is slow to anger *is* better than the mighty;
and he that ruleth his spirit than he that taketh a city.

PROVERBS 16:32

He that hath knowledge spareth his words:
and a man of understanding is of an excellent spirit.

PROVERBS 17:27

**He that *hath* no rule over his own spirit
is like a city *that is* broken down, *and* without walls.**

PROVERBS 25:28

A fool uttereth all his mind:
but a wise *man* keepeth it in till afterwards. PROVERBS 29:11

The benefits of having self-control are numerous. In the New Testament, Paul wrote a personal letter to his ministry partner Titus instructing him to appoint elders in the church gathered on the island of Crete. Self-control, or temperance, as Paul sometimes called it, was a prominent characteristic Titus was to look for in these spiritual leaders. Paul also instructed Titus to call believers of all ages to this virtue, which obviously was much needed in Crete.

To Titus, *mine* own son after the common faith: Grace, mercy, *and* peace, from God the Father and the Lord Jesus Christ our Saviour.

For this cause left I thee in Crete, that thou shouldest set in order the things that are wanting, and ordain elders in every city, as I had appointed thee: If any be blameless, the husband of one wife, having faithful children not accused of riot or unruly. **For a bishop must be blameless, as the steward of God; not selfwilled, not soon angry, not given to wine, no striker, not given to filthy lucre; But a lover of hospitality, a lover of good men, sober, just, holy, temperate;** Holding fast the faithful word as he hath been taught, that he may be able by sound doctrine both to exhort and to convince the gainsayers.   Titus 1:4–9

But speak thou the things which become sound doctrine: That the aged men be sober, grave, temperate, sound in faith, in charity, in patience.

The aged women likewise, that *they be* in behaviour as becometh holiness, not false accusers, not given to much wine, teachers of good things; That they may teach the young women to be sober, to love their husbands, to love their children, *To be* discreet, chaste, keepers at home, good, obedient to their own husbands, that the word of God be not blasphemed.

Young men likewise exhort to be sober minded. In all things shewing thyself a pattern of good works: in doctrine *shewing* uncorruptness, gravity, sincerity, Sound speech, that cannot be condemned; that he that is of the contrary part may be ashamed, having no evil thing to say of you.

Exhort servants to be obedient unto their own masters, *and* to please *them* well in all *things*; not answering again; Not purloining, but shewing all good fidelity; that they may adorn the doctrine of God our Saviour in all things.

For the grace of God that bringeth salvation hath appeared to all men, Teaching us that, denying ungodliness and worldly lusts, we should live soberly, righteously, and godly, in this present world; Looking for that blessed hope, and the glorious appearing of the great God and our Saviour Jesus Christ; Who gave himself for us, that he might redeem us from all iniquity, and purify unto himself a peculiar people, zealous of good works.

These things speak, and exhort, and rebuke with all authority. Let no man despise thee.   TITUS 2:1–15

Paul used several different words—*temperate, discreet, sober minded* and *soberly*—to mean the same thing: *self-controlled.* Underline these words in Titus 2:1–15, remembering that they all encourage self-control. Why do you think self-control is a key virtue required for church leaders?

MODELS OF SELF-CONTROL: BAD AND GOOD

During the days of the judges, the Philistines bullied Israel for 40 years. But time after time God raised up a special person, a judge, to deliver Israel from this oppression. God intervened in the life of a childless Israelite couple and enabled the wife to conceive and give birth to Samson, who would be used by God to set Israel free from this bondage. From conception Samson was a Nazirite—which comes from the Hebrew word meaning "separated"—and God blessed him with supernatural strength. As a spiritual and physical sign of this vow, Samson was never to cut his hair. Interestingly, this special man, one of the last judges of Israel, struggled mightily with self-control over his sexual passions; and ironically, he was particularly attracted to Philistine women. Eventually Samson let his lack of self-control get the best of him.

Then went Samson to Gaza, and saw there an harlot, and went in unto her. *And it was told* the Gazites, saying, Samson is come hither. And they compassed *him* in, and laid wait for him all night in the gate of the city, and were quiet all the night, saying, In the morning, when it is day, we shall kill him.

And Samson lay till midnight, and arose at midnight, and took the doors of the gate of the city, and the two posts, and went away with them, bar and all, and put *them* upon his shoulders, and carried them up to the top of an hill that *is* before Hebron.

And it came to pass afterward, that he loved a woman in the valley of Sorek, whose name *was* Delilah. And the lords of the Philistines came up unto her, and said unto her, Entice him, and see wherein his great strength *lieth*, and by what *means* we may prevail against him, that we may bind him to afflict him: and we will give thee every one of us eleven hundred *pieces* of silver.

And Delilah said to Samson, Tell me, I pray thee, wherein thy great strength *lieth*, and wherewith thou mightest be bound to afflict thee.

And Samson said unto her, If they bind me with seven green withs that were never dried, then shall I be weak, and be as another man.

Then the lords of the Philistines brought up to her seven green withs which had not been dried, and she bound him with them. Now *there were* men lying in wait, abiding with her in the chamber. And she said unto him, The Philistines *be* upon thee, Samson. And he brake the withs, as a thread of tow is broken when it toucheth the fire. So his strength was not known.

And Delilah said unto Samson, Behold, thou hast mocked me, and told me lies: now tell me, I pray thee, wherewith thou mightest be bound.

And he said unto her, If they bind me fast with new ropes that never were occupied, then shall I be weak, and be as another man.

Delilah therefore took new ropes, and bound him therewith, and said unto him, The Philistines *be* upon thee, Samson. And *there were* liers in wait abiding in the chamber. And he brake them from off his arms like a thread.

And Delilah said unto Samson, Hitherto thou hast mocked me, and told me lies: tell me wherewith thou mightest be bound.

And he said unto her, If thou weavest the seven locks of my head with the web. And she fastened *it* with the pin, and said unto him, The Philistines *be* upon thee, Samson. And he awaked out of his sleep, and went away with the pin of the beam, and with the web.

And she said unto him, How canst thou say, I love thee, when thine heart *is* not with me? thou hast mocked me these three times, and hast not told me wherein thy great strength *lieth*. And it came to pass, when she pressed him daily with her words, and urged him, *so* that his soul was vexed unto death;

That he told her all his heart, and said unto her, There hath not come a razor upon mine head; for I *have been* a Nazarite unto God from my mother's womb: if I be shaven, then my strength will go from me, and I shall become weak, and be like any *other* man.

And when Delilah saw that he had told her all his heart, she sent and called for the lords of the Philistines, saying, Come up this once, for he hath shewed me all his heart. Then the lords of the Philistines came up unto her, and brought money in their hand. And she made him sleep upon her knees; and she called for a man, and she caused him to shave off the seven locks of his head; and she began to afflict him, and his strength went from him.

And she said, The Philistines *be* upon thee, Samson.

And he awoke out of his sleep, and said, I will go out as at other times before, and shake myself. And he wist not that the LORD was departed from him.

But the Philistines took him, and put out his eyes, and brought him down to Gaza, and bound him with fetters of brass; and he did grind in the prison house. JUDGES 16:1–21 ⚷

Unlike Samson, Joseph offers one of the best examples in the Bible of a man who exercised excellent self-control. Joseph was sold into slavery at the hands of his jealous brothers. The band of traveling merchants who purchased him took him from his home in Canaan to Egypt to be resold to an important official in Pharaoh's court. Although Joseph was punished by his captors for his self-control, God rewarded his faithfulness.

And Joseph was brought down to Egypt; and Potiphar, an officer of Pharaoh, captain of the guard, an Egyptian, bought him of the hands of the Ishmeelites, which had brought him down thither.

And the LORD was with Joseph, and he was a prosperous man; and he was in the house of his master the Egyptian. And his master saw that the LORD *was* with him, and that the LORD made all that he did to prosper in his hand. And Joseph found grace in his sight, and he served him: and he made him overseer over his house, and all *that* he had he put into his hand. And it came to pass from the time *that* he had made him overseer in his house, and over all that he had, that the LORD blessed the Egyptian's house for Joseph's sake; and the blessing of the LORD was upon all that he had in the house, and in the field. And he left all that he had in Joseph's hand; and he knew not ought he had, save the bread which he did eat.

And Joseph was *a* goodly *person*, and well favoured. And it came to pass after these things, that his master's wife cast her eyes upon Joseph; and she said, Lie with me.

But he refused, and said unto his master's wife, Behold, my master wotteth not what *is* with me in the house, and he hath committed all that he hath to my hand; *There is* none greater in this house than I; neither hath he kept back any thing from me but thee, because thou *art* his wife: how then can I do this great wickedness, and sin against God? And it came to pass, as she spake to Joseph day by day, that he hearkened not unto her, to lie by her, *or* to be with her.

And it came to pass about this time, that *Joseph* went into the house to do his business; and *there was* none of the men of the house there within. And she caught him by his garment, saying, Lie with me: and he left his garment in her hand, and fled, and got him out.

And it came to pass, when she saw that he had left his garment in her hand, and was fled forth, That she called unto the men of her house, and spake unto them, saying, See, he hath brought in an Hebrew unto us to mock us; he came in unto me to lie with me, and I cried with a loud voice: And it came to pass, when he heard that I lifted up my voice and cried, that he left his garment with me, and fled, and got him out.

And she laid up his garment by her, until his lord came home. And she spake unto him according to these words, saying, The Hebrew servant, which thou hast brought unto us, came in unto me to mock me: And it came to pass, as I lifted up my voice and cried, that he left his garment with me, and fled out.

And it came to pass, when his master heard the words of his wife, which she spake unto him, saying, After this manner did thy servant to me; that his wrath was kindled. And Joseph's master took him, and put him into the prison, a place where the king's prisoners *were* bound: and he was there in the prison.

But the LORD was with Joseph, and shewed him mercy, and gave him favour in the sight of the keeper of the prison. And the keeper of the prison committed to Joseph's hand all the prisoners that *were* in the prison; and whatsoever they did there, he was the doer *of it*. The keeper of the prison looked not to any thing *that was* under his hand; because the LORD was with him, and *that* which he did, the LORD made *it* to prosper. GENESIS 39:1–23

THE HOW-TOS

The Bible offers practical instruction on how to grow in the virtue of self-control. One of the primary applications is to "flee"—flee from the person, environment or situation that tempts us to lose control. Corinth was a place given to living without boundaries. In Paul's letter, known to us as 1 Corinthians, he instructed the believers in Corinth to keep themselves out of temptation's way lest they fall.

All things are lawful unto me, but all things are not expedient: all things are lawful for me, but I will not be brought under the power of any. Meats for the belly, and the belly for meats: but God shall destroy both it and them. Now the body *is* not for fornication, but for the Lord; and the Lord for the body. And God hath both raised up the Lord, and will also raise up us by his own power. Know ye not that your bodies are the members of Christ? shall I then take the members of Christ, and make *them* the members of an harlot? God forbid. What? know ye not that he which is joined to an harlot is one body? for two, saith he, shall be one flesh. But he that is joined unto the Lord is one spirit.

Flee fornication. Every sin that a man doeth is without the body; but he that committeth fornication sinneth against his own body. What? know ye not that your body is the temple of the Holy Ghost *which is* in you, which ye have of God, and ye are not your own? For ye are bought with a price: therefore glorify God in your body, and in your spirit, which are God's. 1 CORINTHIANS 6:12–20

Wherefore, **my dearly beloved, flee from idolatry**. I speak as to wise men; judge ye what I say. The cup of blessing which we bless, is it not the communion of the blood of Christ? The bread which we break, is it not the communion of the body of Christ? For we *being* many are one bread, *and* one body: for we are all partakers of that one bread.

Behold Israel after the flesh: are not they which eat of the sacrifices partakers of the altar? What say I then? that the idol is any thing, or that which is offered in sacrifice to idols is any thing? But *I say*, that the things which the Gentiles sacrifice, they sacrifice to devils, and not to God: and I would not that ye should have fellowship with devils. Ye cannot drink the cup of the Lord, and the cup of devils: ye cannot be partakers of the Lord's table, and of the table of devils. Do we provoke the Lord to jealousy? are we stronger than he?

1 Corinthians 10:14–22

Paul reiterated the charge to flee in his letters to Timothy, which he penned to give the young leader instructions regarding how to spiritually guide the church at Ephesus. He wrote about how to avoid false teachers and resist the love of money. He also urged Timothy and the church members not to keep company with people who would draw them into ungodly behaviors.

If any man teach otherwise, and consent not to wholesome words, *even* the words of our Lord Jesus Christ, and to the doctrine which is according to godliness; He is proud, knowing nothing, but doting about questions and strifes of words, whereof cometh envy, strife, railings, evil surmisings, Perverse disputings of men of corrupt minds, and destitute of the truth, supposing that gain is godliness: from such withdraw thyself.

But godliness with contentment is great gain. For we brought nothing into *this* world, *and it is* certain we can carry nothing out. And having food and raiment let us be therewith content. But they that will be rich fall into temptation and a snare, and *into* many foolish and hurtful lusts, which drown men in destruction and perdition. For the love of money is the root of all evil: which while some coveted after, they have erred from the faith, and pierced themselves through with many sorrows.

But thou, O man of God, flee these things; and follow after

righteousness, godliness, faith, love, patience, meekness. Fight the good fight of faith, lay hold on eternal life, whereunto thou art also called, and hast professed a good profession before many witnesses. I give thee charge in the sight of God, who quickeneth all things, and *before* Christ Jesus, who before Pontius Pilate witnessed a good confession; That thou keep *this* commandment without spot, unrebukeable, until the appearing of our Lord Jesus Christ: Which in his times he shall shew, *who is* the blessed and only Potentate, the King of kings, and Lord of lords; Who only hath immortality, dwelling in the light which no man can approach unto; whom no man hath seen, nor can see. 1 TIMOTHY 6:3–16

Flee also youthful lusts: but follow righteousness, faith, charity, peace, with them that call on the Lord out of a pure heart. But foolish and unlearned questions avoid, knowing that they do gender strifes. And the servant of the Lord must not strive; but be gentle unto all *men*, apt to teach, patient, In meekness instructing those that oppose themselves; if God peradventure will give them repentance to the acknowledging of the truth; And *that* they may recover themselves out of the snare of the devil, who are taken captive by him at his will.

This know also, that in the last days perilous times shall come. For men shall be lovers of their own selves, covetous, boasters, proud, blasphemers, disobedient to parents, unthankful, unholy, Without natural affection, trucebreakers, false accusers, incontinent, fierce, despisers of those that are good, Traitors, heady, highminded, lovers of pleasures more than lovers of God; Having a form of godliness, but denying the power thereof: from such turn away.

For of this sort are they which creep into houses, and lead captive silly women laden with sins, led away with divers lusts, Ever learning, and never able to come to the knowledge of the truth.

2 TIMOTHY 2:22—3:7

What does the company we keep have to do
with our ability to be self-controlled?

A second strategy, also defensive in nature, in the fight to preserve self-control is to resist. We can tame our tongues, reduce fights and quarrels among us, control our selfish desires and mitigate against the negative influences of the world and the devil. But ultimately, complete self-control is unattainable. Our sin nature, or flesh, eventually makes us weary and weak. The ultimate solution to gain self-control is "God-control." The believer has God's presence and power within them to guide them and give them strength. As believers, we can use this strength to preserve self-control and live godly lives.

My brethren, be not many masters, knowing that we shall receive the greater condemnation. For in many things we offend all. If any man offend not in word, the same *is* a perfect man, *and* able also to bridle the whole body.

Behold, we put bits in the horses' mouths, that they may obey us; and we turn about their whole body. Behold also the ships, which though *they be* so great, and *are* driven of fierce winds, yet are they turned about with a very small helm, whithersoever the governor listeth. Even so the tongue is a little member, and boasteth great things. Behold, how great a matter a little fire kindleth! And the tongue *is* a fire, a world of iniquity: so is the tongue among our members, that it defileth the whole body, and setteth on fire the course of nature; and it is set on fire of hell.

For every kind of beasts, and of birds, and of serpents, and of things in the sea, is tamed, and hath been tamed of mankind: But the tongue can no man tame; *it is* an unruly evil, full of deadly poison.

Therewith bless we God, even the Father; and therewith curse we men, which are made after the similitude of God. Out of the same mouth proceedeth blessing and cursing. My brethren, these things ought not so to be. Doth a fountain send forth at the same place sweet *water* and bitter? Can the fig tree, my brethren, bear olive berries? either a vine, figs? so *can* no fountain both yield salt water and fresh.

Who *is* a wise man and endued with knowledge among you? let him shew out of a good conversation his works with meekness of wisdom. But if ye have bitter envying and strife in your hearts, glory not, and lie not against the truth. This wisdom descendeth not from above, but *is* earthly, sensual, devilish. For where envying and strife *is*, there *is* confusion and every evil work.

But the wisdom that is from above is first pure, then peaceable, gentle, *and* easy to be intreated, full of mercy and good fruits, without partiality, and without hypocrisy. And the fruit of righteousness is sown in peace of them that make peace.

From whence *come* wars and fightings among you? *come they* not hence, *even* of your lusts that war in your members? Ye lust, and have not: ye kill, and desire to have, and cannot obtain: ye fight and war, yet ye have not, because ye ask not. Ye ask, and receive not, because ye ask amiss, that ye may consume *it* upon your lusts.

Ye adulterers and adulteresses, know ye not that the friendship of the world is enmity with God? whosoever therefore will be a friend of the world is the enemy of God. Do ye think that the scripture saith in vain, The spirit that dwelleth in us lusteth to envy? But he giveth more grace. Wherefore he saith, God resisteth the proud, but giveth grace unto the humble.

Submit yourselves therefore to God. Resist the devil, and he will flee from you. Draw nigh to God, and he will draw nigh to you. Cleanse *your* hands, *ye* sinners; and purify *your* hearts, *ye* double minded. Be afflicted, and mourn, and weep: let your laughter be turned to mourning, and *your* joy to heaviness. Humble yourselves in the sight of the Lord, and he shall lift you up.

JAMES 3:1—4:10

Why are our tongues so difficult to control?

Peter offered similar advice in his first letter to the Christians scattered throughout the region of Asia Minor (modern-day Turkey).

Be sober, be vigilant; because your adversary the devil, as a roaring lion, walketh about, seeking whom he may devour: Whom resist stedfast in the faith, knowing that the same afflictions are accomplished in your brethren that are in the world.

But the God of all grace, who hath called us unto his eternal glory by Christ Jesus, after that ye have suffered a while, make you perfect, stablish, strengthen, settle *you*. To him *be* glory and dominion for ever and ever. Amen. 1 Peter 5:8–11

The apostle Paul presented a different strategy to practice self-control in our lives—particularly in the area of sexual passions: engage these natural desires within the boundaries of God's design.

Now concerning the things whereof ye wrote unto me: *It is* good for a man not to touch a woman. Nevertheless, *to avoid* fornication, let every man have his own wife, and let every woman have her own husband. Let the husband render unto the wife due benevolence: and likewise also the wife unto the husband. The wife hath not power of her own body, but the husband: and likewise also the husband hath not power of his own body, but the wife. Defraud ye not one the other, except *it be* with consent for a time, that ye may give yourselves to fasting and prayer; and come together again, that Satan tempt you not for your incontinency. But I speak this by permission, *and* not of commandment. For I would that all men were even as I myself. But every man hath his proper gift of God, one after this manner, and another after that.

I say therefore to the unmarried and widows, It is good for them if they abide even as I. But if they cannot contain, let them marry: for it is better to marry than to burn.

1 Corinthians 7:1–9

Self-control is truly impossible in our own strength. Our sin nature can wear us down and get the best of us. Thankfully, we as believers have the presence and power of God within us to live a life not undermined by our inner desires and the corruption of the world. In Peter's second letter, he challenged believers to draw on this power to live productive and effective lives.

After you read this passage from Peter (see 2 Peter 1:3–11 below) and the following passage from Paul (see Galatians 5:16–25), describe in your own words how "God-control" works to bring about "self-control" in our lives.

According as his divine power hath given unto us all things that *pertain* unto life and godliness, through the knowledge of him that hath called us to glory and virtue: Whereby are given unto us exceeding great and precious promises: that by these ye might be partakers of the divine nature, having escaped the corruption that is in the world through lust.

And beside this, giving all diligence, add to your faith virtue; and to virtue knowledge; And to knowledge temperance; and to temperance patience; and to patience godliness; And to godliness brotherly kindness; and to brotherly kindness charity. For if these things be in you, and abound, they make *you that ye shall* neither *be* barren nor unfruitful in the knowledge of our Lord Jesus Christ. But he that lacketh these things is blind, and cannot see afar off, and hath forgotten that he was purged from his old sins.

Wherefore the rather, brethren, give diligence to make your calling and election sure: for if ye do these things, ye shall never fall: For so an entrance shall be ministered unto you abundantly into the everlasting kingdom of our Lord and Saviour Jesus Christ.

2 PETER 1:3–11

Paul also stresses the importance of relying on the power of God, walking in the Spirit, to remain in control. The ultimate solution to gain self-control is "God-control."

This I say then, Walk in the Spirit, and ye shall not fulfil the lust of the flesh. For the flesh lusteth against the Spirit, and the Spirit against the flesh: and these are contrary the one to the other: so that ye cannot do the things that ye would. But if ye be led of the Spirit, ye are not under the law.

Now the works of the flesh are manifest, which are *these*; Adultery, fornication, uncleanness, lasciviousness, Idolatry, witchcraft, hatred, variance, emulations, wrath, strife, seditions, heresies, Envyings, murders, drunkenness, revellings, and such like: of the which I tell you before, as I have also told *you* in time past, that they which do such things shall not inherit the kingdom of God.

But the fruit of the Spirit is love, joy, peace, longsuffering, gentleness, goodness, faith, Meekness, temperance: against such there is no law. And they that are Christ's have crucified the flesh with the affections and lusts. If we live in the Spirit, let us also walk in the Spirit. Galatians 5:16–25

The bottom line is that we all struggle and fall. This failure can overwhelm us with guilt that causes us to hide from God. God knows we struggle. He wants us to "come home" to him no matter our condition. This is demonstrated beautifully in the parable of the prodigal son.

⚷ A certain man had two sons: And the younger of them said to *his* father, Father, give me the portion of goods that falleth *to me.* And he divided unto them *his* living.

And not many days after the younger son gathered all together, and took his journey into a far country, and there wasted his substance with riotous living. And when he had spent all, there arose a mighty famine in that land; and he began to be in want. And he went and joined himself to a citizen of that country; and he sent him into his fields to feed swine. And he would fain have filled his belly with the husks that the swine did eat: and no man gave unto him.

And when he came to himself, he said, How many hired servants of my father's have bread enough and to spare, and I perish with hunger! I will arise and go to my father, and will say unto him, Father, I have sinned against heaven, and before thee, And am no more worthy to be called thy son: make me as one of thy hired servants. And he arose, and came to his father.

But when he was yet a great way off, his father saw him, and had compassion, and ran, and fell on his neck, and kissed him.

And the son said unto him, Father, I have sinned against heaven, and in thy sight, and am no more worthy to be called thy son.

But the father said to his servants, Bring forth the best robe, and put *it* on him; and put a ring on his hand, and shoes on *his* feet: And bring hither the fatted calf, and kill *it*; and let us eat, and be merry: For this my son was dead, and is alive again; he was lost, and is found. And they began to be merry.

Luke 15:11–24 ⚷

In what areas of your life do you struggle with self-control?
How do these readings challenge you? How does the
knowledge of God's grace comfort you?

WHAT WE BELIEVE

*If we truly desire to become like Jesus for the sake of others,
we will receive the call and challenge to be self-controlled. As
we read the stories found in the Bible, we see evidence of the
wreckage caused by a lack of self-control, as in the life of Samson. We also see the amazing honor and blessing that comes
with self-control, as in the life of Joseph. How do we free ourselves from addictions and sinful habits? We must learn how
to flee and resist the temptation before us. But the ultimate
producer of self-control is God-control. As we yield our lives to
God's plan, his divine power gives us the strength to say "no" to
ungodliness and "yes" to his will. We have the power, through
Christ, to control ourselves. Yet, when we fall, we can remember
God's grace and run back to him. He will be waiting every time
with welcoming arms.*

CHAPTER

25

Hope

---KEY QUESTION---

How do I deal with the hardships and struggles of life?

--- KEY IDEA ---

I can cope with the hardships of life
because of the hope I have in Jesus Christ.

--- KEY VERSE ---

Which *hope* we have as an anchor of the soul, both sure and
stedfast, and which entereth into that within the veil;
Whither the forerunner is for us entered, *even* Jesus, made
an high priest for ever after the order of Melchisedec.
Hebrews 6:19–20

THE NEED FOR HOPE

It is impossible to cope without hope. Job had lost everything and was running out of strength. He wanted to die. His "friends" came to comfort him. His response to his unhelpful friends is the expression of a man without hope.

But Job answered and said, Oh that my grief were throughly weighed, and my calamity laid in the balances together! For now it would be heavier than the sand of the sea: therefore my words are swallowed up. For the arrows of the Almighty *are* within me, the poison whereof drinketh up my spirit: the terrors of God do set themselves in array against me. Doth the wild ass bray when he hath grass? or loweth the ox over his fodder? Can that which is unsavoury be eaten without salt? or is there *any* taste in the white of an egg? The things *that* my soul refused to touch *are* as my sorrowful meat.

Oh that I might have my request; and that God would grant *me* the thing that I long for! Even that it would please God to destroy me; that he would let loose his hand, and cut me off! Then should I yet have comfort; yea, I would harden myself in sorrow: let him not spare; for I have not concealed the words of the Holy One.

What *is* my strength, that I should hope? and what *is* mine end, that I should prolong my life? *Is* my strength the strength of stones? or *is* my flesh of brass? *Is* not my help in me? and is wisdom driven quite from me?

JOB 6:1–13

Is *there* not an appointed time to man upon earth? *are not* his days also like the days of an hireling? As a servant earnestly desireth the shadow, and as an hireling looketh for *the reward of* his work: So am I made to possess months of vanity, and wearisome nights are appointed to me. When I lie down, I say, When shall I arise, and the night be gone? and I am full of tossings to and fro unto the dawning of the day. My flesh is clothed with worms and clods of dust; my skin is broken, and become loathsome.

My days are swifter than a weaver's shuttle, and are spent without hope.

JOB 7:1–6

Have you ever felt despair like Job's?
What questions did you ask of God?

SOURCES OF FALSE HOPE

Our deep need for hope sometimes leads us to falsely put our hope in unhealthy things. False hope causes people to plan, build and risk for something that is not likely to happen. The Bible identifies several things humans unfortunately place their hope in, only to be disappointed in the end.

As you read about the four sources of false hope,
think about which one you are most susceptible to.
What made you pick the one you did?

False hope ... in riches.
Because of his fearless confidence in God, David was able to hurl condemnation at his enemy who trusted in wealth.

Why boastest thou thyself in mischief, O mighty man?
the goodness of God *endureth* continually.

The tongue deviseth mischiefs;
 like a sharp razor,
 working deceitfully.
Thou lovest evil more than good;
 and lying rather than to speak righteousness.
Thou lovest all devouring words,
 O *thou* deceitful tongue.

God shall likewise destroy thee for ever,
 he shall take thee away,
and pluck thee out of *thy* dwelling place,
 and root thee out of the land of the living.
The righteous also shall see, and fear,
 and shall laugh at him:
Lo, *this is* the man
 ***that* made not God his strength;**
but trusted in the abundance of his riches,
 ***and* strengthened himself in his wickedness.**

But I *am* like a green olive tree
 in the house of God:
I trust in the mercy of God
 for ever and ever.
I will praise thee for ever,
 because thou hast done *it*:
and I will wait on thy name;
 for *it is* good before thy saints.   Psalm 52:1–9

Paul tells Timothy to instruct the believers in Ephesus about the false hope of trusting in riches.

Charge them that are rich in this world, that they be not highminded, nor trust in uncertain riches, but in the living God, who giveth us richly all things to enjoy.   1 Timothy 6:17

False hope ... in people.
 The psalmists tell us that we will be disappointed if we place our hope in people rather than God.

It is better to trust in the LORD
    than to put confidence in man.
It is better to trust in the LORD
    than to put confidence in princes.   PSALM 118:8–9

Put not your trust in princes,
    ***nor* in the son of man, in whom *there* is no help.**
His breath goeth forth, he returneth to his earth;
    in that very day his thoughts perish.   PSALM 146:3–4

The prophet Jeremiah declares the same sentiment.

Thus saith the LORD; **Cursed *be* the man that trusteth in man, and maketh flesh his arm, and whose heart departeth from the LORD.** For he shall be like the heath in the desert, and shall not see when good cometh; but shall inhabit the parched places in the wilderness, *in* a salt land and not inhabited.

                            JEREMIAH 17:5–6

False hope . . . in idols.
    An idol is any object we place above God. The prophet Habakkuk declares how foolish it is to place our hope in such man-made inventions.

What profiteth the graven image that the maker thereof hath graven it; the molten image, and a teacher of lies, that the maker of his work trusteth therein, to make dumb idols? Woe unto him that saith to the wood, Awake; to the dumb stone, Arise, it shall teach! Behold, it *is* laid over with gold and silver, and *there is* no breath at all in the midst of it.   HABAKKUK 2:18–19

False hope . . . in human government.
    It is easy and often more tangible for people to place their trust and hope in nations. Isaiah warns the people of Judah to avoid such a mistake, even with the mighty nation of Egypt.

Woe to them that go down to Egypt for help; and stay on horses, and trust in chariots, because *they are* many; and in horsemen, because they are very strong; but they look not unto the Holy One of Israel, neither seek the LORD! ISAIAH 31:1

Now the Egyptians *are* men, and not God; and their horses flesh, and not spirit. When the LORD shall stretch out his hand, both he that helpeth shall fall, and he that is holpen shall fall down, and they all shall fail together. ISAIAH 31:3

THE SOURCE OF TRUE HOPE

True hope is found only in God.

Hope is only as good as the power and character of the one who guarantees it. The psalmist expresses with deep passion his trust in God as his source of hope when present times were difficult.

As the hart panteth after the water brooks,
    so panteth my soul after thee, O God.
My soul thirsteth for God, for the living God:
    when shall I come and appear before God?
My tears have been my meat
    day and night,
while they continually say unto me,
    Where *is* thy God?
When I remember these *things*,
    I pour out my soul in me:
for I had gone with the multitude,
    I went with them to the house of God,
with the voice of joy and praise,
    with a multitude that kept holyday.

Why art thou cast down, O my soul?
    and *why* art thou disquieted in me?
hope thou in God:
    for I shall yet praise him
    for **the help of his countenance.**

O my God, my soul is cast down within me:
    therefore will I remember thee

from the land of Jordan,
   and of the Hermonites, from the hill Mizar.
Deep calleth unto deep
   at the noise of thy waterspouts:
all thy waves and thy billows
   are gone over me.

Yet the LORD will command his lovingkindness in the
       daytime,
   and in the night his song *shall be* with me,
   and my prayer unto the God of my life.

I will say unto God my rock,
   Why hast thou forgotten me?
why go I mourning because of the
   oppression of the enemy?
As with a sword in my bones,
   mine enemies reproach me;
while they say daily unto me,
   Where *is* thy God?

Why art thou cast down, O my soul?
   and why art thou disquieted within me?
hope thou in God:
   for I shall yet praise him,
   who is **the health of my countenance, and my God.**

PSALM 42:1–11

True hope is found in God's promises.

All the authors of the New Testament wrote on the topic of hope. It is clearly one of the unique and powerful benefits of following God. The writer of Hebrews drew on the character of God to confirm God's promises.

What promises of God can you find in the following
passages from Hebrews 6; Colossians 1; 1 Peter 1;
1 Thessalonians 4 and 1 John 3?

For when God made promise to Abraham, because he could swear by no greater, he sware by himself, Saying, Surely blessing I will bless thee, and multiplying I will multiply thee. And so, after he had patiently endured, he obtained the promise.

For men verily swear by the greater: and an oath for confirmation *is* to them an end of all strife. Wherein God, willing more abundantly to shew unto the heirs of promise the immutability of his counsel, confirmed *it* by an oath: That by two immutable things, in which *it was* impossible for God to lie, we might have a strong consolation, who have fled for refuge to lay hold upon the hope set before us: **Which *hope* we have as an anchor of the soul, both sure and stedfast, and which entereth into that within the veil; Whither the forerunner is for us entered, even Jesus,** made an high priest for ever after the order of Melchisedec.

HEBREWS 6:13–20

Since God's character is rock solid, trustworthy and true, we anchor our hope in his promises to us. Paul wrote a letter to the church at Colosse while he was under house arrest in Rome. God had been unfolding his grand promise of redemption since the fall of Adam and Eve. The true and full content of this promise was a mystery to the people of the Old Testament. Now, God has fulfilled his promise and revealed it to us—the source of our hope has come.

Who now rejoice in my sufferings for you, and fill up that which is behind of the afflictions of Christ in my flesh for his body's sake, which is the church: Whereof I am made a minister, according to the dispensation of God which is given to me for you, to fulfil the word of God; *Even* the mystery which hath been hid from ages and from generations, but now is made manifest to his saints: **To whom God would make known what *is* the riches of the glory of this mystery among the Gentiles; which is Christ in you, the hope of glory:**

Whom we preach, warning every man, and teaching every man in all wisdom; that we may present every man perfect in Christ Jesus: Whereunto I also labour, striving according to his working, which worketh in me mightily.

COLOSSIANS 1:24–29

What God has promised to all believers in Jesus enables us to endure life's hardships. Peter opened his first letter proclaiming this truth. The ultimate promise of God is our future resurrection. The hope of this promise trumps all momentary trials.

Peter, an apostle of Jesus Christ, to the strangers scattered throughout Pontus, Galatia, Cappadocia, Asia, and Bithynia, Elect according to the foreknowledge of God the Father, through sanctification of the Spirit, unto obedience and sprinkling of the blood of Jesus Christ: Grace unto you, and peace, be multiplied.

Blessed *be* the God and Father of our Lord Jesus Christ, which according to his abundant mercy hath begotten us again unto a lively hope by the resurrection of Jesus Christ from the dead, To an inheritance incorruptible, and undefiled, and that fadeth not away, reserved in heaven for you, Who are kept by the power of God through faith unto salvation ready to be revealed in the last time. Wherein ye greatly rejoice, though now for a season, if need be, ye are in heaviness through manifold temptations: That the trial of your faith, being much more precious than of gold that perisheth, though it be tried with fire, might be found unto praise and honour and glory at the appearing of Jesus Christ: Whom having not seen, ye love; in whom, though now ye see *him* not, yet believing, ye rejoice with joy unspeakable and full of glory: Receiving the end of your faith, *even* the salvation of *your* souls.

Of which salvation the prophets have enquired and searched diligently, who prophesied of the grace *that should come* unto you: Searching what, or what manner of time the Spirit of Christ which was in them did signify, when it testified beforehand the sufferings of Christ, and the glory that should follow. Unto whom it was revealed, that not unto themselves, but unto us they did minister the things, which are now reported unto you by them that have preached the gospel unto you with the Holy Ghost sent down from heaven; which things the angels desire to look into.

Wherefore gird up the loins of your mind, be sober, and hope to the end for the grace that is to be brought unto you at the revelation of Jesus Christ; As obedient children, not fashioning yourselves according to the former lusts in your ignorance: But as he which hath called you is holy, so be ye holy in all manner of conversation; Because it is written, Be ye holy; for I am holy.

And if ye call on the Father, who without respect of persons judgeth according to every man's work, pass the time of your sojourning *here* in fear: Forasmuch as ye know that ye were not redeemed with corruptible things, *as* silver and gold, from your vain conversation *received* by tradition from your fathers; But with the precious blood of Christ, as of a lamb without blemish and without spot: Who verily was foreordained before the foundation of the world, but was manifest in these last times for you, Who by him do believe in God, that raised him up from the dead, and gave him glory; that your faith and hope might be in God.

Seeing ye have purified your souls in obeying the truth through the Spirit unto unfeigned love of the brethren, *see that ye* love one another with a pure heart fervently: Being born again, not of corruptible seed, but of incorruptible, by the word of God, which liveth and abideth for ever. For all flesh *is* as grass, and all the glory of man as the flower of grass. The grass withereth, and the flower thereof falleth away: But the word of the Lord endureth for ever.

And this is the word which by the gospel is preached unto you.

1 PETER 1:1–25

The Christians in Thessalonica had misunderstood Paul and thought that all believers would live until Christ returns. That caused them distress when some in the church died. Paul wrote his first letter to them to clear up this matter. The promise to all believers, past and present, of being with the Lord forever is the foundation of our hope.

But I would not have you to be ignorant, brethren, concerning them which are asleep, that ye sorrow not, even as others which have no hope. For if we believe that Jesus died and rose again, even so them also which sleep in Jesus will God bring with him. For this we say unto you by the word of the Lord, that we which are alive *and* remain unto the coming of the Lord shall not prevent them which are asleep. For the Lord himself shall descend from heaven with a shout, with the voice of the archangel, and with the trump of God: and the dead in Christ shall rise first: Then we which are alive *and* remain shall be caught up together with them in the clouds, to meet the Lord in the air: and so shall we ever be with the Lord. Wherefore comfort one another with these words.

1 THESSALONIANS 4:13–18

John echoed the writings of Paul and Peter regarding the hope we have through the promised resurrection. He challenged his readers to live pure lives in anticipation of this guaranteed event.

Behold, what manner of love the Father hath bestowed upon us, that we should be called the sons of God: therefore the world knoweth us not, because it knew him not. Beloved, now are we the sons of God, and it doth not yet appear what we shall be: **but we know that, when he shall appear, we shall be like him; for we shall see him as he is. And every man that hath this hope in him purifieth himself, even as he is pure.** 1 JOHN 3:1–3

THE EFFECT OF HOPE

When we hope in God's promises, the effect on our lives is profound. Even if we are going through difficulties, hope gives us the strength to continue. Isaiah prophesied that the people of Judah were about to go through 70 years of difficulty as captives of the Babylonians. Despite such suffering, Isaiah was able to confidently give the people hope because God had promised to bring them home. The exiles could live full, happy lives in a painful situation because they knew God would keep his promise.

To whom then will ye liken me, or shall I be equal? saith the Holy One. Lift up your eyes on high, and behold who hath created these *things*, that bringeth out their host by number: he calleth them all by names by the greatness of his might, for that *he is* strong in power; not one faileth.

Why sayest thou, O Jacob, and speakest, O Israel, My way is hid from the LORD, and my judgment is passed over from my God? Hast thou not known? hast thou not heard, *that* the everlasting God, the LORD, the Creator of the ends of the earth, fainteth not, neither is weary? *there is* no searching of his understanding. He giveth power to the faint; and to *them that have* no might he increaseth strength. **Even the youths shall faint and be weary, and the young men shall utterly fall: But they that wait upon the LORD shall renew *their* strength; they shall mount up with wings as eagles; they shall run, and not be weary; *and* they shall walk, and not faint.** ISAIAH 40:25–31 ⚷

> *The positive effect of hope is more powerful than we realize. Simeon waited many long years without seeing the fulfillment of his hope, but he carried on, letting hope give him strength for each new day. God and his promises are the reason for our hope. When we embrace this hope, it has a dramatic effect on our daily lives. Simeon's story can give us pause to think about the impact our hope in Christ has on our ability to persevere.*

⚷ And, behold, there was a man in Jerusalem, whose name *was* Simeon; and the same man *was* just and devout, waiting for the consolation of Israel: and the Holy Ghost was upon him. And it was revealed unto him by the Holy Ghost, that he should not see death, before he had seen the Lord's Christ. And he came by the Spirit into the temple: and when the parents brought in the child Jesus, to do for him after the custom of the law, Then took he him up in his arms, and blessed God, and said, Lord, now lettest thou thy servant depart in peace, according to thy word: For mine eyes have seen thy salvation, Which thou hast prepared before the face of all people; A light to lighten the Gentiles, and the glory of thy people Israel.

And Joseph and his mother marvelled at those things which were spoken of him. And Simeon blessed them, and said unto Mary his mother, Behold, this *child* is set for the fall and rising again of many in Israel; and for a sign which shall be spoken against; (Yea, a sword shall pierce through thy own soul also,) that the thoughts of many hearts may be revealed. LUKE 2:25–35 ⚷

What effect did God's promise to Simeon, that he
would see the first arrival of Christ, have on his life?
What effect should God's promise to us, that we will see
the second arrival of Christ, have on our lives?

HOPE ACTIVATES FAITH, FAITH DEEPENS HOPE

Hope is available to all followers of God, but not everyone takes hold of it. It can be hard for us to trust in a God we cannot see and hold fast to fantastic promises yet to come. To activate the power of hope in our lives, we need to have faith in God and his promises. The writer of Hebrews preached this message to his readers. He then listed people from the past who placed their faith in God and experienced amazing results in their lives. God offers this same opportunity to us today. In fact, God has "some better thing" planned for those who know Jesus.

Now faith is the substance of things hoped for, the evidence of things not seen. For by it the elders obtained a good report.

Through faith we understand that the worlds were framed by the word of God, so that things which are seen were not made of things which do appear.

By faith Abel offered unto God a more excellent sacrifice than Cain, by which he obtained witness that he was righteous, God testifying of his gifts: and by it he being dead yet speaketh.

By faith Enoch was translated that he should not see death; and was not found, because God had translated him: for before his translation he had this testimony, that he pleased God. But without faith *it is* impossible to please *him*: for he that cometh to God must believe that he is, and *that* he is a rewarder of them that diligently seek him.

By faith Noah, being warned of God of things not seen as yet, moved with fear, prepared an ark to the saving of his house; by the which he condemned the world, and became heir of the righteousness which is by faith.

By faith Abraham, when he was called to go out into a place which he should after receive for an inheritance, obeyed; and he went out, not knowing whither he went. By faith he sojourned in the land of promise, as *in* a strange country, dwelling in tabernacles with Isaac and Jacob, the heirs with him of the same promise: For he looked for a city which hath foundations, whose builder and maker *is* God. Through faith also Sara herself received strength to conceive seed, and was delivered of a child when she was past age, because she judged him faithful who had promised. Therefore sprang there even of one, and him as good as dead, *so many* as the stars of the sky in multitude, and as the sand which is by the sea shore innumerable.

These all died in faith, not having received the promises, but having seen them afar off, and were persuaded of *them*, and embraced *them*, and confessed that they were strangers and pilgrims on the earth. For they that say such things declare plainly that they seek a country. And truly, if they had been mindful of that *country* from whence they came out, they might have had opportunity to have returned. But now they desire a better *country*, that is, an heavenly: wherefore God is not ashamed to be called their God: for he hath prepared for them a city.

By faith Abraham, when he was tried, offered up Isaac: and he that had received the promises offered up his only begotten *son*, Of whom it was said, That in Isaac shall thy seed be called: Accounting that God *was* able to raise *him* up, even from the dead; from whence also he received him in a figure.

By faith Isaac blessed Jacob and Esau concerning things to come.

By faith Jacob, when he was a dying, blessed both the sons of Joseph; and worshipped, *leaning* upon the top of his staff.

By faith Joseph, when he died, made mention of the departing of the children of Israel; and gave commandment concerning his bones.

By faith Moses, when he was born, was hid three months of his parents, because they saw *he was* a proper child; and they were not afraid of the king's commandment.

By faith Moses, when he was come to years, refused to be called the son of Pharaoh's daughter; Choosing rather to suffer affliction with the people of God, than to enjoy the pleasures of sin for a season; Esteeming the reproach of Christ greater riches than the treasures in Egypt: for he had respect unto the recompence of the reward. By faith he forsook Egypt, not fearing the wrath of the king: for he endured, as seeing him who is invisible. Through faith he kept the passover, and the sprinkling of blood, lest he that destroyed the firstborn should touch them.

By faith they passed through the Red sea as by dry *land*: which the Egyptians assaying to do were drowned.

By faith the walls of Jericho fell down, after they were compassed about seven days.

By faith the harlot Rahab perished not with them that believed not, when she had received the spies with peace.

And what shall I more say? for the time would fail me to tell *of* Gedeon, and *of* Barak, and *of* Samson, and *of* Jephthae; *of* David also, and Samuel, and *of* the prophets: Who through faith subdued kingdoms, wrought righteousness, obtained promises, stopped the mouths of lions, Quenched the violence of fire, escaped the edge of the sword, out of weakness were made strong, waxed valiant in fight, turned to flight the armies of the aliens. Women received their dead raised to life again: and others were tortured, not accepting deliverance; that they might obtain a better resurrection: And others had trial of *cruel* mockings and scourgings, yea, moreover of bonds and imprisonment: They were stoned, they were sawn asunder, were tempted, were slain with the sword: they wandered about in sheepskins and goatskins; being destitute, afflicted, tormented; (Of whom the world was not worthy:) they wandered in deserts, and *in* mountains, and *in* dens and caves of the earth.

And these all, having obtained a good report through faith, received not the promise: God having provided some better thing for us, that they without us should not be made perfect.

Wherefore seeing we also are compassed about with so great a cloud of witnesses, let us lay aside every weight, and the sin which doth so easily beset *us*, and **let us run with patience the race that is set before us, Looking unto Jesus the author and finisher of *our* faith;** who for the joy that was set before him endured the cross, despising the shame, and is set down at the right hand of the throne of God. For consider him that endured such contradiction of sinners against himself, lest ye be wearied and faint in your minds.

HEBREWS 11:1—12:3

According to the writer of Hebrews, what did the
Biblical heroes endure because they had hope in God?
What is the "race that is set before us"?
How is hope dependent on faith?

Unfortunately, too often humans put their hope in things that overpromise and underdeliver—riches, people, idols, government. The only true source of hope is found in Jesus Christ. Christ and his promises become an anchor for our souls and the reason we can persevere. Of all the promises Jesus has made to us, the promise of eternal life with God is the most significant. No matter what we may be going through today, we know what happens in this life is not how our story ends. Our story ends, or really only begins, in the presence of God in his eternal kingdom.

BE

CHAPTER

26

Patience

---------- KEY QUESTION ----------

How does God provide the help I need to deal with stress?

--------------- KEY IDEA ---------------

I am slow to anger and endure patiently
under the unavoidable pressures of life.

--------------- KEY VERSE ---------------

He that is slow to wrath *is* of great understanding:
but *he that is* hasty of spirit exalteth folly.
Proverbs 14:29

417

OUR MAP

As with the beliefs and practices, the first half of the key virtues are more vertical or inward in nature—God plants within us his heart of love, joy, peace, self-control and hope. Now, we turn more outward and consider virtues that are felt by others when we are exhibiting them.

One virtue that is most evident when it is missing is patience. We all have stress triggers—the proverbial buttons that when pushed cause us to lose our patience. Some of these triggers are other people. The way they act, move, talk or even look can set us off. Then there are those triggers of circumstances. We are too busy; we have a wayward family member who is making destructive choices; we suffer from a physical condition or a lingering illness. But if we long to be like Jesus, becoming a more patient person is nonnegotiable. So how does God provide the help we need to deal with stress? That is the focus of the Scripture in this chapter.

In our reading we will learn:

- God Is Patient With Us
- Being Slow to Become Angry
- Persevering Under Pressure

GOD IS PATIENT WITH US

As you might suspect, God models what he desires to see in us.

> But thou, O LORD, *art* a God full of compassion, and gracious,
> longsuffering, and plenteous in mercy and truth.
>
> PSALM 86:15

God loved the Israelites and had a wonderful plan for them. They, however, struggled to trust God even after he proved himself to them repeatedly in mighty ways.

The Israelites had spent 400 long years in Egypt, but now the land God had promised to Abraham for his descendants was ready. But the people had to step forward in faith. God would accomplish the rest. In the book of Exodus, we read how God, through Moses, led the people out of Egypt, and how God even parted the Red Sea.

In the book of Numbers, the people were poised to enter the promised land. They sent 12 spies into the land to scope out the situation. Upon their return, the spies reported that the size and strength of the enemy was too great. Except for Joshua and Caleb, all the spies gave in to their fear and said, "We be not able to go up against the people; for they are stronger than we." After the report was given to the people, they decided they would rather go back to Egypt and subject themselves to slavery than trust God to lay hold of a life of freedom.

As you read the passage below from Numbers 14,
highlight some examples of God's patience.

And all the congregation lifted up their voice, and cried; and the people wept that night. And all the children of Israel murmured against Moses and against Aaron: and the whole congregation said unto them, Would God that we had died in the land of Egypt! or would God we had died in this wilderness! And wherefore hath the LORD brought us unto this land, to fall by the sword, that our wives and our children should be a prey? were it not better for us to return into Egypt? And they said one to another, Let us make a captain, and let us return into Egypt.

Then Moses and Aaron fell on their faces before all the assembly of the congregation of the children of Israel. And Joshua the son of Nun, and Caleb the son of Jephunneh, *which were* of them that searched the land, rent their clothes: And they spake unto all the company of the children of Israel, saying, The land, which we passed through to search it, *is* an exceeding good land. If the LORD delight in us, then he will bring us into this land, and give it us; a land which floweth with milk and honey. Only rebel not ye against the LORD, neither fear ye the people of the land; for they *are* bread for us: their defence is departed from them, and the LORD *is* with us: fear them not.

But all the congregation bade stone them with stones. And the glory of the LORD appeared in the tabernacle of the congregation before all the children of Israel. And the LORD said unto Moses, How long will this people provoke me? and how long will it be ere they believe me, for all the signs which I have shewed among them? I will smite them with the pestilence, and disinherit them, and will make of thee a greater nation and mightier than they.

And Moses said unto the LORD, Then the Egyptians shall hear *it*, (for thou broughtest up this people in thy might from among them;) And they will tell *it* to the inhabitants of this land: *for* they have heard that thou LORD *art* among this people, that thou LORD art seen face to face, and *that* thy cloud standeth over them, and *that* thou goest before them, by day time in a pillar of a cloud, and in a pillar of fire by night. Now *if* thou shalt kill *all* this people as one man, then the nations which have heard the fame of thee will speak, saying, Because the LORD was not able to bring this people into the land which he sware unto them, therefore he hath slain them in the wilderness.

And now, I beseech thee, let the power of my Lord be great, according as thou hast spoken, saying, The LORD *is* longsuffering, and of great mercy, forgiving iniquity and transgression, and by no means clearing *the guilty*, visiting the iniquity of the fathers upon the children unto the third and fourth *generation*. Pardon, I beseech thee, the iniquity of this people according unto the greatness of thy mercy, and as thou hast forgiven this people, from Egypt even until now.

And the LORD said, I have pardoned according to thy word: But *as* truly *as* I live, all the earth shall be filled with the glory of the LORD. Because all those men which have seen my glory, and my miracles, which I did in Egypt and in the wilderness, and have tempted me now these ten times, and have not hearkened to my voice; Surely they shall not see the land which I sware unto their fathers, neither shall any of them that provoked me see it.

NUMBERS 14:1–23

Doubtless ye shall not come into the land, *concerning* which I sware to make you dwell therein, save Caleb the son of Jephunneh, and Joshua the son of Nun. But your little ones, which ye said should be a prey, them will I bring in, and they shall know the land which ye have despised. But *as for* you, your carcases, they shall fall in this wilderness. And your children shall wander in the wilderness forty years, and bear your whoredoms, until your carcases be wasted in the wilderness. NUMBERS 14:30–33

Although God didn't wipe out the rebellious Israelites as they deserved, he made them wander in the wilderness for 40 years — one year for each of the 40 days the spies explored the land. Nevertheless, God patiently demonstrated his commitment to his covenant with Israel and established the next generation in the promised land.

God's patience extends beyond the Israelites to all people. God is just. In Peter's second letter he tells his readers about "the day of the Lord" when Christ will return and bring to consummation all things. This will be the day of judgment for unbelievers, but the day of redemption for believers. God demonstrates his patience toward all humanity by delaying this ultimate and final judgment in order to give more people an opportunity to reach out and take hold of his forgiveness.

This second epistle, beloved, I now write unto you; in *both* which I stir up your pure minds by way of remembrance: That ye may be mindful of the words which were spoken before by the holy prophets, and of the commandment of us the apostles of the Lord and Saviour:

Knowing this first, that there shall come in the last days scoffers, walking after their own lusts, And saying, Where is the promise of his coming? for since the fathers fell asleep, all things continue as *they were* from the beginning of the creation. For this they willingly are ignorant of, that by the word of God the heavens were of old, and the earth standing out of the water and in the water: Whereby the world that then was, being overflowed with water, perished: But the heavens and the earth, which are now, by the same word are kept in store, reserved unto fire against the day of judgment and perdition of ungodly men.

But, beloved, be not ignorant of this one thing, that one day *is* with the Lord as a thousand years, and a thousand years as one day. **The Lord is not slack concerning his promise, as some men count slackness; but is longsuffering to us-ward, not willing that any should perish, but that all should come to repentance.**

But the day of the Lord will come as a thief in the night; in the which the heavens shall pass away with a great noise, and the elements shall melt with fervent heat, the earth also and the works that are therein shall be burned up.

Seeing then *that* all these things shall be dissolved, what manner *of persons* ought ye to be in *all* holy conversation and godliness, Looking for and hasting unto the coming of the day of God, wherein the heavens being on fire shall be dissolved, and the elements shall melt with fervent heat? Nevertheless we, according to his promise, look for new heavens and a new earth, wherein dwelleth righteousness.

Wherefore, beloved, seeing that ye look for such things, be diligent that ye may be found of him in peace, without spot, and blameless. And account *that* the longsuffering of our Lord *is* salvation; even as our beloved brother Paul also according to the wisdom given unto him hath written unto you; As also in all *his* epistles, speaking in them of these things; in which are some things hard to be understood, which they that are unlearned and unstable wrest, as *they do* also the other scriptures, unto their own destruction.

Ye therefore, beloved, seeing ye know *these things* before, beware lest ye also, being led away with the error of the wicked, fall from your own stedfastness. But grow in grace, and *in* the knowledge of our Lord and Saviour Jesus Christ. To him *be* glory both now and for ever. Amen. 2 PETER 3:1–18

BEING SLOW TO BECOME ANGRY

One of the primary ideas behind the virtue of patience is taking a long time to become angry—to overheat. The Greek word carries the idea of a thermometer. If a spiritual thermometer were placed in our mouths as we faced a difficult situation, how long would it take for our temperatures to rise? As we mature, we learn to control our anger and practice patience in all circumstances.

Young David was a threat to King Saul. While popularity was not David's goal, he was beloved by the people of Israel. King Saul burned with anger and jealousy toward David. For the next several years, he pursued David, hoping to capture and kill him. David, forced to become a fugitive, proved he was a "man after

God's own heart" when he waited on God's timing instead of taking matters into his own hands.

As you read 1 Samuel 24, look for examples
of how David waited on God's timing. Why is this
so difficult for many people to do?

And it came to pass, when Saul was returned from following the Philistines, that it was told him, saying, Behold, David *is* in the wilderness of En-gedi. Then Saul took three thousand chosen men out of all Israel, and went to seek David and his men upon the rocks of the wild goats.

And he came to the sheepcotes by the way, where *was* a cave; and Saul went in to cover his feet: and David and his men remained in the sides of the cave. And the men of David said unto him, Behold the day of which the LORD said unto thee, Behold, I will deliver thine enemy into thine hand, that thou mayest do to him as it shall seem good unto thee. Then David arose, and cut off the skirt of Saul's robe privily.

And it came to pass afterward, that David's heart smote him, because he had cut off Saul's skirt. And he said unto his men, The LORD forbid that I should do this thing unto my master, the LORD's anointed, to stretch forth mine hand against him, seeing he *is* the anointed of the LORD. So David stayed his servants with these words, and suffered them not to rise against Saul. But Saul rose up out of the cave, and went on *his* way.

David also arose afterward, and went out of the cave, and cried after Saul, saying, My lord the king. And when Saul looked behind him, David stooped with his face to the earth, and bowed himself. And David said to Saul, Wherefore hearest thou men's words, saying, Behold, David seeketh thy hurt? Behold, this day thine eyes have seen how that the LORD had delivered thee to day into mine hand in the cave: and *some* bade *me* kill thee: but *mine eye* spared thee; and I said, I will not put forth mine hand against my lord; for he *is* the LORD's anointed. Moreover, my father, see, yea, see the skirt of thy robe in my hand: for in that I cut off the skirt of thy robe, and killed thee not, know thou and see that *there is* neither

evil nor transgression in mine hand, and I have not sinned against
thee; yet thou huntest my soul to take it. The LORD judge between
me and thee, and the LORD avenge me of thee: but mine hand shall
not be upon thee. As saith the proverb of the ancients, Wickedness proceedeth from the wicked: but mine hand shall not be upon
thee.

After whom is the king of Israel come out? after whom dost
thou pursue? after a dead dog, after a flea. The LORD therefore
be judge, and judge between me and thee, and see, and plead my
cause, and deliver me out of thine hand.

And it came to pass, when David had made an end of speaking
these words unto Saul, that Saul said, *Is* this thy voice, my son David? And Saul lifted up his voice, and wept. And he said to David,
Thou *art* more righteous than I: for thou hast rewarded me good,
whereas I have rewarded thee evil. And thou hast shewed this day
how that thou hast dealt well with me: forasmuch as when the
LORD had delivered me into thine hand, thou killedst me not. For
if a man find his enemy, will he let him go well away? wherefore
the LORD reward thee good for that thou hast done unto me this
day. And now, behold, I know well that thou shalt surely be king,
and that the kingdom of Israel shall be established in thine hand.
Swear now therefore unto me by the LORD, that thou wilt not cut
off my seed after me, and that thou wilt not destroy my name out
of my father's house.

And David sware unto Saul. And Saul went home; but David
and his men gat them up unto the hold.   1 SAMUEL 24:1–22 ⚷

*Saul returned home, but his jealousy remained. As the days
passed, Saul allowed his anger against David to fester and grow.
Once again Saul led three thousand troops on a mission to capture and kill David.*

And the Ziphites came unto Saul to Gibeah, saying, Doth
not David hide himself in the hill of Hachilah, *which is* before
Jeshimon?

Then Saul arose, and went down to the wilderness of Ziph, having three thousand chosen men of Israel with him, to seek David
in the wilderness of Ziph. And Saul pitched in the hill of Hachilah,

which *is* before Jeshimon, by the way. But David abode in the wilderness, and he saw that Saul came after him into the wilderness. David therefore sent out spies, and understood that Saul was come in very deed.

And David arose, and came to the place where Saul had pitched: and David beheld the place where Saul lay, and Abner the son of Ner, the captain of his host: and Saul lay in the trench, and the people pitched round about him.

Then answered David and said to Ahimelech the Hittite, and to Abishai the son of Zeruiah, brother to Joab, saying, Who will go down with me to Saul to the camp?

And Abishai said, I will go down with thee.

So David and Abishai came to the people by night: and, behold, Saul lay sleeping within the trench, and his spear stuck in the ground at his bolster: but Abner and the people lay round about him.

Then said Abishai to David, God hath delivered thine enemy into thine hand this day: now therefore let me smite him, I pray thee, with the spear even to the earth at once, and I will not *smite* him the second time.

And David said to Abishai, Destroy him not: for who can stretch forth his hand against the LORD's anointed, and be guiltless? David said furthermore, *As* the LORD liveth, the LORD shall smite him; or his day shall come to die; or he shall descend into battle, and perish. The LORD forbid that I should stretch forth mine hand against the LORD's anointed: but, I pray thee, take thou now the spear that *is* at his bolster, and the cruse of water, and let us go.

So David took the spear and the cruse of water from Saul's bolster; and they gat them away, and no man saw *it*, nor knew *it*, neither awaked: for they *were* all asleep; because a deep sleep from the LORD was fallen upon them.

Then David went over to the other side, and stood on the top of an hill afar off; a great space *being* between them: And David cried to the people, and to Abner the son of Ner, saying, Answerest thou not, Abner?

Then Abner answered and said, Who *art* thou *that* criest to the king?

And David said to Abner, *Art* not thou a *valiant* man? and who *is* like to thee in Israel? wherefore then hast thou not kept thy lord the king? for there came one of the people in to destroy the king thy lord. This thing *is* not good that thou hast done. *As* the LORD liveth, ye *are* worthy to die, because ye have not kept your master, the LORD's anointed. And now see where the king's spear *is*, and the cruse of water that *was* at his bolster.

And Saul knew David's voice, and said, *Is* this thy voice, my son David? And David said, *It is* my voice, my lord, O king.

And he said, Wherefore doth my lord thus pursue after his servant? for what have I done? or what evil *is* in mine hand? Now therefore, I pray thee, let my lord the king hear the words of his servant. If the LORD have stirred thee up against me, let him accept an offering: but if *they be* the children of men, cursed *be* they before the LORD; for they have driven me out this day from abiding in the inheritance of the LORD, saying, Go, serve other gods. Now therefore, let not my blood fall to the earth before the face of the LORD: for the king of Israel is come out to seek a flea, as when one doth hunt a partridge in the mountains.

Then said Saul, I have sinned: return, my son David: for I will no more do thee harm, because my soul was precious in thine eyes this day: behold, I have played the fool, and have erred exceedingly.

And David answered and said, Behold the king's spear! and let one of the young men come over and fetch it. The LORD render to every man his righteousness and his faithfulness: for the LORD delivered thee into *my* hand to day, but I would not stretch forth mine hand against the LORD's anointed. **And, behold, as thy life was much set by this day in mine eyes, so let my life be much set by in the eyes of the LORD, and let him deliver me out of all tribulation.**

Then Saul said to David, Blessed *be* thou, my son David: thou shalt both do great *things*, and also shalt still prevail.

So David went on his way, and Saul returned to his place.

1 SAMUEL 26:1–25

Saul was critically wounded in a battle against the Philistines and eventually died after falling on his own sword. When David got

word of the death of Saul and his son Jonathan, he refused to celebrate victory for himself and instead grieved the loss of Israel's
king. In the course of time, David became king of his own tribe,
Judah, and seven years later he was crowned king of all Israel.
During those long years, from when he was chosen to be king at
age 15 to the day of his coronation 15 years later, David waited for
God to work out his plan.

David's son Solomon took the throne of Israel after David's
death. In Proverbs, Solomon shares from his amazing reservoir
of God-instilled wisdom. Listen to and learn from what he wrote
about patience.

As you read Proverbs 14:29; 15:18; 16:32; 19:11 and 25:15 below,
ponder these two questions: How does patience defuse
a conflict? How do impatience and rashness escalate it?

He that is slow to wrath *is* of great understanding:
but *he that is* hasty of spirit exalteth folly.　PROVERBS 14:29

A wrathful man stirreth up strife:
but *he that is* slow to anger appeaseth strife.

PROVERBS 15:18

He that is slow to anger *is* better than the mighty;
and he that ruleth his spirit than he that taketh a city.

PROVERBS 16:32

The discretion of a man deferreth his anger;
and *it is* his glory to pass over a transgression.

PROVERBS 19:11

By long forbearing is a prince persuaded,
and a soft tongue breaketh the bone.　PROVERBS 25:15

In the New Testament, James offers this advice to use in our
relationships with others—particularly those who "push our
buttons."

Wherefore, my beloved brethren, let every man be swift to hear, slow to speak, slow to wrath: For the wrath of man worketh not the righteousness of God. JAMES 1:19–20

PERSEVERING UNDER PRESSURE

Another aspect of patience is holding up under the pressures of life, waiting on the Lord for resolution. The apostle John writes of an elderly man stricken with paralysis who discovered this reality when he met Jesus.

After this there was a feast of the Jews; and Jesus went up to Jerusalem. Now there is at Jerusalem by the sheep *market* a pool, which is called in the Hebrew tongue Bethesda, having five porches. In these lay a great multitude of impotent folk, of blind, halt, withered, waiting for the moving of the water. For an angel went down at a certain season into the pool, and troubled the water: whosoever then first after the troubling of the water stepped in was made whole of whatsoever disease he had. And a certain man was there, which had an infirmity thirty and eight years. When Jesus saw him lie, and knew that he had been now a long time *in that case*, he saith unto him, Wilt thou be made whole?

The impotent man answered him, Sir, I have no man, when the water is troubled, to put me into the pool: but while I am coming, another steppeth down before me.

Jesus saith unto him, Rise, take up thy bed, and walk. And immediately the man was made whole, and took up his bed, and walked: and on the same day was the sabbath.

The Jews therefore said unto him that was cured, It is the sabbath day: it is not lawful for thee to carry *thy* bed.

He answered them, He that made me whole, the same said unto me, Take up thy bed, and walk.

Then asked they him, What man is that which said unto thee, Take up thy bed, and walk?

And he that was healed wist not who it was: for Jesus had conveyed himself away, a multitude being in *that* place.

Afterward Jesus findeth him in the temple, and said unto him, Behold, thou art made whole: sin no more, lest a worse thing come

unto thee. The man departed, and told the Jews that it was Jesus, which had made him whole.
JOHN 5:1–15 🔑

Sometimes the Lord's resolution is physical healing, sometimes it is not. The apostle Paul discovered a different plan from God and came to terms with its good purpose in his life. (Note: Paul did not disclose the specifics of his chronic problem. Some believe it was some sort of eye disease.)

And lest I should be exalted above measure through the abundance of the revelations, there was given to me a thorn in the flesh, the messenger of Satan to buffet me, lest I should be exalted above measure. For this thing I besought the Lord thrice, that it might depart from me. And he said unto me, My grace is sufficient for thee: for my strength is made perfect in weakness. Most gladly therefore will I rather glory in my infirmities, that the power of Christ may rest upon me. Therefore I take pleasure in infirmities, in reproaches, in necessities, in persecutions, in distresses for Christ's sake: for when I am weak, then am I strong.

2 CORINTHIANS 12:7–10

Can you discern why God healed the lame man and not Paul? How does trusting in God's goodness give us the strength to live patiently with our suffering?

In the book of Job we read of a most unusual conversation taking place in heaven between God and Satan. The outcome of this conversation would gravely affect the life of a righteous man named Job. What unfolds is the ultimate test of patience. Will Job curse God or will he offer up his praise to God?

There was a man in the land of Uz, whose name *was* Job; and that man was perfect and upright, and one that feared God, and eschewed evil. And there were born unto him seven sons and three daughters. His substance also was seven thousand sheep, and three thousand camels, and five hundred yoke of oxen, and five hundred she asses, and a very great household; so that this man was the greatest of all the men of the east.

And his sons went and feasted *in their* houses, every one his day; and sent and called for their three sisters to eat and to drink with them. And it was so, when the days of *their* feasting were gone about, that Job sent and sanctified them, and rose up early in the morning, and offered burnt offerings *according* to the number of them all: for Job said, It may be that my sons have sinned, and cursed God in their hearts. Thus did Job continually.

Now there was a day when the sons of God came to present themselves before the LORD, and Satan came also among them. And the LORD said unto Satan, Whence comest thou?

Then Satan answered the LORD, and said, From going to and fro in the earth, and from walking up and down in it.

And the LORD said unto Satan, Hast thou considered my servant Job, that *there is* none like him in the earth, a perfect and an upright man, one that feareth God, and escheweth evil?

Then Satan answered the LORD, and said, Doth Job fear God for nought? Hast not thou made an hedge about him, and about his house, and about all that he hath on every side? thou hast blessed the work of his hands, and his substance is increased in the land. But put forth thine hand now, and touch all that he hath, and he will curse thee to thy face.

And the LORD said unto Satan, Behold, all that he hath *is* in thy power; only upon himself put not forth thine hand.

So Satan went forth from the presence of the LORD.

And there was a day when his sons and his daughters *were* eating and drinking wine in their eldest brother's house: And there came a messenger unto Job, and said, The oxen were plowing, and the asses feeding beside them: And the Sabeans fell *upon them*, and took them away; yea, they have slain the servants with the edge of the sword; and I only am escaped alone to tell thee.

While he *was* yet speaking, there came also another, and said, The fire of God is fallen from heaven, and hath burned up the sheep, and the servants, and consumed them; and I only am escaped alone to tell thee.

While he *was* yet speaking, there came also another, and said, The Chaldeans made out three bands, and fell upon the camels, and have carried them away, yea, and slain the servants with the edge of the sword; and I only am escaped alone to tell thee.

While he *was* yet speaking, there came also another, and said, Thy sons and thy daughters *were* eating and drinking wine in their eldest brother's house: And, behold, there came a great wind from the wilderness, and smote the four corners of the house, and it fell upon the young men, and they are dead; and I only am escaped alone to tell thee.

Then Job arose, and rent his mantle, and shaved his head, and fell down upon the ground, and worshipped, And said, Naked came I out of my mother's womb, and naked shall I return thither: the LORD gave, and the LORD hath taken away; blessed be the name of the LORD.

In all this Job sinned not, nor charged God foolishly.

Again there was a day when the sons of God came to present themselves before the LORD, and Satan came also among them to present himself before the LORD. And the LORD said unto Satan, From whence comest thou?

And Satan answered the LORD, and said, From going to and fro in the earth, and from walking up and down in it.

And the LORD said unto Satan, Hast thou considered my servant Job, that *there is* none like him in the earth, a perfect and an upright man, one that feareth God, and escheweth evil? and still he holdeth fast his integrity, although thou movedst me against him, to destroy him without cause.

And Satan answered the LORD, and said, Skin for skin, yea, all that a man hath will he give for his life. But put forth thine hand now, and touch his bone and his flesh, and he will curse thee to thy face.

And the LORD said unto Satan, Behold, he *is* in thine hand; but save his life.

So went Satan forth from the presence of the LORD, and smote Job with sore boils from the sole of his foot unto his crown. And he took him a potsherd to scrape himself withal; and he sat down among the ashes.

Then said his wife unto him, Dost thou still retain thine integrity? curse God, and die.

But he said unto her, Thou speakest as one of the foolish

women speaketh. What? shall we receive good at the hand of God, and shall we not receive evil?

In all this did not Job sin with his lips.

Now when Job's three friends heard of all this evil that was come upon him, they came every one from his own place; Eliphaz the Temanite, and Bildad the Shuhite, and Zophar the Naamathite: for they had made an appointment together to come to mourn with him and to comfort him. And when they lifted up their eyes afar off, and knew him not, they lifted up their voice, and wept; and they rent every one his mantle, and sprinkled dust upon their heads toward heaven. So they sat down with him upon the ground seven days and seven nights, and none spake a word unto him: for they saw that *his* grief was very great.   JOB 1:1—2:13

> *Job's three friends did their best work when they merely sat silently with Job in the ashes. But they didn't stay silent. They felt an obligation to open their mouths and interpret the tragedy that befell Job. They suggested it could only be Job's sin that would cause such a catastrophe. Of course, this wasn't true. Understandably, Job contemplated giving up; he also had straightforward questions for God and defended himself. But Job never cursed God as Satan claimed he would. Job's patience in the face of trials is a model for us. In the end, God restored Job.*

And it was *so*, that after the LORD had spoken these words unto Job, the LORD said to Eliphaz the Temanite, My wrath is kindled against thee, and against thy two friends: for ye have not spoken of me *the thing that is* right, as my servant Job *hath*. Therefore take unto you now seven bullocks and seven rams, and go to my servant Job, and offer up for yourselves a burnt offering; and my servant Job shall pray for you: for him will I accept: lest I deal with you *after your* folly, in that ye have not spoken of me *the thing which is* right, like my servant Job. So Eliphaz the Temanite and Bildad the Shuhite *and* Zophar the Naamathite went, and did according as the LORD commanded them: the LORD also accepted Job.

And the LORD turned the captivity of Job, when he prayed for his friends: also the LORD gave Job twice as much as he had before.

Then came there unto him all his brethren, and all his sisters, and all they that had been of his acquaintance before, and did eat bread with him in his house: and they bemoaned him, and comforted him over all the evil that the LORD had brought upon him: every man also gave him a piece of money, and every one an earring of gold.

So the LORD blessed the latter end of Job more than his beginning: for he had fourteen thousand sheep, and six thousand camels, and a thousand yoke of oxen, and a thousand she asses. He had also seven sons and three daughters. And he called the name of the first, Jemima; and the name of the second, Kezia; and the name of the third, Keren-happuch. And in all the land were no women found *so* fair as the daughters of Job: and their father gave them inheritance among their brethren.

After this lived Job an hundred and forty years, and saw his sons, and his sons' sons, *even* four generations. So Job died, *being* old and full of days.

JOB 42:7–17

Do you struggle more with being patient with other people or dealing with unavoidable pressures in your life? What is one thing you learned from this chapter that might help you?

WHAT WE BELIEVE

Not all our stories are the same, yet we are all called to respond with patience. Patience is a key virtue that we must work to develop. Our cultivation of it pleases God, who is patient with us. Showing patience positively affects our relationships and brings great joy to our lives and community. If we trust God and have a passion to treat others the way he treats us, we will learn more each day how to be slow to anger and tolerate the unavoidable pressures of life.

BE

CHAPTER

27

Kindness/Goodness

——————— KEY QUESTION ———————

What does it mean to do the right thing? How do I know?

——————— KEY IDEA ———————

I choose to be kind and good
in my relationships with others.

——————— KEY VERSE ———————

See that none render evil for evil unto any *man*;
but ever follow that which is good,
both among yourselves, and to all *men*.
1 Thessalonians 5:15

OUR KIND AND GOOD GOD

As with all the virtues, our God is the perfect example. This psalm was likely written after the Israelites returned from captivity in Babylon and was recited each year at one of the annual religious festivals. Throughout their history the Israelites cried out to God for mercy and help. Each time God responded from a tender and kind heart. As we look back on our own life we will see the same pattern of response from God.

O give thanks unto the LORD, for *he is* good:
for his mercy *endureth* for ever.

Let the redeemed of the LORD say *so*,
   whom he hath redeemed from the hand of the enemy;
And gathered them out of the lands,
   from the east, and from the west,
   from the north, and from the south.

They wandered in the wilderness in a solitary way;
   they found no city to dwell in.
Hungry and thirsty,
   their soul fainted in them.
Then they cried unto the LORD in their trouble,
   and he delivered them out of their distresses.
And he led them forth by the right way,
   that they might go to a city of habitation.
Oh that *men* would praise the LORD *for* his goodness,
   and *for* his wonderful works to the children of men!
For he satisfieth the longing soul,
   and filleth the hungry soul with goodness.

Such as sit in darkness and in the shadow of death,
   being bound in affliction and iron;
Because they rebelled against the words of God,
   and contemned the counsel of the most High:
Therefore he brought down their heart with labour;
   they fell down, and *there was* none to help.
Then they cried unto the LORD in their trouble,
   and he saved them out of their distresses.
He brought them out of darkness and the shadow of death,
   and brake their bands in sunder.
Oh that *men* would praise the LORD *for* his goodness,
   and *for* his wonderful works to the children of men!
For he hath broken the gates of brass,
   and cut the bars of iron in sunder.

Fools because of their transgression,
   and because of their iniquities, are afflicted.
Their soul abhorreth all manner of meat;
   and they draw near unto the gates of death.
Then they cry unto the LORD in their trouble,
   and he saveth them out of their distresses.

He sent his word, and healed them,
   and delivered *them* from their destructions.
Oh that *men* would praise the LORD *for* his goodness,
   and *for* his wonderful works to the children of men!
And let them sacrifice the sacrifices of thanksgiving,
   and declare his works with rejoicing.

They that go down to the sea in ships,
   that do business in great waters;
These see the works of the LORD,
   and his wonders in the deep.
For he commandeth, and raiseth the stormy wind,
   which lifteth up the waves thereof.
They mount up to the heaven, they go down again to the
      depths:
   their soul is melted because of trouble.
They reel to and fro, and stagger like a drunken man,
   and are at their wit's end.
Then they cry unto the LORD in their trouble,
   and he bringeth them out of their distresses.
He maketh the storm a calm,
   so that the waves thereof are still.
Then are they glad because they be quiet;
   so he bringeth them unto their desired haven.
Oh that *men* would praise the LORD *for* his goodness,
   and *for* his wonderful works to the children of men!
Let them exalt him also in the congregation of the people,
   and praise him in the assembly of the elders.

He turneth rivers into a wilderness,
   and the watersprings into dry ground;
A fruitful land into barrenness,
   for the wickedness of them that dwell therein.
He turneth the wilderness into a standing water,
   and dry ground into watersprings.
And there he maketh the hungry to dwell,
   that they may prepare a city for habitation;
And sow the fields, and plant vineyards,
   which may yield fruits of increase.

He blesseth them also, so that they are multiplied greatly;
and suffereth not their cattle to decrease.

Again, they are minished and brought low through
oppression,
affliction, and sorrow.
He poureth contempt upon princes,
and causeth them to wander in the wilderness, *where
there is* no way.
Yet setteth he the poor on high from affliction,
and maketh *him* families like a flock.
The righteous shall see *it*, and rejoice:
and all iniquity shall stop her mouth.

Whoso *is* wise, and will observe these *things*,
even they shall understand the lovingkindness
of the LORD.   PSALM 107:1–43

Write your own psalm. Start with the same opening words
of Psalm 107: "O give thanks unto the LORD, for *he is* good:
for his mercy *endureth* for ever. Let the redeemed
of the LORD say *so*." Then record an act of kindness
and goodness that God has shown toward you.

STORIES OF KINDNESS: RAHAB

*The Bible contains many stories of kindness throughout its pages.
In the Old Testament, Joshua, Israel's great and courageous
leader, sent two spies to scope out the land of Canaan in preparation for the conquest. While they were deep in enemy territory,
God used a most unusual character to show them kindness.*

And Joshua the son of Nun sent out of Shittim two men to spy
secretly, saying, Go view the land, even Jericho. And they went,
and came into an harlot's house, named Rahab, and lodged there.
And it was told the king of Jericho, saying, Behold, there came
men in hither to night of the children of Israel to search out the
country. And the king of Jericho sent unto Rahab, saying, Bring

forth the men that are come to thee, which are entered into thine house: for they be come to search out all the country.

And the woman took the two men, and hid them, and said thus, There came men unto me, but I wist not whence they *were*: And it came to pass *about the time* of shutting of the gate, when it was dark, that the men went out: whither the men went I wot not: pursue after them quickly; for ye shall overtake them. But she had brought them up to the roof of the house, and hid them with the stalks of flax, which she had laid in order upon the roof. And the men pursued after them the way to Jordan unto the fords: and as soon as they which pursued after them were gone out, they shut the gate.

And before they were laid down, she came up unto them upon the roof; And she said unto the men, I know that the LORD hath given you the land, and that your terror is fallen upon us, and that all the inhabitants of the land faint because of you. For we have heard how the LORD dried up the water of the Red sea for you, when ye came out of Egypt; and what ye did unto the two kings of the Amorites, that *were* on the other side Jordan, Sihon and Og, whom ye utterly destroyed. And as soon as we had heard *these things*, our hearts did melt, neither did there remain any more courage in any man, because of you: for the LORD your God, he *is* God in heaven above, and in earth beneath.

Now therefore, I pray you, swear unto me by the LORD, since I have shewed you kindness, that ye will also shew kindness unto my father's house, and give me a true token: And *that* ye will save alive my father, and my mother, and my brethren, and my sisters, and all that they have, and deliver our lives from death.

And the men answered her, Our life for yours, if ye utter not this our business. And it shall be, when the LORD hath given us the land, that we will deal kindly and truly with thee.

Then she let them down by a cord through the window: for her house *was* upon the town wall, and she dwelt upon the wall. And she said unto them, Get you to the mountain, lest the pursuers meet you; and hide yourselves there three days, until the pursuers be returned: and afterward may ye go your way.

And the men said unto her, We *will be* blameless of this thine oath which thou hast made us swear. Behold, *when* we come into the land, thou shalt bind this line of scarlet thread in the window which thou didst let us down by: and thou shalt bring thy father, and thy mother, and thy brethren, and all thy father's household, home unto thee. And it shall be, *that* whosoever shall go out of the doors of thy house into the street, his blood *shall be* upon his head, and we *will be* guiltless: and whosoever shall be with thee in the house, his blood *shall be* on our head, if *any* hand be upon him. And if thou utter this our business, then we will be quit of thine oath which thou hast made us to swear.

And she said, According unto your words, so *be* it.

And she sent them away, and they departed: and she bound the scarlet line in the window.

And they went, and came unto the mountain, and abode there three days, until the pursuers were returned: and the pursuers sought *them* throughout all the way, but found *them* not. So the two men returned, and descended from the mountain, and passed over, and came to Joshua the son of Nun, and told him all *things* that befell them: And they said unto Joshua, Truly the LORD hath delivered into our hands all the land; for even all the inhabitants of the country do faint because of us.   JOSHUA 2:1–24

> With the hand of God obviously on their side, the Israelites con-
> quered the city of Jericho, and Rahab was rewarded for her act
> of kindness.

And Joshua rose early in the morning, and the priests took up the ark of the LORD. And seven priests bearing seven trumpets of rams' horns before the ark of the LORD went on continually, and blew with the trumpets: and the armed men went before them; but the rereward came after the ark of the LORD, *the priests* go-ing on, and blowing with the trumpets. And the second day they compassed the city once, and returned into the camp: so they did six days.

And it came to pass on the seventh day, that they rose early about the dawning of the day, and compassed the city after the same manner seven times: only on that day they compassed the city seven times. And it came to pass at the seventh time, when the priests blew with the trumpets, Joshua said unto the people,

Shout; for the LORD hath given you the city. And the city shall be accursed, *even* it, and all that *are* therein, to the LORD: only Rahab the harlot shall live, she and all that *are* with her in the house, because she hid the messengers that we sent. And ye, in any wise keep *yourselves* from the accursed thing, lest ye make *yourselves* accursed, when ye take of the accursed thing, and make the camp of Israel a curse, and trouble it. But all the silver, and gold, and vessels of brass and iron, *are* consecrated unto the LORD: they shall come into the treasury of the LORD.

So the people shouted when *the priests* blew with the trumpets: and it came to pass, when the people heard the sound of the trumpet, and the people shouted with a great shout, that the wall fell down flat, so that the people went up into the city, every man straight before him, and they took the city. And they utterly destroyed all that *was* in the city, both man and woman, young and old, and ox, and sheep, and ass, with the edge of the sword.

But Joshua had said unto the two men that had spied out the country, Go into the harlot's house, and bring out thence the woman, and all that she hath, as ye sware unto her. And the young men that were spies went in, and brought out Rahab, and her father, and her mother, and her brethren, and all that she had; and they brought out all her kindred, and left them without the camp of Israel.

And they burnt the city with fire, and all that *was* therein: only the silver, and the gold, and the vessels of brass and of iron, they put into the treasury of the house of the LORD. **And Joshua saved Rahab the harlot alive, and her father's household, and all that she had; and she dwelleth in Israel *even* unto this day; because she hid the messengers, which Joshua sent to spy out Jericho.**

JOSHUA 6:12–25

How do you reconcile Rahab's decision to lie about the spies' whereabouts with her act of kindness?

STORIES OF KINDNESS: DAVID

The prophet Samuel anointed David, when he was just a teenager, to be Israel's next king. His coronation, however, was a number of years away. Over the next several years God would use the rebellious heart of King Saul to grow David's trust in God. Before David took off running from King Saul, Jonathan, Saul's son and successor to the throne, had a sobering conversation with David. Jonathan acknowledged and accepted God's plan for David, not himself, to be the next king. However, he made one request of the future king of Israel.

[Jonathan said,] If it please my father *to do* thee evil, then I will shew it thee, and send thee away, that thou mayest go in peace: and the LORD be with thee, as he hath been with my father. **And thou shalt not only while yet I live shew me the kindness of the LORD, that I die not: But *also* thou shalt not cut off thy kindness from my house for ever: no, not when the LORD hath cut off the enemies of David every one from the face of the earth.**

So Jonathan made *a covenant* with the house of David, *saying*, Let the LORD even require *it* at the hand of David's enemies.

1 SAMUEL 20:13–16

Fast-forward many years. Saul and Jonathan were both dead, and David was king. All potential threats from the old royal house of Saul had been neutralized, and David remembered his promise to Jonathan.

And David said, Is there yet any that is left of the house of Saul, that I may shew him kindness for Jonathan's sake?

And *there was* of the house of Saul a servant whose name *was* Ziba. And when they had called him unto David, the king said unto him, *Art* thou Ziba?

And he said, Thy servant *is he.*

And the king said, *Is* there not yet any of the house of Saul, that I may shew the kindness of God unto him?

And Ziba said unto the king, Jonathan hath yet a son, *which is* lame on *his* feet.

And the king said unto him, Where *is* he?

And Ziba said unto the king, Behold, he *is* in the house of Machir, the son of Ammiel, in Lo-debar.

Then king David sent, and fetched him out of the house of Machir, the son of Ammiel, from Lo-debar.

Now when Mephibosheth, the son of Jonathan, the son of Saul, was come unto David, he fell on his face, and did reverence.

And David said, Mephibosheth.

And he answered, Behold thy servant!

And David said unto him, Fear not: for I will surely shew thee kindness for Jonathan thy father's sake, and will restore thee all the land of Saul thy father; and thou shalt eat bread at my table continually.

And he bowed himself, and said, What *is* thy servant, that thou shouldest look upon such a dead dog as I *am*?

Then the king called to Ziba, Saul's servant, and said unto him, I have given unto thy master's son all that pertained to Saul and to all his house. Thou therefore, and thy sons, and thy servants, shall till the land for him, and thou shalt bring in *the fruits*, that thy master's son may have food to eat: but Mephibosheth thy master's son shall eat bread alway at my table. Now Ziba had fifteen sons and twenty servants.

Then said Ziba unto the king, According to all that my lord the king hath commanded his servant, so shall thy servant do. As for Mephibosheth, *said the king*, he shall eat at my table, as one of the king's sons.

And Mephibosheth had a young son, whose name *was* Micha. And all that dwelt in the house of Ziba *were* servants unto Mephibosheth. So Mephibosheth dwelt in Jerusalem: for he did eat continually at the king's table; and was lame on both his feet.

2 SAMUEL 9:1–13 ⚷

STORIES OF KINDNESS: THE DINNER GUEST

The Jewish religious leaders in Jesus' day held exclusive dinner parties. Only invited guests of significant public standing were allowed to attend. Upon arrival, the host would seat guests in order of importance. On one occasion when Jesus was invited to eat at the table of a well-known Pharisee, he took advantage of the opportunity to teach a lesson, first about humility and then about the kind of people who should be on the guest list of such occasions.

And it came to pass, as [Jesus] went into the house of one of the chief Pharisees to eat bread on the sabbath day, that they watched him.   LUKE 14:1

And [Jesus] put forth a parable to those which were bidden, when he marked how they chose out the chief rooms; saying unto them, When thou art bidden of any *man* to a wedding, sit not down in the highest room; lest a more honourable man than thou be bidden of him; And he that bade thee and him come and say to thee, Give this man place; and thou begin with shame to take the lowest room. But when thou art bidden, go and sit down in the lowest room; that when he that bade thee cometh, he may say unto thee, Friend, go up higher: then shalt thou have worship in the presence of them that sit at meat with thee. For whosoever exalteth himself shall be abased; and he that humbleth himself shall be exalted.

Then said he also to him that bade him, When thou makest a dinner or a supper, call not thy friends, nor thy brethren, neither thy kinsmen, nor *thy* rich neighbours; lest they also bid thee again, and a recompence be made thee. **But when thou makest a feast, call the poor, the maimed, the lame, the blind: And thou shalt be blessed; for they cannot recompense thee: for thou shalt be recompensed at the resurrection of the just.**   LUKE 14:7–14

Jesus was teaching us to do exactly what David
did for Mephibosheth. Why does it matter that
we invite people into our lives who cannot reciprocate?
Can you think of a way to include someone
in your activities who is usually left out?

STORIES OF KINDNESS: PAUL, ONESIMUS AND PHILEMON
While Paul was in prison, likely in Rome, he met a slave named Onesimus, who may have stolen from his master before running away. Through Paul's ministry, Onesimus became a Christian and eventually returned to his master. As it turned out, the master, a man name Philemon, was a Christian and Paul's close friend. Paul sent Onesimus home with a personal letter he had written to give

to Philemon. The letter encouraged Philemon to exercise kindness toward his slave and accept Onesimus, not as a slave but as a Christian brother.

As you read Philemon 1–25 below, note how Paul models kindness in his appeal to Philemon. Would you have honored Paul's request? Why or why not?

Paul, a prisoner of Jesus Christ, and Timothy *our* brother,

Unto Philemon our dearly beloved, and fellowlabourer, And to *our* beloved Apphia, and Archippus our fellowsoldier, and to the church in thy house: Grace to you, and peace, from God our Father and the Lord Jesus Christ.

I thank my God, making mention of thee always in my prayers, Hearing of thy love and faith, which thou hast toward the Lord Jesus, and toward all saints; That the communication of thy faith may become effectual by the acknowledging of every good thing which is in you in Christ Jesus. For we have great joy and consolation in thy love, because the bowels of the saints are refreshed by thee, brother.

Wherefore, though I might be much bold in Christ to enjoin thee that which is convenient, Yet for love's sake I rather beseech *thee*, being such an one as Paul the aged, and now also a prisoner of Jesus Christ. I beseech thee for my son Onesimus, whom I have begotten in my bonds: Which in time past was to thee unprofitable, but now profitable to thee and to me:

Whom I have sent again: thou therefore receive him, that is, mine own bowels: Whom I would have retained with me, that in thy stead he might have ministered unto me in the bonds of the gospel: But without thy mind would I do nothing; that thy benefit should not be as it were of necessity, but willingly. For perhaps he therefore departed for a season, that thou shouldest receive him for ever; Not now as a servant, but above a servant, a brother beloved, specially to me, but how much more unto thee, both in the flesh, and in the Lord?

If thou count me therefore a partner, receive him as myself. If he hath wronged thee, or oweth *thee* ought, put that on mine account; I Paul have written *it* with mine own hand, I will repay *it*: albeit I do not say to thee how thou owest unto me even thine own self besides. Yea, brother, let me have joy of thee in the Lord: refresh my bowels in the Lord. Having confidence in thy obedience I wrote unto thee, knowing that thou wilt also do more than I say.

But withal prepare me also a lodging: for I trust that through your prayers I shall be given unto you.

There salute thee Epaphras, my fellowprisoner in Christ Jesus; Marcus, Aristarchus, Demas, Lucas, my fellowlabourers.

The grace of our Lord Jesus Christ *be* with your spirit. Amen.

PHILEMON 1–25

STORIES OF KINDNESS: ONESIPHORUS

While Paul spent his years in ministry encouraging others to show kindness, from time to time he found himself on the receiving end and was grateful. At the end of his ministry and life, from a cold dungeon Paul penned his last letter to his prodigy Timothy, who was pastoring the church at Ephesus. Life in this season had been extremely hard for Paul. In the letter he shared with Timothy his gratitude for one particular believer.

This thou knowest, that all they which are in Asia be turned away from me; of whom are Phygellus and Hermogenes. **The Lord give mercy unto the house of Onesiphorus; for he oft refreshed me, and was not ashamed of my chain: But, when he was in Rome, he sought me out very diligently, and found *me.*** The Lord grant unto him that he may find mercy of the Lord in that day: and in how many things he ministered unto me at Ephesus, thou knowest very well.   2 TIMOTHY 1:15–18

TEACHINGS ON GOODNESS

Jesus left us instructions for being good to others that are both practical and radical. Remember that kindness is doing something that the recipient feels positively about, but goodness means doing the right thing for a person, even when it may not make them feel good. Goodness is sometimes called "tough love," because it involves speaking the truth or withholding something harmful for the ultimate benefit of the recipient.

Write down a list of every principle you discover from the teachings of Jesus, Peter and Paul on how to not only do the kind thing but also the right thing in our relationships. Which principle speaks to you the most? Why?

But I say unto you which hear, Love your enemies, do good to them which hate you, Bless them that curse you, and pray for them which despitefully use you. And unto him that smiteth thee on the *one* cheek offer also the other; and him that taketh away thy cloak forbid not *to take thy* coat also. Give to every man that asketh of thee; and of him that taketh away thy goods ask *them* not again. **And as ye would that men should do to you, do ye also to them likewise.**

For if ye love them which love you, what thank have ye? for sinners also love those that love them. And if ye do good to them which do good to you, what thank have ye? for sinners also do even the same. And if ye lend *to them* of whom ye hope to receive, what thank have ye? for sinners also lend to sinners, to receive as much again. But love ye your enemies, and do good, and lend, hoping for nothing again; and your reward shall be great, and ye shall be the children of the Highest: for he is kind unto the unthankful and *to* the evil. Be ye therefore merciful, as your Father also is merciful.

Judge not, and ye shall not be judged: condemn not, and ye shall not be condemned: forgive, and ye shall be forgiven: Give, and it shall be given unto you; good measure, pressed down, and shaken together, and running over, shall men give into your bosom. For with the same measure that ye mete withal it shall be measured to you again.

And he spake a parable unto them, Can the blind lead the blind? shall they not both fall into the ditch? The disciple is not above his master: but every one that is perfect shall be as his master.

And why beholdest thou the mote that is in thy brother's eye, but perceivest not the beam that is in thine own eye? Either how canst thou say to thy brother, Brother, let me pull out the mote that is in thine eye, when thou thyself beholdest not the beam that is in thine own eye? Thou hypocrite, cast out first the beam out of thine own eye, and then shalt thou see clearly to pull out the mote that is in thy brother's eye.

For a good tree bringeth not forth corrupt fruit; neither doth a corrupt tree bring forth good fruit. For every tree is known by his own fruit. For of thorns men do not gather figs, nor of a bramble bush gather they grapes. **A good man out of the good treasure of his heart bringeth forth that which is good; and an evil man out of the evil treasure of his heart bringeth forth that which is evil: for of the abundance of the heart his mouth speaketh.**

LUKE 6:27–45

Two good men who were followers of Jesus—the apostles Peter and Paul—offered instruction to the early believers on living a life of kindness and goodness. The Scripture passages below remind us how the goodness we show to others can enlighten the world about our good God. In other words, the way we treat people is a reflection of our relationship with God.

Finally, *be ye* all of one mind, having compassion one of another, love as brethren, *be* pitiful, *be* courteous: Not rendering evil for evil, or railing for railing: but contrariwise blessing; knowing that ye are thereunto called, that ye should inherit a blessing. For, he that will love life, and see good days, let him refrain his tongue from evil, and his lips that they speak no guile: Let him eschew evil, and do good; let him seek peace, and ensue it. For the eyes of the Lord *are* over the righteous, and his ears *are open* unto their prayers: but the face of the Lord *is* against them that do evil.

And who *is* he that will harm you, if ye be followers of that which is good? But and if ye suffer for righteousness' sake, happy *are ye*: and be not afraid of their terror, neither be troubled; But sanctify the Lord God in your hearts: and *be* ready always to *give* an answer to every man that asketh you a reason of the hope that is in you with meekness and fear: Having a good conscience; that, whereas they speak evil of you, as of evildoers, they may be ashamed that falsely accuse your good conversation in Christ. For *it is* better, if the will of God be so, that ye suffer for well doing, than for evil doing.

1 PETER 3:8–17

We then that are strong ought to bear the infirmities of the weak, and not to please ourselves. Let every one of us please *his* neighbour for *his* good to edification.   Romans 15:1–2

All things are lawful for me, but all things are not expedient: all things are lawful for me, but all things edify not. **Let no man seek his own, but every man another's *wealth*.**   1 Corinthians 10:23–24

And let us not be weary in well doing: for in due season we shall reap, if we faint not. As we have therefore opportunity, let us do good unto all *men*, especially unto them who are of the household of faith.   Galatians 6:9–10

Let all bitterness, and wrath, and anger, and clamour, and evil speaking, be put away from you, with all malice: **And be ye kind one to another, tenderhearted, forgiving one another, even as God for Christ's sake hath forgiven you.** Be ye therefore followers of God, as dear children; And walk in love, as Christ also hath loved us, and hath given himself for us an offering and a sacrifice to God for a sweetsmelling savour.   Ephesians 4:31—5:2

See that none render evil for evil unto any *man*; but ever follow that which is good, both among yourselves, and to all *men*.
                                    1 Thessalonians 5:15

In all things [shew] thyself a pattern of good works: in doctrine [*shew*] uncorruptness, gravity, sincerity.   Titus 2:7

Put them in mind to be subject to principalities and powers, to obey magistrates, to be ready to every good work, To speak evil of no man, to be no brawlers, *but* gentle, shewing all meekness unto all men.

For we ourselves also were sometimes foolish, disobedient, deceived, serving divers lusts and pleasures, living in malice and envy, hateful, *and* hating one another. **But after that the kindness and love of God our Saviour toward man appeared, Not by works of righteousness which we have done, but according to his mercy he saved us,** by the washing of regeneration, and renewing of the Holy Ghost; Which he shed on us abundantly through Jesus Christ our Saviour; That being justified by his grace, we should be made heirs according to the hope of eternal life. *This is* a faithful saying, and these things I will that thou affirm constantly, that they which have believed in God might be careful to maintain good works. These things are good and profitable unto men. TITUS 3:1–8

And let ours also learn to maintain good works for necessary uses, that they be not unfruitful. TITUS 3:14

WHAT WE BELIEVE

Throughout history God has consistently showed his kindness and goodness to all people. If God's love is in us, we will seek to show that love to the people in our lives. Most often we will engage in positive acts of kindness toward others. However, occasionally we can help someone by issuing some tough love—a confrontation, a rebuke, a refusal. We have many great examples in the Bible to look to, including Rahab, David, Jesus, Paul and Onesiphorus. We have also been given many practical principles to guide our demonstration of both random and intentional acts of goodness and kindness. Pick one principle and one person in your life with the most need and give it a try!

CHAPTER

28

Faithfulness

———— KEY QUESTION ————

Why is it important to be loyal
and committed to God and others?

———— KEY IDEA ————

I have established a good name with God
and others based on my loyalty to those relationships.

———— KEY VERSE ————

Let not mercy and truth forsake thee: bind them about thy neck;
write them upon the table of thine heart: So shalt thou find
favour and good understanding in the sight of God and man.
Proverbs 3:3 – 4

As with all the other key virtues, faithfulness benefits the people in our lives. When we are faithful to them, they are blessed. And over time, as our key verse expresses, our faithfulness to others also has a reciprocal benefit. First, we win favor. As needs emerge in our lives, people will be inclined to help us. Second, we establish a good name. When our name is mentioned, even when we are not present, it is spoken with high regard. A good name established through a life of faithfulness is a boundless gift to pass on to our children. Most of all, faithfulness pleases God, who is always loyal and committed to us. Our loyalty and commitment to others reflects the love God has shown us. Yet because of our sinful nature, we struggle to be faithful. That is where God and his presence in our lives come into play.

In this chapter we will read Scripture passages that address the following subjects to instruct and inspire us:

- *God's Faithfulness*
- *Called to Faithfulness*
- *Stories of Faithfulness: Joseph*
- *Stories of Faithfulness: Ruth*
- *Stories of Faithfulness: Mary*

GOD'S FAITHFULNESS

Many of the authors of the Bible recorded their reflections about God's faithfulness. In the Song of Moses, recorded in Deuteronomy 32, Moses exalts the faithfulness of the covenant-keeping God.

As you read the passages below from Deuteronomy 32; Psalm 36 and Lamentations 3, highlight the phrases that best express God's faithfulness to you.

Give ear, O ye heavens, and I will speak; and hear, O earth, the words of my mouth. My doctrine shall drop as the rain, my speech shall distil as the dew, as the small rain upon the tender herb, and as the showers upon the grass: Because I will publish the name of the LORD: ascribe ye greatness unto our God. *He is* the Rock, his work *is* perfect: for all his ways *are* judgment: **a God of truth and without iniquity, just and right *is* he.** DEUTERONOMY 32:1–4

Likewise, while living in a world with so much uncertainty, the author of Psalm 36 took great comfort in the extent of God's devotion.

Thy mercy, O LORD, *is* in the heavens;
   ***and* thy faithfulness *reacheth* unto the clouds.**
Thy righteousness *is* like the great mountains;
   thy judgments *are* a great deep:
   O LORD, thou preservest man and beast.
How excellent *is* thy lovingkindness, O God!
   therefore the children of men put their trust under the
      shadow of thy wings.
They shall be abundantly satisfied with the fatness of thy
      house;
   and thou shalt make them drink of the river of thy
      pleasures.
For with thee *is* the fountain of life:
   in thy light shall we see light. PSALM 36:5–9

While God always remained faithful, the Israelites did not, and he disciplined them for it. God called the prophet Jeremiah to warn the southern kingdom of Judah of God's just punishment. In 586 BC Jerusalem and the temple were destroyed and the people were exiled to Babylon. The author (ancient tradition credits Jeremiah with writing Lamentations) of this series of alphabetic acrostic poems lamented about what he saw and felt but also reminded the people of God's consistent faithfulness.

Remembering mine affliction and my misery, the wormwood and the gall. My soul hath *them* still in remembrance, and is humbled in me. This I recall to my mind, therefore have I hope.

***It is of* the LORD's mercies that we are not consumed, because his compassions fail not. *They are* new every morning: great *is* thy faithfulness.** The LORD *is* my portion, saith my soul; therefore will I hope in him. LAMENTATIONS 3:19–24

CALLED TO FAITHFULNESS

The writers of the wisdom books call the reader to a life of faith-fulness and also highlight its rich rewards in their lives.

My son, forget not my law;
    but let thine heart keep my commandments:
For length of days, and long life,
    and peace, shall they add to thee.

Let not mercy and truth forsake thee:
    bind them about thy neck;
    write them upon the table of thine heart:
So shalt thou find favour and good understanding
    in the sight of God and man.

Trust in the LORD with all thine heart;
    and lean not unto thine own understanding.
In all thy ways acknowledge him,
    and he shall direct thy paths.   PROVERBS 3:1–6

Most men will proclaim every one his own goodness:
    but a faithful man who can find?   PROVERBS 20:6

A faithful man shall abound with blessings:
    but he that maketh haste to be rich shall not be
        innocent.   PROVERBS 28:20

Why will a faithful person be richly blessed,
and one eager to get rich be punished?

The calling Paul shared with the Corinthians concerning his own life applies to all followers of Christ.

Let a man so account of us, as of the ministers of Christ, and stewards of the mysteries of God. Moreover it is required in stewards, that a man be found faithful.   1 CORINTHIANS 4:1–2

STORIES OF FAITHFULNESS: JOSEPH

God built Israel from scratch, starting with Abraham, to reveal his plan to provide a way for people to come back into a relationship with him. Israel's faithfulness to God over the next 2,000 years was sketchy at best. However, a few Israelites, such as Joseph, did display a tenacious faithfulness both to God and to others.

At the age of seventeen, Joseph, one of the twelve sons of Jacob, had two consecutive dreams in which his brothers bowed down to him. The brothers were furious with their younger brother, whom their dad already favored. So they plotted together one day and sold Joseph to a caravan of Ishmaelites who ultimately sold him into slavery in Egypt. The brothers returned home and lied to their father, telling him that Joseph had been mauled to death by a ferocious animal. Jacob was crushed. Joseph, however, was prospering despite his brothers' jealous attempts to destroy him.

As you read Joseph's story, look back
at our key verse from Proverbs 3:3–4.
How did Joseph live out the truth of this verse?

And Joseph was brought down to Egypt; and Potiphar, an officer of Pharaoh, captain of the guard, an Egyptian, bought him of the hands of the Ishmeelites, which had brought him down thither. And the LORD was with Joseph, and he was a prosperous man; and he was in the house of his master the Egyptian. And his master saw that the LORD *was* with him, and that the LORD made all that he did to prosper in his hand. And Joseph found grace in his sight, and he served him: and he made him overseer over his house, and all *that* he had he put into his hand. And it came to pass from the time *that* he had made him overseer in his house, and over all that he had, that the LORD blessed the Egyptian's house for Joseph's sake; and the blessing of the LORD was upon all that he had in the house, and in the field. And he left all that he had in Joseph's hand; and he knew not ought he had, save the bread which he did eat.

GENESIS 39:1–6

As part of God's master plan, Joseph rose again only to be cast into another "pit." Potiphar's wife tried to seduce Joseph, but Joseph maintained his integrity and faithfulness to both Potiphar and God by resisting the temptation. Because he rejected her, Potiphar's wife made false accusations against Joseph, and he was thrown into prison. But God was with him there too and lifted him up yet again.

And it came to pass after these things, *that* the butler of the king of Egypt and *his* baker had offended their lord the king of Egypt. And Pharaoh was wroth against two *of* his officers, against the chief of the butlers, and against the chief of the bakers. And he put them in ward in the house of the captain of the guard, into the prison, the place where Joseph *was* bound. And the captain of the guard charged Joseph with them, and he served them: and they continued a season in ward.

And they dreamed a dream both of them, each man his dream in one night, each man according to the interpretation of his dream, the butler and the baker of the king of Egypt, which *were* bound in the prison.

And Joseph came in unto them in the morning, and looked upon them, and, behold, they *were* sad. And he asked Pharaoh's officers that *were* with him in the ward of his lord's house, saying, Wherefore look ye *so* sadly to day?

And they said unto him, We have dreamed a dream, and *there is* no interpreter of it.

And Joseph said unto them, *Do* not interpretations *belong* to God? tell me *them*, I pray you.

And the chief butler told his dream to Joseph, and said to him, In my dream, behold, a vine *was* before me; And in the vine *were* three branches: and it *was* as though it budded, *and* her blossoms shot forth; and the clusters thereof brought forth ripe grapes: And Pharaoh's cup *was* in my hand: and I took the grapes, and pressed them into Pharaoh's cup, and I gave the cup into Pharaoh's hand.

And Joseph said unto him, This *is* the interpretation of it: The three branches are three days: Yet within three days shall Pharaoh lift up thine head, and restore thee unto thy place: and thou shalt deliver Pharaoh's cup into his hand, after the former manner when thou wast his butler. But think on me when it shall be well with thee, and shew kindness, I pray thee, unto me, and make mention of me unto Pharaoh, and bring me out of this house: For indeed I was stolen away out of the land of the Hebrews: and here also have I done nothing that they should put me into the dungeon.

When the chief baker saw that the interpretation was good, he said unto Joseph, I also *was* in my dream, and, behold, *I had* three white baskets on my head: And in the uppermost basket *there was* of all manner of bakemeats for Pharaoh; and the birds did eat them out of the basket upon my head.

And Joseph answered and said, This *is* the interpretation thereof: The three baskets *are* three days: Yet within three days shall Pharaoh lift up thy head from off thee, and shall hang thee on a tree; and the birds shall eat thy flesh from off thee.

And it came to pass the third day, *which was* Pharaoh's birthday, that he made a feast unto all his servants: and he lifted up the head of the chief butler and of the chief baker among his servants. And he restored the chief butler unto his butlership again; and he gave the cup into Pharaoh's hand: But he hanged the chief baker: as Joseph had interpreted to them.

Yet did not the chief butler remember Joseph, but forgat him.

GENESIS 40:1–23

Joseph sat in prison two more years. It wasn't until Pharaoh had a dream that none of his magicians or wise men could interpret that the restored butler finally remembered Joseph, and Joseph was brought from the dungeon to explain the dream's meaning. As he stood before the king, Joseph maintained his faithfulness to God.

Then Pharaoh sent and called Joseph, and they brought him hastily out of the dungeon: and he shaved *himself,* and changed his raiment, and came in unto Pharaoh.

And Pharaoh said unto Joseph, I have dreamed a dream, and *there is* none that can interpret it: and I have heard say of thee, *that* thou canst understand a dream to interpret it.

And Joseph answered Pharaoh, saying, *It is* not in me: God shall give Pharaoh an answer of peace.

And Pharaoh said unto Joseph, In my dream, behold, I stood upon the bank of the river: And, behold, there came up out of the river seven kine, fatfleshed and well favoured; and they fed in a meadow: And, behold, seven other kine came up after them, poor and very ill favoured and leanfleshed, such as I never saw in all the land of Egypt for badness: And the lean and the ill favoured kine did eat up the first seven fat kine: And when they had eaten them up, it could not be known that they had eaten them; but they *were* still ill favoured, as at the beginning. So I awoke.

And I saw in my dream, and, behold, seven ears came up in one stalk, full and good: And, behold, seven ears, withered, thin, *and* blasted with the east wind, sprung up after them: And the thin ears devoured the seven good ears: and I told *this* unto the magicians; but *there was* none that could declare *it* to me.

And Joseph said unto Pharaoh, The dream of Pharaoh *is* one: God hath shewed Pharaoh what he *is* about to do. The seven good kine *are* seven years; and the seven good ears *are* seven years: the dream *is* one. And the seven thin and ill favoured kine that came up after them *are* seven years; and the seven empty ears blasted with the east wind shall be seven years of famine.

This *is* the thing which I have spoken unto Pharaoh: What God *is* about to do he sheweth unto Pharaoh. Behold, there come seven years of great plenty throughout all the land of Egypt: And there shall arise after them seven years of famine; and all the plenty shall be forgotten in the land of Egypt; and the famine shall consume the land; And the plenty shall not be known in the land by reason of that famine following; for it *shall be* very grievous. And for that the dream was doubled unto Pharaoh twice; *it is* because the thing *is* established by God, and God will shortly bring it to pass.

Now therefore let Pharaoh look out a man discreet and wise, and set him over the land of Egypt. Let Pharaoh do *this*, and let him appoint officers over the land, and take up the fifth part of the land of Egypt in the seven plenteous years. And let them gather all the food of those good years that come, and lay up corn under the hand of Pharaoh, and let them keep food in the cities. And that food shall be for store to the land against the seven years of famine, which shall be in the land of Egypt; that the land perish not through the famine.

And the thing was good in the eyes of Pharaoh, and in the eyes of all his servants. And Pharaoh said unto his servants, Can we find *such a one* as this *is*, a man in whom the Spirit of God *is*?

And Pharaoh said unto Joseph, Forasmuch as God hath shewed thee all this, *there is* none so discreet and wise as thou *art*: Thou shalt be over my house, and according unto thy word shall all my people be ruled: only in the throne will I be greater than thou.

And Pharaoh said unto Joseph, See, I have set thee over all the land of Egypt. And Pharaoh took off his ring from his hand, and put it upon Joseph's hand, and arrayed him in vestures of fine linen, and put a gold chain about his neck; And he made him to ride in the second chariot which he had; and they cried before him, Bow the knee: and he made him *ruler* over all the land of Egypt.

And Pharaoh said unto Joseph, I *am* Pharaoh, and without thee shall no man lift up his hand or foot in all the land of Egypt. And Pharaoh called Joseph's name Zaphnath-paaneah; and he gave him to wife Asenath the daughter of Poti-pherah priest of On. And Joseph went out over *all* the land of Egypt.

And Joseph *was* thirty years old when he stood before Pharaoh king of Egypt. And Joseph went out from the presence of Pharaoh, and went throughout all the land of Egypt. GENESIS 41:14–46

Just as Joseph had predicted, seven years of bumper crops were followed by seven years of famine throughout the land. Joseph made sure Egypt saved up enough food during the good years to survive the hard years. Although he was now a rich and influential man, Joseph stayed faithful to his promise to help Egypt survive the famine. Meanwhile, back in Joseph's homeland, his father and brothers began to talk about where they might be able to find more food for their families. Joseph's long-ago dream was about to come true.

Now when Jacob saw that there was corn in Egypt, Jacob said unto his sons, Why do ye look one upon another? And he said, Behold, I have heard that there is corn in Egypt: get you down thither, and buy for us from thence; that we may live, and not die.

And Joseph's ten brethren went down to buy corn in Egypt. But Benjamin, Joseph's brother, Jacob sent not with his brethren; for he said, Lest peradventure mischief befall him. And the sons of Israel came to buy *corn* among those that came: for the famine was in the land of Canaan.

And Joseph *was* the governor over the land, *and* he *it was* that sold to all the people of the land: and Joseph's brethren came, and bowed down themselves before him *with* their faces to the earth. GENESIS 42:1–6 ⊙—π

From pit to pinnacle. It took 21 years for Joseph's dreams to come to pass, but through it all God was faithful. Joseph also stayed faithful to God, whether his circumstances were terribly unjust or tremendously prosperous. Through the faithfulness of God and Joseph, the emerging nation of Israel survived the famine. As a result, Joseph was reunited with his father and enjoyed a position of prosperity and blessing for more than 70 years until his death.

Throughout the Bible, God never calls us to be successful. He calls us to be faithful. As we saw in Joseph's life, sometimes success follows faithfulness, sometimes it doesn't. What do you think about this? How are you doing at being faithful?

STORIES OF FAITHFULNESS: RUTH

Fast-forward to the period in Israel's history when the Israelites occupied the land of Canaan. One of the most heartwarming stories of faithfulness and loyalty does not involve an Israelite but a young Moabite woman.

Now it came to pass in the days when the judges ruled, that there was a famine in the land. And a certain man of Beth-lehem-judah went to sojourn in the country of Moab, he, and his wife, and his two sons. And the name of the man *was* Elimelech, and the name of his wife Naomi, and the name of his two sons Mahlon and Chilion, Ephrathites of Beth-lehem-judah. And they came into the country of Moab, and continued there.

And Elimelech Naomi's husband died; and she was left, and her two sons. And they took them wives of the women of Moab; the name of the one *was* Orpah, and the name of the other Ruth: and they dwelled there about ten years. And Mahlon and Chilion died also both of them; and the woman was left of her two sons and her husband.

Then she arose with her daughters in law, that she might return from the country of Moab: for she had heard in the country of Moab how that the LORD had visited his people in giving them bread. Wherefore she went forth out of the place where she was, and her two daughters in law with her; and they went on the way to return unto the land of Judah.

And Naomi said unto her two daughters in law, Go, return each to her mother's house: the LORD deal kindly with you, as ye have dealt with the dead, and with me. The LORD grant you that ye may find rest, each *of you* in the house of her husband.

Then she kissed them; and they lifted up their voice, and wept. And they said unto her, Surely we will return with thee unto thy people.

And Naomi said, Turn again, my daughters: why will ye go with me? *are* there yet *any more* sons in my womb, that they may be your husbands? Turn again, my daughters, go *your way*; for I am too old to have an husband. If I should say, I have hope, *if* I should have an husband also to night, and should also bear sons; Would ye tarry for them till they were grown? would ye stay for them from having husbands? nay, my daughters; for it grieveth me much for your sakes that the hand of the LORD is gone out against me.

And they lifted up their voice, and wept again: and Orpah kissed her mother in law; but Ruth clave unto her.

And she said, Behold, thy sister in law is gone back unto her people, and unto her gods: return thou after thy sister in law.

And Ruth said, Intreat me not to leave thee, *or* to return from following after thee: for whither thou goest, I will go; and where thou lodgest, I will lodge: thy people *shall be* my people, and thy God my God: Where thou diest, will I die, and there will I be buried: the LORD do so to me, and more also, *if ought* but death part thee and me. When she saw that she was stedfastly minded to go with her, then she left speaking unto her.

So they two went until they came to Beth-lehem. And it came to pass, when they were come to Beth-lehem, that all the city was moved about them, and they said, *Is* this Naomi?

And she said unto them, Call me not Naomi, call me Mara: for the Almighty hath dealt very bitterly with me. I went out full, and the LORD hath brought me home again empty: why *then* call ye me Naomi, seeing the LORD hath testified against me, and the Almighty hath afflicted me?

So Naomi returned, and Ruth the Moabitess, her daughter in law, with her, which returned out of the country of Moab: and they came to Beth-lehem in the beginning of barley harvest. RUTH 1:1–22

God demonstrated his faithfulness to Naomi and Ruth through Boaz, their near relative, who provided for their needs and married Ruth. Boaz and Ruth had a son named Obed, who had a son named Jesse, who had a son named David—who became the greatest king of Israel.

STORIES OF FAITHFULNESS: MARY

The prophet Micah prophesied that the Messiah would come from David's town of Beth-lehem. A thousand years after David lived, the time had come for the Messiah to be born from the tribe of Judah, the family of David, in the city of Beth-lehem. God would pull this off through Ruth's very young descendant Mary. Her response to a shocking announcement shows us her heart of faithfulness.

And in the sixth month the angel Gabriel was sent from God unto a city of Galilee, named Nazareth, To a virgin espoused to a man whose name was Joseph, of the house of David; and the virgin's name *was* Mary. And the angel came in unto her, and said, Hail, *thou that art* highly favoured, the Lord *is* with thee: blessed *art* thou among women.

And when she saw *him,* she was troubled at his saying, and cast in her mind what manner of salutation this should be. **And the angel said unto her, Fear not, Mary: for thou hast found favour with God. And, behold, thou shalt conceive in thy womb, and bring forth a son, and shalt call his name JESUS. He shall be great, and shall be called the Son of the Highest: and the Lord God shall give unto him the throne of his father David: And he**

shall reign over the house of Jacob for ever; and of his kingdom there shall be no end.

Then said Mary unto the angel, How shall this be, seeing I know not a man?

And the angel answered and said unto her, The Holy Ghost shall come upon thee, and the power of the Highest shall overshadow thee: therefore also that holy thing which shall be born of thee shall be called the Son of God. And, behold, thy cousin Elisabeth, she hath also conceived a son in her old age: and this is the sixth month with her, who was called barren. For with God nothing shall be impossible.

And Mary said, Behold the handmaid of the Lord; be it unto me according to thy word. And the angel departed from her.

And Mary arose in those days, and went into the hill country with haste, into a city of Juda; And entered into the house of Zacharias, and saluted Elisabeth. And it came to pass, that, when Elisabeth heard the salutation of Mary, the babe leaped in her womb; and Elisabeth was filled with the Holy Ghost: And she spake out with a loud voice, and said, Blessed *art* thou among women, and blessed *is* the fruit of thy womb. And whence *is* this to me, that the mother of my Lord should come to me? For, lo, as soon as the voice of thy salutation sounded in mine ears, the babe leaped in my womb for joy. And blessed *is* she that believed: for there shall be a performance of those things which were told her from the Lord.

And Mary said, My soul doth magnify the Lord, And my spirit hath rejoiced in God my Saviour. For he hath regarded the low estate of his handmaiden: for, behold, from henceforth all generations shall call me blessed. For he that is mighty hath done to me great things; and holy *is* his name. And his mercy *is* on them that fear him from generation to generation. He hath shewed strength with his arm; he hath scattered the proud in the imagination of their hearts. He hath put down the mighty from *their* seats, and exalted them of low degree. He hath filled the hungry with good things; and the rich he hath sent empty away. He hath holpen his servant Israel, in remembrance of *his* mercy; As he spake to our fathers, to Abraham, and to his seed for ever.

And Mary abode with her about three months, and returned to her own house. LUKE 1:26–56

Mary committed herself, as "the handmaid of the Lord," to be faithful to God's plan, and she extolled God's faithfulness. After visiting her relative Elizabeth, Mary—now about three months pregnant—returned to her home in Nazareth. But Nazareth was at least a three-day trip from Bethlehem. How then was the prophecy, that the Messiah would come from the town of Bethlehem, going to be fulfilled?

And it came to pass in those days, that there went out a decree from Caesar Augustus, that all the world should be taxed. (*And* this taxing was first made when Cyrenius was governor of Syria.) And all went to be taxed, every one into his own city.

And Joseph also went up from Galilee, out of the city of Nazareth, into Judaea, unto the city of David, which is called Bethlehem; (because he was of the house and lineage of David:) To be taxed with Mary his espoused wife, being great with child. And so it was, that, while they were there, the days were accomplished that she should be delivered. And she brought forth her firstborn son, and wrapped him in swaddling clothes, and laid him in a manger; because there was no room for them in the inn.

And there were in the same country shepherds abiding in the field, keeping watch over their flock by night. And, lo, the angel of the Lord came upon them, and the glory of the Lord shone round about them: and they were sore afraid. And the angel said unto them, Fear not: for, behold, I bring you good tidings of great joy, which shall be to all people. For unto you is born this day in the city of David a Saviour, which is Christ the Lord. And this *shall be* a sign unto you; Ye shall find the babe wrapped in swaddling clothes, lying in a manger.

And suddenly there was with the angel a multitude of the heavenly host praising God, and saying, Glory to God in the highest, and on earth peace, good will toward men.

And it came to pass, as the angels were gone away from them into heaven, the shepherds said one to another, Let us now go even unto Bethlehem, and see this thing which is come to pass, which the Lord hath made known unto us.

And they came with haste, and found Mary, and Joseph, and the babe lying in a manger. And when they had seen *it*, they made known abroad the saying which was told them concerning this child. And all they that heard *it* wondered at those things which were told them by the shepherds. But Mary kept all these things, and pondered *them* in her heart. And the shepherds returned, glorifying and praising God for all the things that they had heard and seen, as it was told unto them.

And when eight days were accomplished for the circumcising of the child, his name was called JESUS, which was so named of the angel before he was conceived in the womb.   Luke 2:1–21

Based on what you have learned about faithfulness, who are some of the most faithful people you know? How have they found honor and a good name in your sight? In the sight of others? If it is possible, let them know.

WHAT WE BELIEVE

Throughout the Bible, God called believers to be faithful to his assignments for them, no matter how difficult. In fact, it was often amid the difficult seasons that they discovered the trustworthiness of God the most. When they aligned their lives to God's story, he was with them and accomplished great things through them. All believers have the opportunity to open their lives to God's will and demonstrate their faithfulness. The results of such faithfulness can be both great and beautiful as God works through those who believe.

CHAPTER

29

Gentleness

––––––––– KEY QUESTION –––––––––

How do I demonstrate thoughtfulness
and consideration?

––––––––– KEY IDEA –––––––––

I am thoughtful, considerate and calm
in my dealings with others.

––––––––– KEY VERSE –––––––––

Let your moderation be known unto all men.
The Lord *is* at hand.
Philippians 4:5

O U R   M A P

Nothing kills a family, a friendship, a neighborhood or even a church like pride, arrogance, anger, closed ears and raised voices. Since God is all about community, he calls his followers to be gentle. The New Testament word for "gentleness" comes from a medical word and is associated with a mild medication. Essentially, we might say a gentle person is someone who is easy on our stomachs. The person who lacks gentleness causes our stomach to double up in knots. God wants us to be healing agents in the lives of those around us. So how do we learn how to demonstrate thoughtfulness and consideration to others? That is the focus of this chapter, with Scripture concentrated on:

- Gentle Jesus
- Nuggets on Gentleness
- Stories of Gentleness: Abigail
- Stories of Gentleness: David
- Stories of Gentleness: Paul

Look at the key verse again. Why do you think
Paul put these two sentences together?

GENTLE JESUS

Throughout the Bible we find stories and people who reinforce the fact that gentleness is a character trait that God has intended for us. Jesus, of course, is our greatest example of someone who displayed gentleness in his dealings with others. This is particularly true in his relationship with Peter. At the Last Supper on the night before Jesus was crucified, Peter told Jesus he would die for him. Jesus, predicting Peter's future betrayal, corrected him. Jesus had already predicted the betrayal of Judas, who had just stepped out of the room.

Therefore, when [Judas] was gone out, Jesus said, Now is the Son of man glorified, and God is glorified in him. If God be glorified in him, God shall also glorify him in himself, and shall straightway glorify him.

Little children, yet a little while I am with you. Ye shall seek me: and as I said unto the Jews, Whither I go, ye cannot come; so now I say to you.

A new commandment I give unto you, That ye love one another; as I have loved you, that ye also love one another. By this shall all *men* know that ye are my disciples, if ye have love one to another.

Simon Peter said unto him, Lord, whither goest thou?

Jesus answered him, Whither I go, thou canst not follow me now; but thou shalt follow me afterwards.

Peter said unto him, Lord, why cannot I follow thee now? I will lay down my life for thy sake.

Jesus answered him, Wilt thou lay down thy life for my sake? Verily, verily, I say unto thee, The cock shall not crow, till thou hast denied me thrice.   John 13:31–38

> *Peter could not imagine betraying his master. He had left everything to follow Jesus. However, when Jesus was arrested later that evening Peter's fear overcame his faith.*

Then the band and the captain and officers of the Jews took Jesus, and bound him, And led him away to Annas first; for he was father in law to Caiaphas, which was the high priest that same year. Now Caiaphas was he, which gave counsel to the Jews, that it was expedient that one man should die for the people.

And Simon Peter followed Jesus, and *so did* another disciple: that disciple was known unto the high priest, and went in with Jesus into the palace of the high priest. But Peter stood at the door without. Then went out that other disciple, which was known unto the high priest, and spake unto her that kept the door, and brought in Peter.

Then saith the damsel that kept the door unto Peter, Art not thou also *one* of this man's disciples?

He saith, I am not.

And the servants and officers stood there, who had made a fire of coals; for it was cold: and they warmed themselves: and Peter stood with them, and warmed himself.

The high priest then asked Jesus of his disciples, and of his doctrine.

Jesus answered him, I spake openly to the world; I ever taught in the synagogue, and in the temple, whither the Jews always resort; and in secret have I said nothing. Why askest thou me? ask them which heard me, what I have said unto them: behold, they know what I said.

And when he had thus spoken, one of the officers which stood by struck Jesus with the palm of his hand, saying, Answerest thou the high priest so?

Jesus answered him, If I have spoken evil, bear witness of the evil: but if well, why smitest thou me? Now Annas had sent him bound unto Caiaphas the high priest.

And Simon Peter stood and warmed himself. They said therefore unto him, Art not thou also *one* of his disciples?

He denied it, and said, I am not.

One of the servants of the high priest, being *his* kinsman whose ear Peter cut off, saith, Did not I see thee in the garden with him? Peter then denied again: and immediately the cock crew. JOHN 18:12–27

Sometime between Jesus' resurrection and ascension to heaven, he appeared to seven of his disciples who had gone fishing. With a heart of gentleness, Jesus restored Peter's relationship with him and reinstated Peter to a position of special responsibility in the church.

After these things Jesus shewed himself again to the disciples at the sea of Tiberias; and on this wise shewed he *himself.* There were together Simon Peter, and Thomas called Didymus, and Nathanael of Cana in Galilee, and the *sons* of Zebedee, and two other of his disciples. Simon Peter saith unto them, I go a fishing. They say unto him, We also go with thee. They went forth, and entered into a ship immediately; and that night they caught nothing.

But when the morning was now come, Jesus stood on the shore: but the disciples knew not that it was Jesus.

Then Jesus saith unto them, Children, have ye any meat?

They answered him, No.

And he said unto them, Cast the net on the right side of the ship, and ye shall find. They cast therefore, and now they were not able to draw it for the multitude of fishes.

Therefore that disciple whom Jesus loved saith unto Peter, It is the Lord. Now when Simon Peter heard that it was the Lord, he girt *his* fisher's coat *unto him*, (for he was naked,) and did cast himself into the sea. And the other disciples came in a little ship; (for they were not far from land, but as it were two hundred cubits,) dragging the net with fishes. As soon then as they were come to land, they saw a fire of coals there, and fish laid thereon, and bread.

Jesus saith unto them, Bring of the fish which ye have now caught. Simon Peter went up, and drew the net to land full of great fishes, an hundred and fifty and three: and for all there were so many, yet was not the net broken. Jesus saith unto them, Come *and* dine. And none of the disciples durst ask him, Who art thou? knowing that it was the Lord. Jesus then cometh, and taketh bread, and giveth them, and fish likewise. This is now the third time that Jesus shewed himself to his disciples, after that he was risen from the dead.

So when they had dined, Jesus saith to Simon Peter, Simon, *son* of Jonas, lovest thou me more than these?

He saith unto him, Yea, Lord; thou knowest that I love thee.

He saith unto him, Feed my lambs.

He saith to him again the second time, **Simon, *son* of Jonas, lovest thou me?**

He saith unto him, Yea, Lord; thou knowest that I love thee.

He saith unto him, Feed my sheep.

He saith unto him the third time, **Simon, *son* of Jonas, lovest thou me?**

Peter was grieved because he said unto him the third time, Lovest thou me? And he said unto him, Lord, thou knowest all things; thou knowest that I love thee.

Jesus saith unto him, Feed my sheep. Verily, verily, I say unto thee, When thou wast young, thou girdedst thyself, and walkedst whither thou wouldest: but when thou shalt be old, thou shalt stretch forth thy hands, and another shall gird thee, and carry *thee* whither thou wouldest not. This spake he, signifying by what death he should glorify God. And when he had spoken this, he saith unto him, Follow me.   JOHN 21:1–19

Some have suggested that Jesus asked Simon Peter
if he loved him three times to help restore Peter
from the three times he had denied Jesus. Do you think
this was Jesus' intent? Do you think this would have
helped you if you were in Peter's sandals?

Peter's relationship was fully restored by Jesus' gentle invitation. The rest of the New Testament tells us how Peter fulfilled this mission given to him by Jesus. He spoke the Word of God boldly and provided leadership to God's people. Peter isn't the only one Jesus spoke to with gentleness. Jesus invites all people to receive his gift of peace and rest.

Come unto me, all *ye* that labour and are heavy laden, and I will give you rest. Take my yoke upon you, and learn of me; for I am meek and lowly in heart: and ye shall find rest unto your souls. For my yoke *is* easy, and my burden is light.

MATTHEW 11:28–30

NUGGETS ON GENTLENESS

The New Testament offers us wonderful nuggets on being thoughtful, considerate and calm. Jesus offered up powerful insights and encouragement in the Sermon on the Mount.

As you read Jesus' nuggets of wisdom
on gentleness, identify the one that most speaks
to you. Why did you choose this one?

Blessed *are* the meek: for they shall inherit the earth.

MATTHEW 5:5

Ye have heard that it hath been said, An eye for an eye, and a tooth for a tooth: But I say unto you, That ye resist not evil: but

whosoever shall smite thee on thy right cheek, turn to him the other also. And if any man will sue thee at the law, and take away thy coat, let him have *thy* cloak also. And whosoever shall compel thee to go a mile, go with him twain. Give to him that asketh thee, and from him that would borrow of thee turn not thou away.

MATTHEW 5:38–42

Judge not, that ye be not judged. For with what judgment ye judge, ye shall be judged: and with what measure ye mete, it shall be measured to you again.

And why beholdest thou the mote that is in thy brother's eye, but considerest not the beam that is in thine own eye? Or how wilt thou say to thy brother, Let me pull out the mote out of thine eye; and, behold, a beam *is* in thine own eye? Thou hypocrite, first cast out the beam out of thine own eye; and then shalt thou see clearly to cast out the mote out of thy brother's eye.   MATTHEW 7:1–5

Inspired by the life and teaching of Jesus and led by the Spirit, the apostles offered further understanding of and encouragement about gentleness.

But the fruit of the Spirit is love, joy, peace, longsuffering, gentleness, goodness, faith, Meekness, temperance: against such there is no law.   GALATIANS 5:22–23

Walk worthy of the vocation wherewith ye are called. With all lowliness and meekness, with longsuffering, forbearing one another in love.   EPHESIANS 4:1–2

Be ye angry, and sin not: let not the sun go down upon your wrath: Neither give place to the devil. Let him that stole steal no more: but rather let him labour, working with *his* hands the thing which is good, that he may have to give to him that needeth. **Let no corrupt communication proceed out of your mouth, but that which is good to the use of edifying, that it may minister grace unto the hearers.** And grieve not the holy Spirit of God, whereby ye are sealed unto the day of redemption. Let all bitterness, and wrath, and anger, and clamour, and evil speaking, be put away from you, with all malice: And be ye kind one to another, tenderhearted, forgiving one another, even as God for Christ's sake hath forgiven you.   EPHESIANS 4:26–32

And, ye fathers, provoke not your children to wrath: but bring them up in the nurture and admonition of the Lord.

                                                    EPHESIANS 6:4

Put on therefore, as the elect of God, holy and beloved, bowels of mercies, kindness, humbleness of mind, meekness, longsuffering.

                                                COLOSSIANS 3:12

This *is* a true saying, If a man desire the office of a bishop, he desireth a good work. A bishop then must be blameless, the husband of one wife, vigilant, sober, of good behaviour, given to hospitality, apt to teach; Not given to wine, no striker, not greedy of filthy lucre; but patient, not a brawler, not covetous; One that ruleth well his own house, having his children in subjection with all gravity.   1 TIMOTHY 3:1–4

Rebuke not an elder, but intreat *him* as a father; *and* the younger men as brethren; The elder women as mothers; the younger as sisters, with all purity.   1 TIMOTHY 5:1–2

For the love of money is the root of all evil: which while some coveted after, they have erred from the faith, and pierced themselves through with many sorrows.

But thou, O man of God, flee these things; and follow after righteousness, godliness, faith, love, patience, meekness.

                                            1 TIMOTHY 6:10–11

And the servant of the Lord must not strive; but be gentle unto all *men*, apt to teach, patient, In meekness instructing those that oppose themselves; if God peradventure will give them repentance to the acknowledging of the truth; And *that* they may recover themselves out of the snare of the devil, who are taken captive by him at his will.   2 TIMOTHY 2:24–26

Put them in mind to be subject to principalities and powers, to obey magistrates, to be ready to every good work, To speak evil of no man, to be no brawlers, *but* gentle, shewing all meekness unto all men.

TITUS 3:1–2

But the wisdom that is from above is first pure, then peaceable, gentle, *and* easy to be intreated, full of mercy and good fruits, without partiality, and without hypocrisy. And the fruit of righteousness is sown in peace of them that make peace.

JAMES 3:17–18

Look at Ephesians 4:26–32 again. How do we give the devil a place in our lives when we let the sun go down while we are still angry?

Paul encouraged two Christian women in the church at Philippi to reconcile their differences and then urged the entire congregation to put their gentleness on public display in light of the Lord's arrival.

I beseech Euodias, and beseech Syntyche, that they be of the same mind in the Lord. And I intreat thee also, true yokefellow, help those women which laboured with me in the gospel, with Clement also, and *with* other my fellowlabourers, whose names *are* in the book of life.

Rejoice in the Lord alway: *and* again I say, Rejoice. **Let your moderation be known unto all men. The Lord *is* at hand.**

PHILIPPIANS 4:2–5

Likewise, Peter told his readers that a thoughtful, considerate and calm gentleness is key in a marriage relationship.

Likewise, ye wives, *be* in subjection to your own husbands; that, if any obey not the word, they also may without the word be won by the conversation of the wives; While they behold your chaste conversation *coupled* with fear. **Whose adorning let it not be that outward *adorning* of plaiting the hair, and of wearing of gold,** or of putting on of apparel; But *let it be* the hidden man of the heart, in that which is not corruptible, *even the ornament* of a meek and quiet spirit, which is in the sight of God of great price.

1 Peter 3:1–4

Likewise, ye husbands, dwell with *them* according to knowledge, giving honour unto the wife, as unto the weaker vessel, and as being heirs together of the grace of life; that your prayers be not hindered.

1 Peter 3:7

Stories of Gentleness: Abigail

As you read the next three stories from 1 Samuel 25;
2 Samuel 16 and 1 Thessalonians 2,
find the ways anger is stirred up and look for
how gentleness affects tense situations.

Samuel anointed young David to be the next king of Israel, but the reigning King Saul hated David, causing David to flee as a fugitive. David was on the run from Saul when he encountered a couple who displayed opposite qualities—Abigail was wise and gentle, while Nabal was foolish and cruel. When David asked Nabal for reasonable payment for the protection that he and his men had voluntarily rendered for Nabal's benefit, Nabal's response was harsh and rude. Abigail repaired the situation with gentleness and diplomacy.

And Samuel died; and all the Israelites were gathered together, and lamented him, and buried him in his house at Ramah. And David arose, and went down to the wilderness of Paran.

And *there was* a man in Maon, whose possessions *were* in Carmel; and the man *was* very great, and he had three thousand sheep, and a thousand goats: and he was shearing his sheep in Carmel. Now the name of the man *was* Nabal; and the name of his wife Abigail: and *she was* a woman of good understanding, and of a beautiful countenance: but the man *was* churlish and evil in his doings; and he *was* of the house of Caleb.

And David heard in the wilderness that Nabal did shear his sheep. And David sent out ten young men, and David said unto the young men, Get you up to Carmel, and go to Nabal, and greet him in my name: And thus shall ye say to him that liveth *in prosperity*, Peace *be* both to thee, and peace *be* to thine house, and peace *be* unto all that thou hast.

And now I have heard that thou hast shearers: now thy shepherds which were with us, we hurt them not, neither was there ought missing unto them, all the while they were in Carmel. Ask thy young men, and they will shew thee. Wherefore let the young men find favour in thine eyes: for we come in a good day: give, I pray thee, whatsoever cometh to thine hand unto thy servants, and to thy son David.

And when David's young men came, they spake to Nabal according to all those words in the name of David, and ceased.

And Nabal answered David's servants, and said, Who *is* David? and who *is* the son of Jesse? there be many servants now a days that break away every man from his master. Shall I then take my bread, and my water, and my flesh that I have killed for my shearers, and give *it* unto men, whom I know not whence they *be*?

So David's young men turned their way, and went again, and came and told him all those sayings. And David said unto his men, Gird ye on every man his sword. And they girded on every man his sword; and David also girded on his sword: and there went up after David about four hundred men; and two hundred abode by the stuff.

But one of the young men told Abigail, Nabal's wife, saying, Behold, David sent messengers out of the wilderness to salute our master; and he railed on them. But the men *were* very good unto us, and we were not hurt, neither missed we any thing, as long as we were conversant with them, when we were in the fields: They were a wall unto us both by night and day, all the while we were with them keeping the sheep. Now therefore know and consider what thou wilt do; for evil is determined against our master, and against all his household: for he *is such* a son of Belial, that *a man* cannot speak to him.

Then Abigail made haste, and took two hundred loaves, and

two bottles of wine, and five sheep ready dressed, and five measures of parched *corn*, and an hundred clusters of raisins, and two
hundred cakes of figs, and laid *them* on asses. And she said unto
her servants, Go on before me; behold, I come after you. But she
told not her husband Nabal.

And it was *so*, *as* she rode on the ass, that she came down by
the covert of the hill, and, behold, David and his men came down
against her; and she met them. Now David had said, Surely in vain
have I kept all that this *fellow* hath in the wilderness, so that nothing was missed of all that *pertained* unto him: and he hath requit-
ed me evil for good. So and more also do God unto the enemies of
David, if I leave of all that *pertain* to him by the morning light any
that pisseth against the wall.

And when Abigail saw David, she hasted, and lighted off the
ass, and fell before David on her face, and bowed herself to the
ground, And fell at his feet, and said, Upon me, my lord, *upon* me
let this iniquity *be*: and let thine handmaid, I pray thee, speak in
thine audience, and hear the words of thine handmaid. Let not
my lord, I pray thee, regard this man of Belial, *even* Nabal: for as
his name *is*, so *is* he; Nabal *is* his name, and folly *is* with him: but
I thine handmaid saw not the young men of my lord, whom thou
didst send. Now therefore, my lord, *as* the LORD liveth, and *as* thy
soul liveth, seeing the LORD hath withholden thee from coming to
shed blood, and from avenging thyself with thine own hand, now
let thine enemies, and they that seek evil to my lord, be as Nabal.
And now this blessing which thine handmaid hath brought unto
my lord, let it even be given unto the young men that follow my
lord.

I pray thee, forgive the trespass of thine handmaid: for the
LORD will certainly make my lord a sure house; because my lord
fighteth the battles of the LORD, and evil hath not been found in
thee *all* thy days. Yet a man is risen to pursue thee, and to seek
thy soul: but the soul of my lord shall be bound in the bundle of
life with the LORD thy God; and the souls of thine enemies, them
shall he sling out, *as out* of the middle of a sling. And it shall come
to pass, when the LORD shall have done to my lord according to
all the good that he hath spoken concerning thee, and shall have

appointed thee ruler over Israel; That this shall be no grief unto thee, nor offence of heart unto my lord, either that thou hast shed blood causeless, or that my lord hath avenged himself: but when the LORD shall have dealt well with my lord, then remember thine handmaid.

And David said to Abigail, Blessed *be* the LORD God of Israel, which sent thee this day to meet me: And blessed *be* thy advice, and blessed *be* thou, which hast kept me this day from coming to *shed* blood, and from avenging myself with mine own hand. For in very deed, *as* the LORD God of Israel liveth, which hath kept me back from hurting thee, except thou hadst hasted and come to meet me, surely there had not been left unto Nabal by the morning light any that pisseth against the wall.

So David received of her hand *that* which she had brought him, and said unto her, Go up in peace to thine house; see, I have hearkened to thy voice, and have accepted thy person.

And Abigail came to Nabal; and, behold, he held a feast in his house, like the feast of a king; and Nabal's heart *was* merry within him, for he *was* very drunken: wherefore she told him nothing, less or more, until the morning light. But it came to pass in the morning, when the wine was gone out of Nabal, and his wife had told him these things, that his heart died within him, and he became *as* a stone. And it came to pass about ten days *after*, that the LORD smote Nabal, that he died.

And when David heard that Nabal was dead, he said, Blessed *be* the LORD, that hath pleaded the cause of my reproach from the hand of Nabal, and hath kept his servant from evil: for the LORD hath returned the wickedness of Nabal upon his own head.

And David sent and communed with Abigail, to take her to him to wife. And when the servants of David were come to Abigail to Carmel, they spake unto her, saying, David sent us unto thee, to take thee to him to wife.

And she arose, and bowed herself on *her* face to the earth, and said, Behold, *let* thine handmaid *be* a servant to wash the feet of the servants of my lord. And Abigail hasted, and arose, and rode upon an ass, with five damsels of hers that went after her; and she went after the messengers of David, and became his wife.

1 SAMUEL 25:1–42

STORIES OF GENTLENESS: DAVID

Our gentleness toward others is tested most when things are not going well for us—when we are frustrated, tired or discouraged. David was now king of Israel, but his son Absalom had conspired against him to take the throne. Uncertain of the extent of Absalom's support, David feared being trapped in Jerusalem and wanted to spare the city a bloodbath. So he fled as a fugitive once again. On his way out of Jerusalem, David experienced a situation that was nearly unbearable. How would he respond?

And when king David came to Bahurim, behold, thence came out a man of the family of the house of Saul, whose name *was* Shimei, the son of Gera: he came forth, and cursed still as he came. And he cast stones at David, and at all the servants of king David: and all the people and all the mighty men *were* on his right hand and on his left. And thus said Shimei when he cursed, Come out, come out, thou bloody man, and thou man of Belial: The LORD hath returned upon thee all the blood of the house of Saul, in whose stead thou hast reigned; and the LORD hath delivered the kingdom into the hand of Absalom thy son: and, behold, thou *art taken* in thy mischief, because thou *art* a bloody man.

Then said Abishai the son of Zeruiah unto the king, Why should this dead dog curse my lord the king? let me go over, I pray thee, and take off his head.

And the king said, What have I to do with you, ye sons of Zeruiah? so let him curse, because the LORD hath said unto him, Curse David. Who shall then say, Wherefore hast thou done so?

And David said to Abishai, and to all his servants, Behold, my son, which came forth of my bowels, seeketh my life: how much more now *may this* Benjamite *do it*? let him alone, and let him curse; for the LORD hath bidden him. It may be that the LORD will look on mine affliction, and that the LORD will requite me good for his cursing this day.

And as David and his men went by the way, Shimei went along on the hill's side over against him, and cursed as he went, and threw stones at him, and cast dust. And the king, and all the people that *were* with him, came weary, and refreshed themselves there.

2 SAMUEL 16:5–14

STORIES OF GENTLENESS: PAUL

Like David, Paul carried great responsibility on his shoulders and was often challenged by others and undermined in his work. It would have been easy for Paul to lose his temper with the new believers he sought to encourage in Christ. But he didn't. In his first letter to the church of Thessalonica, Paul laid out his effective approach of gentleness in ministering to them. It's an approach we would be wise to emulate with the people God has placed in our lives.

For yourselves, brethren, know our entrance in unto you, that it was not in vain: But even after that we had suffered before, and were shamefully entreated, as ye know, at Philippi, we were bold in our God to speak unto you the gospel of God with much contention. For our exhortation *was* not of deceit, nor of uncleanness, nor in guile: But as we were allowed of God to be put in trust with the gospel, even so we speak; not as pleasing men, but God, which trieth our hearts. For neither at any time used we flattering words, as ye know, nor a cloak of covetousness; God *is* witness: Nor of men sought we glory, neither of you, nor *yet* of others, when we might have been burdensome, as the apostles of Christ.

But we were gentle among you, even as a nurse cherisheth her children: So being affectionately desirous of you, we were willing to have imparted unto you, not the gospel of God only, but also our own souls, because ye were dear unto us. For ye remember, brethren, our labour and travail: for labouring night and day, because we would not be chargeable unto any of you, we preached unto you the gospel of God. Ye *are* witnesses, and God *also*, how holily and justly and unblameably we behaved ourselves among you that believe: As ye know how we exhorted and comforted and charged every one of you, as a father *doth* his children, That ye would walk worthy of God, who hath called you unto his kingdom and glory.

For this cause also thank we God without ceasing, because, when ye received the word of God which ye heard of us, ye received *it* not *as* the word of men, but as it is in truth, the word of God, which effectually worketh also in you that believe.

1 THESSALONIANS 2:1–13

WHAT WE BELIEVE

Gentleness is rooted in our belief in humanity. When we see people the way God sees them, we are compelled to treat them well. A gentle person, according to God's vision, is thoughtful. They think before they talk or act. A gentle person is considerate. They consistently put themselves in other people's shoes and act accordingly. A gentle person is calm. They are known for their even temper and positive energy. Jesus modeled this for us in so many of his relationships. We can also find positive examples of gentleness in the stories of Abigail, David and Paul. Also pay attention to the lives of men like Nabal. Sometimes looking at a negative example can be eye-opening. Go back to the nuggets on gentleness you read earlier in the chapter. Pick just one suggestion and try it for seven days and see if it doesn't make a difference in your life and the lives of those God has purposefully placed around you.

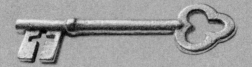

CHAPTER

30

Humility

KEY QUESTION

What does it mean to value others before myself?

KEY IDEA

I choose to esteem others above myself.

KEY VERSE

Let nothing *be done* through strife or vainglory;
but in lowliness of mind let each esteem
other better than themselves.
Look not every man on his own things,
but every man also on the things of others.
Philippians 2:3 – 4

482

OUR MAP

Humility is a driving virtue in the Christian life and community. Choosing to esteem others above oneself encourages harmony and love. The opposite of humility is pride. Prideful people typically believe they are better than others. They strive to get their way at the expense of others or boast as a way of boosting low self-esteem. When a person possesses Biblical humility, they draw from internal "God-esteem." They have received God's unconditional love and embraced their inherent worth as God's child—their identity in Christ. From this belief they are capable of lifting others up. This chapter will provide us with God's Word on the matter:

- Christ As Our Example
- God Resists the Proud, Gives Grace to the Humble
- The Paradox of Humility
- God's Requirement

CHRIST AS OUR EXAMPLE

Jesus is our supreme example of humility. The God of the universe could have ridden into our world on a white horse with a serious entourage and fanfare. Instead he came to us as a baby born in a stable to poor parents.

And it came to pass in those days, that there went out a decree from Caesar Augustus, that all the world should be taxed. (*And this taxing was first made when Cyrenius was governor of Syria.*) And all went to be taxed, every one into his own city.

And Joseph also went up from Galilee, out of the city of Nazareth, into Judaea, unto the city of David, which is called Bethlehem; (because he was of the house and lineage of David:) To be taxed with Mary his espoused wife, being great with child. And so it was, that, while they were there, the days were accomplished that she should be delivered. **And she brought forth her firstborn son, and wrapped him in swaddling clothes, and laid him in a manger; because there was no room for them in the inn.**

And there were in the same country shepherds abiding in the field, keeping watch over their flock by night. And, lo, the angel of the Lord came upon them, and the glory of the Lord shone round about them: and they were sore afraid. And the angel said unto them, Fear not: for, behold, I bring you good tidings of great joy, which shall be to all people. For unto you is born this day in the city of David a Saviour, which is Christ the Lord. And this *shall be* a sign unto you; Ye shall find the babe wrapped in swaddling clothes, lying in a manger.

And suddenly there was with the angel a multitude of the heavenly host praising God, and saying, Glory to God in the highest, and on earth peace, good will toward men.

And it came to pass, as the angels were gone away from them into heaven, the shepherds said one to another, Let us now go even unto Bethlehem, and see this thing which is come to pass, which the Lord hath made known unto us.

And they came with haste, and found Mary, and Joseph, and the babe lying in a manger. And when they had seen *it*, they made known abroad the saying which was told them concerning this child. And all they that heard *it* wondered at those things which were told them by the shepherds. But Mary kept all these things, and pondered *them* in her heart. And the shepherds returned, glorifying and praising God for all the things that they had heard and seen, as it was told unto them.   LUKE 2:1–20

As Jesus was coming to the end of his time on earth, he wanted to impress upon his disciples the importance of humility. He does so in an unforgettable way.

☦—π Now before the feast of the passover, when Jesus knew that his hour was come that he should depart out of this world unto the Father, having loved his own which were in the world, he loved them unto the end.

And supper being ended, the devil having now put into the heart of Judas Iscariot, Simon's *son*, to betray him; **Jesus knowing that the Father had given all things into his hands, and that he was come from God, and went to God; He riseth from supper, and laid aside his garments; and took a towel, and girded himself. After that he poureth water into a bason, and began to wash the disciples' feet, and to wipe *them* with the towel wherewith he was girded.**

Then cometh he to Simon Peter: and Peter saith unto him, Lord, dost thou wash my feet?

Jesus answered and said unto him, What I do thou knowest not now; but thou shalt know hereafter.

Peter saith unto him, Thou shalt never wash my feet.

Jesus answered him, If I wash thee not, thou hast no part with me.

Simon Peter saith unto him, Lord, not my feet only, but also *my* hands and *my* head.

Jesus saith to him, He that is washed needeth not save to wash *his* feet, but is clean every whit: and ye are clean, but not all. For he knew who should betray him; therefore said he, Ye are not all clean.

So after he had washed their feet, and had taken his garments, and was set down again, he said unto them, Know ye what I have done to you? Ye call me Master and Lord: and ye say well; for *so* I am. If I then, *your* Lord and Master, have washed your feet; ye also ought to wash one another's feet. For I have given you an example, that ye should do as I have done to you. Verily, verily, I say unto you, The servant is not greater than his lord; neither he that is sent greater than he that sent him. If ye know these things, happy are ye if ye do them.

JOHN 13:1–17

Servant leadership is what Jesus modeled while on earth. What other ways can we demonstrate this principle besides washing someone's feet?

Following in the steps of his Savior, the apostle Paul wrote a tender letter to the church at Philippi instructing them to practice humility. He cited Jesus as their model.

If *there be* therefore any consolation in Christ, if any comfort of love, if any fellowship of the Spirit, if any bowels and mercies, Fulfil ye my joy, that ye be likeminded, having the same love, *being* of one accord, of one mind. *Let* nothing *be done* through strife or vainglory; but in lowliness of mind let each esteem other better than themselves. Look not every man on his own things, but every man also on the things of others.

Let this mind be in you, which was also in Christ Jesus: Who, being in the form of God, thought it not robbery to be equal with God: But made himself of no reputation, and took upon him the form of a servant, and was made in the likeness of men: And being found in fashion as a man, he humbled himself, and became obedient unto death, even the death of the cross.

Wherefore God also hath highly exalted him, and given him a name which is above every name: That at the name of Jesus every knee should bow, of *things* in heaven, and *things* in earth, and *things* under the earth; And *that* every tongue should confess that Jesus Christ *is* Lord, to the glory of God the Father.

Wherefore, my beloved, as ye have always obeyed, not as in my presence only, but now much more in my absence, work out your own salvation with fear and trembling. For it is God which worketh in you both to will and to do of *his* good pleasure.

PHILIPPIANS 2:1–13

What do you think was involved when Jesus "made himself of no reputation?" What was he before? Why did he do this?

GOD RESISTS THE PROUD, GIVES GRACE TO THE HUMBLE

Throughout the Bible we find a pattern—God resists the proud but gives grace to the humble. The following passages from Psalms and Proverbs are brief, but their messages are powerful.

As you read the Scripture passages below
from Psalms and Proverbs, write down all the ways God
resists the proud and gives grace to the humble.

The wicked in *his* pride doth persecute the poor:
let them be taken in the devices that they have
imagined.
For the wicked boasteth of his heart's desire,
and blesseth the covetous, *whom* the LORD abhorreth.
The wicked, through the pride of his countenance,
will not seek *after God*: God *is* not in all his thoughts.

PSALM 10:2–4

For thou wilt save the afflicted people;
　　but wilt bring down high looks.　　　　　PSALM 18:27

Good and upright *is* the LORD:
　　therefore will he teach sinners in the way.
The meek will he guide in judgment:
　　and the meek will he teach his way.　　　PSALM 25:8–9

The LORD lifteth up the meek:
　　he casteth the wicked down to the ground.　PSALM 147:6

The curse of the LORD *is* in the house of the wicked:
　　but he blesseth the habitation of the just.
Surely he scorneth the scorners:
　　but he giveth grace unto the lowly.　　　PROVERBS 3:33–34

When pride cometh, then cometh shame:
　　but with the lowly *is* wisdom.　　　　　PROVERBS 11:2

**Pride *goeth* before destruction,
　　and an haughty spirit before a fall.**

Better *it is to be* of an humble spirit with the lowly,
　　than to divide the spoil with the proud.　PROVERBS 16:18–19

Before destruction the heart of man is haughty,
　　and before honour *is* humility.　　　　　PROVERBS 18:12

An high look, and a proud heart,
　　and the plowing of the wicked, *is* sin.　PROVERBS 21:4

Proud *and* haughty scorner *is* his name,
　　who dealeth in proud wrath.　　　　　　PROVERBS 21:24

**By humility *and* the fear of the LORD
　　are riches, and honour, and life.**　　　PROVERBS 22:4

Put not forth thyself in the presence of the king,
　　and stand not in the place of great *men*:

> For better *it is* that it be said unto thee, Come up hither;
> than that thou shouldest be put lower in the presence of
> the prince whom thine eyes have seen.
>
> PROVERBS 25:6–7

> A man's pride shall bring him low:
> but honour shall uphold the humble in spirit.
>
> PROVERBS 29:23

An example of God resisting the proud and giving grace to the humble can be found in the story of a young Hebrew man named Daniel, who was taken captive from Jerusalem to Babylon in 605 BC. There, after three years of training, Daniel was given a responsible post in King Nebuchadnezzar's service. Through divine wisdom, Daniel was able to interpret dreams, and he soon became one of the most prominent figures in the royal court. God used Daniel to teach Nebuchadnezzar a memorable lesson in humility. The book of Daniel includes the following letter that the king wrote to his subjects regarding his experience.

Nebuchadnezzar the king, unto all people, nations, and languages, that dwell in all the earth; Peace be multiplied unto you.

I thought it good to shew the signs and wonders that the high God hath wrought toward me. How great *are* his signs! and how mighty *are* his wonders! his kingdom *is* an everlasting kingdom, and his dominion *is* from generation to generation.

I Nebuchadnezzar was at rest in mine house, and flourishing in my palace: I saw a dream which made me afraid, and the thoughts upon my bed and the visions of my head troubled me. Therefore made I a decree to bring in all the wise *men* of Babylon before me, that they might make known unto me the interpretation of the dream. Then came in the magicians, the astrologers, the Chaldeans, and the soothsayers: and I told the dream before them; but they did not make known unto me the interpretation thereof. But at the last Daniel came in before me, whose name *was* Belteshazzar, according to the name of my god, and in whom *is* the spirit of the holy gods: and before him I told the dream, *saying*,

O Belteshazzar, master of the magicians, because I know that the spirit of the holy gods *is* in thee, and no secret troubleth thee, tell me the visions of my dream that I have seen, and the interpretation thereof. Thus *were* the visions of mine head in my bed; I saw, and behold a tree in the midst of the earth, and the height thereof *was* great. The tree grew, and was strong, and the height thereof reached unto heaven, and the sight thereof to the end of all the earth: The leaves thereof *were* fair, and the fruit thereof much, and in it *was* meat for all: the beasts of the field had shadow under it, and the fowls of the heaven dwelt in the boughs thereof, and all flesh was fed of it.

I saw in the visions of my head upon my bed, and, behold, a watcher and an holy one came down from heaven; He cried aloud, and said thus, Hew down the tree, and cut off his branches, shake off his leaves, and scatter his fruit: let the beasts get away from under it, and the fowls from his branches: Nevertheless leave the stump of his roots in the earth, even with a band of iron and brass, in the tender grass of the field.

And let it be wet with the dew of heaven, and *let* his portion *be* with the beasts in the grass of the earth: Let his heart be changed from man's, and let a beast's heart be given unto him; and let seven times pass over him.

This matter *is* by the decree of the watchers, and the demand by the word of the holy ones: to the intent that the living may know that the most High ruleth in the kingdom of men, and giveth it to whomsoever he will, and setteth up over it the basest of men.

This dream I king Nebuchadnezzar have seen. Now thou, O Belteshazzar, declare the interpretation thereof, forasmuch as all the wise *men* of my kingdom are not able to make known unto me the interpretation: but thou *art* able; for the spirit of the holy gods *is* in thee.

Then Daniel, whose name *was* Belteshazzar, was astonied for one hour, and his thoughts troubled him. The king spake, and said, Belteshazzar, let not the dream, or the interpretation thereof, trouble thee.

Belteshazzar answered and said, My lord, the dream *be* to them that hate thee, and the interpretation thereof to thine enemies. The tree that thou sawest, which grew, and was strong, whose height reached unto the heaven, and the sight thereof to all the earth; Whose leaves *were* fair, and the fruit thereof much, and in it *was* meat for all; under which the beasts of the field dwelt, and upon whose branches the fowls of the heaven had their habitation: It *is* thou, O king, that art grown and become strong: for thy greatness is grown, and reacheth unto heaven, and thy dominion to the end of the earth.

And whereas the king saw a watcher and an holy one coming down from heaven, and saying, Hew the tree down, and destroy it; yet leave the stump of the roots thereof in the earth, even with a band of iron and brass, in the tender grass of the field; and let it be wet with the dew of heaven, and *let* his portion *be* with the beasts of the field, till seven times pass over him;

This *is* the interpretation, O king, and this *is* the decree of the most High, which is come upon my lord the king: That they shall drive thee from men, and thy dwelling shall be with the beasts of the field, and they shall make thee to eat grass as oxen, and they shall wet thee with the dew of heaven, and seven times shall pass over thee, till thou know that the most High ruleth in the kingdom of men, and giveth it to whomsoever he will. And whereas they commanded to leave the stump of the tree roots; thy kingdom shall be sure unto thee, after that thou shalt have known that the heavens do rule. **Wherefore, O king, let my counsel be acceptable unto thee, and break off thy sins by righteousness, and thine iniquities by shewing mercy to the poor; if it may be a lengthening of thy tranquillity.**

All this came upon the king Nebuchadnezzar. At the end of twelve months he walked in the palace of the kingdom of Babylon. The king spake, and said, Is not this great Babylon, that I have built for the house of the kingdom by the might of my power, and for the honour of my majesty?

While the word *was* in the king's mouth, there fell a voice from heaven, *saying*, O king Nebuchadnezzar, to thee it is spoken; The kingdom is departed from thee. And they shall drive thee from men, and thy dwelling *shall be* with the beasts of the field: they shall make thee to eat grass as oxen, and seven times shall pass over thee, until thou know that the most High ruleth in the kingdom of men, and giveth it to whomsoever he will.

The same hour was the thing fulfilled upon Nebuchadnez-zar: and he was driven from men, and did eat grass as oxen, and his body was wet with the dew of heaven, till his hairs were grown like eagles' *feathers,* **and his nails like birds'** *claws.*

And at the end of the days I Nebuchadnezzar lifted up mine eyes unto heaven, and mine understanding returned unto me, and I blessed the most High, and I praised and honoured him that liveth for ever, whose dominion *is* an everlasting dominion, and his kingdom *is* from generation to generation: And all the inhabitants of the earth *are* reputed as nothing: and he doeth according to his will in the army of heaven, and *among* the inhabitants of the earth: and none can stay his hand, or say unto him, What doest thou?

At the same time my reason returned unto me; and for the glory of my kingdom, mine honour and brightness returned unto me; and my counsellors and my lords sought unto me; and I was established in my kingdom, and excellent majesty was added unto me. Now I Nebuchadnezzar praise and extol and honour the King of heaven, all whose works *are* truth, and his ways judgment: **and those that walk in pride he is able to abase.**   DANIEL 4:1–37 🔑

James, the brother of Jesus, wrote a practical book of application for the first followers of Jesus. Contained in the letter is a "cost-benefit" analysis between pride and humility from which all of us can learn.

From whence *come* wars and fightings among you? *come they* not hence, *even* of your lusts that war in your members? Ye lust, and have not: ye kill, and desire to have, and cannot obtain: ye fight and war, yet ye have not, because ye ask not. Ye ask, and receive not, because ye ask amiss, that ye may consume *it* upon your lusts.

Ye adulterers and adulteresses, know ye not that the friendship of the world is enmity with God? whosoever therefore will be a friend of the world is the enemy of God. Do ye think that the scripture saith in vain, The spirit that dwelleth in us lusteth to envy? But he giveth more grace. Wherefore he saith, **God resisteth the proud, but giveth grace unto the humble.**

Submit yourselves therefore to God. Resist the devil, and he will flee from you. Draw nigh to God, and he will draw nigh to you. Cleanse *your* hands, *ye* sinners; and purify *your* hearts, *ye* double minded. Be afflicted, and mourn, and weep: let your laughter be turned to mourning, and *your* joy to heaviness. Humble yourselves in the sight of the Lord, and he shall lift you up.

Speak not evil one of another, brethren. He that speaketh evil of *his* brother, and judgeth his brother, speaketh evil of the law, and judgeth the law: but if thou judge the law, thou art not a doer of the law, but a judge. There is one lawgiver, who is able to save and to destroy: who art thou that judgest another?

Go to now, ye that say, To day or to morrow we will go into such a city, and continue there a year, and buy and sell, and get gain: Whereas ye know not what *shall be* on the morrow. For what *is* your life? It is even a vapour, that appeareth for a little time, and then vanisheth away. For that ye *ought* to say, If the Lord will, we shall live, and do this, or that. But now ye rejoice in your boastings: all such rejoicing is evil. Therefore to him that knoweth to do good, and doeth *it* not, to him it is sin.   JAMES 4:1–17

In Peter's first letter to the growing group of Christians in Asia Minor, he instructed believers of all ages to practice the virtue of humility.

The elders which are among you I exhort, who am also an elder, and a witness of the sufferings of Christ, and also a partaker of the glory that shall be revealed: Feed the flock of God which is among you, taking the oversight *thereof*, not by constraint, but willingly; not for filthy lucre, but of a ready mind; Neither as being lords over *God's* heritage, but being ensamples to the flock. And when the chief Shepherd shall appear, ye shall receive a crown of glory that fadeth not away.

Likewise, ye younger, submit yourselves unto the elder. Yea, all *of you* be subject one to another, and be clothed with humility: **for God resisteth the proud, and giveth grace to the humble. Humble yourselves therefore under the mighty hand of God, that he may exalt you in due time.**   1 PETER 5:1–6

THE PARADOX OF HUMILITY

A paradox is a statement that seems contrary to common sense and yet is true. Some might believe that a humble person always loses out, gets overlooked and comes in dead last, while someone with less humility always wins, gets noticed and comes in first. But the Bible teaches the opposite. There are great blessings in store for people who demonstrate humility. It doesn't mean humble people will always "win" or "come in first" in a worldly sense, but it does mean that they will experience true contentment and joy.

As you read the Scripture passage from Matthew 5 below, identify all of God's paradoxes (such as, rejoice when people persecute you). Have you seen the truth in any of these paradoxes in your own experience?

And seeing the multitudes, he went up into a mountain: and when he was set, his disciples came unto him: And he opened his mouth, and taught them, saying, Blessed *are* the poor in spirit: for theirs is the kingdom of heaven. Blessed *are* they that mourn: for they shall be comforted. **Blessed *are* the meek: for they shall inherit the earth**. Blessed *are* they which do hunger and thirst after righteousness: for they shall be filled. Blessed *are* the merciful: for they shall obtain mercy. Blessed *are* the pure in heart: for they shall see God. Blessed *are* the peacemakers: for they shall be called the children of God. Blessed *are* they which are persecuted for righteousness' sake: for theirs is the kingdom of heaven.

Blessed are ye, when *men* shall revile you, and persecute *you*, and shall say all manner of evil against you falsely, for my sake. Rejoice, and be exceeding glad: for great *is* your reward in heaven: for so persecuted they the prophets which were before you.

MATTHEW 5:1–12

It was not uncommon for large crowds of people to follow and gather around Jesus to hear him teach and watch him perform all kinds of miracles. On one such occasion, after Jesus healed a demon-possessed boy, a disagreement broke out among the disciples. Before pride got the best of them, Jesus reiterated the role of humility in a believer's life.

And it came to pass, that on the next day, when they were come down from the hill, much people met him. And, behold, a man of the company cried out, saying, Master, I beseech thee, look upon my son: for he is mine only child. And, lo, a spirit taketh him, and he suddenly crieth out; and it teareth him that he foameth again, and bruising him hardly departeth from him. And I besought thy disciples to cast him out; and they could not.

And Jesus answering said, O faithless and perverse generation, how long shall I be with you, and suffer you? Bring thy son hither.

And as he was yet a coming, the devil threw him down, and tare *him*. And Jesus rebuked the unclean spirit, and healed the child, and delivered him again to his father. And they were all amazed at the mighty power of God.

But while they wondered every one at all things which Jesus did, he said unto his disciples, Let these sayings sink down into your ears: for the Son of man shall be delivered into the hands of men. But they understood not this saying, and it was hid from them, that they perceived it not: and they feared to ask him of that saying.

Then there arose a reasoning among them, which of them should be greatest. And Jesus, perceiving the thought of their heart, took a child, and set him by him, And said unto them, **Whosoever shall receive this child in my name receiveth me: and whosoever shall receive me receiveth him that sent me: for he that is least among you all, the same shall be great.**

LUKE 9:37–48

This question of which of Jesus' disciples would be the greatest arose on a number of occasions. You would think the message would have eventually sunk in, but it hadn't. As Jesus was on his way to Jerusalem for the last time, the brothers James and John — two disciples from Jesus' inner circle — approached him with a request.

And James and John, the sons of Zebedee, come unto him, saying, Master, we would that thou shouldest do for us whatsoever we shall desire.

And he said unto them, What would ye that I should do for you?

They said unto him, Grant unto us that we may sit, one on thy right hand, and the other on thy left hand, in thy glory.

But Jesus said unto them, Ye know not what ye ask: can ye drink of the cup that I drink of? and be baptized with the baptism that I am baptized with?

And they said unto him, We can.

And Jesus said unto them, Ye shall indeed drink of the cup that I drink of; and with the baptism that I am baptized withal shall ye be baptized: But to sit on my right hand and on my left hand is not mine to give; but *it shall be given to them* for whom it is prepared.

And when the ten heard *it*, they began to be much displeased with James and John. But Jesus called them *to him*, and saith unto them, Ye know that they which are accounted to rule over the Gentiles exercise lordship over them; and their great ones exercise authority upon them. But so shall it not be among you: but whosoever will be great among you, shall be your minister: **And whosoever of you will be the chiefest, shall be servant of all. For even the Son of man came not to be ministered unto, but to minister, and to give his life a ransom for many.**   Mark 10:35–45

Jesus did acknowledge one individual who got it right. What he said next was in keeping with the paradox of humility.

Verily I say unto you, Among them that are born of women there hath not risen a greater than John the Baptist: notwithstanding he that is least in the kingdom of heaven is greater than he.

Matthew 11:11

What was John's secret to success? John gave perhaps the most succinct description of how to become humble in a powerful conversation with his disciples.

After these things came Jesus and his disciples into the land of Judaea; and there he tarried with them, and baptized. And John also was baptizing in Aenon near to Salim, because there was much water there: and they came, and were baptized. For John was not yet cast into prison. Then there arose a question between *some* of John's disciples and the Jews about purifying. And they came unto John, and said unto him, Rabbi, he that was with thee beyond Jordan, to whom thou barest witness, behold, the same baptizeth, and all *men* come to him.

John answered and said, A man can receive nothing, except it be given him from heaven. Ye yourselves bear me witness, that I said, I am not the Christ, but that I am sent before him. He that hath the bride is the bridegroom: but the friend of the bridegroom, which standeth and heareth him, rejoiceth greatly because of the bridegroom's voice: this my joy therefore is fulfilled. **He must increase, but I must decrease.**

He that cometh from above is above all: he that is of the earth is earthly, and speaketh of the earth: he that cometh from heaven is above all. JOHN 3:22–31

People who struggle with humility are often caught boasting or bragging about themselves. In 2 Corinthians, Paul responded to criticism he received about his ministry. Using a unique style of writing, almost tongue-in-cheek, Paul introduced his readers to a proper form of boasting.

I speak as concerning reproach, as though we had been weak. Howbeit whereinsoever any is bold, (I speak foolishly,) I am bold also. Are they Hebrews? so *am* I. Are they Israelites? so *am* I. Are they the seed of Abraham? so *am* I. Are they ministers of Christ? (I speak as a fool) I *am* more; in labours more abundant, in stripes above measure, in prisons more frequent, in deaths oft. Of the Jews five times received I forty *stripes* save one. Thrice was I beaten with rods, once was I stoned, thrice I suffered shipwreck, a night and a day I have been in the deep; *In* journeyings often, in perils of waters, *in* perils of robbers, *in* perils by *mine own* countrymen, *in* perils by the heathen, *in* perils in the city, *in* perils in the wilderness, *in* perils in the sea, *in* perils among false brethren; In weariness and painfulness, in watchings often, in hunger and thirst, in fastings often, in cold and nakedness. Beside those things that are without, that which cometh upon me daily, the care of all the churches. Who is weak, and I am not weak? who is offended, and I burn not?

If I must needs glory, I will glory of the things which concern mine infirmities.
2 CORINTHIANS 11:21–30

And lest I should be exalted above measure through the abundance of the revelations, there was given to me a thorn in the flesh, the messenger of Satan to buffet me, lest I should be exalted above measure. For this thing I besought the Lord thrice, that it might depart from me. And he said unto me, My grace is sufficient for thee: for my strength is made perfect in weakness. Most gladly therefore will I rather glory in my infirmities, that the power of Christ may rest upon me. Therefore I take pleasure in infirmities, in reproaches, in necessities, in persecutions, in distresses for Christ's sake: **for when I am weak, then am I strong.**
2 CORINTHIANS 12:7–10

Although he eventually became one of Christ's most trusted followers, Paul had not always been a humble servant of Jesus. He once had been arrogant and violent, a vehement persecutor of Christians. In his first letter to Timothy, the apostle wrote honestly and openly about this amazing shift in his life.

And I thank Christ Jesus our Lord, who hath enabled me, for that he counted me faithful, putting me into the ministry; Who was before a blasphemer, and a persecutor, and injurious: but I obtained mercy, because I did *it* ignorantly in unbelief. And the grace of our Lord was exceeding abundant with faith and love which is in Christ Jesus.

This *is* a faithful saying, and worthy of all acceptation, that Christ Jesus came into the world to save sinners; of whom I am chief. **Howbeit for this cause I obtained mercy, that in me first Jesus Christ might shew forth all longsuffering, for a pattern to them which should hereafter believe on him to life everlasting.** Now unto the King eternal, immortal, invisible, the only wise God, *be* honour and glory for ever and ever. Amen. 1 TIMOTHY 1:12–17

GOD'S REQUIREMENT

What does God require from us? Micah, a prophet to Israel and Judah in the eighth century BC, answered this question with convicting succinctness. What God required then, he still requires of us today.

Wherewith shall I come before the LORD, *and* bow myself before the high God? shall I come before him with burnt offerings, with calves of a year old? Will the LORD be pleased with thousands of rams, *or* with ten thousands of rivers of oil? shall I give my firstborn *for* my transgression, the fruit of my body *for* the sin of my soul? He hath shewed thee, O man, what *is* good; and **what doth the LORD require of thee, but to do justly, and to love mercy, and to walk humbly with thy God?** MICAH 6:6–8

Micah tells us that God requires us to do justly, love mercy and walk humbly with him. How are these actions related?

WHAT WE BELIEVE

One of the most amazing pieces of evidence that we are becoming more and more like Jesus is the virtue of humility. Believers do not lift others up because they think lowly of themselves. No, they are able to esteem others above themselves because they have accepted the high esteem they have found through faith in Christ. Because we are freed from the struggle to prove we are somebody special, we can humble ourselves and look instead to build up others. When we do, it signals God's presence within us. Look to the supreme example of Jesus. Remember, God resists the proud but gives grace to the humble. Don't let the world fool you; a humble person wins out at the end of the day and at the end of eternity. God requires his followers to do justly, love mercy and walk humbly before him. It's a requirement that leads to great blessing. Remember, "I can do all things through Christ which strengthenth me" (Philippians 4:13).

Epilogue

You have just finished reading stories of real people who lived in ancient times and encountered the one true God. They were invited to take part in the unfolding of God's Grand Love Story.

Many believed; many did not. But for all it was a journey. We see this in one particular story from the Bible. A man brought his boy to Jesus to deliver him from demon possession. Jesus asked the father how long his son had been like this. The father replied that he had been afflicted since childhood. "'And ofttimes it hath cast him into the fire, and into the waters, to destroy him: but if thou canst do any thing, have compassion on us, and help us.'

"Jesus said unto him, 'If thou canst believe, all things *are* possible to him that believeth.' And straightway the father of the child cried out, and said with tears, 'Lord, I believe; help thou mine unbelief'" (Mark 9:22 – 24).

Right now, Jesus invites you to believe — to believe in him and to believe the truths taught in the pages of Scripture that guide our lives daily and into eternity. Be honest, like the man who spoke with Jesus. Tell Jesus about your doubts and invite him to help you with your unbelief. He will. He doesn't want you to merely believe these truths are the right answer. He wants you to take them in your heart where they will affect how you will live.

Here is the promise: what you once thought was impossible will now be possible. The more you believe, the more you see and discover the power of God. The more you believe, the more he changes you from the inside out to become the kind of person you have only dreamed about — filled with love, joy, peace, longsuffering, gentleness, goodness, faith, meekness and temperance. These virtues are displayed in your life like fruit on a tree for others to taste and enjoy.

When we *think* and *act* like Jesus, empowered by his presence within us, little by little we *become* like Jesus. This is not only the most truthful and abundant way to live, but it is truly the best gift we can give to our family and others whom God sovereignly places into our lives.

So, spiritual pilgrim, BELIEVE.

O taste and see that the LORD is good (Psalm 34:8).

499

Chart of References

Chapter 1: God

Genesis 1:1
Psalm 19:1–4
Romans 1:20
Deuteronomy 6:1–9
Joshua 24:1–31
1 Kings 18:16–40
Genesis 2:4–9

Genesis 2:15–24
John 1:1–5
Luke 3:1–6
Luke 3:15–18
Luke 3:21–23
Acts 17:16–34
2 Corinthians 13:14

Chapter 2: Personal God

Genesis 16:1–16
Genesis 21:1–21
Psalm 8:1–9
Psalm 23:1–6
Psalm 139:1–18
Psalm 145:1–21
2 Kings 20:1–7

Jeremiah 1:1–19
Jeremiah 29:1–14
Matthew 6:25–34
Romans 8:12–13
Romans 8:26–39
James 1:1–18

Chapter 3: Salvation

Genesis 2:8–9
Genesis 2:15–17
Genesis 3:1–24
Exodus 11:1—12:13
Exodus 12:21–31
Isaiah 52:13—53:12
Matthew 26:1–4

Matthew 27:27—28:10
John 3:1–21
Acts 2:36–41
Romans 5:12–21
Romans 10:1–13
Ephesians 1:3–14

Chapter 4: The Bible

Exodus 3:1—4:17
Luke 24:27–49
2 Peter 1:1–21
Exodus 19:1–9
Exodus 19:16–19
Exodus 20:1–21
Matthew 4:1–11

2 Timothy 3:10–17
Isaiah 40:6–8
Isaiah 55:6–13
Hebrews 4:12–13
Deuteronomy 4:1–2
Proverbs 30:5–6
Revelation 22:18–19

Chapter 5: Identity in Christ

Genesis 17:1–7
Genesis 17:17
Genesis 17:19
Genesis 21:1–7
Jeremiah 31:31–34
John 1:9–13
Hebrews 10:1–18
Luke 19:1–9
Romans 3:10–26
Romans 5:1–2

Romans 5:6–11
Romans 6:1–7
Romans 8:1–25
Ephesians 2:1 — 3:21
1 Corinthians 3:16–17
1 Corinthians 6:19
1 Corinthians 12:12–14
1 Peter 1:1–5
1 Peter 1:22–23
1 Peter 2:4–10

Chapter 6: Church

Genesis 12:1–9
Genesis 15:1–6
Genesis 15:7–21
Matthew 16:13–19
Acts 1:1–11
Acts 2:1–41
Acts 8:1–8
Acts 8:14–17
Acts 8:25

Acts 9:31
Acts 11:1–18
Acts 11:19–26
Acts 13:1–3
Acts 13:38–52
Acts 20:17 — 21:1
Ephesians 4:1–16
Revelation 2:1–7

Chapter 7: Humanity

Genesis 1:1–31
Genesis 4:1–5
Genesis 4:6–16
Jude 1–16
Romans 1:18–32
Romans 2:17–24
Romans 3:9–20
Hosea 1:1–3
Hosea 3:1–3
Hosea 11:1–11
John 1:4
John 1:7
John 1:11–12
John 3:16
John 3:36

John 4:14
John 5:24
John 6:35
John 6:37
John 6:51
John 6:54
John 7:38
John 8:12
John 8:51
John 10:9
John 11:26
John 12:31–32
Matthew 18:1–14
Luke 6:27–36
Philemon 1–25

CHAPTER 8: COMPASSION

Nehemiah 9:1–38
Romans 3:21–26
1 John 4:7–10
Deuteronomy 24:10–15
Deuteronomy 24:17–22
Deuteronomy 25:5–10

Ruth 2:1–23
Ruth 4:13–17
Luke 10:25–37
Matthew 25:31–46
James 1:19—2:13

CHAPTER 9: STEWARDSHIP

Psalm 24:1–10
Psalm 50:1–23
Matthew 25:14–30
Genesis 1:26–30
1 Samuel 1:1–28
1 Samuel 2:18–21
Deuteronomy 12:5–7
Malachi 3:6–12
Luke 16:1–15

Mark 12:41–44
1 Kings 17:1–24
Romans 12:12–13
Hebrews 13:2
1 Peter 4:9
3 John 2–8
1 Corinthians 6:12–20
1 Corinthians 10:23—11:1

CHAPTER 10: ETERNITY

2 Kings 2:1–18
Luke 16:19–31
1 Corinthians 15:1–28
1 Corinthians 15:35–58

1 Thessalonians 4:13—5:11
2 Peter 3:1–18
Revelation 20:11—22:21
John 14:1–7

CHAPTER 11: WORSHIP

Psalm 95:1–7
Isaiah 1:11–20
Matthew 23:1–28
Exodus 15:1–21
Daniel 6:1–27

Acts 16:16–35
Hebrews 10:1–25
Luke 22:7–30
Colossians 3:1–17

CHAPTER 12: PRAYER

Psalm 66:16–20
Mark 1:32–35
Luke 6:12–16
Mark 6:39–46
Matthew 26:36–46
Psalm 77:1–20
Ecclesiastes 5:1–3

Judges 6:1—7:22
Psalm 25:1–15
Genesis 18:20–33
2 Kings 20:1–11
Luke 11:1–13
Philippians 4:6–9

CHAPTER 13: BIBLE STUDY

Deuteronomy 6:13–25
Deuteronomy 31:9–13
Joshua 1:1–9
Nehemiah 7:73—9:3
Psalm 19:7–14
Psalm 119:9–24
Psalm 119:33–40

Psalm 119:97–112
Matthew 13:1–23
John 14:15–27
1 Corinthians 2:1–16
1 Timothy 4:1–16
2 Timothy 2:14–16
Hebrews 5:9—6:3

CHAPTER 14: SINGLE-MINDEDNESS

Exodus 20:2–3
Deuteronomy 6:1–9
Matthew 6:19–24
Philippians 3:1–14
2 Chronicles 20:1–30
John 8:12–30

Matthew 14:22–33
Acts 5:12–42
Deuteronomy 29:16—30:20
Romans 12:1–2
Colossians 3:1–4
Colossians 3:15–17

CHAPTER 15: TOTAL SURRENDER

Exodus 20:1–7
Daniel 3:1–28
Esther 3:1—4:16
Luke 9:23–26

Luke 22:24–62
Acts 6:8—7:60
Acts 21:4–14
Philippians 1:12–21

CHAPTER 16: BIBLICAL COMMUNITY

Genesis 2:4–25
Ecclesiastes 4:8–12
Exodus 25:1–9
Exodus 40:1–17
Exodus 40:34–35
2 Chronicles 7:1–3
Ephesians 2:11–22
Acts 2:1–4
Acts 2:42–47
Acts 4:32–37
Hebrews 10:19–25
Matthew 18:20
Nehemiah 2:11—3:32
Nehemiah 6:15
Romans 12:4–5
Romans 12:10
Romans 13:8

Romans 15:5–7
Romans 15:14
Galatians 5:13
Galatians 6:2
Ephesians 4:1–2
Ephesians 5:21
1 Thessalonians 5:9–11
Hebrews 13:1–3
Hebrews 13:15–16
Acts 18:1–3
Acts 18:18–19
Acts 18:24–26
1 Corinthians 16:19
Romans 16:3–4
1 John 1:1–7
1 John 2:7–11
1 John 3:16–18

Chapter 17: Spiritual Gifts

Exodus 35:30—36:1
Daniel 2:1–47
John 14:15–31
Acts 2:1–21
Romans 12:4–8

1 Corinthians 12:4–31
Matthew 25:14–30
1 Peter 4:7–11
Ephesians 4:1–16

Chapter 18: Offering My Time

Jonah 1:1—2:10
Haggai 1:1–15
Luke 2:41–52
Exodus 16:1–30
Exodus 18:5–27

Proverbs 31:10–31
John 7:1–16
Matthew 25:31–46
Ephesians 5:15–17
Galatians 6:7–10

Chapter 19: Giving My Resources

Genesis 28:10–22
Exodus 35:4–29
Exodus 36:3–7
1 Chronicles 29:1–18
Proverbs 3:9–10
Proverbs 11:24–25
Proverbs 11:28
Ecclesiastes 5:10–20

Matthew 2:1–12
Matthew 6:1–4
Matthew 6:19–24
Luke 12:13–21
Mark 12:41–44
Luke 6:32–36
Acts 4:32–37
2 Corinthians 8:1—9:15

Chapter 20: Sharing My Faith

Genesis 12:1–4
2 Corinthians 5:14–21
2 Kings 5:1–15
Matthew 5:13–16
Acts 2:42–47
1 Corinthians 9:19–23
Psalm 40:1–10
Acts 1:1–8

Acts 8:1–8
Acts 8:26–40
Acts 20:17–24
Ephesians 6:19–20
Colossians 4:2–6
Jonah 3:1—4:11
John 4:3–42
Romans 10:1–15

Chapter 21: Love

1 Corinthians 13:1–13
Deuteronomy 6:4–9
Leviticus 19:17–18
Mark 12:28–34
John 13:31–35
Galatians 5:13–25
1 John 4:7–21

Matthew 5:43–48
Romans 13:8–10
Matthew 18:21–35
1 Samuel 18:1–4
1 Samuel 19:1–7
1 Samuel 20:1–42
John 10:14–18

CHAPTER 22: JOY

Psalm 16:1–11
Luke 2:1–21
John 15:1–11
Nehemiah 8:13–17
1 Chronicles 16:7–36
Habakkuk 3:16–19
John 13:1
John 16:16–24
James 1:2–17
Philippians 1:1–8

Philippians 1:12–19
Philippians 2:14–18
Philippians 3:1–21
Philippians 4:1
Philippians 4:4
Philippians 4:10–13
1 Peter 1:3–9
1 Peter 4:12–16
1 Peter 5:6–11

CHAPTER 23: PEACE

Isaiah 9:6–7
Romans 5:1–11
Ephesians 2:1–22
Genesis 13:1–18
1 Kings 3:3–15
1 Kings 4:20–25
Matthew 5:21–26
Romans 14:1—15:13

Colossians 3:1–17
Romans 12:17–21
1 Timothy 2:1–8
Titus 3:1–11
Matthew 6:25–34
Mark 4:35–41
Philippians 4:4–9

CHAPTER 24: SELF-CONTROL

Proverbs 16:32
Proverbs 17:27
Proverbs 25:28
Proverbs 29:11
Titus 1:4–9
Titus 2:1–15
Judges 16:1–21
Genesis 39:1–23
1 Corinthians 6:12–20

1 Corinthians 10:14–22
1 Timothy 6:3–16
2 Timothy 2:22—3:7
James 3:1—4:10
1 Peter 5:8–11
1 Corinthians 7:1–9
2 Peter 1:3–11
Galatians 5:16–25
Luke 15:11–24

CHAPTER 25: HOPE

Job 6:1–13
Job 7:1–6
Psalm 52:1–9
1 Timothy 6:17
Psalm 118:8–9
Psalm 146:3–4
Jeremiah 17:5–6
Habakkuk 2:18–19
Isaiah 31:1
Isaiah 31:3

Psalm 42:1–11
Hebrews 6:13–20
Colossians 1:24–29
1 Peter 1:1–25
1 Thessalonians 4:13–18
1 John 3:1–3
Isaiah 40:25–31
Luke 2:25–35
Hebrews 11:1—12:3

CHAPTER 26: PATIENCE

Psalm 86:15
Numbers 14:1–23
Numbers 14:30–33
2 Peter 3:1–18
1 Samuel 24:1–22
1 Samuel 26:1–25
Proverbs 14:29
Proverbs 15:18

Proverbs 16:32
Proverbs 19:11
Proverbs 25:15
James 1:19–20
John 5:1–15
2 Corinthians 12:7–10
Job 1:1—2:13
Job 42:7–17

CHAPTER 27: KINDNESS/GOODNESS

Psalm 107:1–43
Joshua 2:1–24
Joshua 6:12–25
1 Samuel 20:13–16
2 Samuel 9:1–13
Luke 14:1
Luke 14:7–14
Philemon 1–25
2 Timothy 1:15–18
Luke 6:27–45

1 Peter 3:8–17
Romans 15:1–2
1 Corinthians 10:23–24
Galatians 6:9–10
Ephesians 4:31—5:2
1 Thessalonians 5:15
Titus 2:7
Titus 3:1–8
Titus 3:14

CHAPTER 28: FAITHFULNESS

Deuteronomy 32:1–4
Psalm 36:5–9
Lamentations 3:19–24
Proverbs 3:1–6
Proverbs 20:6
Proverbs 28:20
1 Corinthians 4:1–2

Genesis 39:1–6
Genesis 40:1–23
Genesis 41:14–46
Genesis 42:1–6
Ruth 1:1–22
Luke 1:26–56
Luke 2:1–21

CHAPTER 29: GENTLENESS

John 13:31–38
John 18:12–27
John 21:1–19
Matthew 11:28–30
Matthew 5:5
Matthew 5:38–42
Matthew 7:1–5
Galatians 5:22–23
Ephesians 4:1–2
Ephesians 4:26–32
Ephesians 6:4
Colossians 3:12

1 Timothy 3:1–4
1 Timothy 5:1–2
1 Timothy 6:10–11
2 Timothy 2:24–26
Titus 3:1–2
James 3:17–18
Philippians 4:2–5
1 Peter 3:1–4
1 Peter 3:7
1 Samuel 25:1–42
2 Samuel 16:5–14
1 Thessalonians 2:1–13

CHAPTER 30: HUMILITY

Luke 2:1–20
John 13:1–17
Philippians 2:1–13
Psalm 10:2–4
Psalm 18:27
Psalm 25:8–9
Psalm 147:6
Proverbs 3:33–34
Proverbs 11:2
Proverbs 16:18–19
Proverbs 18:12
Proverbs 21:4
Proverbs 21:24
Proverbs 22:4

Proverbs 25:6–7
Proverbs 29:23
Daniel 4:1–37
James 4:1–17
1 Peter 5:1–6
Matthew 5:1–12
Luke 9:37–48
Mark 10:35–45
Matthew 11:11
John 3:22–31
2 Corinthians 11:21–30
2 Corinthians 12:7–10
1 Timothy 1:12–17
Micah 6:6–8

BELIEVE

POWERED BY ▮ ZONDERVAN®

Dear Reader,

Notable researcher George Gallup Jr. summarized his findings on the state of American Christianity with this startling revelation: "Churches face no greater challenge…than overcoming biblical illiteracy, and the prospects for doing so are formidable because **the stark fact is, many Christians don't know what they believe or why."**

The problem is not that people lack a hunger for God's Word. Research tells us that the number one thing people want from their church is for it to help them understand the Bible, and that Bible engagement is the number one catalyst for spiritual growth. Nothing else comes close.

This is why I am passionate about the book you're holding in your hands: *Believe*— a Bible engagement experience to anchor every member of your family in the key teachings of Scripture.

The *Believe* experience helps you answer three significant questions: Can you clearly articulate the essentials of the faith? Would your neighbors or coworkers identify you as a Christian based on their interactions with you and your family? Is the kingdom of God expanding in your corner of the world?

Grounded in Scripture, *Believe* is a spiritual growth experience for all ages, taking each person on a journey toward becoming more like Jesus in their beliefs, actions, and character. There is one edition for adults, one for students, and two versions for children. All four age-appropriate editions of *Believe* unpack the 10 key beliefs, 10 key practices, and 10 key virtues of a Christian, so that everyone in your family and your church can learn together to be more like Jesus.

When these timeless truths are understood, believed in the heart, and applied to our daily living, they will transform a life, a family, a church, a city, a nation, and even our world.

Imagine thousands of churches and hundreds of thousands of individuals all over the world who will finally be able to declare—**"I know what I believe and why, and in God's strength I will seek to live it out all the days of my life."** It could change the world. It has in the past; it could happen again.

In Him,

Randy Frazee
General Editor, *Believe*

LIVING THE STORY OF THE BIBLE TO BECOME LIKE JESUS

Teach your whole family how to live the story of the Bible!

- **Adults** – Unlocks the 10 key beliefs, 10 key practices, and 10 key virtues that help people live the story of the Bible. Bible Study DVD and Study Guide also available.
- *Think, Act, Be Like Jesus* – A companion to *Believe*, this fresh resource by pastor Randy Frazee will help readers develop a personal vision for spiritual growth and a simple plan for getting started on the *Believe* journey.
- **Students** – This edition contains fewer Scriptures than the adult edition, but with transitions and fun features to engage teens and students. Bible Study DVD also available.
- **Children** – With a Kids' Edition for ages 8-12, a Storybook for ages 4-8, a coloring book for toddlers, and four levels of curriculum for toddlers, preschool, early elementary, and later elementary, children of all ages will learn how to think, act, and be like Jesus.
- **Churches** – *Believe* is flexible, affordable, and easy to use with your whole church.
- **Spanish** – All *Believe* resources are also available in Spanish.

FOR ADULTS

9780310443834   9780310250173

FOR STUDENTS

9780310745617

FOR CHILDREN

Ages 8–12   Ages 4–8   Ages 2–5
9780310746010   9780310745907   9780310752226

FOR CHURCHES

Campaign Kit 9780310681717

BelieveTheStory.com

BELIEVE
POWERED BY ZONDERVAN

THE STORY

POWERED BY ■ ZONDERVAN®

READ THE STORY. EXPERIENCE THE BIBLE.

Here I am, 50 years old. I have been to college, seminary, engaged in ministry my whole life, my dad is in ministry, my grandfather was in ministry, and **The Story has been one of the most unique experiences of my life**. The Bible has been made fresh for me. It has made God's redemptive plan come alive for me once again.

—Seth Buckley, Youth Pastor,
Spartanburg Baptist Church, Spartanburg, SC

As my family and I went through *The Story* together, the more I began to believe and the more real [the Bible] became to me, and **it rubbed off on my children and helped them with their walk with the Lord**. *The Story* inspired conversations we might not normally have had.

—Kelly Leonard, Parent, Shepherd of the Hills Christian Church, Porter Ranch, CA

We have people reading *The Story*—**some devour it and can't wait for the next week**. Some have never really read the Bible much, so it's exciting to see a lot of adults reading the Word of God for the first time. I've heard wonderful things from people who are long-time readers of Scripture. They're excited about how it's all being tied together for them. It just seems to make more sense.

—Lynnette Schulz,
Director of Worship
Peace Lutheran Church,
Eau Claire, WI

FOR ADULTS

9780310950974

FOR TEENS

Ages 13+
9780310722809

FOR KIDS

Ages 8–12
9780310719250

Dive into the Bible in a whole new way!

The Story is changing lives, making it easy for any person, regardless of age or biblical literacy level, to understand the Bible.

The Story comes in five editions, one for each age group from toddlers to adults. All five editions are organized chronologically into 31 chapters with selected Scripture from Genesis to Revelation. The additional resources create an engaging group Bible-reading experience, whether you read *The Story* with your whole church, in small groups, or with your family.

- **Adults** – Read the Bible as one compelling story, from Genesis to Revelation. Available in NIV, KJV, NKJV, large print, imitation leather, and audio editions. Curriculum DVD and Participant's Guide also available.
- **Teens** – Teen edition of *The Story*, with special study helps and features designed with teens in mind. Curriculum DVD also available.
- **Children** – With a Kids' Edition for ages 8-12, a Storybook Bible for ages 4-8, a Storybook Bible for toddlers, fun trading cards, and three levels of curriculum for preschool, early elementary, and later elementary, children of all ages will learn how their story fits into God's story.
- **Churches** – *The Story* is flexible, affordable, and easy to use with your church, in any ministry, from nursery to adult Sunday school, small groups to youth group…and even the whole church.
- **Spanish** – *The Story* resources are also available in Spanish.

FOR CHILDREN

Ages 4–8
9780310719755

Ages 2–5
9780310719274

FOR CHURCHES

Campaign Kit   9780310941538